Meiji Japan

Routledge Library of Modern Japan

Education and Training in Japan
Meiji Japan
Showa Japan
The Japanese Economy, Part 1
The Japanese Economy, Part 2
Banking in Japan

Meiji Japan

Political, economic and social history 1868–1912

Edited and with an introduction
by Peter Kornicki

Volume I
The emergence of the Meiji state

ROUTLEDGE

London and New York

First published 1998
by Routledge
11 New Fetter Lane, London EC4P 4EE

Simultaneously published in the USA and Canada
by Routledge
29 West 35th Street, New York, NY 10001

Typeset in Times by RefineCatch Limited, Bungay, Suffolk
Printed and bound in Great Britain by
TJ International Ltd, Padstow, Cornwall

British Library Cataloguing in Publication Data
A catalogue record for this book is available from the British Library

Library of Congress Cataloging in Publication Data

Meiji Japan / edited and with an introduction by Peter Kornicki.
p. cm.
1. Japan – History – Meiji period, 1868–1912. 2. Japan – Politics and government – 1868–1912. 3. Japan – Economic conditions – 1868–1918. 4. Japan – Social conditions – 1868–
I. Kornicki, Peter F. (Peter Francis)
DS882.M3835 1998
952.03′ 1–dc21 97–37916
CIP

ISBN 0–415–15618–1 (4 volume set)
ISBN 0–415–15619–X (Volume I)
ISBN 0–415–15620–3 (Volume II)
ISBN 0–415–15621–1 (Volume III)
ISBN 0–415–15622–X (Volume IV)

Contents

Part II Economic change

VOLUME II: THE GROWTH OF THE MEIJI STATE

Part I Political and ideological change

Part II Economic development

Acknowledgements

The publishers would like to thank the following for permission to reprint their material:

American Historical Association for permission to reprint from the *American Historical Review*, vol. 85, no. 3 (June 1990), pp. 535-556.

The Asiatic Society of Japan for permission to reprint from J. L. Huffman, 'Freedom and the Press in Meiji-Taisho Japan', *Transactions of the Asiatic Society of Japan*, series 3, vol. 19 (1984), pp. 137–171.

The Association for Asian Studies, Inc. for permission to reprint from the *Journal of Asian Studies*, vol. 31, no. 4 (1972), pp. 793–819; vol. 37, no. 4 (1978), pp. 677–696; vol. 33, no. 1 (1973), pp. 51–65.

Associated University Press for permission to reprint from H. Conroy, S. T. W. Davis and W. Patterson (eds) *Japan in Transition: Thought and Action in the Meiji Era* (1984), pp. 96–112.

Cambridge University Press for permission to reprint from G. M. Wilson, 'Plots and motives in Japan's Meiji Restoration', *Comparative Studies in Society and History*, vol. 25, pp. 407–427 (1983); R. P. Dore, 'The modernizer as a special case: Japanese factory legislation 1882–1922', *Comparative Studies in Society and History*, vol. 11, pp. 433–450 (1969); Y. Yamamura, 'The role of the samurai in the development of modern banking in Japan', *Journal of Economic History*, vol. 27, pp. 198–220 (1967); S. S. Large, 'Labor's image of the past in 1919–1920', pp. 11–30 in *Organized Workers and Socialist Politics in Interwar Japan* (1981); M. B. Jansen, 'The Meiji Restoration', *Cambridge History of Japan*, vol. 5, pp. 308–366 (1989); E. S. Crawcour, 'Industrialization and technological change, 1885–1920', *Cambridge History of Japan*, vol. 6, pp. 385–450 (1989); J. Breen, 'Shintoists in Restoration Japan', *Modern Asian Studies*, vol. 24, pp. 579–602 (1989); C. L. Yates, 'Saigo Takamori in the emergence of Meiji Japan', *Modern Asian Studies*, vol. 28, pp. 449–474 (1994); A. A. Altman, 'The press and social cohesion during a period of change: the case of early Meiji Japan', *Modern Asian Studies*, vol. 15, pp. 865–876 (1981); M. W. Steele, 'From custom to right: the politicization of the village in early Meiji Japan, *Modern Asian Studies*, vol. 23, pp. 729–748 (1989); E. P. Tsurumi, 'Meiji primary school language and ethics textbooks: old values for a new society', *Modern Asian Studies*, vol. 8, pp. 247–261 (1974); Thomas C. Smith, 'The right to benevolence: dignity and Japanese workers, 1890–1930', *Comparative Studies in Society and History*, Vol. 26 (1984).

Frank Cass & Co. Ltd for permission to reprint from *Business History*, vol. 26, pp. 139–155 (1984), published by Frank Cass & Company, 900 Eastern Avenue, Ilford, Essex, England. Copyright Frank Cass & Co Ltd.

Harvard University Press for permission to reprint from Peter Duus, *Party Rivalry and Political Change in Taisho Japan*, pp. 6–27, © 1968 the President and Fellows of Harvard College.

Dr R. H. P. Mason for permission to reprint from R. H. P. Mason, 'The Peace Preservation Ordinance and the first Meiji Diet, 1980–92', *Papers in Far Eastern History*, vol. 31 (1985), pp. 117–167.

Oxford University Press for permission to quote from Hedley Bull and Adam Watson (eds) *The Expansion of International Society*, pp. 185–199, © 1984 Hedley Bull and Adam Watson.

Pantheon Books, a division of Random House, Inc. for permission to reprint from Mikiso Hane, *Peasants, Rebels and Outcastes*, pp. 172–206, © 1982 Mikiso Hane.

Princeton University Press for permission to reprint from T. R. H. Havens, *Farm and Nation in Modern Japan: Agrarian Nationalism 1870–1940*, pp. 5–55, © 1974 Princeton University Press; W. W. Lockwood (ed) *The State and Economic Enterprise in Japan*, pp. 209–247, © 1965 Princeton University Press; M. B. Jansen and G. Rozman (eds) *Japan in Transition: from Tokugawa to Meiji*, pp. 168–194, © 1986 Princeton University Press; R. E. Ward (ed) *Political Development in Modern Japan*, pp. 65–97, © 1968 (Princeton University Press; D. H. Shively (ed) *Tradition and Modernization in Japanese Culture*, pp. 121–175, © 1971 Princeton University Press; P. Duus, R. H. Myers and M. R. Peattie (eds), *The Japanese Informal Empire in China, 1895–1937*, pp. 101–132, © 1989 Princeton University Press; B. S. Silberman and H. D. Harootunian (eds) *Japan in Crisis: Essays on Taisho*, pp. 3–28, © 1974 Princeton University Press; A. Iriye (ed) *The Chinese and the Japanese*, pp. 184–198, © 1980 Princeton University Press; T. Najita and J. V. Koschmann (eds) *Conflict in Modern Japanese History: the Neglected Tradition*, pp. 295–341, © 1982 Princeton University Press.

Routledge for permission to reprint from P. Francks, 'Peasantry, proletariat or private enterprise? – the Japanese farmer in the industrialisation process', *Japan Forum* 2i (1990), British Association for Japanese Studies, pp. 91–104; P. Francks, *Japanese Economic Development: Theory and Practice*, chapters 6 and 7 (1990); R. Siddle, *Race, Resistance and the Ainu of Japan*, pp. 51–75 (1996).

Stanford University Press for permission to reprint from Byron K. Marshall, *Capital and Nationalism in Prewar Japan,* pp. 13–29, © 1967 the Board of Trustees of the Leland Stanford Junior University; Sharon L. Sievers, *Flowers in Salt: the Beginnings of Feminist Consciousness in Modern*

Japan, chapter 8, © 1983 the Board of Trustees of the Leland Stanford Junior University.

University of California Press for permission to reprint from Irwin Scheiner, *Christian Converts and Social Protest in Meiji Japan*, pp. 41–66, © 1970 The Regents of the University of California; Gail Bernstein, *Recreating Japanese Women 1600–1945*, pp. 151–174, © 1991 The Regents of the University of California.

University of Chicago Press for permission to reprint from *Signs*, 6 (1981), pp. 602–616.

University of Washington for permission to reprint from the *Journal of Japanese Studies*, vol. 8, no. 2 (1982), pp. 307–42; vol. 3, no. 1 (1977), pp. 71–97; vol. 1, no. 1 (1974), pp. 127–164; vol. 1, no. 1 (1974), 113–125; vol. 1, no. 2 (1975), pp. 351–383.

The publishers have made every effort to contact authors/copyright holders of works reprinted in *Meiji Japan*. This has not been possible in every case, however, and we would welcome correspondence from those individuals/companies we have been unable to trace.

General introduction

Peter Kornicki

JAPAN AND 'MODERNITY'

Nobody needs to be reminded these days that all historical boundaries are artificial and that they inevitably encourage an emphasis on change and an underappreciation of continuities. But some boundaries are tyrannical, and none more so in the history of Japan than the year 1868, that of the Meiji Restoration. The Restoration, as widely presented, was a pivotal event in Japanese history, perhaps the one crucial event, but it has also come to be a determining event in perceptions of the past and in the historiography of Japan. It is the event that divides the 'modern' from the 'pre-modern', or the 'traditional', not only in history but in literature and a host of other fields, establishing an almost impermeable disciplinary boundary. It may be inappropriate to think of Japan in terms of a nineteenth century, a perspective that may make some sense in the context of Europe or North America. But it is undoubtedly desirable to challenge the tyranny of the year 1868, to take the long view and to rethink the history of Japan on both sides of the Restoration not as fragments about to end or just beginning but as parts of a longer continuity.

We have become used to many comfortable and convenient ways of imagining the history of Japan in the nineteenth century, some of which smack of ethnocentricity. One such is the 'open/closed rhythm to Japanese history' based on perceptions of Japanese receptivity to influences from outside, that is, from Europe or North America. This has its origins in the representation of Japan as a 'closed' country during the Tokugawa period by Western historians who considered, wrongly, that Japan had been closed to European influences during that period. Not only was this view mistaken, in that European influences not only permeated Japan but also stimulated intellectual developments of great importance, but it was also misconceived, for Japanese contacts with China, Korea and the Ryūkyū islands (now Okinawa, a prefecture of Japan) continued to be important.[1] And yet the 'open/closed rhythm' continues to shape our perceptions of the long march of Japanese history and to provide a framework for both popular and academic books.[2]

Arguably none of these convenient ways of imagining Japan has been more insidious and recently contentious than the notion that 'modern' Japan starts in 1868. It should be noted that this notion itself is of relatively recent origin. When Count Ōkuma Shigenobu's grand survey of the fifty years that had passed since the 'opening' of Japan was published in an English version in 1909, it was entitled *Fifty years of new Japan*. Since 1945, however, the tendency has been without question to associate the recent history of Japan with 'modernity'. Thus the late Hugh Borton's thorough summation of the last hundred years of Japanese history, published in 1955, bore the title *Japan's modern century*, and drew a distinction between the 'secluded, semi-feudal, agrarian country' that was pre-modern Japan and the 'modern industrial state' that Japan had become.[3] This perception was set in concrete by the modernization series of conferences that resulted in the highly influential set of volumes published by Princeton University Press in the 1960s and 1970s. These were set in motion by a conference held in 1960 at Hakone, which sought to apply modernization theory to Japan, adopting a holistic approach that positively appraised Japan's economic development and convergence with the capitalist economies. It is not fanciful to see behind the whole endeavour the coloration of the tensions of the Cold War world, and the desire of the US State Department to keep Japan in the 'Western' camp, but that is not to dismiss the scholarship contained in the volumes, the first of which was *Changing Japanese attitudes towards modernization* (1965); rather, it is to draw attention to the intellectual and political circumstances that shaped their agendas.[4]

Perhaps the most important point to notice here about these modernization volumes is that 'modernization' was a code word for Westernization. The equation of 'modernity' with Western modernity was unquestioned, and the unstated assumption was that Japan became 'modern' by virtue of its encounter with the 'West' and its willingness to embrace the paraphernalia of Western civilization. This unilinear perception of modernity is one that is still remarkably influential, and one that ignores the changes that had taken place in Japanese society in the second half of the Tokugawa period. To be sure, many of these changes and developments were repudiated in favour of Western models in the Meiji period: the sophisticated financial operations of Japanese banking institutions were transformed in the Meiji period with the introduction of Western-style banks, and the vigorous publishing industry was similarly transformed by the introduction of Western-style movable-type printing technology and the steam press.[5] But it is at least arguable that Japan was in certain senses becoming a 'modern' society well before the Westernization of the Meiji period, albeit in its own terms. It was certainly not the primitive society suggested by Borton's crude contrast, and it is not helpful either to see the Tokugawa period teleologically as a 'preparation' for modernization, as many have done. Rather, it is perhaps important to recognize that Japan was in functional terms going through a parallel but quite distinct process that was turning it into a society with a thriving print culture, a range of financial services, and so on; in other words a 'modern' society but one not dependent on Western models of modernity.

However that may be, even if we accept, for a moment, the proposition that Japan's modernity is defined by its confrontation with the West, that is with the Great Powers of the nineteenth century, with their ideologies and with their technologies, it is still embarrassingly clear that 1868 simply will not do. The intellectual history of the Tokugawa period is one of a gradual disengagement with China, brought about partly by a new empiricism and partly by the rise of the Kokugaku or Nativist movement that conceived for the first time of a Japanocentric world. Ironically, the disengagement with China, incomplete though it was until the end of the nineteenth century, made possible, and was facilitated by, the encounter with the West. That encounter, beginning at the end of the seventeenth century, initially involved only scientific disciplines of demonstrable practical value, such as medicine and calendrical astronomy. By the middle of the nineteenth century, however, it encompassed a much wider range of disciplines and had stimulated, for example, the experimental marriage of Western surgical techniques and Chinese pharmacology that led in 1804 to the first surgical operation to make use of a general anaesthetic anywhere in the world.[6]

In our approach to the history of Japan in modern times it is inevitable that we will be swayed or determined by the cultural constructs and political realities of our time, but it is clearly time to question many of the assumptions that have pervaded postwar writing on Japan and unavoidably colour some of the essays reprinted in these volumes. We need to question the bipolarity of our facile opposition of 'Japan' and the 'West' and the constructs that underpin our notion of the 'West' itself, and to unravel some of the narratives written by historians. The essays contained in the recently-published volume *Multicultural Japan* do just this, and so does Fujitani's *Splendid monarchy*, which demonstrates how official narratives become accepted as 'history' and exposes the 'invented traditions' that have obscured the history of the imperial institution in the Meiji period.[7]

Of course, the very notion of a 'Meiji period', tied as it is to the reign of the emperor Meiji (1868–1912), is as questionable as its successors, the Taishō and Shōwa 'periods': such conceptions of time defined monarchically are at least distracting for the historian and frequently obscure important continuities. It is for this reason that these volumes, although for the most part concerned with the events and issues of the Meiji period, deal also with the final years of the Tokugawa Bakufu, the government of samurai that ruled Japan from 1600 until 1867, and with the Taishō period that takes its name from the emperor Taishō, who reigned from 1912 to 1926.

The various considerations outlined above must guide our response to earlier work on the history of Japan in the Meiji period and lead us to new questions and new approaches. The essays contained in these volumes need to be seen in this light, appreciated for their insights and for the problems they raise and at the same time critically assessed for weaknesses and for indications of areas where further work and thought are needed. They represent a selection taken from the many articles and books on the Meiji period which have been published in the last thirty or so years, and they have obviously been chosen primarily for their quality and the intellectual challenges they pose. Nevertheless, no selection such as this can be an ideal one, firstly and most obviously because authors and publishers are not always willing to permit the inclusion of their texts in anthologies. A second reason is that it was not thought desirable to include more than two pieces by any one author, in order to ensure that there is a plurality of viewpoints and approaches represented; consequently, some good essays have been omitted simply because two pieces by the same author have already been included. Thirdly, some topics that ought to be covered in these volumes have simply not inspired work that is good enough to be included or have hitherto been ignored by scholars writing in English. For these reasons, then, readers are advised to adopt a critical approach not only to the individual pieces but also to the selection as a whole and to supplement it with reference to the attached reading lists, which contain much additional material.

The selection as a whole obviously represents a form of narrative, albeit a patchy one and one that has many lacunae. That narrative needs to be fleshed out and to be fitted into a context of alternative narratives, and that will be the task of the remainder of this introduction. Reference will be made to authors whose works are included in these volumes, and whose names will therefore be given in bold type, and to other writers, whose works will be mentioned in the footnotes.

VOLUME I: THE EMERGENCE OF THE MEIJI STATE

For reasons that have already been explained above, the first volume starts with several pieces that deal with the period before the Meiji Restoration and so before the start of the Meiji period: the first part is entitled 'The collapse of the Bakufu and the Meiji Restoration'. The tensions that brought down the Tokugawa Bakufu were both internal and external: the interplay between the two is a matter of debate, but historians are agreed that both the growing domestic crisis and the sudden diplomatic crisis that developed in the 1850s contributed to the increasing difficulty of the Bakufu's position. On the one hand there were the financial crises facing the Bakufu and the domains in the provinces, the rising tide of peasant unrest breaking out more and more often into revolt and armed confrontation, and the increasingly obvious lack of political will and understanding to resolve these difficulties, and on the other there was the pressure from abroad for the establishment of trading relationships like those that had been established between the Western powers and China after the Opium Wars had put China at their mercy. It is commonplace to assert that it was Commodore Perry who was responsible for 'opening' Japan in 1853–4, but this is misleading, and not only because Japan was never really completely 'closed', owing to the Dutch presence in Nagasaki and the active trade conducted by Japan with China and Korea. More important is the fact that Japan was under pressure not solely from the United States, but from several nations whose territorial and other interests were leading them to converge in Japanese waters. After all, just one month after Perry reached Japan, Admiral Putyatin arrived in Nagasaki harbour on an identical mission inspired by Russia's long-standing and serious interest in East Asia and in the end gained a more favourable treaty than Perry did. Furthermore, the British were active in Hong Kong and, since the time of Earl Macartney's mission to China in 1793, had been interested in establishing relations with Japan, while French missionaries had been active in the Ryūkyū islands since the 1840s.[8] It is therefore more appropriate to see the pressures upon Japan as international in nature, and stemming from the expansionist drive which was working itself out among the Great Powers, and to understand the changes in Japan's position in the world that took place at that time as 'Japan's entry into international society', as the title of **Suganami**'s piece puts it. These changes provoked within Japan a different perception of the outside world which in turn had very considerable domestic repercussions: **Totman**'s article, which picks up and refines the analysis presented by Beasley in 1955, demonstrates the shifts that ensued in foreign policy in the final years of the Bakufu.[9]

The Meiji Restoration, to give it the rather misleading name that has become established in English usage, conventionally took place in 1868, but all scholars take a much longer view of the events of that year and see it as the outcome of forces that had been building up for some time. For some it is the intellectual shifts that are important as Kokugaku, or Nativism as it is often called in English, developed into a nationalistic and emperor-focused ideology, while others give the economic and political bankruptcy of the Bakufu greater prominence; further, as Beasley's major study of the Restoration suggested, the momentum of the Restoration carries on for some years, making it desirable to see the 'Restoration' as a package of social changes rather than simply a political event.[10] The historiography of the Restoration encompasses a rich variety of perspectives, from that of Huber and others who have seen it as a revolutionary movement to the view of it as a 'revolution from above' proposed by **Jansen**.[11] The use of the word 'revolution', while problematic in certain respects, usefully associates the events in Japan with sudden political changes in other cultures and invites comparisons, but **Wilson** draws attention to the multiplicity of 'stories' of the events of the Restoration years and the unreliability of a clear narrative line. Some historians have drawn attention to the pacific character of the Meiji Restoration, but the supposed lack of violence or opposition has been much exaggerated and we need to take account of the violence of the campaign against Buddhist temples, which were perceived as complicit with the Tokugawa régime, and of the continuing resistance to the changes.[12] Recent work, especially by **Breen**, two of whose essays are included in this volume, has focused attention on the ways in which political changes were represented ritually and on the importance assumed by questions of religion in the early Meiji period, and particularly the prominence in the new régime of a number of Shintō activists. This has reminded us among other things of the fragility and instability of the early Meiji régime as symbolized by the frequent changes of policy and the constant realignments of political factions inside and outside the government.

The final two pieces in the first section focus on two further dimensions of the early years of the Meiji state. **Mayo**'s account of the Korean crisis of 1873, which took place when many members of the government were on a fact-finding and diplomatic mission to the West led by Count Iwakura, reveals not only the internal policy divisions within the ruling élite but also the continuing importance of Japan's search for an appropriate place in the hierarchical world order. It is salutary to be reminded of the instability of the new régime, for even recent studies of the Meiji state have attributed to it a sense of definite purpose and unanimity it did not have. **Yates**, on the other hand, examines the role of Saigō Takamori, who was one of the defeated proponents of an invasion of Korea in 1873 and who led the Satsuma rebellion of 1877. Although he was branded a traitor and his samurai army was roundly defeated by the new conscript army, he came later to be perceived as one of the heroes of the time in an acknowledgment of the significance of the movements opposed to the Meiji régime and as the 'last samurai', a man whose values had been left behind by the rapid pace of change in early Meiji Japan. Both pieces, therefore, expose some of the myth-making that has surrounded the early years of the Meiji period, and Fujitani's recent book, referred to above, takes this further.

The second part of this volume explores the economic changes of the early Meiji period, although the first essay by **Crawcour** focuses on the antecedents in the Tokugawa period. The perspective which sees the Tokugawa period as 'Japan's preparation for modem economic growth', as his title puts it, is not without problems and can lend itself to an underappreciation of how far the economy had developed by the late Tokugawa period. On the other hand it is essential to appreciate that the economic growth of the Meiji period was no 'miracle' and was firmly rooted in the commercial experiences and infrastructure of the previous decades. This is not to say that the translation was smooth, for, to take one example, the introduction of steam-powered manufacturing processes in factories and of railways running to fixed timetables required a new understanding of time; and the adoption of Western banking and industrial practices created a dislocation, a distance from earlier practices. Nevertheless, the consensus is that the developed commercial economy of the Tokugawa period provided a matrix of skills and experiences that 'modern economic growth' could build upon. This understanding has been an important development, for the view of the economic growth of the Meiji period as a 'miracle' was built upon the eurocentric perception that Japan was 'backward' simply because it lacked the visible props familiar in the West.

The involvement of Japan in the world economy in the early Meiji period was facilitated by two factors, one of which was the involvement of European and North American capital, entrepreneurs and businesses, which is partly the subject of the paper by the **Checklands**. The other was the participation in the international exhibition movement. The international exhibitions began with the Great Exhibition of 1851 in the Crystal Palace and in the course of the nineteenth century they became regular events which had important roles to play in the search for new markets and for competitive advantage. Japan's participation in these exhibitions in various cities from Melbourne to Vienna and Philadelphia, costly though it was, created a public image of Japan as a producer of tea, porcelain and other items that constituted Japan's first export products and in addition gave the accompanying officials an unrivalled opportunity to acquaint themselves with the most recent technological and industrial developments that were proudly on display and to conduct research on possible markets for Japanese exports. Much work has been done in Japanese on these subjects, and on the role of Japanese consulates abroad in collecting valuable commercial intelligence, but so far there have been few explorations in English of the international context in which the Meiji economy made its first faltering steps.[13]

Although the agricultural sector has sometimes been seen as the 'victim' of the industrialization process of the Meiji period, and it is true that farming was no longer seen as the foundation of the economy as it had been in the Tokugawa period, **Havens** demonstrates the importance of the agrarian movement, and of the agrarian response to the government's desire to industrialize agriculture, as factors that led to rising agricultural output. The pieces by **Yamamura** and **Marshall** bringing this volume to a close focus on individuals in the emerging economy, the former demonstrating that not only former samurai but also commoners played significant roles in the creation of the new financial institutions of Meiji Japan. **Marshall** shows that entrepreneurs accepted government intervention in economic life because of the government's commitment to the encouragement of private business initiatives and that they had little reason, except when they perceived that their interests were at stake, to press for laissez-faire economics.

VOLUME II: THE GROWTH OF THE MEIJI STATE

This volume opens with a part devoted to 'Political and ideological change' in the 1870s and 1880s. These were years of turmoil, debate and repression and they reached a climax with the promulgation in 1889 of the Constitution, which remained in force until it was superseded by the new Constitution promulgated in 1946, and with the holding of the first parliamentary elections in 1890, albeit on a very limited franchise. The conceptual understanding of the political sphere in those years has grown enormously in sophistication over the last twenty years. Gluck's work, for example, has made us much more conscious of the shifting ideologies that underpinned the state, of the politicization of Meiji, the first of the modern emperors, and of his symbolic manipulation, and Fujitani's work, mentioned earlier, has added new dimensions to that with an account of the processes whereby new traditions were generated for their symbolic value.[14]

By this time the existence of translations of a large range of Western political texts and the personal experiences of Japanese, mostly men, who had travelled to the West, not to mention the presence of numerous foreigners hired by the government for their intellectual abilities, had added to the range of available models for consideration. Indeed, given the process of conscious selection practised by the Meiji government, which was clearly aware of the plurality of the 'West', it is unhelpful to argue that the 'West' was serving as a political model. The article by **Akita** and **Hirose** is a case study of the use of the British model of a monarchical system for consideration with regard to the Japanese monarchy, though the Japanese monarchy is widely held to have developed in the Meiji period under the influence of the more autocratic Prussian system. The conscious selectivity applied to foreign models is often forgotten and it is salutary to take note of the possible models that were not selected. It is also important to note the ever-increasing geographical and social accessibility of texts and information that held a mirror up to Japan, showing how things could be different, how Japan's future could be rethought. The political novels of the 1880s were particularly effective in this respect: original works of fiction explored future possibilities and depicted an imaginary Japan, and even the translations were more akin to adaptations carefully worked to extend the domestic political vocabulary and draw domestic lessons. But the newspapers and magazines which sprung up in large numbers in the early Meiji period and which circulated widely throughout Japan by means of networks of reading rooms and private libraries had much the same effect, although subject to increasingly stringent censorship regulations. **Steele**'s article on the 'politicization of the village in early Meiji Japan' demonstrates how quickly and effectively political and legal language spread, although this must have been dependent on the comparatively high literacy rates found in the late Tokugawa period and on pre-existing networks for the distribution of books and information.

Sievers's article on Kishida Toshiko raises the interesting and so far little-explored issue of Meiji feminism. Indeed, women's history and feminist history are still topics that deserve much more attention in the study of the history of Japan even in the scholarship published in Japan, let alone the Western-language scholarship. As Bernstein has put it, 'the need to link women and the family to the new nation-state has been a major preoccupation of political leadership in the past century: excluded from politics, women have rarely been excluded from political considerations or bureaucratic concerns', and there is at least an urgent need to integrate these issues into our understanding of the Meiji state. Sievers saw her pioneering book *Flowers in salt: the beginnings of feminist consciousness in modern Japan*, as little more than an introduction and looked forward to the time 'when the experience of Japanese women becomes a routine part of the growing international dialogue on women in the modern period'.[15] To some extent that is happening with regard to women in twentieth-century, and particularly post-war, Japan, but there is still very little in English on women in nineteenth-century Japan, let alone in earlier periods. The collection of essays edited by Gail Lee Bernstein under the title *Recreating Japanese women, 1600–1945* has extended the horizons of the history of Japanese women with a number of case studies which in the first half throw much light on the situation of rural and urban women in the Tokugawa period, but there is still much work to be done, for example on the political and ideological perceptions of women during that period: did they remain as static as we are usually asked to suppose or were there changes? We need a better understanding of gender relations and their underpinnings at the end of the Tokugawa period before we can begin to appreciate and assess the significance of the changes that took place in the Meiji period.

The possibility of a public role for women had emerged as early as 1872, when the Iwakura mission to the United States and Europe set off. With the party were five young women, who were deposited with families and educational institutions on the east coast of the United States. This was the idea of Mori Arinori, who was later to become Minister of Education but at the time was the Japanese diplomatic representative in Washington, and Kuroda Kiyotake of the Hokkaidō Development Bureau, who made an investigative trip to the United States. Both men were convinced by their perceptions of American women that it was desirable to pay more attention to the education of Japanese women in order to further the development of Japan; this was a novel enough idea at the time, but it was not supported by any expectation that women would play a more prominent public or political role in a future Japan. Rather, the thinking was that better educated women would be better mothers. Some of these five women undertook postgraduate work and were the first Japanese women to be educated abroad; they were also the last to be educated abroad for some years to come. Upon their return to Japan their experiences were disappointing in terms of the expectations that had been raised in them but several of them did succeed in creating a public role for themselves some years later.

As Rose has argued, 'in associating motherhood with race, civilization, colonization, and national strength, Kuroda indicated the main elements of the emerging rationale for educating women'.[16] But even this sort of argument failed to convince some segments of the population and the very idea of women's education had its opponents to the end of the century and beyond: in their view educating women rendered them less likely to marry and to bear children. The new education Act of 1872 provided for compulsory education for both boys and girls and in addition private institutions, some run by foreign missionaries, were established to provide for further education for women: female students became a familiar part of the Meiji scene and even inspired novels in the 1880s centred around the lives of women students.[17] However, the low attendance rates of girl pupils at the compulsory elementary schools demonstrate that many remained unconvinced of the need to educate women.

The whole question of the role women were to play in Meiji society clearly exercised the government as early as the 1870s, as the passage of bills relating to the liberation of prostitutes or to the regulation of women's hairstyles shows. In these years, however, the public debate was conducted by men, such as the members of the Meirokusha, a society of intellectuals founded in 1873, some of whom drew on their knowledge of Western societies to develop a positive appreciation of the domestic roles of women.[18] However, the example of Kishida Toshiko, who addressed her first public meeting in 1882 at the age of twenty, shows that by the 1880s women were beginning to articulate their own agendas and later, as the Freedom and Popular Rights movement grew in strength, to demand political rights. As Sievers's book demonstrates, there was undeniably a feminist consciousness emerging in Meiji Japan, even though the aspirations it aroused were to be denied in the Constitution promulgated in 1889, and the Meiji state sought increasingly to propagate its conservative notion of the roles women could play in Japanese society.

Quite separate from the feminist critiques of the Meiji state were the criticisms of liberals who, in the years leading up to the promulgation of the Constitution, argued and campaigned vigorously for a parliamentary democracy of a much more liberal stamp than that which was finally adopted. Much of the ideological background to these campaigns was inspired by readings of the 'West' by such enthusiastic propagators of liberal values and the notion of progress as Tokutomi Sohō, who had in fact never visited any Western country and who is the subject of **Pierson**'s article. One of the means used to expound their ideas, apart from meetings, speeches and journalism, which were all subject to strict government controls, was political novels, some of which were translations of the works of Western writers such as Disraeli and Bulwer-Lytton adapted to convey particular messages to Japanese readers.[19] There can be no doubt that the radical politics and vigour of the various components of the freedom and popular rights movement represented a serious challenge to the government, and it was one which it met both with repression and with argument, including, as **Mehl**'s article demonstrates, the use of history to justify and validate the constitutional framework that was emerging.

The second part of this volume deals with the economy during these years. As has become evident from the study of Japan's participation in the international exhibitions and from the focus of the domestic exhibitions for the encouragement of industry, of which the first was held in Tokyo in 1877, it was 'traditional' craft industries that were perceived as the most promising source of export earnings. They were encouraged by the government, and the importance of this sector has recently been underlined by **Howe** in the chapter included here from his book *The origins of Japanese trade supremacy*. This development required some market research, for it became apparent to the responsible government agencies that 'Western' and Japanese tastes in Japanese craft wares did not necessarily coincide, and it undoubtedly contributed to the development of an image of Japan as 'quaint', as traced in the case of

Britain by Yokoyama.[20] But simultaneously even the craft industries were being transformed by the introduction of new technology, especially the steam engine which not only raised the productive capacity of the textile industry but also created new patterns of work and new relations to the workplace. In the new steam-powered textile factories, which were visually exciting enough to inspire colour prints, female workers living in dormitories constituted the bulk of the labour force: on the one hand this has been seen as having foreshadowed the possibility of economic independence for women and having provided the impetus for a fledgling Japanese export industry, but on the other hand the conditions have been deplored and the industrial enslavement has been seen as part of the 'dark side' of the process of industrialization in the Meiji period, as is clear from **Hane**'s essay. A 'dark side' there certainly was, as documented for example in the stories of Higuchi Ichiyō, and this has hitherto received insufficient attention.[21] On the other hand, the incorporation of industrial technology and patterns of work and the implementation of Western models for social and economic institutions such as banks, together with the emergence of entrepreneurs such as Shibusawa Eiichi, the subject of **Hirschmeier**'s paper, who were able to ride the rapidly changing economic environment, undoubtedly resulted in conditions that were favourable for economic growth in the urban, industrial sector of the economy. To some extent the agricultural sector was the loser, and the frequency of rural riots indicates that some of the burden for industrialization fell on that sector in the form of a heavy weight of taxation, but **Francks** argues in her piece on the Japanese farmer in the industrialization process that the conflict of interests between the agricultural and industrial sectors has been exaggerated and that there has been an inadequate appreciation of the ways in which farmers adapted to the spread of market conditions in agriculture.

The pieces contained in the final section of this volume cover various aspects of social and cultural change in the Meiji period and inevitably address the engagement with the West. There is, perhaps surprisingly, still much work to be done in this area, particularly with regard to the sources and nature of the information reaching a Japan in which first-hand knowledge was confined to a few, and to the ways in which that information was mediated. How accurate were the translations and what slants do they put on the originals, and how did Japanese read foreign texts, whether in the original or in translation? The Iwakura Mission, which has already been mentioned above, was undoubtedly of crucial importance in exposing senior members of the government not only to the realities of life in Western countries but also to the political realities governing relationships with the Great Powers. One such was the problem of Christianity, for the Meiji government had preserved the Bakufu's ban on proselytization but was forced to reconsider and lift the ban when members of the Iwakura Mission became aware of the importance attached to this issue in the West. As **Scheiner**'s book *Christian converts and social protest in Meiji Japan* shows, the impact that Protestant Christianity had on Tokutomi Sohō and other thinkers in the first half of the Meiji period was considerable, although not long-lasting, and the Meiji government made efforts to restrict its capacity for growth by recreating Shintō into more of an organized state religion and later promulgating the Imperial Rescript on Education, in which, as **Nolte**'s piece shows, morality is conceived in national terms that leave little room for attachment to 'foreign' religions.

Military organization had already been undergoing changes in the 1850s and 1860s as the Tokugawa Bakufu tried to develop a Western-style army, composed of infantry, cavalry and artillery, with which to meet potential foes internal and external. **Westney**'s article shows how this was translated into a national army based on conscription in the early Meiji period, depriving the samurai of the hereditary right to bear arms and creating the foundations for a modern professional army, and later navy. In many other aspects of Meiji social and cultural life there is a detectable tension between existing practice and Western practices and these tensions are resolved in very different ways. Banking, insurance and many other institutions were reformed or established in the Meiji period with reference to Western practices, and it was in these years too that the press, described in **Altman**'s article, began to come into its own and that the first challenges were posed to the traditional position of women in Japanese society, but by men such as Fukuzawa Yukichi, whose views on the subject are discussed by **Hane**. Along with these changes came new attitudes towards work and the notion of the 'self-made man' which, as **Kinmonth** demonstrates in the piece included here and in his book on the subject, derived from the writings of Samuel Smiles and was integrated into the idea of the self in Japan with the help of existing elements in perceptions of the social role of the samurai.[22]

VOLUME III: THE MATURE MEIJI STATE

This volume takes the reader up to the Russo-Japanese war, and so encompasses the Sino-Japanese war of 1894–5, the Triple Intervention of 1895 by which Russia, France and Germany forced Japan to give up one of the gains of the war with China, the formation of the Anglo-Japanese alliance in 1902 which brought Japan to a relationship of parity with a Western power for the first time, and the clash with Russia in 1904–5. It was at this time that enthusiasm for the West began to dim as the realities of international politics began to make themselves felt, and that the military consequences of modernization began to be apparent in the first mechanized trench war which provided a foretaste of things to come on the Western Front in 1916. The first section contains five pieces on various aspects of the political control exercised by successive Meiji governments as they moved towards a more repressive and less tolerant posture.

The first article by **Hackett** considers the role played by group leadership, rather than the leadership of a charismatic individual, in the political processes of the Meiji period, with special attention to the *genrō*, or 'elder statesmen'. This was a small and informal body of senior politicians who operated as a group outside the Constitution and who kept no record of their deliberations but who exerted considerable influence behind the scenes. Towards the end of the Meiji period their exercise of power outside the framework provided by the Constitution came under criticism, and there is no denying that their political leverage undermined even the limited provisions of the Constitution and that they resisted the development of representative government in Japan, but, as Hackett emphasizes, they also by their very continuity added an element of stability to a turbulent political system. Whether, as he suggests, this system was 'the one best suited to the leadership needs and capacities of Japan during the process of political modernization' is another matter. After all, the Meiji state had limited sympathy with the notion of participatory government, as **Mason** shows in his study of the Peace Preservation Ordinance of 1887, which had an immediate and devastating effect on the government's critics. Similarly, **Westney**, in her study of the development of the Tokyo police force along the lines of the Paris Prefecture of Police, demonstrates the appeal of a force that was centralized and performed functions of social and political control in addition to regular policing. **Iriye** and **Siddle** both tackle the expansion of Japanese political control and its consequnces, the former focusing on the increasingly expansionist policies of the Meiji government and Japan's emergence as a 'great power', and the latter considering the colonization of the northernmost island of Japan, Hokkaidō, by Japanese, which he dubs an 'internal colonization', and the suppression of Ainu identity and culture.

The next part contains four papers examining some of the consequences of industrialization. **Notehelfer**'s paper deals with the first pollution incident in Japan to become a political issue. Pollution as such was, of course, not new, and even in 1880 it was becoming clear that the Ashio copper mine was destroying not only the fish in the local rivers but also the livelihoods of the fishing communities that depended upon them. In 1891 the issue of pollution associated with the Ashio mine came before the Diet and was the subject of parliamentary discussion, but in spite of scientific reports demonstrating the connection between the pollution effects observed in rivers and the effluents from the mine, the government took no action. Later in the 1890s public protest became more strident and the mine and the pollution it was causing became a national issue as Christians and socialists protested about the human cost of unrestrained industrialization. **Smith**'s article, by contrast, deals with the effects of industrialization and the factory system on the workforce. In the first part of the Meiji period the majority of industrial workers had been women, employed in the textile industry, which was traditionally seen as women's work. It was in that context of low wages, poor working conditions and exploitation that the women workers began to turn to protest and resistance: the first strike in Japan took place in 1886 at the Amamiya silk mill in Kōfu, and after four days the managers accepted many of the demands of the women workers.[23] In the course of the 1880s and 1890s there was a growing awareness among industrial workers of the need to organize, but the union movement was still in a weak and uncertain state, and successful major strikes, such as that of 1899 which pitted the Japan Railway Company against a well-organized workforce, had nothing to do with the nascent labour unions. As **Smith** points out, at this stage, and up to the 1920s, industrial action was not so much based on modern perceptions of 'rights' as on pre-existing concepts of the 'benevolence' inferiors could expect from superiors in an unequal relationship such as that of the workplace. Finally, two chapters from **Francks**'s book on Japanese economic development offer new perspectives on the successful development of the agricultural sector within the overall economy and the impact on agricultural practice of technical changes and the application of scientific methods.

The final part in this volume focuses on social and cultural changes. In the first essay **Keene** deals with the cultural impact of the first important overseas war fought by Japan, that with China in the years 1894–5, which has recently been re-examined by Lone.[24] Japan's victory against a much larger neighbour was unexpected in the West and precipitated a new awareness of Japan as a military power as well as injecting a nationalist flavour into many forms of cultural production in Japan, such that, for example, the sinified literary language was replaced by a more colloquial style that owed less to Chinese diction. **Huffman**'s study of the press in the Meiji and Taishō periods shows how this nationalist agenda gradually overcame the resistance of the press to government control. By the time of the Russo-Japanese war the press had swung round in support of the government and not only attacked the one newspaper, Kōtoku Shūsui's *Heimin shinbun*, that opposed the war but even questioned its right to exist: the concept of a free press, that had been so strongly advocated earlier in the Meiji period was in the early twentieth century all but defunct. The final paper by **Tsurumi** considers changes in the content of education in the Meiji period and argues that the Westernization found in the textbooks produced during the early years gave way to a more pluralist set of values. It is true that the government decided in 1882 to switch the focus of education to ethics and that both Confucian and nationalist motifs began to be re-emphasized in textbooks, but she rejects the argument that the textbooks of the Meiji period moved to a position of simple indoctrination of the values of the state: the spread of nationalist feeling in late nineteenth-century Japan was more subtle in its methods and motives.

VOLUME IV: THE END OF MEIJI AND EARLY TAISHŌ

Within the scope of this volume come not only the last years of the Meiji period, but also the early part of the Taishō period, roughly up to the end of the First World War. It will thus end at the point at which the companion volumes on *Shōwa Japan*, edited by Stephen Large, take up the story. It will therefore cover the period marked by the Russo-Japanese war, the annexation of Korea in 1910 and the growth of the Japanese colonial empire, the Kōtoku treason trial of 1911 (the Dreyfus Affair of Japan) and the alienation of writers and intellectuals. Although these are all important subjects there are few good, self-contained essays that proved amenable to inclusion in this volume, so it might be helpful here to run lightly over the historical background.

Japan's victory in the Russo-Japanese war came as a shock, a profound shock to most European observers and governments, though not to members of the foreign military missions which accompanied the Japanese troops in the field and were impressed by the high levels of training and preparedness they found.[25] It was a shock because it was the first time that a European power had been defeated by an Asian one, and because it established Japan firmly on the Asian mainland as a significant colonial player. It had an electrifying effect on Russia's oppressed neighbours, such as Finland and Poland, and in Asia it suggested the reversal of the old order of things: Jawaharlal Nehru, the first prime minister of India after independence in 1947, noted in his autobiography that the Japanese victory came as an inspiration.[26] Russia had, since the eighteenth century, been establishing itself in East Asia, at first through the economic activities of the Russian–America Company and the lucrative fur trade with China, and had, in the course of the nineteenth century, acquired the Maritime Province and founded the port of Vladivostok. It was during the Sino-Japanese war, and particularly its aftermath, that the conflicting interests of Japan and Russia came to the fore, as they both sought control over Korea. Russia was eager to secure a warm-water port (Vladivostok was icebound in winter) at Port Arthur on the Liaotung peninsula just to the west of Korea, while Japan aimed to ensure that its closest neighbour was under its own control for reasons of security. This is to put it too simply, and the reader is advised to turn for a fuller account to Nish's detailed study.[27] The war began, before any declaration had been made, on 8 February 1904 when Japanese naval units launched a torpedo attack on the Russian Pacific fleet at Port Arthur. The naval side of the war ran overwhelmingly in Japan's favour, especially when the Russian Baltic fleet, which had sailed around the world from St Petersburg, was annihilated by the Imperial Japanese Navy off the Tsushima islands between Japan and Korea in May 1905. But the land war proved far more intractable and brought heavy casualties to both sides: it was a grim introduction to the horrors of mechanized warfare that were later to become commonplace on the Western Front during the First World War. Once the war was over, Japan secured a much-enhanced extension of the Anglo-Japanese Alliance, which would now secure the one partner's assistance in the case of any attack on the other partner's territories in India or East Asia. The conclusions of the Portsmouth Peace Conference convened by President Roosevelt to establish peace between Japan and Russia were, however, perceived as disappointing in Japan. Japan's economic and political interests in Korea were recognized and Japan acquired the Liaotung peninsula, including Port Arthur, and the South Manchuria Railway, which is the subject of **Myers**'s article, but there was no indemnity: there were riots in

Tokyo and some newspapers called for rejection of the treaty, in spite of Japan's financial exhaustion as a result of the war.

In the years following the Russo-Japanese war Japan consolidated its position in Korea until finally, in 1910, the decision was taken to annex Korea and to make it an integral part of the Japanese empire. For the next thirty-five years Korea remained under Japanese military rule, and Koreans lost their identity: the Korean winner of the marathon at the notorious Berlin Olympics of 1936 was therefore classed officially as a Japanese.[28] The two years following the annexation of Korea were marked by two sensational events. Firstly, in January 1911 Kōtoku Shūsui and eleven others, including the radical woman activist Kanno Sugako, were executed for their supposed involvement in a plot to assassinate the emperor: they had all in their various ways been articulating their resistance to the state and its suppression of thought, and many had turned to socialism and anarchism in their search for an ideology with which to confront the intellectual apparatus of the Meiji state; the severity of their sentences was a clear signal that radicals could expect no tolerance or mercy, and led inevitably to a decade of quiescence and retreat for the nascent left-wing in Japan.[29] And secondly, the following year, on 30 July 1912, the emperor Meiji died: as the hero of Natsume Sōseki's novel *Kokoro* put it, 'I felt as though the spirit of the Meiji era had begun with the Emperor and had ended with him. I was overcome with the feeling that I and the others, who had been brought up in that era, were now left behind to live as anachronisms.'[30] As Fujitani has noted, 'the Meiji imperial funeral rites . . . were modern creations that ignored conventions which had been followed for almost all of recorded Japanese history' in that they were purged of Buddhist elements and thus gave expression to the new sense of national identity that had emerged over the course of Meiji's reign, one which owed less and less to China or to the West.[31]

Meiji was succeeded by his mentally incapacitated son whose reign was given the name Taishō and who reigned until his early death in 1926, when he was succeeded by Hirohito, now known as the emperor Shōwa. As **Harootunian** argues in the essay included in the first part, there was in 1912 not only a sense of a portentous end but also one of a new departure and there were calls for a new politics to replace those of the Meiji period. The Taishō period is indeed now often associated with what is known as 'Taishō democracy', and it is certainly true, as **Duus** argues, that the political parties achieved a new degree of acceptance and respectability in the Taishō period, to the point that in 1918 for the first time the leader of the largest political party in the Diet, a commoner called Hara Kei, was appointed as prime minister to lead a cabinet composed of party members. This is not, however, to say that the political parties achieved any great measure of trust or that the 'democracy' they represented was anything but severely circumscribed: after all, universal manhood suffrage, giving all male citizens above the age of twenty-five the right to vote, was not introduced until 1925, and it was not until 1945 that women gained the right to vote.

The First World War of 1914–18 did not directly involve Japan, but Japan entered the war against Germany in 1914, partly to comply with the terms of the Anglo-Japanese Alliance and partly to seize German territorial possessions in China. The collapse of the Manchu dynasty in China in 1912 and now the preoccupation of the European powers with their own struggle presented Japan with an opportunity to strengthen its hold on China, which took the form of the Twenty-one Demands. The Demands, presented to China by the Japanese government in 1915, covered the transfer of German rights in China to Japan, enhanced opportunities for Japanese economic exploitation of Manchuria, and even the appointment of Japanese advisers to the Chinese republican government, and most of the provisions were accepted, under duress, by the Chinese government. These gains were, for the most part, accepted at the post-war Peace Conference and enshrined in the Versailles Treaty of 1919. The demands are discussed in **Okamoto**'s paper in the context of Ishibashi Tanzan's vociferous opposition to his government's imperialist expansion on the mainland.

It is against the background of these events, then, that the papers in the first part of this volume, on political and institutional change, need to be read. **Pyle** tackles the role of the bureacracy in fostering nationalism in the early years of the twentieth century in order simultaneously to promote continued economic development and to prevent industrialization from having the same damaging social consequences in Japan as it was perceived to have had in the West. In his study of the Local Improvement Movement he reveals one of the concrete mechanisms by which nationalist ideologies were disseminated at local level. Censorship was, of course, the ever-present negative component of the ideological machine and the chapter included here from **Mitchell**'s book on *Censorship in Imperial Japan* recounts the inexorable development of Japan into a 'surveillance state' and in particular notes the manic response, in the light of the Kōtoku Shūsui High Treason trial, to all expressions of socialist ideas in books, newspapers or magazines. He concludes bleakly that 'the state not only denied writers political freedom, but it also stunted their artistic growth', drawing attention to the need, when considering all forms of cultural production in pre-war Japan, to take full account of a climate that presented writers and artists with stark choices and undoubtedly encouraged at least a measure of self-censorship.

The second part focuses on the economy, and consists of four classic pieces that have established our fundamental understanding of the trajectory of growth in the early twentieth century and its consequences for the workforce. **Goldsmith**, unlike some other historians, takes the period leading up to the outbreak of the First World War as the first stage in the growth of the modern Japanese economy, arguing that the changed international economic conditions brought about by the onset of war mark the start of a new phase of growth based on munitions and war-related materials. By that time Japan had by international standards achieved high rates of growth with little dependence on foreign funds and had developed in just thirty years a range of sophisticated financial institutions on a par with those to be found in Western countries. On the other hand, income per head was still much lower than was the case in Western Europe and North America, factory working conditions remained brutal and harsh, and unionization was still at a low level. **Large**'s chapter, from his book *Organized workers and socialist politics in interwar Japan*, explores some of these topics, starting with the formation of the first labour union in 1897, and demonstrates that the friendly societies and labour unions of the early twentieth century benefited from, among other things, the greater tolerance shown by factory owners who were more inclined to make concessions in the interest of avoiding disputes and maintaining production. The papers by **Dore** and **Pyle** explore some of the consequences of the fact that Japan was a 'late-developer': on the one hand technological developments were ready to be adopted wholesale without the need to be reinvented in Japan and the pitfalls into which others had fallen could be avoided, but on the other hand there were the problems of national identity occasioned by dependence on the West and the constant tension between what were perceived as Western and Japanese values. **Dore** examines the difficulties encountered in this connection by supporters of factory legislation, who had to make concessions to textile manufacturers and others seeking exemptions to permit the employment of minors and delays in other provisions before the final passage of the Factory Act in 1911. **Pyle**, on the other hand, tackles the views of certain bureaucrats and intellectuals who were familiar with German thinking on social policy and took advantage of the fact, as they saw it, that Japan was following the same path as the Western economies to adopt a preventive posture, one that they hoped would enable Japan to avoid some of the problems they detected in the West. These 'problems' included class consciousness and industrial conflict, and the preventive measures considered were ones that were inclined towards the inculcation of nationalism and restrictions on the freedom of expression.

The final section contains five essays dealing with the impact of the state on cultural and social life in the early twentieth century. **Okamoto**'s paper on Ishibashi Tanzan's opposition to the Twenty-one Demands, which have already been mentioned above, explores the roots of his independent stance at a time when few were questioning the growth of Japanese imperialism in China. Women also found themselves increasingly confronted by a state that sought to fit them into a rigid model of womanhood and in 1890 forbade them to attend political meetings in any capacity whatsoever, a measure that remained in force until 1922. **Nolte** and **Hastings** in their essay explore the gradual tightening of the screw in the decades leading up to the end of the Meiji period; to their account can be added the Civil Code of 1898, which tied women to the patriarchal *ie* household system and left married women without legal status or the rights to take legal action and control their own property. As in other societies at similar stages of development, the women's movement, such as it was, was fragmented and there was little, if any, contact between, for example, the women textile workers pressing for more humane working conditions and the intellectuals agitating for their political rights. Hiratsuka Raichō and the women who founded the magazine *Seitō,* or 'Bluestocking', were, as **Sievers** demonstrates, initially more interested in developing a literary forum for women but gradually became more politicized.

The last two essays deal with intellectual life in Meiji Japan. **Marshall** examines the Meiji academic élite, concentrated at Tokyo Imperial University, and their close integration with the state via the Ministry of Education, which was their employer. By the early twentieth century, academics had begun to distance themselves from the state and the first clashes between the government and some Tokyo University professors took place: the professors were attempting to force the government to take a firmer line against Russia and the government's response, which included the dismissal of one of the professors, produced a vigorous response from which it is clear that the academic élite had already a strong commitment to their intellectual independence of the government. Finally **Bartholomew** considers the clash between the bureaucracy and the interests of experimental science in Japan, focusing on the successful career of Kitasato Shibasaburō, who was the first to isolate the plague bacillus but whose scientific methodology was not in harmony with that of the scientific bureaucracy.

This volume ends, then, on a cautious note. The Meiji state had gradually turned itself into a highly centralized, closely controlled and bureaucratically efficient state and in the process found itself at odds with segments of the population who resisted the encroachments of state power and rejected the monocultural uniformity imposed from above. The outcome of the High Treason Trial showed how high the stakes were and how far the government was prepared to go in order to suppress criticism, and in a sense how false and superficial the concept of 'Taishō democracy' really is. For the fate of that fragile and limited democracy, and the rise of the military in the early Shōwa period, the reader is advised to turn to the companion volumes edited by Stephen Large, *The Shōwa period.*

Peter Kornicki
Cambridge, England, 10 May 1997

NOTES

1 On this issue see Ronald P. Toby, *State and diplomacy in early modern Japan: Asia in the development of the Tokugawa Bakufu* (Princeton: Princeton University Press, 1984).

2 See Derek Massarella, 'Some reflections on identity formation in East Asia in the sixteenth and seventeenth centuries', in Donald Denoon, Mark Hudson, Gavan McCormack and Tessa Morris-Suzuki, eds, *Multicultural Japan: palaeolithic to postmodern* (Cambridge: Cambridge University Press, 1996), pp. 135—6.

3 Shigenobu Ōkuma, *Fifty years of new Japan*, 2 vols (London: Smith, Elder & Co., 1909); Hugh Borton, *Japan's modern century* (New York: Ronald Press, 1955), p. v.

4 For a useful discussion of the Westernization volumes and modernization theory, see Ross Mouer and Yoshio Sugimoto, *Images of Japanese society: a study in the structure of social reality* (London: KPI, 1986), esp. pp. 27–32, 47–9, and 'Introduction: modernization and beyond', in Gavan McCormack and Yoshio Sugimoto, eds, *The Japanese trajectory: modernization and beyond* (Cambridge: Cambridge University Press, 1988), pp. 1–14.

5 On the banks see Norio Tamaki, *Japanese banking*, 1859–1959 (Cambridge: Cambridge University Press, 1995).

6 Grant K. Goodman, *Japan; the Dutch experience* (London: Athlone Press, 1986), and Masayoshi Sugimoto and David L. Swain, *Science and culture in traditional Japan:* A.D. 600–1854 (Cambridge, Mass.: MIT Press, 1978).

7 For *Multicultural Japan* see note 2; T. Fujitani, *Splendid monarchy: power and pageantry in modern Japan* (Berkeley: University of California Press, 1996).

8 On the Russians, Macartney and the French see respectively G. A. Lensen, *The Russian push toward Japan; Russo-Japanese relations, 1697–1875* (Princeton: Princeton University Press, 1959), J. L. Cranmer-Byng, 'Russian and British interests in the Far East, 1791–1793', *Canadian Slavonic Papers* 10 (1968): 357–75, and Patrick Beillevaire, 'Heavenly affinities and discrepancies: Fr Leturdu's early ethnographic account of Okinawa (1846–1848)', in P. F. Kornicki and I. J. McMullen, eds, *Religion in Japan: arrows to heaven and earth* (Cambridge: Cambridge University Press, 1996), pp. 156–78.

9 W. G. Beasley, *Select documents on Japanese foreign policy, 1853–68* (Oxford: Oxford University Press, 1955).

10 W. G. Beasley, *The Meiji Restoration* (Stanford: Stanford University Press, 1972).

11 T. M. Huber, *The Revolutionary origins of modern Japan* (Stanford: Stanford University Press, 1981).

12 On these issues see Martin Collcutt, 'Buddhism: the threat of eradication', in M. B. Jansen and G. Rozman, eds, *Japan in transition: from Tokugawa to Meiji* (Princeton: Princeton University Press, 1986), pp. 143–67, and Stephen Vlastos, 'Opposition movements in early Meiji, 1868–1885', in Marius B. Jansen, ed., *The Cambridge history of Japan,* Vol. 5 (Cambridge: Cambridge University Press, 1989), pp. 367–431.

13 On the exhibitions and Japan see P. F. Kornicki, 'Public display and changing values in nineteenth-century Japan: exhibitions in the early Meiji period and their precursors', *Monumenta Nipponica* 49 (1994): 167–96, and 'Japan at the Australian exhibitions', *Australian Studies* 8 (1994):15–60.

14 Carol Gluck, *Japan's modern myths: ideology in the late Meiji period* (Princeton: Princeton University Press, 1985).

15 S. L. Sievers, *Flowers in salt: the beginnings of feminist consciousness in modern Japan* (Stanford: Stanford University Press, 1983), p. xiv.

16 Barbara Rose, *Tsuda Umeko and women's education in Japan* (New Haven: Yale University Press, 1992), p. 11; the story of another of these women, Yamakawa Sutematsu, is told in Akiko Kuno, *Unexpected destinations: the poignant story of Japan's first Vassar graduate,* trans. Kirsten McIvor (Tokyo: Kodansha International, 1993).

17 See P. F. Kornicki, *The reform of fiction in Meiji Japan* (London: Ithaca Press, 1982), pp. 51–2.

18 William Braisted, *Meiroku zasshi: journal of the Japanese enlightenment* (Cambridge, Mass.: Harvard University Press, 1976), pp. 401–4.

19 On the political novels, see P. F. Kornicki, 'Disraeli and the Meiji novel', *Harvard Journal of Asiatic Studies* 44 (1984): 29–55.

20 Toshio Yokoyama, *Japan in the Victorian mind: a study of sterotyped images of a nation, 1850–80* (London: Macmillan, 1987).

21 A number of Ichiyō's stories are translated in Robert Lyons Danly, *In the shade of*

spring leaves: the life and writings of Higuchi Ichiyō, a woman of letters in Meiji Japan (New Haven: Yale University Press, 1981).

22 E. H. Kinmonth, *The self-made man in Meiji Japanese thought: from samurai to salary man* (Berkeley: University of Califomia Press, 1981).

23 S. L. Sievers, *Flowers in salt: the beginnings of feminist consciousness in modern Japan* (Stanford: Stanford University Press, 1983), pp. 81–2.

24 S. Lone, *Japan's first modern war: army and society in the conflict with China, 1894–95* (London: St Martin's Press, 1994).

25 See for example Lt-Gen. Sir Ian Hamilton's account in *A staff officer's scrap-book during the Russo-Japanese War*, 2 vols (London: Edward Arnold, 1905–7).

26 Jawaharlal Nehru, *Toward freedom* (New York: Cornwall, 1941), pp. 29–30.

27 Ian Nish, *The origins of the Russo-Japanese war* (London: Longman, 1985).

28 On the Japanese control of Korea see H. Conroy, *The Japanese seizure of Korea: 1868–1910* (University of Pennsylvania Press, 1960); A. C. Nahm, ed., *Korea under Japanese colonial rule* (Center for Korean Studies, Western Michigan University, 1973); and Peter Duus, *The abacus and the sword: the Japanese penetration of Korea, 1895–1910* (Berkeley: University of California Press, 1995).

29 On the High Treason case, see F. G. Notehelfer, *Kōtoku Shūsui: portrait of a Japanese radical* (Cambridge: Cambridge University Press, 1971) and S. L. Sievers, *Flowers in salt the beginnings of feminist consciousness in modern Japan* (Stanford: Stanford University press, 1983), pp. 139–62.

30 Natsume Soseki, *Kokoro*, trans. Edwin McClellan (Tokyo: Tuttle, 1969), p. 245.

31 T. Fujitani, *Splendid monarchy: power and pageantry in modern Japan* (Berkeley: University of California Press, 1996), p. 152.

Part I

The collapse of the Bakufu and the Meiji Restoration

1 Japan's entry into international society*

The expansion of international society

H. Suganami

*Source: Headley Bull and A. Watson (eds), *The Expansion of International Society* (Oxford: Clarendon Press, 1984), Ch. 12, pp. 185–99.

Commodore Perry's arrival in Japan in 1853 may be commonly remembered as the starting-point of Japan's relations with the Western Powers, but her first encounter with the West began with the 'discovery' of Japan by Portuguese castaways in the mid-sixteenth century. From then on Japan's foreign relations went through three stages.

In the first stage, lasting to the early decades of the seventeenth century, there was a great deal of interaction between the Japanese and foreigners inhabiting the Far East. In the second stage, up to the mid-nineteenth century, Japan under the House of Tokugawa adopted the policy of seclusion. During the third stage, from the mid-nineteenth century onwards, Japan reluctantly abandoned the seclusion policy and later strove for equality and Great Power status in international society. Here we shall concentrate on Japan's relations with the outside world during the seclusion and post-seclusion periods up to the end of the First World War.

THE PERIOD OF SECLUSION

The years from 1603 to 1868 are known in Japanese history as the Edo Period. Edo, renamed Tokyo in 1868, was where the House of Tokugawa, a warrior clan, having terminated a long period of war among feudal lords, established the central administration of Japan, called the 'Bakufu'. The Bakufu was headed by a 'Shogun', which in the ancient time was the title of the Emperor's *ad hoc* military deputy, but which had come to mean the supreme feudal lord formally authorized by the Emperor to rule Japan. The office of Shogun was hereditary in the House of Tokugawa throughout the Edo Period. The Imperial Family and Court Nobles survived in the ancient capital of Kyoto, but were politically impotent until the very last phase of the Edo Period.

A part of Japan was under direct Tokugawa rule, and the rest was divided up into feudal domains governed by the 'Daimyos', or feudal lords. There were three classes of Daimyos: those of Tokugawa blood; those descended from the vassals of Ieyasu, the founder of the Tokugawa Bakufu, during his rise to power; and those who submitted to Tokugawa control after the battle of Sekigahara in 1600 which won Ieyasu the title of Shogun. The Tokugawas treated the third category of Daimyos with suspicion. It was chiefly to prevent them from allying with foreign powers against the Tokugawa hegemony, and gaining power through foreign trade, that in the early part of the seventeenth century the Bakufu introduced the policy of seclusion.

According to the official doctrine of the seclusion period, foreigners were divided into three categories. The Dutch and the Chinese were classified as 'Tsusho-no-kuni', or 'nations-for-trading'. Korea and Ryukyu came under the category of 'Tsushin-no-kuni', or countries whose official envoys were invited as state guests to Edo on important ceremonial occasions for the exchange of goodwill. The rest of the world was to be repelled.[1] Despite their classification as 'Tsusho-no-kuni', however, the Dutch and the Chinese were not treated in the same way by the Japanese; nor were the positions of Korea and Ryukyu the same *vis-à-vis* Japan despite their title 'Tsushin-no-kuni'.

At the beginning of the seventeenth century, there were four European nations which had relations with Japan: the Portuguese, Spanish, English, and Dutch. The first two were expelled by the Tokugawa seclusion edicts, while the third temporarily withdrew on account of the lack of profit. When in 1673 the English attempted to resume trade, the Bakufu's seclusion policy had become too rigid to allow for their return despite the Charter of Privileges accorded them earlier by the first two Tokugawa Shoguns. This left the Dutch as the sole Europeans to be accepted in Japan.

The Dutch were confined to Dejima, an artificial island in the port of Nagasaki, and subjected to all manner of restrictions. They did, however, share one burden with the Daimyos, which by that very fact was a sign of privilege. This was the Shogun's audience. The Daimyos, with certain exceptions, had an obligation to alternate their residence between Edo and their fiefs, leaving their families as hostages in Edo. On their arrival, the Daimyos were to be conducted to the Shogun's presence in Edo Castle to pay their respects. Similarly, the Dutch Factory had to send envoys regularly to Edo with presents to pay their respects to the Shogun. The head of the Factory was brought into the Shogun's presence in a manner similar to that in which the Daimyos were introduced, and although he had to perform obeisance to the Shogun, which might have seemed undignified from the European viewpoint, he was at least on a par with any of the great Daimyos in this respect.

The Chinese were in a different position. There were no formal relations of 'Tsushin' (communication of goodwill through official envoys) between China and Japan during the Edo Period; by the mid-sixteenth century this form of intercourse, which Japan had maintained with the Ming in the early part of the fifteenth century in order to facilitate trade, had fallen into desuetude. The Bakufu's desire to re-establish 'Tsushin' with China through Korean mediation was not fulfilled. Nevertheless Chinese merchants continued to visit Japanese ports for private trading. In 1636 Nagasaki was declared the only port open to them, but no envoys were sent to Edo from the

Chinese community, which thrived in Nagasaki. In the relationship with the Chinese, therefore, we find a purer example of 'Tsusho' (trade).

In the case of relations between Korea and Japan in the Edo Period there were three principal actors: the Korean Court, the Bakufu, and Tsushima, an island midway between Korea and Japan. The Bakufu invited envoys from Korea, while Tsushima traded with her, maintained a small settlement in Pusan, and acted as an intermediary for Japanese–Korean relations. The relationship between Japan and Korea was not a product of the seclusion period. There had been similar relations between them since the fifteenth century. It is of interest that the Bakufu's relations with Korea were conducted on the basis of formal diplomatic equality, and that the protocol was worked out in detail by the Bakufu's official Confucian scholars.[2]

There were twelve missions from Korea throughout the Edo Period, each of which contained a large number of delegates. The first mission, for instance, that of 1607, consisted of 467 members, including circus riders and musicians.[3] The nearest contemporary equivalent of the Korean missions may be found in the practice of sending special envoys to attend important occasions, such as state funerals, or in the exchange of cultural missions for the promotion of goodwill. It is important to note, however, that the main aim of the Bakufu in inviting missions from Korea was political. The Bakufu attempted to enhance its prestige, and reinforce its legitimacy, by means of international recognition, which was to be obtained from the Korean envoys' occasional visits to the Shogun's capital.

In contast to the case of Korea, Japan's relations with the Ryukyu islands were not based on equality, as the King of Ryukyu had been subjugated by Satsuma, Japan's southernmost domain, in 1609. Ryukyu maintained a tributary relationship with China, which facilitated trade, but Satsuma, far from objecting to the islands' formal subservience to another country, positively encouraged it, because Satsuma's chief aim in subjugating the islands had been to establish an indirect trading link with China. Satsuma even directed the Ryukyu authorities to conceal their relationships with Japan from the Chinese lest the disclosure of the Ryukyu King's double loyalty should displease the Chinese and result in the loss of trade.[4] The King of Ryukyu began to send congratulatory missions to Edo in 1644, which heightened the prestige both of the Bakufu and of Satsuma.[5] Japan under the Meiji Government was to declare full sovereignty over the islands in 1871, originally incorporating them in the Kagoshima Prefecture, a former Satsuma domain, and shortly afterwards according them the status of the Okinawa Prefecture. However, unlike the Meiji Government, equipped with the modern notion of absolute territorial jurisdiction by the state, the feudalist Tokugawas tolerated a less exclusive relationship with what was, after all, their vassal's vassal in a distant place.

In addition to contacts with these four peoples, there was also some trade between Matusmae, Japan's northernmost domain, and the Ainu, who traded between themselves and brought animal pelts from the northern Kuril islands and Kamchatka.[6] All these, however, were exceptions to the rule. Under the strict policy of seclusion, all other nations were to be refused any contact with the Japanese. Naturally, the effectiveness of this policy depended not only on the power of the Bakufu to enforce its laws but also upon the willingness of the foreign countries to acquiesce. Unfortunately for the Bakufu's seclusion policy, ships began to approach the coast of Japan from Russia, Britain, and the United States in increasing numbers from the early part of the eighteenth century. The official treatment of unwanted foreigners arriving on the ships reflected to a large extent the laws that the Bakufu enacted to implement its policy of seclusion.[7]

The first such law was the edict of 1791, which consolidated customary rules that had begun to develop in the treatment of foreign vessels approaching Japan. Given the general principle that foreigners were not allowed to visit Japan, the tone of the 1791 edict was relatively moderate, although it severely restricted the freedom of those who arrived.

The Bakufu was impressed by the willingness to comply with the laws of Japan shown by two Russian envoys (Laxman in 1792 and Rezanov in 1804). This led to the revision of the Bakufu attitude in 1806 in favour of the Russians. The new edict recommended a particularly gentle treatment of the Russians, although all it amounted to was an instruction that the Japanese officials should try to be as gentle as possible in telling them to depart and never to return.

However, the Bakufu's special favour to the Russians was soon abandoned in response to the Khvostov/Davidov affair of 1806–7, when two naval officers seconded to the Russian-American Company, of which Rezanov was a leading figure, attacked Japanese settlements in Sakhalin and the southern Kuril islands. They had acted under the personal instruction of Rezanov, who had been outraged by the fact that his painstaking effort to open trade with Japan had completely failed. The Bakufu now decreed that all Russian ships must be repelled, and failing this, their crews detained, or executed in case of resistance.

Another unfortunate event occurred in 1824 when some English whalers attacked Satsuma officials, attempting to steal some bullocks for food. Insignificant though it might appear as a political event, this, in fact, caused the Bakufu to promulgate in 1825 the most uncompromising repulsion edict of all. All foreign vessels approaching the Japanese coast were to be repelled unconditionally. The Bakufu, however, did hardly anything to strengthen coastal defence and the edict's efficacy was precarious.

Meanwhile, European naval and military capabilities were developing rapidly. Already in 1840 the news of the Opium War had reached Japan through the Dutch Factory and shaken the Bakufu's confidence in China's status as a Great Power, and *a fortiori*, its confidence in its own power to maintain the 1825 edict. Moreover, the idea of an unconditional repulsion was thought by the Bakufu's official Confucian scholar to be unreasonable and contrary to moral obligation towards foreign countries. A report, which had reached

Japan through the Dutch Factory, that the *Morrison*, which had been repelled in 1837 in accordance with the 1825 edict, in fact intended among other things to return some Japanese castaways raised a strong sense of shame among some Bakufu officials. The result was the abolition in 1842 of the unconditional repulsion edict and reversion to the decree of 1806. Aid to ships in distress was assured, although landings were firmly refused.

The Bakufu legislations generally proscribed unnecessary violence. However, some degree of violence was necessary for the very implementation of the seclusion policy. This, and some inaccurate reporting by the castaways who had been imprisoned (or quarantined) in Japan, as well as unfortunate incidents during the unconditional repulsion period, caused the Western nations, particularly the Americans, who were the most frequent victims, to regard the Japanese as barbaric in their treatment of foreigners. This explains much of Commodore Perry's uncompromising attitude towards Japan and his conviction that civilization must be forced upon the Japanese. Perry determinedly refused to comply with the usual restrictions that the Bakufu had imposed upon foreigners approaching Japan, and resisted all attempts by the Bakufu officials to employ their customary techniques of hindrance and procrastination. Perry's approach worked because the Bakufu, intimidated by his show of superior force, concluded that there was little it could do to avoid accepting some of his demands, at least temporarily. The Bakufu did not attempt to resist Perry by force because it thought that it would be even more undignified to accept the American terms after having been seen to have lost a battle.

ENTRY INTO INTERNATIONAL SOCIETY

As we saw, during the seclusion period, Japan operated what might be called an ethnocentric system with herself at the centre surrounded by Korea, Ryukyu, the Chinese, and the Dutch. In addition, there were sporadic contacts with Russia, Britain, and America. These relationships did not constitute an 'international society' of the kind which existed in the West. However, Japan by the end of the century had transformed her uncertain relationship with the West into a full 'societal' one, while her traditional ethnocentric system lost its practical relevance. The question arises as to when this transformation took place.

It is to be noted that between 1853 and 1858, during the Bakumatsu (End-of-the-Bakufu) Period, treaties were negotiated and concluded between Japan and the Western Powers, and consuls were sent to Japan. Thus during this period Japan can be said to have begun to participate in the operation of some of the basic rules and practices of international society. However, her knowledge of these rules and practices, or institutions, was very limited. She did not appreciate the value of preserving these institutions, or indeed of becoming a member of an international society with such institutions. The strong anti-foreign factions in Japan still maintained that the Bakufu should pursue the policy of seclusion, that any concessions offered by the Bakufu to the Western Powers through the treaties of 1854–8 were temporary measures, and that, when Japan had rebuilt her strength to match the West, she should revert to the ancient laws of seclusion. The Western Powers, on their part, as is clear from the terms of these treaties, did not regard the Japanese state as an equal member of their international society. Thus, despite her gradual abandonment of the policy of seclusion, it is doubtful whether Japan can be said to have become a member of international society in any proper sense during the Bakumatsu Period.

Meanwhile, the Tokugawas continued to exhibit their inability to revert to the seclusion policy. The anti-Tokugawa forces in Japan used this weakness of the Bakufu to their best advantage. The Tokugawas were now being shown to be unfit to govern Japan, for they could not abide by their own ancestral laws, and failed to protect Japan from the encroachment of the 'barbarians'. The Tokugawas fell, and the power of government was restored to the Emperor in 1868, because they were outbalanced by the coalition of anti-Tokugawa factions who rallied round the slogan, 'Revere the Emperor; Expel the Barbarians.' It was argued that only through unification under the leadership of the Emperor could Japan rebuild her strength to repel the Western Powers. Although the leading factions of the anti-Tokugawa forces had come to realize by 1864 the futility of attempting to repel the Western Powers, they clung to the latter half of the slogan because it effectively disclosed the Bakufu's weaknesses.

The policy of seclusion, however, was not a realistic alternative for the newborn Government of Emperor Meiji. Contrary to Japanese expectation, that the new government would adopt a seclusionist policy, it announced that the goal of the whole nation should be to restore the glory of Japan in the eyes of all nations, that the iniquitous aspects of the treaties the Bakufu had concluded with the West would be revised, but that foreign relations should be conducted in accordance with the law of nations.[8]

Japan can be said to have entered international society somewhere between this time and the turn of the century, when she finally managed to persuade the West that the 'unequal' treaties imposed upon Tokugawa Japan should be revised. In 1868 Japan declared her intention to become a member of international society by formally abandoning the policy of seclusion and undertaking to comply with Western rules and the practices of foreign intercourse. Some thirty years later the Western Powers upgraded Japan from an inferior status by agreeing to revise the 'unequal' treaties.

THE ADVANCEMENT OF JAPAN IN INTERNATIONAL SOCIETY

The development of Japan's foreign relations from the arrival of Perry to the early decades of the twentieth century can be divided into three stages.

In the first, between Perry's initial visit (1853) and the Iwakura Mission to the West (1871–3),Japan was still learning to understand Western conceptions and the methods of foreign relations.[9] At the beginning of this stage, Japan's attitude was that of an unwilling pupil, but practical necessity soon turned her into a keen student of Western diplomacy. After the Meiji Restoration of 1868 the process was irreversible. By the end of this stage Japan was engaged in an earnest endeavour to adopt the behaviour appropriate to the Western-dominated international society in order to be accepted as one of its full members.

The quest for equality, which has its roots in the formal abandonment of the seclusion policy by the Meiji Government, is the predominant theme of the second stage in Japan's foreign relations after Perry. It stretches from the time of the Iwakura Mission (1871–3) to 1911, when Japan, having abolished consular jurisdiction in 1899 (an agreement to terminate it had been reached in 1894), finally succeeded in removing the restrictions on her tariff autonomy.

Japan's transition during these two stages necessitated change in her relations with Korea and China. No formal relations existed between Japan and China, and 'Tsushin' with Korea had ended in the early part of the nineteenth century. One of the first diplomatic acts of the Meiji Government was to attempt to establish full relations on the European model with the governments of these countries.

It is to be noted that Meiji Japan's intercourse with these countries closely resembled that between the Western Powers and the Tokugawa authorities in both form and substance: in form, it was based on treaty obligations; in substance, it was an exercise in power politics. Just as Japan was at the receiving end of 'unequal' treaties with the West, so she herself imposed an 'unequal' treaty upon Korea in 1876, thereby ending the seclusion of that country and, in 1896, gained most-favoured-nation status in relation to China. Thus this second stage of Japan's foreign relations is one in which she began to apply what she had learnt from the West in her external affairs. Clearly, Japan's success in putting into practice what she had learnt was the major source of her advancement in international society.

The most significant events during this stage, from the viewpoint of Japan's status in international society, included war with China (1894–5), participation alongside the European powers and the United States in the Boxer Intervention (1900–1), the Anglo-Japanese Alliance (1902), war with Russia (1904–5), and the annexation of Korea (1910). Japan's meticulous observance of international law during the Sino-Japanese War, the Boxer Intervention, and the Russo-Japanese War was also an important factor in helping her win a reputation among the Western Powers as a civilized nation, while the formation of the Anglo-Japanese Alliance gave her not only international prestige but also a pretext under which she was later to participate in the First World War against Germany. Clearly, by the end of the second stage, Japan had begun to behave like a Great Power, and to be accepted by the Western Great Powers as a member of the ruling directorate of international society.

In the third stage of Japan's foreign relations after Perry, which is from about the second decade of the twentieth century, she tried to consolidate her position in international society as a Great Power of Asia equal in importance to those of the West. Japan secured a formal expression of such a status by becoming a permanent member of the Council of the League of Nations after the First World War, while her Twenty-One Demands to China during the War were a clear indication of the imperialist path Japan had set out to follow in the decades to come.

WESTERNIZATION IN JAPAN'S FOREIGN RELATIONS

We must now examine how the Japanese came to accept Western practices of foreign relations which were entirely alien to them during the period of seclusion. When the Westerners approached the Japanese in the Bakumatsu Period there was a gap between the foreign visitors and the Japanese governing class as regards the purpose of foreign intercourse: the Japanese saw very little, for the tradition of seclusion had been accompanied by the cultivation not only of an inarticulate anti-foreign sentiment, but, combined with it, a belief in autarky. It came to be held, except by a negligible minority, that what foreigners brought were unnecessary luxuries, that they took away what Japan could hardly spare, and that therefore foreign trade was harmful to the Japanese economy and society. This belief was reinforced by the warrior ethos, which emphasized austerity and disdained commerce.

Thus the reluctant abandonment of the seclusion policy in the Bakumatsu Period, and the radical departure from it in the Meiji Period, involved Japanese acceptance of the Western conception of the purpose of foreign intercourse, which reflected the current Western international economic theory and practice.[10] In this sense the abandonment of the policy of seclusion can itself be said to have involved Westernization.

Westernization in Japan's purposes in engaging in foreign intercourse was accompanied by the Western Powers' imposition of their formal methods, or institutions, of foreign relations. This had already begun with the arrival of Perry, who successfully ignored the traditional Japanese methods of dealing with unwanted foreigners. Among these new methods, or institutions, introduced by the West, the most fundamental were the diplomatic/consular system and international law.

The idea of sending letters and envoys abroad had existed among the Japanese prior to seclusion, and the practice of receiving missions from overseas continued in the Edo Period. But the distinctively European idea of a permanently resident diplomatic mission or consul was entirely alien to the Japanese. Perry's proposal to set up a US Consulate in Japan was strongly resisted because the Bakufu assumed a consul to be just an alien civil administrator incompatible with Japan's sovereignty.

However, Perry was also insistent. A solution was found in what appears to be a deliberate mistranslation: the English text of the 1854 US–Japanese treaty secured to the US government the right to send 'consuls or agents to reside in Shimoda' automatically after the expiration of eighteen months from the date of signature, whereas the Japanese text made this conditional on an agreement between the two governments after the eighteen months' period.

There was no provision in the treaty indicating which of the four versions was the original text: the Dutch, English, Chinese, or Japanese. Through such an arrangement, Perry obtained what he wanted, while the Japanese negotiators appear to have tried to cover up their weaknesses.[11]

In accordance with the English provision, Harris arrived in Shimoda in 1856 as a US consul-general. The Bakufu officials strongly protested against his arrival, and severely restricted his freedom, but in the end acquiesced in his presence. By 1858 commercial treaties had been concluded with the West, and the Western Powers secured the right to keep resident diplomatic and consular agents in Japan and obtained extraterritorial rights for their nationals. These developments owe much to Harris's negotiating skills, while the growth of the anti-seclusion party in the Bakufu was also decisive. Japan herself, however, did not send resident missions abroad till the Meiji Period when the policy of seclusion was finally discarded without reservation.

Given its initial insistence that a resident diplomatic or consular agent was incompatible with Japan's sovereignty, it is curious that the Bakufu should have given away extraterritorial rights to foreign nationals on a non-reciprocal basis. Three reasons may be noted here. First, the Japanese negotiators did not have sufficient power to avoid such an arrangement. Second, they negotiated within the seclusionist frame of mind, which meant that, with the one notable exception of the 1855 Russo-Japanese Friendship Treaty, all the treaties envisaged the existence of foreigners in Japan, but not that of the Japanese abroad. This one-sidedness in the balance of interest seems to have reinforced that of the balance of power. Third, the Japanese negotiators were so ignorant of the workings of international relations that they could not foresee the inconvenience and injustices that could result from the arrangement. It should be noted in this connection that Japanese ignorance also explains in part why they unquestioningly gave away the most-favoured-nation clause to Perry, and accepted fixed tariff rates in the negotiations with Harris.[12]

Compared with the case of the resident diplomatic/consular system, the Japanese acceptance of international law went more smoothly, despite the fact that the existence of international law was totally unknown to them. This was because some understanding of international law was essential to the Bakufu in order to cope with the new concepts and rules employed by the West since the arrival of Perry. Moreover, when the Meiji Government was established, it was popularly expected to carry out the expulsion of foreigners, because the anti-Tokugawa forces had used chauvinistic slogans as a means of pressure upon the Bakufu. The new government, however, had neither the power nor the intention to revert to the policy of seclusion, and thus felt the need to justify its foreign policy as soon as it came to power. In this respect, the concept of the law of nations was most appropriate because the Government could try to pacify the people with the idea that the Western Powers complied with the law of nations and should not be regarded as lawless barbarians. The fact that most textbooks of international law imported to Japan had Natural Law overtones suited the Government well, because the Western Natural Law vocabulary was translated into Japanese through the basic language of Confucianism, which added grandiosity to the new body of rules.[13]

It should also be noted that the Meiji Government used international law both to defend Japan against Western interference in her domestic affairs and as a means of breaking up China's suzerainty over Korea. The Japanese were to achieve this through the use of force, but they also tried to make use of the basic conceptual tools of the Western theory of international relations embodied in international law, such as sovereign equality, independence, and non-intervention, to which the Chinese idea of suzerainty was opposed. At the same time, Japan tried to impress the Western Powers by meticulous observance of international law. Two eminent Japanese jurists were attached to the Army and the Navy respectively during the Sino-Japanese War as the legal adviser of each headquarters. In the Russo-Japanese War many more advisers were involved, some of whom worked at the front.[14] There was a tendency among the Japanese élite to respect international law as part of their West-worship.

FACTORS FAVOURABLE TO JAPAN

Several factors favoured Japan in her struggle in the Western-dominated international society. A comparison with China is particularly instructive.

First, we may compare the two nations' self-images. The Chinese divided the world into the civilized centre, where the Emperor's rule was effective, and the barbaric periphery, where, they thought, Chinese influence had not brought up the standard of morality and living. It is important to note that this division was cultural rather than territorial or ethnic.[15]

The Japanese also had a sense of national superiority. In particular, the scholars of the Japanese classics who were self-consciously opposed to Chinese culture became influential in the nineteenth century. They argued for Japan's uniqueness and superiority on the grounds of Shinto beliefs: that the Japanese Emperor was descended from the Sun-Goddess, that the Japanese Islands and people were also of divine origin, and that therefore Japan was superior to the rest of the world. The Japanese sense of superiority, by contrast with that of the Chinese, was thus closely bound up with the unity of the race and the integrity of the territory in which they had developed their peculiar blend of culture.

This difference between the two nations favoured Japan over China as the Japanese authorities, being more conscious of territory and race than their Chinese counterparts, could perceive the threat from outside more vividly. The 'Black Ships' created an acute sense of crisis among the Japanese leaders, while the Chinese appear to have seen them rather as just another source of nuisance.

A second factor which favoured Japan over China was the difference in the nature of the leadership. Japan was governed by the warrior class. Although 200 years of domestic peace had made Samurais redundant in their original functions as fighters, and turned them virtually into civil administrators, they maintained their traditional mode of thinking as military experts. This helped the Japanese leaders rule out strategically irrational options in responding to the Western threat, and encouraged them to import superior Western technology. By contrast, the Chinese civilian mandarinate had almost no interest in military and technological matters, and even disdained them.

Compared with the Bakufu leaders, anti-foreign factions of the powerful Satsuma and Choshu domains were more deeply misguided by their chauvinism; but through the events of 1863 and 1864, in which they exchanged fire with Western naval forces, they too had to come to realize their impotence in the face of new Western technology, and therefore speeded up their efforts to modernize their forces through foreign aids. In this connection it may also be noted that, unlike their counterparts in China, peasant uprisings in Japan did not develop into a large-scale anti-foreign movement, which would not only have cost Japan military intervention by the Western Powers but would also have led to further curtailment of her political independence.

A third factor is the Japanese readiness to learn from abroad, which the Japanese sense of national superiority was not so overwhelming as to rule out. In fact, even during the seclusion period, strong West-worship developed among the so-called Dutch scholars, especially after the middle of the eighteenth century. Although few in number, they nevertheless illustrate the Japanese readiness to seek any new form of knowledge regardless of its cultural or ethnic origins. One tangible result of the scholars' efforts was the production of modern cannon in one of the domains in 1853, the year of Perry's arrival. Westernization in technology and military science, however, was negligible during the Edo Period. The Meiji Period saw a systematic effort by the government and people to import from the West all necessary artefacts and paraphernalia to qualify as a civilized, modern, nation.

A fourth factor was a peculiar structure of dual authority in Japan: the presence of the Emperor in addition to the Shogun. As we saw, the opening up of Japan went side by side with the decline in the power and authority of the Bakufu, but, fortunately for Japan, the Emperor provided a rallying-point for the anti-Tokugawa factions and enabled Japan to avoid a long period of national division. Moreover, a timely change in the government provided Japan with an opportunity to reform its political institutions along Western lines. In China, by contrast, there was no similar second authority to make such a transition possible. The view that the revitalization of China in the face of the Western encroachment required the modernization of her political institutions as well as the importation of Western technology was defeated by the conservative intellectual outlook of the ruling class and the inertia of the old institutions.[16]

Westernization in both technology and institutions distinguishes the experience of Japan in the nineteenth century from that of China. This institutional Westernization helped Japan to attain the position of equality with the Western Powers because the revision of 'unequal' treaties had been made conditional upon her internal law reforms on the Western model. Moreover, the abolition of the feudal system and introduction of a centralized form of land-taxation by the Meij Government gave Japan a national basis for state-led industrialization.

How real this institutional Westernization has been in Japan since the latter part of the nineteenth century is a question that cannot be dealt with in this chapter. It should be noted, however, that at the level of ethics, traditional Confucian values were stressed through state-controlled education, and at the deeper level of social psychology, the Japanese conceptions of personal relationships appear to have remained largely unchanged despite the West-worship of the Meiji Period.

Fifthly, geographical factors and their implications should be noted. Japan was far smaller than China and, viewed from Europe, lay beyond the Chinese subcontinent. This had made China the more compelling centre of attraction for European capitalism and its first victim in the Far East. The resultant time-lag was valuable for Japan. It enabled some enlightened Japanese leaders of the Bakumatsu Period, who learnt about the developments in the neighbouring country through the Dutch Factory, to try their utmost to avoid repeating China's mistakes.

Moreover, Japan managed to maintain the policy of seclusion precariously in a distant corner of the world until the leading European Powers' expansion began to slow down. Britain and France had enough on their hands in China, as witnessed by their involvement in the Taiping Rebellion and the Arrow War. In addition, Britain, France, and Russia became engaged in the Crimean War. This momentary deceleration in European expansionism left America to take the initiative in the opening up of Japan. Fortunately for Japan, the change in the United States Presidency from Fillmore, a Republican, to Pierce, a Democrat, reduced the militancy of American policy towards the Far East. What the Americans saw in Japan was chiefly port facilities, vital for their trade with China, and for their whaling industry in the Northern Pacific, but not a territory to colonize.[17]

In addition, the small size of Japan made it relatively easy, when the new government came to power, for it to extend its rule effectively to the whole territory and to maintain a centralized-system – something that was much more difficult for China partly because of her sheer bulk.

A number of other factors can be added to the above list, for example, the level of Japanese economic development, and that of literacy in the Bakumatsu and early Meiji Periods. The above analysis tends to show, however, that Japan's advancement in international society is due partly to a fortunate set of circumstances and partly also to Japan's conscious effort to strengthen herself and respond rationally to the pressure from outside. Her eagerness to satisfy Western standards of civilization in external affairs was also vital. The proofs that she had achieved these standards included not only her acceptance of international law and the diplomatic system but also the winning of wars against China and Russia. As Martin Wight remarks, 'as the head-hunters of Borneo entered into manhood by taking their first head, so a power becomes a great power by successful war against another great power'.[18] The case of Japan was no exception.

NOTES

1 *Tsūkō-ichiran* (Tokyo, 1912), vol. l, preface, p. 1.

2 Hidetaka Nakamura, *Nissen-kankei-shi no Kenkyu*, 3 vols. (Tokyo, 1969), vol. iii, chapters 3 and 8.

3 Ibid., pp. 302–3.

4 Eishō Miyagi, *Ryūkyū no Rekishi* (Tokyo, 1977), pp. 94 ff.

5 Nakamura, op. cit., vol. iii, p. 540.

6 John Stephan, *The Kuril Islands* (Oxford, 1974), pp. 52 ff.

7 Kiyoshi Tabohashi, *Kindai Nihon Gaikoku-kankei-shi*, rev. edn. (Tokyo, 1943, reprinted 1976), chapter 13.

8 Sakuzō Yoshino, 'Waga-kuni Kindaishi ni okeru Seiji-ishiki no Hassei', in his *Sūfu to Naikaku* (Tokyo, 1950), pp. 85–6.

9 On the Iwakura Mission, see W. G. Beasley, *The Modern History of Japan*, 2nd edn. (London, 1967), pp. 113–14.

10 Note Harris's effort to teach basic principles of international trade to the Bakufu administrators. See Toshio Ueda, 'Nihon no Kaikoku to Chūgoku', in *Kokusaihō Gaikō Zassi*, vol. xlix (1950), nos. 2, 4, and 5, pp. 347 ff., esp. p. 355; p. 471.

11 See Tabohashi, op. cit., p. 631.

12 Takashi Ishii, *Nihon Kaikoku-shi* (Tokyo, 1972), pp. 230 and 276–7. Tabohashi, op. cit., p. 630.

13 Yoshino, op. cit.

14 J. Shinobu, 'Vicissitudes of International Law in the Modern History of Japan', in *Kokusaihō Gaikō Zassi*,vol. 1 (1951), no. 1, pp. 217 ff.

15 Michiari Uete, 'Taigaikan no Tenkai', in Bunsō Hashikawa and Sannosuke Matsumoto, *Kindai Nihon Seiji Shisōshi*, 2 vols. (Tokyo, 1971), vol. i, pp. 33–74, esp. p. 36.

16 Shinkichi Etō, *Kindai Chūgoko Seijishi Kenkyu* (Tokyo, 1968), pp. 235 ff.

17 Ueda, op. cit., pp. 129 ff. and 474 ff.

18 Martin Wright, *Power Politics*, ed. Hedley Bull and Carsten Holbraad (Leicester, 1978), p. 46.

2 From *sakoku* to *kaikoku*

The transformation of foreign-policy attitudes, 1853–1868*

C. Totman†

*Source: *Monumenta Nipponica* 35 (1980): 1–19.

This year marks the twenty-fifth anniversary of the publication of one of the major pioneer English-language studies of Japanese history, W. G. Beasley's *Select Documents on Japanese Foreign Policy, 1853–1868*, Oxford University Press, 1955. The volume consists of a complex, compact ninety-three-page Introduction and about two hundred pages of documents in translation. It was the first truly scholarly English-language study of the *bakumatsu*, or late Tokugawa, years, and it was splendidly executed, a lucid, perceptive, and sophisticated analysis of an extremely complicated era.

So successful was Beasley's work that in the twenty-five years since its appearance, although selected aspects of *bakumatsu* foreign relations have been dealt with in greater detail, no one writing in English has chosen to re-examine the subject as a whole. Subsequent scholarly studies of domestic aspects of *bakumatsu* history have qualified some elements of his interpretation, but his basic approach to foreign policy has remained intact. It seems to me, however, that the topic does merit reconsideration because the way in which Beasley chose to deal with it left somewhat obscure the nature of the change in Japanese foreign-policy attitudes and the relationship of that change to more general changes of political perception.

BEASLEY'S *JŌI–KAIKOKU* AXIS

Beasley analyzed Japanese attitudes toward foreign policy during the *bakumatsu* period in terms of 'the rival policies of *kaikoku* and *jōi*' (p. 15). He attempted at the outset to spell out and contrast the substance of the two positions. He described advocates of *kaikoku*, or 'open the country', as arguing, in essence, that in the face of foreign pressure it would be impossible to refuse the demands for foreign diplomatic, commercial, and ancillary relations. Some advocates, he maintained, even saw such relations as positively desirable for a variety of reasons, not least of which was the fiscal advantage to those in power. He described advocates of *jōi*, or 'expel the barbarian', as considering foreign trade harmful to the Japanese economy, and Western customs and religions debilitating to the ethical basis of Japanese society. An important element in the position of many advocates of *jōi*, he indicated, was a desire to revitalize what they saw as a decadent polity and society. Because of that desire, 'Despite its obvious roots in chauvinism and xenophobia, the *jōi* movement became more and more preoccupied with political disputes in which advocacy of expulsion . . . proved an invaluable weapon against the Tokugawa Bakufu' (p. 15).

Lest readers should interpret the terms *jōi* and *kaikoku* too literally, Beasley took great care to spell out the limits of their dissimilarity. Advocates of both policies, he wrote, 'acted from the same motives and towards the same objective. They differed, in fact, not about the end but about the means of attaining it' (p. 15). 'The leaders, in fact, of whatever party, had more in common than it would appear from a superficial reading of the arguments they used' (p. 91).

Beasley was saying then that the main lines of conflict over foreign policy pitted against one another adherents of two viewpoints that were rooted in differing estimates of what was possible, what was tolerable, and how particular interests were best served. He warned, moreover, that both viewpoints had much internal diversity, and that they also changed over time as the immediate diplomatic context changed. Finally, because they became bound up with domestic political disputes after 1858,

> The pattern of ideas that had been built up around the words *jōi* and *kaikoku* was necessarily distorted by forcing it into a political framework with which it only loosely corresponded. So, too, was the distribution of those ideas in Japanese society. The result was to set a gulf, wider even than before, between what men said and what they meant. (pp. 92–93)

What we seem to have, then, are two positions that are really one in fundamentals, differing essentially on questions of tactics. We have, moreover, a situation in which it is very difficult to determine who properly is labeled a supporter of *jōi* or *kaikoku* and what it really signifies to have so identified him. However, having settled upon the *jōi–kaikoku* frame of reference, all the qualifications notwithstanding, Beasley has left us with two definable and conflicting viewpoints, and they serve as fixed points of reference that are to give us bearing as we follow the historical narrative from 1853 to 1868.

These two points of reference present interpretative difficulties not only because their meaning and applicability are difficult to ascertain but also because they embody awkward value judgments. The *kaikoku–jōi* rivalry emerges from Beasley's study as a contest between a rational, responsible, progressive attempt to adjust to a new, inevitable, and implicitly preferable world of Western-style state relations and an irrational 'xenophobic' impulse to hold back the tide of historical progress. In what was perhaps an attempt to soften the judgments inherent in the analysis, Beasley chose to maximize the presence of progressive thought even before 1853 and to find as much of a progressive impulse under the rhetoric of *jōi* as he could.

Thus, for example, he wrote that Abe Masahiro, the bakufu leader who accepted Commodore Perry's treaty, 'had for some years favoured opening of the ports, largely on the grounds that to refuse would involve Japan in a catastrophic war' (pp. 21–22). Really now, Abe did not favor opening the ports. What he favored was avoiding war, and to that end he would, however reluctantly, make such minimal concessions as were necessary. It was a position he held in common with such earlier leaders as Matsudaira Sadanobu.[1] Change was not welcome, and minimizing the scope and dangers of change was the point of it all. Even Abe's concessiveness had its limits; he did reluctantly accept Perry's demands, but those of Townsend Harris, notably his demand of 1857 to enter the city of Edo, were too much for him, and Abe died unreconciled to them.[2] And in Abe's day, few politically conscious Japanese were more responsive to the idea of contact with Western nations than he. Besides attempting to show that there was substantial pro-*kaikoku* sentiment among informed leaders as early as 1853, Beasley stressed the amount of crypto-*kaikoku* sentiment among informed advocates of *jōi*. Of *jōi* proponents he wrote,

> [their advocacy of explusion] did not always or necessarily imply that Japan must rid herself, by war, of all foreigners. It meant a firmer attitude to foreign demands, even at the risk of war. . . . But to the few, at least, it was to be employed as a stimulus rather than as an imperative.[3]
>
> These remarks, of course, apply only to a very small minority. It is an important minority, both for its political influence in the period we are discussing and because it later provided the leadership for the new Japan. But it must not be taken as typical of the whole. Against the handful of leaders we must set the background of hundreds or even thousands of the rank and file who implicitly believed the catchwords and slogans of the age. Nor was the minority itself entirely unaffected by the emotional content of the expressions it habitually used. Only gradually did the idea of Japan as an active participant in world affairs win wider acceptance. More particularly, it took time and the pressure of events to remove the initial delusions and weld the varied and often conflicting elements of thought into what could be regarded as a national foreign policy. The working out of that process is in large part the theme of this book. (pp. 17–18)

Beasley thus argued that the advocates of *jōi* whom he was treating individually were at base rational men whose words did not necessarily mean what they said. It was obscure followers, duped by their delusions and by the emotional content of catchwords and slogans, who were the irrational ones truly seeking to throw the barbarian out. Hence the struggle between the rational and irrational was not the struggle between the proponents of *kaikoku* and *jōi* but rather between the rationality demonstrated by those who really rejected the ideals of *jōi* and the irrationality inherent in the sincere *jōi* of the faceless mob. But will this do? Can we dismiss the unexamined rank and file as gullible dupes? After all, was it unreasonable for Japanese observers of the 1850s and 1860s to fear that their world would very likely change for the worse if Westerners obtained what they wanted from Japan? Given their understanding of war and their knowledge of the military threat, moreover, were they being irrational in advocating expulsion, or at least attempted expulsion, by force?[4]

In the end, however, the most serious drawback in the *jōi–kaikoku* axis is that while it helps us follow the evolving dialogue of political debate, it also obscures the character and scope of change in foreign-policy attitudes that occurred in *bakumatsu* Japan. It does so because the strategy of giving the terms *jōi* and *kaikoku* a fixed content and making their rivalry the axis of the historical dialectic created a static intellectual tableau in which conceptual change could not be presented effectively. Beasley attempted to escape that cul-de-sac by pointing out that the two terms were ill-defined at the time, meant different things to different people and in different contexts, had a number of subtle psychological functions, and represented something other than specific policy positions. That the outcome of the *bakumatsu* diplomatic experience was widespread Japanese acceptance of a new foreign-policy position Beasley made explicit, but why that result came to pass did not emerge clearly from the study.

To grasp the magnitude and character of the change in foreign-policy ideas that occurred during the *bakumatsu* years, it will be helpful to adumbrate the larger context of thought within which those ideas evolved and to examine salient characteristics of that process of evolution. For purposes of verbal convenience the prevailing foreign-policy position of 1853 can be labeled *sakoku* ('closed country')[5] and that of 1868 *kaikoku* ('open country'). The process of intellectual change that led from *sakoku* to *kaikoku* had roots that long antedated 1853, of course, and intellectual holdouts lingered on long after 1868. It was during the fifteen years after 1853, however, that the center of gravity moved dramatically from the one position to the other, and in consequence it is by examining this period that one best illuminates the dynamics of the transformation.

FROM *SAKOKU* TO *KAIKOKU*: ONE ASPECT OF A TRANSFORMATIONAL EXPERIENCE

During the years from 1853 to 1868 basic structual elements of the established Japanese societal ideal went through a process of disintegration, transition, and reconstruction, forming by 1868 a sharply altered ideal whose supporters were spread all across the political spectrum.[6] The change in thinking on foreign relations was part and parcel of that broader transformation and entailed a fundamental transvaluation of foreign-policy positions.

The elements of the broader societal ideal that disintegrated after 1853 were no less than those that gave form to the full blown philosophical vision of the Tokugawa social order. Domestically those elements included the order's fountainhead in a benign imperial legacy and its institutional expression in the *bakuhan taisei* (the decentralized or *hōken* system of bakufu and *han*). The foreign-policy element was the image of a society whose boundaries were delineated and whose character was protected by the policy of *sakoku*, which restricted Japanese-foreign contact almost entirely to a closely regulated trade with Dutchmen and Chinese at Nagasaki, with China via the Ryukyus, and with Korea via Tsushima.

The elements as reconstructed constituted a radically altered vision of the social order. It was an order rooted in an active imperial legacy. It was manned by the people of Japan, who were united not by the *bakuhan taisei* but through their communal support of that imperial legacy and the ethnic virtues it embodied. It was delineated not by *sakoku* but by Japanese ethnic distinctiveness. And it was protected not by *sakoku* but by the people's capacity to mobilize their own resources and master the secrets of the West through a policy of *kaikoku* or Western-style foreign relations. Using those secrets as necessary, the emperor and his people would replace the obsolete *hōken* system with a *gunken seidō*, a centralized polity that would again give stable operational form to society. As these comments imply, the foreign policies that we have identified by the terms *sakoku* and *kaikoku* were instrumental devices designed to realize broader social ideals, and the transvaluation of those policies was organically tied to the transformation of the broader ideals.

BASIC FEATURES OF THE SHIFT FROM *SAKOKU* TO *KAIKOKU*

The shift from *sakoku* to *kaikoku* had three principal dimensions. It involved a dramatic increase in the level of public engagement in foreign-policy debate. It involved a shift from widespread support for *sakoku* to widespread support for *kaikoku*. It involved an ethical transvaluation that transferred virtue from *sakoku* to *kaikoku*.

The change in level of public engagement might be called social mobilization in that it was a process wherein vast numbers of samurai who thitherto had accepted *sakoku* passively began to take an active interest in the fate of all that *sakoku* implied. This activated interest was expressed through the vocabulary of *son'nō jōi* ('revere the Emperor, expel the barbarian'). Initially *jōi* meant in almost all cases a positive and vociferous advocacy of the core principles of the Tokugawa social order and hence of the general principles of *sakoku*. Once that active engagement in affairs had begun, however, men found the tensions of the day leading them to a serious questioning of *sakoku* as concrete policy and to a more fundamental questioning of the *bakuhan taisei* and its underlying social order.

In other words, *jōi* was basically a statement of political commitment, in contrast to passivity, and not a statement of a specific policy position. Because that commitment was made in a period of profound contextual stress, moreover, the content of *son'nō jōi* as a foreign-policy position was from the very outset in a state of flux. That flux gave *jōi* its appearance of contradiction and confusion, and that, of course, is why people have had such trouble nailing down its meaning, some arguing with Beasley that it stood in the main for xenophobic expulsionism, others finding in it nearly the opposite meaning.[7]

The second basic dimension of change in foreign-policy attitudes, namely the shift from support for *sakoku* to support for *kaikoku*, is implicit in what has already been said. That shift seems to have progressed ideal-typically from passive acceptance of *sakoku* to active advocacy of it and thence to resentful acquiescence in *kaikoku* and finally to active support for it. The process was occurring in the minds of individuals, however, and so there was much confusion, ambiguity, and sequential overlap in attitudes.

Despite the confusion and ambiguity, this shift in policy preference sooner or later entailed an ethical transvaluation. That transvaluation cannot be dismissed as an obvious corollary of the change in policy positions because it meant that people who at one point advocated *kaikoku* on grounds of necessity, *faute de mieux*, in due course came to advocate it as intrinsically desirable. In the end general acceptance of this argument was essential to the survival of the new *kaikoku* posture. More specifically, from the time of Perry until well into the sixties proponents of the treaties could be, and were, vilified as corrupt, spineless men lacking in elemental notions of civilization and honor. Unsurprisingly, few officials wanted to assume diplomatic responsibilities, and those who did not have to do so usually kept as much distance as possible from the whole deadly business. Defenders of the treaties were in consequence a lonely and vulnerable group, even within officialdom. By contrast those who seized the pro-*sakoku* banner, especially after the ports opened in 1859, found themselves able to mobilize widespread support even among vassals of the shogun. They were able to neutralize the growing numbers of daimyo and others who really considered the whole expulsionist rhetoric dangerous and wrong-headed but who had no political need to say as much. And they were able to confuse, demoralize, and intimidate their vulnerable opponents within officialdom and the scholarly community. To use Levenson's phrase, a tension between history and value existed.[8] It was a tension between the unavoidableness of the treaties and the virtue of a pre-treaty ideal. Until there emerged a new ideal embracing treaty relations, the tension would persist and proponents of treaties would be under perpetual attack.

In due course, however, that new ideal was formulated, and it came to be accepted by ever larger numbers of samurai. By the latter half of the sixties defenders of the treaties were beginning to discover persuasive ethical grounds on which to base their arguments, and these principled grounds emerged as integral parts of the broader statements of a new societal ideal. The ethical transvaluation thus constitutes the third principal dimension of the shift in foreign-policy attitudes. The substance of that transvaluation can be suggested simply enough. As of 1853 *sakoku* was an expression of ethnic virtue, and it embodied a strategy for preserving that virtue. *Kaikoku* was an expression of tactical prudence, but it made no pretense to embodying virtue. By 1867 *sakoku* was well on the way to becoming an expression of archaic parochialism, and *kaikoku* was rapidly acquiring credibility as an expression of ethnic virtue and sound strategy.

Because the process of abandoning *sakoku* in favor of *kaikoku* involved confusion, ambiguity, and sequential overlap, it does not break down into neat stages. Nevertheless, one can probe it more deeply by examining it in terms of general phases in which the old ideal was defended, then discredited, and finally displaced as a new ideal found effective expression. During the first phase, which covered the years from 1853 to about 1858, leaders of the polity maneuvered as best they could to minimize the disruptive impact of the foreigners' demands in hopes of preserving the essential character of the established order. By 1858, however, their inability to do so was becoming more widely recognized, and an active concern for *sakoku* and all it represented began to spread within the samurai class. That concern led to intense political activism, repeated failures, massive disillusionment, and eventually the discrediting of *sakoku* and much of what it stood for. From about 1864 this phase of disillusionment gave way to a more constructive phase in which the ideals imbedded in *sakoku* and *kaikoku* experienced a high degree of transvaluation as part of the process in which men forged a new vision of the future. By 1868 a new diplomatic ideal had emerged as the dominant one in Japan.

THE DEFENSE OF *SAKOKU*, 1853–1858

The ethical poverty of pro-treaty arguments was evident during the Perry crisis of 1853–54. The only effective argument in support of a treaty, the one used by Abe Masahiro, was the observation that its rejection would invite war and defeat while accommodation would buy time in which to prepare a defense of the established order. From the outset of the crisis a pervasive sense of Japanese vulnerability was evident, with men of all persuasions warning that yielding to Perry, even if such were the least malign of alternatives, would damage bakufu prestige, undermine public morale, and expose society to all sorts of dangers. The foreign assault on *sakoku* was clearly seen as a fundamental cultural threat and a menace to the whole social order.

It is worth noting that among those pervasive fears concern with the economics of trade was almost a negligible factor. Because trade was the *raison d'être* of mid-nineteenth-century imperialism, trade negotiations bulked large in the diplomatic correspondence, but during the 1850s economics was a minor concern from the Japanese viewpoint, except in the eyes of those officials, notably the finance magistrates (*kanjō bugyō*) whose responsibilities were of a fiscal nature. Men in both the *jōi* and *kaikoku* categories of Beasley's analysis could accept trade, but they wished it to be handled by the Japanese going overseas, not by foreigners coming into Japan. People as varied as Sakuma Shōzan, Ii Naosuke, and Tokugawa Nariaki were in agreement on that point. They could agree on the wisdom of trading abroad because from the outset of the Perry crisis it was the issue of foreign penetration and residence, not the issue of trade, that was at the heart of the deepest fear and most bitter quarrels. Trading abroad appeared to be the best way to meet the foreign menace with the least danger of civilization's being subverted. It was a strategy that proposed to modify a relatively minor aspect of the customary content of *sakoku* in order to preserve its larger instrumental function.

The strategy of trading abroad was not implemented, and in hindsight one can safely say that *sakoku* as the policy delineating the extent and protecting the character of society was, in fact, confounded by Perry in 1854. Nevertheless, the consensus that persisted for three years thereafter postulated that at worst concessions must be limited to those already given, and that at best, after defenses had been strengthened, something akin to the pre-1853 situation could be restored. This containment policy was threatened, however, by Dutch trade negotiations in 1857, and it was routed by Townsend Harris's efforts of 1857–58.

Harris, unlike Perry, sought directly to open Japan to trade. Despite the movement of the trade issue to the center of diplomacy, however, it was still the penetration of foreigners and foreign influence into Japan and not commercial matters per se that alarmed people and gave rise to heated disputes. The issue of foreign penetration, moreover, began to change its character. The older diffuse opposition to any penetration anywhere in Japan rapidly acquired a set of priorities. At the time of Perry the immediate threat had been to the Edo area, seat of the bakufu, and it was defense of Edo Bay that commanded the most attention. Three years later during the Harris negotiations Edo itself seemed threatened by foreign demands for ministerial residence in the city proper, and that issue quickly was supplemented by foreign interest in an open port in the Kinai (Kyoto-Osaka) region, near the imperial capital. Both matters led to intense domestic quarreling. The emergence and rapid increase in concern about the Kinai issue both reflected and contributed to a growing centrality of the imperial institution in political thought. As we note later, it foreshadowed crucial political and diplomatic developments of the sixties.

The concern about foreign penetration was evident in the tortuous argumentation of the bakufu diplomat Iwase Tadanari, whom Beasley spoke of as one of the most progressive officials in 1850s Japan.[9] When Harris sought to open a trading port near Edo and to gain diplomatic admission to the city itself in 1857, most bakufu officials opposed his request. Iwase, however, in a memorandum that he addressed to the senior councilors near the end of the year, took a more subtle position.[10] In his memorandum he was arguing basically the 'unavoidableness' of accepting Harris's demand, and much of his essay was an attempt to mollify the anger of those infuriated by Harris's bullying tactics. But then he argued that refusal to open a port near Edo would be counterproductive because it would lead inevitably to later demands for ministerial residence in Edo itself and for trade centers in 'Ōsaka or some place in the vicinity of Edo' (p. 175). To avoid such demands would require shrewd diplomacy, not obduracy. He presented his strategy for keeping ministers out of Edo and trade out of Ōsaka in this way.

> It appears from what has been said during the negotiations that from the beginning the fundamental aim of all foreign countries has been the opening of a port in the vicinity of Edo. However, in the belief that conditions within Japan make it quite impossible for the Bakufu to accede to this, it seems that in the first place they insist only on the residence of ministers there. If, therefore, the Bakufu were to take the foreigners completely by surprise by stating categorically that it intends agreeing to the major step of opening Yokohama and admitting foreigners of all countries to our ports, then it is probable that the question of the residence of ministers would be but a trifling problem and that a settlement could be reached without undue difficulty. It is not, after all, simply that the foreigners would gladly agree to the opening of Yokohama. There is also the point that while ostensibly keeping the foreigners away from the Imperial Palace, the shrine territories, and the private fiefs and demonstrating its sense of responsibility by undertaking a task of such importance to the whole country, the Bakufu would in fact be reasserting its authority in overall supervision of national affairs, would be carrying out a policy that would be to our lasting advantage, and would be laying the foundations of national wealth and strength. (p. 176)

Iwase was saying, then, that the Edo ministerial demand was a stalking horse that likely could be evaded by opening Yokohama to trade and residence. Doing that, moreover, would help to keep foreigners away from 'the Imperial Palace, the shrine territories, and the private fiefs', which is to say much of the rest of Japan and especially the Kinai region, to which Osaka was the gateway. And by doing that the established order could be preserved. Another tactical adjustment of *sakoku* could thus be used to sustain its larger customary purpose.

SAKOKU DISCREDITED: 1858–1864

It would be misleading to imply that the difficulties of preceding years had had no impact on official attitudes by 1858. A statement by the bakufu leader Hotta Masayoshi revealed what might be labeled the most 'advanced' diplomatic thought of the day, meaning that which was closest to a *kaikoku* orientation. In a memorandum that he probably prepared a few days before Iwase's, Hofta summed up and dismissed as worse than useless the two most widely recommended policies of the time: a policy of resistance by force and a policy of grudging accommodation. He then went on to assert, 'Of recent times a change has come over world conditions in general. All countries are alike in concluding treaties by which they make friendly alliances, open trade, exchange their products, and help each other in difficulties' (pp. 166–67). After expanding on that proposition a little, Hotta went on to argue that Japan should understand those conditions and act accordingly because,

> . . . military power always springs from national wealth, and means of enriching the country are principally to be found in trade and commerce. I am therefore convinced that our policy should be to stake everything on the present opportunity, to conclude friendly alliances, to send ships to foreign countries everywhere and conduct trade, to copy the foreigners where they are at their best and so repair our own shortcomings, to foster our national strength and complete our armaments, and so gradually subject the foreigners to our influence until in the end all the countries of the world know the blessings of perfect tranquillity and our hegemony is acknowledged throughout the globe. (p. 167)

Clearly Hotta was proposing to abandon the policy of *sakoku* in a way that Abe could not have done. In his attempt to sell that heretical view, however, he still stressed the going out of Japanese rather than the entering of foreigners, and he said nothing to suggest that this change in foreign policy would necessarily have significant domestic ramifications. To the contrary, it would avoid the calamitous consequences of war and defeat. Nevertheless, to make even this much of a policy change, he felt pressed, as had earlier advocates of trading abroad, to describe a future of such Wagnerian dimensions as to make the sortie from Valhalla acceptable. It was a beginning, but only a beginning, of transvaluation, and it did not result in an abandonment of the two preferred policies of resistance by force and grudging accommodation.

Despite the enduring opposition to *kaikoku* trade treaties were reluctantly signed in 1858, and foreign trade at Yokohama and foreign residence in Edo began the following year. During the next five years foreign affairs became extremely complicated, as men attempted to achieve at least the minimal goal of preventing further foreign inroads by successfully implementing either the policy of grudging accommodation or that of resistance by force.

The proponents of resistance by force were led by a heterogeneous, volatile, and occasionally organized 'party' of zealously committed anti-treaty activists. Mostly excluded from decision-making positions in government, they undertook desperate strategems – including coercive lobbying, putsches, assassination of leaders such as Ii Naosuke and foreigners such as Harris's secretary Hendrik Heusken, and other forms of terrorism – in attempts to reverse the massive ethical erosion represented by the 1858 treaty concessions and the incipient *kaikoku* thought evident in Hotta's opinion. At the very least, these proponents hoped, the cowardly men in power could be induced to halt the erosion. At best the whole disgraceful process of the 1850s could be reversed, its perpetrators punished, and the old order restored or reformed in some way that would re-establish the elemental virtue of society.

This anti-treaty policy was linked to domestic political activity through the formula *son'nō jōi*, whose domestic political aspect, *son'nō*, was a desire to realize national unity through a vigorous rallying of all people to the imperial banner. The movement gained momentum after the assassination of Ii

Naosuke in 1860 and reached its greatest influence in an abortive Imperial Restoration in 1863.

Standing opposed to the proponents of *jōi* were the advocates of grudging accommodation, a much smaller collection of men, most of them high-ranking officials of bakufu and daimyo domain and most caught in the transitional dilemma of Hotta: convinced that *sakoku* could never be restored, but doubtless wishing in their heart of hearts to throw the barbarian out, and in any case still lacking a credible alternative vision of how to assure Japanese well-being. Their accommodationist policy was linked to domestic political activity through the formula *kōbu gattai*, a concept that proposed to achieve national unity through a coalition of high-ranking members of the imperial nobility and samurai class. This strategy, first pursued by Ii Naosuke, also gained momentum after his death and led to a series of unsuccessful attempts at coalition by daimyo, bakufu, and court.

Neither the *son'nō jōi* nor *kōbu gattai* policy for national unification was successful during the early sixties, and neither of the associated foreign policies proved effective against the foreigners. In consequence frustration, bitterness, and distrust intensified and erupted in sporadic armed conflict. This conflict repeatedly stopped short of open civil war, however, in part because influential men such as Matsudaira Shungaku of Fukui were able to appeal effectively to the general fear that foreigners might exploit internal disorder to extend their positions in Japan.

The desire to prevent further foreign advances into Japan applied particularly to the Kinai region and the vicinity of the throne. Concern with the Kinai, which had emerged during discussion of the Harris treaty proposal, had utterly displaced concern with Edo by the early sixties, and the major accomplishment of Japanese diplomacy during those years was the preservation of Kinai immunity. This accomplishment came at a severe price, however. During 1862–63 defense of the Kinai became the focus of attempts to strengthen the military and consumed vast amounts of wealth and energy. During 1864 the bakufu agreed to pay millions of dollars in indemnities rather than allow foreigners to open a port there. In 1865, when a foreign armada at last anchored off Hyōgo in Osaka Bay and by threat of aggression extracted imperial approval of the treaties previously negotiated, the one issue on which the court still refused to yield was the opening of Hyōgo to foreigners. In subsequent months, moreover, although the bakufu agreed to a ruinous revision of tariff schedules, it continued to resist opening Hyōgo or any other Kinai port because the intensity of domestic opposition made such an action politically unacceptable.

The successful preservation of Kinai immunity was ruinously expensive, and still it could not conceal the more general pattern of diplomatic failure. The treaty ports were growing. More and more foreign troops were being stationed in Japan. More and more foreign activities were taking place on Japanese soil: trade, tourism, teaching, religious proselytizing, and arms-selling. And there seemed no way for the Japanese to stop the trend. The same general point was made more bluntly by a series of major diplomatic reverses, notably foreign coercion of the bakufu in 1863 and the bombardments of Satsuma and Chōshū in 1863 and 1864. The overwhelming evidence of failure discredited both the policy of forceful expulsion and that of grudging concessiveness. Those bakufu officials and others who had struggled so hard to stem the foreign assault by measures short of war found themselves repeatedly thwarted, humiliated, and discredited. By late 1864 they had abandoned all faith in such tactics and were moving to a new posture. At the same time the zealous advocates of expulsion were being forced by several sorts of adversity through a rapid process of change.[11] Some were slain in the turmoil of the day. Others withdrew or were driven from active political participation. Yet others, finding old hopes blasted, became receptive to new ideas. By 1865 it was clear to samurai throughout the country that all Japan, court and Kinai included, was open to foreign plunder and that *sakoku*, however attempted, simply would not work. The cumulative effect of the early 1860s experience had been to discredit *sakoku*, paving the way for the triumph of *kaikoku*.

A brief digression on the matter of Kinai defense seems appropriate here. The deep and widespread concern about the Kinai has not been properly investigated, but its pervasiveness suggests its importance. It cut across all political lines, involving people at all levels of the samurai class, as well as many of lesser status, and including people throughout the polity, whether members of the bakufu, *fudai*, *shinpan*, or *tozama* houses. Men came to defend Kyoto from all over Japan: from Hirosaki, Shōnai, Sendai, Aizu, Mito, Utsunomiya, *hatamoto* fiefs, Edo, Hikone, Kii, Tottori, Tosa, Chōshū, Saga, Satsuma. They came as *han* vassals, as bakufu vassals, as *rōnin*, singly and in groups, as Shinsengumi, as soldiers, and as officials. Accordingly, while these following comments are speculative, the centrality of the matter to 1860s developments seems to warrant speculation.

To say it in a phrase, engagement in the question of Kinai defense seems to have been the act that enabled many samurai to abandon the dying vision of the old order in favor of a new vision and, as a corollary, to make the intellectual leap from support of *sakoku* to support of *kaikoku*. For many the Kinai seems to have been at the outset the last non-negotiable defense line of the old order, but it subtly evolved into the first defense line of the new. Perhaps because the single tangible task of defending the Kinai could be undertaken for two such dissimilar reasons, it became the event in the lives of ordinary samurai and regular officials and would-be officials that enabled them to change purposes in mid-act, so to say, to behave consistently while abandoning one larger purpose that was hopeless in favor of another larger purpose that resonated with promise of fulfillment.

To elaborate, protection of the Kinai was the last defense line of the old order in the sense that during the early 1860s the imperial institution emerged the only unsullied part of the Tokugawa policy. With treaties signed, ports opened, and Edo defiled, the Kinai district became by 1860 the undisputed inner heart of an endangered order. Keeping foreigners away from the court became the last attenuated expression of *sakoku*'s function as the policy protecting civilization. If the Kinai could be saved from foreign despoilment, one could hope in due course to restore the whole order. If not, then the last vestigial hope for the Tokugawa order was lost.

The imperial institution was not merely the irreplaceable heart of the Tokugawa order, however. It had also begun to acquire validity as to what might be called the core element in a diffuse ethnic consciousness that had been forced into being by the imperialist onslaught and that was tied to neither the structure of the *bakuhan taisei* nor the more basic integrated cultural construct underlying the Tokugawa social order. This perception of the imperial institution was prompted initially by the existing body of nativist propositions about the special character and historic significance of the imperial institution. Then during the 1850s and sixties the inability of *bakuhan* leaders to control the foreigners reinforced interest in the court as distraught men cast about for effective instruments of political action. As men directed their concern more fully to defense of the Kinai, going there as soldiers and activists and thinking of tactics and policies in terms of Kinai defense, their commitment to the preservation of imperial honor (*son'nō*) was strengthened. As repeated diplomatic reverses discredited the *bakuhan taisei* and destroyed the credibility of *sakoku*, men took psychic refuge in the imperial institution as the foundation of a new, still unarticulated order that would somehow handle the crisis of the day and thereby accommodate the needs of a conscious ethnic awareness. Preservation of that institution, then, became the new order's first line of defense because the rest of the order being unarticulated, its lines of defense could not be identified. And *sakoku* having lost instrumental credibility, men were prepared to consider the merit of *kaikoku* as a means of accomplishing that task.

THE TRIUMPH OF *KAIKOKU*: 1864–1868

From about 1864 the conviction that both *sakoku* and its underlying Tokugawa ideal were fundamentally unworthy as well as unworkable began to spread rapidly among the leaders and would-be leaders of Japan. In their place the vision of *kaikoku* and a new order began to shape men's choices. The diplomatic dimension of this new approach to affairs was suggested in an opinion paper presented by the bakufu official Ikeda Nagaaki (Chōhatsu) in 1864. Having just returned from a mission to Europe, he was trying to convince his superiors of the advantages of more extensive foreign relations. He discussed with considerable sophistication the complexity of interstate relations, the dangers inherent in any European alliance against Japan, and the necessity therefore of accommodating certain French demands. He continued,

Speaking generally, for the Bakufu to lay the foundations of national independence it is fundamental that national unity be attained within Japan. Special attention must be paid to the equipment of our land and sea forces, of course, and also to our relations with foreign countries. And the Bakufu must be resolute in performing its engagements. It is thus of the first importance that we study conditions abroad. In our view, therefore, the following steps are desirable:

1. that Resident Ministers be sent to all the countries of Europe;
2. that treaties be concluded not only with European countries but also with all other independent countries; and that we plan in the event of need to ally ourselves with some when in conflict with others;
3. that in order to avail ourselves of Western skills in land and sea warfare, students be sent abroad to study these things;
4. that we subscribe to the various Western newspaper organizations and so inform ourselves of world conditions;
5. that our people be permitted to travel freely to foreign countries, both to trade and to make themselves familiar with conditions overseas. (p. 281)

Again the predominant theme was of the Japanese going abroad, not of foreigners penetrating Japan. However, whereas Hotta had betrayed only a general understanding of what a permanent abandonment of *sakoku* would involve, Ikeda had a much more fully developed appreciation of the complications and implications of the new diplomatic order. Moreover, whereas Hotta's arguments had failed to change the two preferred policies of resistance and grudging accommodation, the bakufu began to implement policies in line with Ikeda's ideas within months of his return.[12] During the next two years connections between bakufu officials and foreigners grew apace, and by the summer of 1867 the bakufu had gone well beyond Ikeda's ideas. It had established permanent embassies in London and Paris, was developing a regular passport system, was expanding rapidly its foreign study programs both in Japan and abroad, was attempting to develop close ties with France, was adopting Western copyright regulations and economic contractual arrangements, was opening more of the country – including the Kinai – to foreigners, and was granting unrestricted Japanese–foreign marriage rights.

This final acceptance of *kaikoku* practice was not merely a bakufu phenomenon. It was equally visible in the rhetoric and action of leaders and activists in Satsuma, Chōshu, and other daimyo domains.[13] As the institution responsible for diplomatic affairs, however, the bakufu, not surprisingly, was the first to give full institutional expression to the new posture. The shogun Yoshinobu, moreover, gave the new policy one of its most elegant formulations. In 1867, when he was trying to persuade the court to approve the opening of Hyōgo, he presented a lengthy memorial in defense of the action. He first reiterated two points made by senior councilor Manabe Akikatsu back in 1859 when he had tried to persuade the court to accept the Harris treaty – namely, that to refuse the treaties would be to invite war, defeat, and disastrous punishment, and that to renege on treaties already signed would be to disgrace Japan. Then, however, Yoshinobu went on to outline a whole new mode of reasoning. He wrote,

> What is more, treaties are the basis of international relations. If there were to be no permanent and lasting rules, the large would in the end overcome the small, the weak would be dominated by the strong. Among the countries of the West there are both great and small, both strong and weak. But they lay great stress on keeping faith. They show respect for treaties. Thus they do not suffer from annexation and aggression and all preserve their national independence. . . .
>
> As I have often reported, world conditions have changed. Yet if you study those conditions closely, both past and present, you will find that while there are differences both of territory and of customs among nations, all experience the same process of evolution, all experience alike the span of life from birth to death. In this there is no difference between one and another. All are born of the same womb. Thus to keep faith with one another is to conform to divine justice. Moreover, as an island Japan holds a vital position in the world, in the eyes both of East and of West. At this time other countries are making steady progress. Distance is no obstacle to them and they communicate freely with each other. If we alone, at such a time, cling to outworn customs and refrain from international relations of a kind common to all countries, our action will be in conflict with the natural order of things. We will, I think, soon find ourselves in great difficulties. Now is our opportunity, therefore, to change this state of affairs. It is desirable that the Court should guide itself by the ancient saying, 'since all men are brothers treat all with the same benevolence', that Court and Empire together should begin afresh. By so doing we shall exert all our efforts to wipe out the evil practices of the past. Before many years are out our wealth and strength will be assured, our military prestige will have expanded and increased. And so the Emperor's mind will be set at rest. (pp. 309–310)

Universal virtue existed and was embodied in *kaikoku*. Through adherence to the principles of *kaikoku* the well-being of Japan could be assured. History and value were one. It was a statement that would have won a ringing endorsement in the Tokyo of 1890, but it would have been inconceivable in the Edo of 1853.

AN EXPLANATION OF *KAIKOKU*'S TRIUMPH

How does one explain the triumph of *kaikoku*? Why did the decay of *sakoku* not simply lead to confusion and disorder? An explanation is rooted in the instrumental character of both *sakoku* and *kaikoku* as policies designed to protect the larger societal ideal. To explain the triumph of *kaikoku* one must explain the larger intellectual reorientation of *bakumatsu* Japan and then show the instrumental utility of *kaikoku* to the new vision.

A critical factor in that larger reorientation was the political experience of the age. The political and diplomatic failures of the early sixties – the failures of bakufu policy and also of *kōbu gattai* and *son'nō jōi* politics – had disillusioned men about the value of the established order and had made them receptive to alternative possibilities.

Such possibilities were available because they were imbedded in the established corpus of Tokugawa political wisdom. One crucial idea was that of an emperor-centered policy. It had underlain the abortive Restoration of 1863 and subsequently had been fostered by the crisis of Kinai defense. As Harootunian has pointed out,[14] that idea had been so redefined by nineteenth-century scholars as to convert the emperor from a passive source of political legitimation into an active font of authority. During the 1860s this new view spread rapidly, and by the latter sixties it was for all practical purposes universally accepted throughout the samurai class.

Of equal significance was the idea of a centralized bureaucratic state, or *gunken seidō*. This idea, which is of Confucian origin, had long been taboo, having been dismissed during the seventeenth century as inappropriate to Tokugawa Japan. It was associated with ancient Japan and dynastic China, both of which were contrasted invidiously with the decentralized *hōken* or 'feudal' system of samurai governance. By the nineteenth century political thinkers such as Satō Nobuhiro were advocating policies more appropriate to a *gunken* than a *hōken* order, but as late as 1865 talk of *gunken seidō* could still provoke bitter hostility from defenders of feudal privilege. Doubtless, however, that very hostility was a measure of the extent to which the idea of a centralized policy had acquired attractiveness as the key to a new strategy for coping with Japan's problems. Indeed, by 1866 the most dynamic members of the bakufu and of the emerging leadership within the domains were working to achieve just such a unification.

Interest in an emperor-centered *gunken* system was stimulated by the political battering of the early sixties and was heightened further by the expansion of foreign contacts, which brought information that seemed to validate these once-fugitive ideas. Surely the discovery that the most dynamic states of Europe, the France of Napoleon III and Victorian England, to say nothing of Czarist Russia and burgeoning Prussia, were monarchies could only have strengthened belief in the merit of imperial rule. As Japanese diplomats and students learned ever more about European society, moreover, they reached the conclusion that the power of European states, and hence their ability to ravage Japan, stemmed from their social and political organization. The polities were centralized and highly structured. They were rooted in popular support, in armies composed of commoners, and in tax systems that exploited all forms of economic activity. They stood in sharp contrast to the *hōken* system of the Tokugawa order and seemed analogous to the classic *gunken seidō*.

These three factors – a political experience that discredited the *bakuhan taisei*, a political legacy that embodied an alternative vision, and an external example that seemed to validate that vision – seem to have been crucial to the emergence of the new political ideal. What, then, was it that made *kaikoku* rather than *sakoku* appear the better instrument for establishing that ideal?

Again, the political disasters of the early sixties played a key role because they discredited the ideal (inherent in both *kōbu gattai* and *son'nō jōi*) of cooperative voluntaristic political action. More and more people came to regard coercion, even civil war if necessary, as the only adequate mode of political action. The maximizing of military effectiveness for domestic, as distinct from international, purposes came to be a crucial tactical factor in political calculations. It was clear that foreigners were the source of the most effective military technology, and in their quest for it Japanese leaders and would-be leaders began to develop close bilateral foreign connections. Those connections brought to Japan weapons and other war material, information on techniques of warfare, and instructors to teach their use. During the mid-sixties more and more Japanese visitors sent informative letters home from Europe, missions returned from there, and officials talked with foreigners in Japan. Such figures as Kurimoto Kon, Oguri Tadamasa, and Ikeda Nagaaki at Edo, and Itō Hirobumi and Inoue Kaoru of Chōshū, for example, began to formulate and advocate new ideas about both foreign policy and the political order.

The quest for new modes of warfare and governance was thus accorded a new and great importance to access to foreign knowledge, foreign technology, and foreign social models, all phenomena that *sakoku* had sought to restrict and that *kaikoku* made accessible. In the eyes of protagonists the advantages of diplomatic ties were thus coming to outweigh the dangers of foreign association.[15] *Kaikoku*, a feasible policy, was becoming a more valuable instrument than the unworkable policy of *sakoku*. Active commitment to a policy of *kaikoku* was thus congruent with the broader transformation of political values, the commitment to a new order, and the search for means to establish that order. The transvaluation of foreign-policy attitudes, so dramatically illustrated in the statement of Yoshinobu, was well on the way to completion.

* * * * *

In the Edo of 1853 most samurai had taken *sakoku* for granted. Their leaders favored it more actively, convinced that the larger social configuration that *sakoku* was designed to protect deserved to be perpetuated. Accordingly when Perry demanded that *sakoku* be abandoned, they resisted as best they could, hoping to avoid war while still minimizing change. By the early 1860s the situation had changed considerably. Most samurai, leaders and followers alike, saw *sakoku* as in fundamental danger, and most believed that by one strategy or another it must be revitalized so it could fulfill its larger social purpose. On the other hand a steadily growing number were becoming convinced that it could not be revitalized. This conclusion left most of them in limbo, however, and uncertain how to proceed, because very few were ready to assert that the larger purpose of *sakoku* – the preservation of the Tokugawa social order with or without modest changes – was intrinsically unworthy and therefore ought not to be pursued. By 1867, however, basic convictions about the character of the desired society and hence of the desired Japanese–foreign relationship had been transformed. The *sakoku* consensus of 1853 with its underlying commitment to the old order had disintegrated, to be replaced by a rapidly emerging *kaikoku* consensus and commitment to a new order.

NOTES

† Quotations from Professor Beasley's work are made by permission of Oxford University Press.

1 Herman Ooms, *Charismatic Bureaucrat: A Political Biography of Matsudaira Sadanobu, 1758–1829*, University of Chicago Press, 1975, pp. 120–1. *Dai Nihon Ishin Shiryō*, Series 1, Vol. 2, pp. 1–9, contains the data on Abe's wish to avoid war in 1848 by allowing trade in the Ryukyus.

2 Watanabe Shūjirō, *Abe Masahiro Jiseki*, 1910, I, pp. 304–13.

3 Beasley reiterated this position at the close of his introduction, p. 92.

4 Beasley suggested, pp. 10–11, that to the 'Western mind' there was a logical contradiction in the argument that Japan could be revitalized only by accepting the risk of war and defeat. Does the problem not lie with the 'mid-twentieth-century mind' rather than the 'Western mind'? The idea of total war, in which conflict continues until one side or the other is totally defeated and subjected to total conquest, was not a nineteenth-century idea.

As the battles of Shimonoseki and Kagoshima showed, those who chose to accept war were also capable of deciding when to terminate it. The *jōi* notion that Japan might be well served if the samurai class were bloodied in war was, sad to say, not necessarily irrational. And the argument of the Aizawa school that capitulationism was an open-ended risk was very well taken.

5 For a brief statement on the etymology of the word *sakoku*, see Ronald B. Toby, 'Reopening the Question of *Sakoku*: Diplomacy in the Legitimation of the Tokugawa Bakufu', in *The Journal of Japanese Studies*, III:2, 1977, pp. 323–4, n. 1.

Although the term is of nineteenth-century origins, the policy that it was designed to express dated from the seventeenth century. The central intent of that policy was straightforward – to keep foreigners and foreign influences, especially Western, from moving about Japan at will and to keep daimyo from consorting freely with foreigners. To that end the bakufu regulated Japanese–foreign contacts carefully.

Within the limits dictated by the central intent of policy, however, some latitude was permitted on specific issues, such as the extent of trade, the varieties and volume of admissible foreign knowledge, and the tactics for handling unauthorized visitors.

6 Much of the interpretation in this article, especially regarding the 1860s, grows out of a lengthy study entitled *The Collapse of the Tokugawa Bakufu, 1862–1868*, University Press of Hawaii, 1979.

7 Thus Tetsuo Najita in *Japan*, Prentice-Hall, Englewood Cliffs, N.J., 1974, pp. 47–8, argues that in 1825 Aizawa Seishisai felt, 'Seclusionism was not a practical strategy against the West,' and that, 'As a matter of practical strategy, Japan must break out of its present seclusion to confront that threat.'

The implication, perhaps unintended but surely wrong, is that Aizawa would have accepted Western-style diplomatic relations as a permanent alternative. What he sought was an effective strategy for achieving the objectives sought by *sakoku* as currently implemented.

8 Joseph R. Levenson makes this theme central to his book, *Liang Ch'i-ch'ao and the Mind of Modern China*, Harvard U.P., 1959.

9 Beasley puts a far more pro-*kaikoku* interpretation on Iwase's views than I do here. He writes that during treaty negotiations with the Dutch in 1857, Iwase 'came down strongly on the side of major concessions'. Concerning Harris's demands, Beasley says that Iwase supported them in 'a response [to arguments against doing so] which is startling in the frankness of its attack on such "trifling arguments about detail." Iwase's own concern was that the Bakufu should revise its whole attitude to foreign affairs, reasserting its leadership by a decision to conform in substance with Harris's views and confining its efforts to the discussion of points that had a real importance' (pp. 28–33).

10 Beasley, p. 175, dates this ca. 4 January 1858 (i.e., ca. Ansei 4/11/20).

11 In his more recent book on the Restoration, Beasley stresses that 'there *was* a change of atmosphere that one can plainly date from 1864.' He is referring to proponents of *jōi* losing their commitment to expulsion, not to the broader pattern I am seeking to suggest. W. G. Beasley, *The Meiji Restoration*, Stanford U.P., 1971, p. 208.

12 It is true that Ikeda was formally repudiated and placed under house arrest after presenting his argument, but that was due to domestic problems of the moment and was not a basic repudiation of his diplomatic vision.

13 In his *Mori Arinori*, Harvard U.P., 1973, Ivan Parker Hall illustrates very nicely young Mori's growing interest in change during the mid-1860s.

14 Harry Harootunian's book, *Toward Restoration*, University of California Press, 1970, is an examination of this theme.

15 The displacement of *sakoku/bakuhan taisei* ideals by *kaikoku*/Emperor-centered *gunken* ideals had dramatic diplomatic consequences, amounting to a diplomatic revolution. That revolution marked the end – temporarily – of the basic diplomatic pattern in which Japanese were pitted as a group against foreigners as a group.

Instead a new pattern appeared during 1866 in which cross-cutting alignments pitted some Japanese backed by some foreigners against other Japanese backed by other foreigners. Most notably the bakufu developed ties with France; and Satsuma and Chōshū, ties with England. It was a dangerous situation, fraught with risks of imperialist exploitation of Japanese civil strife, as Matsudaira Shungaku and others repeatedly pointed out. Hence it was not an adequate long-range position, but it was perhaps an inescapable transitional means of linking the post-*sakoku* treaty system to an emerging domestic order.

3 Plots and motives in Japan's Meiji Restoration*

G. M. Wilson

*Source: *Comparative Studies in Society and History* 25 (1983): 407–27.

The French Revolution as commonly conceived never took place.
——Claude Lévi-Strauss

Like other dramatic and discontinuous historical processes, the Meiji Restoration of 1868 possesses the inherent fascination to sustain yet another rehearsal of its basic course of events. The present one differs from others in several ways. It does not center on samurai heroes and villains contesting foreign incursion. Instead it identifies fully four groups that acted during the late Tokugawa era, the years 1850–68, known by the generic periodizing word *bakumatsu* – "the end of the bakufu," that is, of the shogun's government situated at Edo. It presents each group according to the experiences and motives of its members. It points to the interactions between the four narrative structures, the plots or *mythoi*, but without homogenizing them into a unitary historiographical line. It also recognizes the necessary prefiguration of the historian's field but tries nevertheless to convey the perceived intentions of the four groups of historical actors.

Using the last decade of the bakumatsu period as an example of an historic watershed, this essay thus sketches a novel method for appreciating the onset of large-scale political and social change. The basis of the method lies in establishing the four *mythoi* and then narrating these plots or story lines that historical agents and agencies (human beings and social institutions) experienced during the final years of Tokugawa bakufu control over Japan. Long-lived as it was, lasting from 1600 to 1868, the Tokugawa era retained its synchronic unity for some two centuries after the system was fixed. But the period ended with Japan in profound disarray. It is that ending to which we will turn our attention.

Bakumatsu Japan is known for its confusions. A cacophony of voices expressed differing perceptions of the world. These voices proposed actions emanating from a multitude of motivations. Real people, of course, do not live "stories." They live in the here and now and generally make the best of it. But historians must construct narratives that make sense of the random data handed along from the past, data that represent something of the aspirations of historical actors. The point of this article is to emphasize the differential roles of interacting groups on the eve of the Meiji Restoration.

In a passage remarkable for capturing the surface contradictions of a time of confusion, George Sansom observes that during the bakumatsu period "a fantastic ethos prevails throughout the land." He continues with a catologue of the seeming paradoxes that puzzle the retrospective analyst who wants to understand the era:

> The domestic politics of this period were described by more than one contemporary writer in works with such titles as *Yumemonogatari*, or *Story of a Dream*. That, though not so intended, was a fitting description of the plots and counterplots, the quarrels and arguments, the confusion between names and things, the misunderstandings and bewilderments which characterize this uneasy epoch. It is full of episodes that seem not to belong to waking life, but have the plausible inconsequence, the unearthly logic, of events in a dream.[1]

If what Sansom means by all this is that he and others have encountered difficulty in comprehending the course of events between the arrival of the American Commodore Matthew Perry in 1853 and the Meiji Restoration of 1868, then he is surely right. As the bakufu approached what was to be the end of its time in power, the historian looking backward finds it troublesome to formulate a coherent narrative. The chronology gets "hot," as Claude Lévi-Strauss would say, because stunning and memorable events follow one after another with dizzying speed.[2]

The various ideas comprising the collective ethos of the Japanese who lived at the time are hard to summarize, harder to analyze, and harder still to compress into a single orderly system. Victor Turner has persuasively characterized periods such as this as "liminal,"[3] pointing out that reason and logic rarely govern what happens in major historical transitions. More often, myth works its way to the fore, appealing to the psychological need for stability and deep-seated truth – a truth more compelling than the superficial facts of existence, which themselves may well be transitory – shared by elites and masses alike. "Myths treat of origins but derive from transitions," Turner writes. "Myths relate how one state of affairs become another . . . how chaos became cosmos."[4] And myths reassure people when events threaten the viability of the social or political order, for myth promises recurrence, the return of fundamental virtues and heroic action.

No liminal period in world history is more rife with myth and the quest for redemption than bakumatsu Japan. There are numberless accounts of what happened, concurring in skeletal outline of facts and events but not in what those facts and events mean. Although the chronology is not in serious doubt, there are many schools of interpretation, several of them blooming while others wither, but none convincing enough to close the books. Social scientists disagree about the "revolutionary" character of the Meiji Restoration. Writers who judge the Restoration a failure, or simply deem it defective, usually deny that it constituted a revolution. Others who applaud the experiments of the Restoration leaders take refuge in a thesis that the revolution may have been made from above, by an oligarchy, yet it did do wonders for Japan and therefore deserves high praise.[5]

A working historian confronted with the multitude of versions of how the bakumatsu period proceeded and the Meiji Restoration came to occur must despair about what any retrospective investigator can really know. Whether we can draw any valid conclusions at all is a challenging question, and the issue may turn into one of faith or of ideology. The facts are there, but how they are strung together is what produces an interpretation. An attempt to present "just the facts" will fall short of a coherent interpretation and disappoint even the most rudimentary survey in a history course. In recent years the social science models developed by Western scholars and the economic determinism that has prevailed among the Japanese have added a wealth of information about events and situations but have only muddied the issue of what the Meiji Restoration finally signifies.

The search for another way to comprehend the bakumatsu years and the Restoration tends to draw the historian back to first principles, or, quite literally, to the principals themselves – the actors who took part in the dramas of bakumatsu Japan. R. G. Collingwood points the way by defining the objective thus: the historian must remember, Collingwood writes, that an action is "the unity of the outside and inside of an event," that is, of its exterior happenings and movements and its interior "thought"; therefore the historian's "main task is to think himself into this action, to discern the thought of its agent."[6] And Kenneth Burke cautions readers that those who would understand human motivation must bear in mind "a pentad of key terms": act, scene, agent, agency, and purpose.[7] In short the intent in this essay is to go back and reconstruct the history of bakumatsu Japan according to the perceptions and purposes of the "agents" – the groups of actors who participated in the stories that go with the era.

But this formulation raises the question, how many dramas? The Greeks, and H. W. Fowler, would forever remind us that no drama can have more than a single protagonist.[8] Yet the necessarily simultaneous occurrence of many histories within the larger history of bakumatsu Japan allows us license to speak of several protagonists, several dramas. By a further leap into the arbitrary realm of assigning literary plots to the aspirations of historical actors, we may try to characterize the kind of story that each group lived through. The trick is to limit the number of groups we treat in such a way as to be able to construct a coherent combined narrative.

It is a commonplace that people must make sense of events by construing them in story form. "We tell ourselves stories in order to live," observes Joan Didion. "We interpret what we see, select the most workable of the multiple choices. We live entirely . . . by the imposition of a narrative line upon disparate images, by the 'ideas' with which we have learned to freeze the shifting phantasmagoria which is our actual experience."[9] The people of bakumatsu

Japan were obliged to make sense of their life situations if for no other reason than the very novelty of much of what they faced. Excited and confused, their lives altered by forces that were inscrutable to them, they experienced different stories depending on the attitudes and goals they brought to their rapidly changing world. And no one of these groups experienced the same Meiji Restoration as any other. Different motives and perceptions yielded different results, ranging from defeat and frustration to success and jubilation. Lévi-Strauss, referring to another period that has always been viewed as liminal, puts the point boldly:

> When one proposes to write a history of the French Revolution one knows (or ought to know) that it cannot, simultaneously and under the same heading, be that of the Jacobin and that of the aristocrat. *Ex hypothesi*, their respective totalizations . . . are equally true. One must therefore . . . give up the attempt to find in history a totalization of the set of partial totalizations; or alternatively one must recognize them all as equally real: but only to discover that the French Revolution as commonly conceived never took place.[10]

So it was also with the Meiji Restoration. Many restorations occurred, not just one, despite the fact that we routinely speak of "The Restoration" as if it were a uniform process.

Most people have written the history of the Restoration from the standpoint of the winners, those hardy dreamers who lived out their passionate ambitions imbued with myths about Japan and its destiny.[11] But the winners were not alone in living so close to myth. Turner has written that by its nature "liminality is . . . a period of structural impoverishment and symbolic enrichment" when people take stock of their cultural inventory and seize upon myths that relate to life crises and milieus outside of normal rules and regulations.[12] For such a period, then, I propose to focus on four sets of actors – four protagonists – who lived four separate story lines that require four kinds of orientation toward the world with four different ideological outlooks.[13] To be sure, this scheme excludes some groups, and it also lumps individuals into groups for purposes of clarity. But the dangers in conducting this exercise are minimal compared to the advantage of being able to look at the Restoration through the lenses of a defined set of groups of actors.

A full elaboration of this method would yield an extended exercise in "thick description," a phrase Clifford Geertz borrowed from Gilbert Ryle in order to characterize the sort of ethnography that exposes the multiple layers of meaning of behavior when it is seen in its cultural context.[14] But this article will be descriptively lean rather than thick, because its object is to concentrate on the method, not on the content, of the historical period in question.

By the terms of this method, the protagonists of the several dramas on the eve of the Meiji Restoration divide neatly into four groups: (1) the Western envoys and traders, (2) the bakufu and its allies, even when they disagreed, so that this one group perforce includes both the imperial court and the chief feudal lords, or *daimyo*, (3) the followers of popular millennial and other "religious" movements, and (4) the men who called themselves imperial loyalists, who finally did "seize the jewel" that was the Meiji emperor and made the Restoration in his name. Adapting from Northrop Frye, it can be argued that the foreigners sought reconciliation – on their own terms, of course – and lived the story line of comedy. Not that theirs was a funny story; it just turned out right, from their standpoint, because it reintegrated a disordered Japan and made it possible to resume stable trade relations. The other narrative forms or story lines are those of irony on the part of the bakufu and leading daimyo, of tragedy for the popular movements that were suppressed or redirected after the Restoration, and of romance or adventure for the self-proclaimed patriots who quested after and finally found the grail that betokened success.[15]

Now, these four agents, or groups of historical actors, perceived and explained their own actions and intentions very differently, in conformity with their disparate views of the scene in which they acted and with the discrete purposes that animated them. This is not a formal psychological judgment, but one based on simple cognition and perception.[16] Geertz might say that their world views conflicted, that the four groups of actors construed sheer reality in quite different and incompatible ways.[17] To hold that they saw reality in either (1) an integrated manner or (2) a dispersed manner gives us an analytical handle for comparing the four groups. The use of integration and dispersion as opposed tendencies among the groups can be summarized thus:

Western envoys	Integrative
Bakufu and daimyo	Dispersive
Popular revivalists	Integrative
Imperial loyalists	Dispersive

All four groups of actors sought the unity of Japan and the restoration of stability, but any particular group's basic cognitive attitude toward social action was either "integrative" or "dispersive" depending on whether that group saw its fundamental welfare residing in the ethnic collectivity of Japan or simply in itself.[18]

Western envoys who came to Japan as representatives of their governments knew that the Japanese were no match militarily for the force of arms and technological sophistication that then characterized the European nations and the United States. Yet the Japanese seemed an uncommonly volatile lot, forever subject to shifts of mood despite their demure and polite external behavior. The traders who followed the envoys when the commercial treaties went into effect felt much the same way.

What these foreigners wanted was the ability to deal with Japan unfettered by concern about personal security or the ramifications of internal Japanese political disturbances. Theirs was the start of a mission of deliverance: the best of them – the American consul, Townsend Harris; the English minister, Harry Parkes; or the French minister, Léon Roches – hoped that the Japanese government could be induced to bring the country into the community of civilized nations and end the "barbarism" of ancient ways, which heretofore had kept Japan in feudal bondage. Ethnocentrists to the core, they encountered nothing in Japan to jolt their faith in civilization and progress. They wondered how the Japanese would ever be qualified to pursue these twin muses of nineteenth-century Western social gospel.

When in 1853 the officials of the Tokugawa bakufu had looked with disfavor on Commodore Perry's assertion that Japan must abandon its long seclusion, he threatened them with the possibility of the destruction of Edo, which held a large and vulnerable population of more than a million. Perry's return in 1854 resulted in the hurried signing of the Treaty of Kanagawa, binding Japan and the United States in ties of mutual "amity and friendship."

Later Western dealings with Japan also featured heavy reliance on persuasion by force. In 1862 several samurai serving the daimyo of the Satsuma domain murdered an English merchant named Richardson. The British punished Satsuma with a naval bombardment of its capital, Kagoshima, the following summer.[19] Four Western powers – the United States, Britain, France, and the Netherlands – sent a joint flotilla to the domain of Chōshū in the summer of 1864. This naval force bombarded the port city of Shimonoseki to punish Chōshū authorities who had given orders to fire on Western shipping in a vain effort to "repel the barbarians" after the imperial court at Kyoto had proclaimed 25 June 1863 as the date when foreign trade must cease and all foreigners leave Japan.

Parkes and Roches took to forging alliances rather than bombarding ports as the military strategy of choice for treating with the Japanese. Roches made overtures to the Tokugawa bakufu; France even loaned money to the Edo government for military improvements.[20] The British hedged but gradually cast their lot with Satsuma and Chōshū, the two southwestern feudal domains that finally ended the bakufu's dominion over Japanese foreign and domestic policies. The outcome was probably unchanged by this foreign intervention, though no one should doubt its importance: the Westerners made themselves felt,

By displaying their military superiority over their Japanese hosts, the foreigners not only underscored their presence but also tipped their hand. Whether French or English, pro- or anti-bakufu, the Westerners considered Japan a small piece in the puzzle of the world's balance of power. The games they played were ideologically conservative in the extreme, and no wonder: their purpose was always to protect their own advantage. To assure themselves of success, they needed to preserve the status quo. As France saw it, this meant bakufu hegemony over Japan. Through British eyes the restoration of stability could better be accomplished by new leaders – but stability was the coin of the realm for all the foreigners. A Japan in chaos was an impossible market into which to export and sell foreign goods.

On this point – the protection of stability – the Westerners agreed with the officials of the Tokugawa bakufu and most of the major daimyo until 1866.

Both the foreigners and the Japanese leaders approached events from a standpoint of situational congruence: they could live with the status quo if only they could revive it.[21] However they might tamper, neither the foreigners nor the bakufu and daimyo wanted to forgo Japan's essential stability.

While the Westerners were intent on securing Japan as a trading partner under duress, the Japanese authorities worried more about internal stability and its requisite political underpinning. Bakufu officials and leading daimyo shared a common concern with the status quo, and they made policies meant to maintain it. An occasional maverick like Ii Naosuke, lord of Hikone and grand councillor of the bakufu from 1858 until his assassination in 1860, aimed to turn back the clock and restore a status quo ante that had become too hard to defend. The point here, though, is that all Japanese leaders favored the existing political configuration. Their notion of situational congruence varied in details from domain to domain, and within the chambers and councils of the bakufu where lesser officials ambitious for power concocted schemes for maximizing the bakufu's authority. But situational congruence was still to be its own reward, a fitting objective for politicians to pursue, and a fully sanctioned one in a Confucian hierarchical political order.

It is true that some Japanese leaders did strive to change the political system, and this very disposition toward change sets them apart from the foreigners, who were anxious not to disturb the status quo any more than necessary to perpetuate their trade advantage. Bakufu and domain officials played opposing forces off one another in order to disperse threats and resolve disputes through subsumption of the conflicting parties into the overall context. The more they worked at this strategy, the harder it became to keep things in any kind of order. The best of these Japanese officials were what we might call "liberal" because of their desire to spread benefits and authority, thereby co-opting potential opponents into an effective consensus with the bakufu still at its head. Abe Masahiro had tried this tack while he was chief councillor of the bakufu from 1845 to 1855, and his successor, Hotta Masayoshi, followed the same line until Ii Naosuke forcibly intervened in mid-1858. After Ii's death at the hands of samurai whose lords he had treated harshly during his so-called Ansei Purge of 1858–59, new bakufu leaders resumed the strategy of temporizing, consulting, and inviting both court and daimyo to join new tactical arrangements that begged the question of full-scale systemic reform.

The geniuses of this "liberal" approach were Tokugawa Yoshinobu and Matsudaira Shungaku, who were the lords of Hitotsubashi and Fukui and direct relatives of the main shogunal line. During 1857–58 they combined to build a small alliance of influential daimyo and bakufu and court officials who tried to secure the shogunal succession for Tokugawa Yoshinobu. When Ii Naosuke's purge blocked this strategem, they awaited another opportunity. It came in 1862. As advisers extraordinaire they attempted simultaneously to rebuild feudal morale and to strengthen the bakufu. By ending the feudal obligation of alternate attendance that forced the daimyo to shuttle between

Edo and their own domains, they saved money for the fiscally pressed daimyo at home; but their plan backfired as Edo turned into a partially depopulated city beset by economic depression, which led to an unsuccessful attempt to reinstitute alternate attendance. By January of 1867, however, Tokugawa Yoshinobu did become shogun and began to work with ambitious middle-level officials to maintain the bakufu's supremacy while somehow acknowledging the daimyo's claims of feudal autonomy. The height of this policy was reached in the fall of 1867. The bakufu announced *taisei hōkan*, a decision to return governing power to the imperial court. According to this plan, the shogun would step down and join all the feudal lords in a new participatory political system based on a council that would "advise" the imperial court on actual policy formulation. And the Tokugawa house would remain at the apex of wealth with its landholdings undiminished despite the political change.

This conciliar scheme might have worked if Satsuma and Chōshū, acting through the court on 3 January 1868, had not forcibly restored imperial rule on their own very different, imperial loyalist terms. But in a fickle age liberal reformers are always ripe candidates for an unhappy end. Ample resources and a political culture favorably disposed to compromise are the sine qua non of liberal politics, and bakumatsu Japan was running short of both. Beset by external troubles, and pressed to adopt sometimes contradictory domestic policies, the bakufu and those daimyo who cooperated with it confronted a problem whose only cure appeared to be the use of force. The liberals did not want to compel their detractors to support the status quo, yet they were quite willing to divide and conquer: they would discriminate against feudal lords who were recalcitrant, even though the ultimate support of all the daimyo was necessary for the success of the liberal line. Against heavy odds the liberals made a valiant effort, though it was one they might as well have given up as hopeless. The problem is nicely demonstrated by a statement attributed to Tokugawa Yoshinobu in 1863, when the British crisis with Satsuma over Richardson's murder reached a climax. Nothing can happen, he wrote to the Council of Elders, that will help the bakufu. If hostilities break out between Satsuma and Britain, "victory for the English would be a disgrace for the country, victory for Satsuma a blow to the Bakufu's prestige."[22]

Nothing could illustrate the liberal dilemma more plainly. Because the feudal domains were outside the bakufu, the bakufu could not punish Satsuma for the killing of the hapless Richardson. But because Satsuma was a part of Japan, Japan as a whole could only lose if Satsuma were injured by the British, and Japan's loss was necessarily also the bakufu's. For the bakufu was *primus inter pares*, first among equals in a feudal order and the source of authority to which all foreigners looked as they tried to wrench Japan into the international system they were erecting all around the world.

The same dilemma became more acute later when the bakufu twice tried to punish Chōshū because it practiced radical policies that infuriated some foreigners and some Japanese, but most of all because these policies threatened bakufu authority. First in 1864 in response to the imperial court's wishes, then again in 1866, the bakufu mobilized troops and mounted punitive expeditions against Chōshū. In 1866 the bakufu forces were repulsed, to the very great embarrassment of the whole political system, which depended on ultimate bakufu military supremacy within Japan. Yet far from calming the fears of other domains, this pair of assaults on Chōshū sparked the far greater fear among the daimyo that if the bakufu had dared to move against Chōshū, it might soon attempt to make their own feudal autonomy an anachronism. Satsuma therefore came to rethink its traditional cosy relationship with the bakufu; in 1866 it decided to make common cause with Chōshū in a secret new alliance whose existence eventually made possible the coup d'état of 3 January 1868 – the Meiji Restoration in its classic form. All the complexities of this political situation were well understood by the bakufu, whose officials possessed the greatest familiarity with the outside world and had even established schools and offices for analyzing the sources of Western military, political, and economic strength. But the 1860s in Japan were to witness a massive outburst of simplistic yet powerful emotional distress at the condition of the country. And this outburst was finally directed against the bakufu, despite its wealth of knowledge and information.

The great simplifiers had taken the field. It was a time when many complex truths would be ignored in favor of noble motives and heroic deeds. As William Thompson has said of the Irish revolutionaries of 1916, "the agents must be great simplifiers if they are to rise to the purity of heart that is to hate one thing";[23] or, we might add, to *love* one thing, such as the cause of imperial loyalism in Japan. But simplification was not confined to the samurai elites or to purely partisan politics.

The common people of course constituted the bulk of Japan's population of some thirty-five million, and as an undifferentiated mass they came to stand on grounds just as situationally transcendent as those of the most dedicated anti-bakufu imperial loyalist samurai. But the common people are not properly described as an undifferentiated mass. Many millions felt little or nothing in direct response to the troubled times. Their lives continued more or less without change. Other millions, however, searched for new ways to cope with the perverse present, for novel behaviors that might afford the hope of a better future.

Some of these millions created or were persuaded to adopt new religious convictions. Roads filled with pilgrims mark this period as well as certain earlier decades, but the pilgrimages of the 1860s – to sites such as the Sun Goddess Amaterasu's Grand Shrine at Ise in central Japan – were redolent with the anxieties of a population in flux. It was a time when new sects came into being, old faiths were abandoned, and all sorts of movements burst into flower. Uncertain people look for answers in untraditional conduct, and bakumatsu Japan was a laboratory for popular pessimism, fear, and fervent hopes. It was a time of *yonaoshi*, a millennial urge to "remake the world." World renewal movements varied from farmer and townsman rebellions to the fanatical pursuit of new or refurbished deities. Religious sects like

Tenrikyō began to claim thousands of adherents. Carnivals often accompanied the pilgrimages. By the latter half of 1867, after two years of bad harvests were followed by an improvement, a carnival atmosphere pervaded the streets of Japan's major cities in the form of the *ee ja nai ka* ("right on!") commotions that coincided with the political events attending the death of the bakufu and the proclamation of a restored emperor as ruler over all Japan.

Let us take just the example of one sect, Tenrikyō, which the Japanese religious historian Murakami Shigeyoshi calls "the representative entity among popular religions established during the bakumatsu and Restoration period."[24] Founded in 1838 by Nakayama Miki, wife of a prosperous merchant-farmer in a central Japanese village located between the metropolises of Osaka and Kyoto, Tenrikyō stressed "heavenly wisdom" (*tenri*) as embodied in a benevolent creator god, Tenri Ōnomikoto. A happy family life, amelioration of financial woes, and community togetherness became hallmarks of the new sect. Nakayama Miki, who had found her calling in the midst of a faith-healing episode, was the earthly mediator between man and Tenri Ōnomikoto. In its monotheism, its founding by a charismatic personality, its appeal to the rural poor and impoverished urbanites, its emphasis on family and individual irrespective of sex or social status, its message of universal salvation through faith, and even its eschatological anticipation of the achievement of a millenarian *yonaoshi* in this world, Tenrikyō differed profoundly from the existing Buddhist sects as well as from the Confucian ideological orientation of the samurai elites.[25] Thousands of pilgrims descended on the new town of Tenri that eventually sprang up around Nakayama's rural home, and that location itself became Tenrikyōs so-called *jiba* (place of places), the font of creation where mankind and this world as we know it were supposed to have originated.

No sensible estimate can be made of the number of followers that Tenrikyō ultimately attracted, but contemporary and retrospective commentators agree that the community of the faithful was rapidly enhanced during the mid-1860s. Not only did the new religion promise a millennial change for the better here on earth, it also aided its community in the interim by providing loans and jobs to many who were hard hit by the economic difficulties of bakumatsu Japan. The sect served as a kind of credit union and employment security agency for its neediest converts. Some of the new religious movements were first known as *kō* or *kōsha*, terms denoting a mutual financial association for community benefit.[26] Tenrikyō thus attended to both spiritual and mundane requirements among its faithful, and the religion grew, as did the ranks of the poor and needy.

Nakayama Miki is thought to have welcomed the Meiji Restoration as the advent of the millennium.[27] She had witnessed *okagemairi*, "pilgrimages of thanksgiving," through central Japan ever since the massive migration to Ise that occurred in 1830.[28] The carnivals that came along in late 1867, with their common catch phrase, "*ee ja nai ka*," struck Nakayama as portents of the millennium.[29] Yet the fate of Tenrikyō, its foundress, and its followers, while hardly tragic in the literal sense, was pathetic indeed compared to their expectations. The new government after 1868 turned on Tenrikyō with special vigor, sapped its foundress's hope of heaven on earth, and eventually registered the sect as an unorthodox variant of Shinto, a status it did not escape until the era of religous freedom that followed World War II.[30] The triumph and the millennium had failed. And Tenrikyō was never the only target. All the mass religious movements were viewed with disfavor by the Meiji government in Tokyo (the new name for Edo). So were mass movements of people for any purpose, whether religious, such as the pilgrimages, or economic, as with the rural uprisings, or social in nature.

Ee ja nai ka celebrations in the cities also wound down after the new government came to power in January of 1868.[31] This strange antinomian phenomenon, in which the urban masses flouted prevailing mores and expressed contempt for existing institutions of law and order, appeared late in the summer of 1867 and totally ceased by the following spring. The celebrations, often likened to spontaneous carnivals, began near Nagoya, then spread from Yokohama and Edo in the east through Kyoto, Osaka, and Hiroshima in the west, right across Japan's widest belt of urban population density. The carnivals started when pieces of paper bearing the names of Shinto deities (*ofuda*) fell out of the sky on surprised – and "charmed" – downtown urban populaces. Launched by persons unknown, these religious talismans were distributed far too widely and spontaneously to have resulted from a political plot, even though the city crowds clearly favored the anti-bakufu forces over the representatives of the old order.[32] The recipients of these tokens of good fortune from on high quickly got together to hold parties, feasts for relatives and friends, and above all dancing and singing orgies that ran on through day and night and clogged the central districts of major Japanese cities.

"*Ee ja nai ka*" is the phrase that concluded every verse of the improvised songs to which the merrymakers danced. Usually without political meaning, these verses were occasionally directed against usurious rice and saké merchants or others whom the crowds disliked. Sometimes a verse castigated the foreigners, whose economic intervention had disrupted many local commercial routines in the port cities where overseas trade was beginning. But normally, the phrase "*ee ja nai ka*" was just a linking stanza, a means of assuring the crowd that the jollity of the moment would continue as new songs were sung and more fun would be had by one and all.

Students of *ee ja nai ka* acknowledge its importance in perpetuating the mood of *yonaoshi* yearning that marked the pilgrimages, the rise of new religions, and the bitter rural and urban riots of the middle 1860s. Itō Tadao, for instance, writes that *ee ja nai ka* was inseparably bound up with the hope of *yonaoshi* felt by the people at large in their disgust with the old regime. Itō points out that the number of rural uprisings declined from a record 106 in 1866 to a mere 34 in 1867 – the year of the *ee ja nai ka* celebrations – before climbing to a new peak of 108 in 1868.[33]

The records of the city of Kyoto illustrate how divisive the *ee ja nai ka* frenzies could be at a crucial time in Japanese political history. The city was beset in 1867 not only by the intrigues that would result in the imperial restoration, but also by real economic hardship. White rice indexed at 304.6 in 1865 jumped nearly fourfold to a price indexed at 1147.6 for 1867. Soy sauce was up about 150 percent in two years, saké almost 200 percent, while *miso* or bean paste tripled in price.[34] At this point, in the tenth month of 1867, "popular *ee ja nai ka* activity, with no warning at all, suddenly, and with unpredictable scale and duration, appeared as a storm of . . . mass hysteria." But the compilers of the history of Kyoto will not consign *ee ja nai ka* to the category of inexplicable hysterical behavior. "When this activity is investigated closely, it becomes clear that it is activity in which the populace rejects the forms, values, and ethical norms of everyday life, [causing] society itself to tremble from the ground up."[35] More than 60 places throughout Kyoto were sites of continuing *ee ja nai ka* frenzies, almost all of them commercial neighborhoods and many in the city's busiest centers – Pontochō, Gion, Teramachi, Sanjō, Gojo, Horikawa. While the frenzies in Kyoto declined during the eleventh month, they did not stop until the new government took over the city in January of 1868.[36]

Such efforts to defy public mores and mold new realities amount to political acts of violence against the old regime. This is so whether or not the commoners involved were subjectively trying to attack the status quo. All these new mass phenomena involved acts of radical desperation committed by people whose world view transcended the existing situation in Japan. Through the disorders in which they took part, they were attempting to design new patterns for the ultimate purpose of reintegrating Japan. The effect, they hoped, would be to realign their conception of the world with the cultural ethos through which they experienced reality. For world view and ethos had gotten out of alignment in the distress of the bakumatsu perils.[37]

Popular participation in disorders, pilgrimages, and carnivals was deeply unsettling to all samurai and all political leaders, whether of the old regime or the new one that was forming. Few of these leaders could see the people as a constructive force, and in the general Confucian frame of ideological perception such manifestations of popular discontent were regarded as improper and dangerous. Uprisings in the countryside and city crowds and mobs conveyed this sense of unsettled lives and political malaise. Such happenings frightened the imperial loyalists as much as they did the bakufu and the daimyo.[38] In principle one might try to argue a causal link between the rise of chiliastic behavior among commoners and the increased militancy of the loyalist samurai, but there is no reliable evidence to confirm a connection. It is true, though, that the loyalists concluded that the bakufu and its attendant systems were bankrupt just at the time when the *ee ja nai ka* carnivalers were making nonsense out of the downtown streets of many large Japanese cities, in the autumn of 1867.

But imperial loyalist sentiment arose earlier in quite a different context – among samurai who were willing to court anarchy in order to accomplish their objectives. These were very different figures from the cautious officials of the bakufu and the feudal domains. These samurai saw a black-and-white world that badly needed changing. Their appreciation of politics was tempered by a highly formal view of society, community, and the world as a congeries of dispersed idiographic entities. In chaos they quested for redemption, not order. Their overriding motive was to redeem the honor of Japan; a lesser one was to pacify the country, though that task too was part of the redeemer's role.

A profile of the imperial loyalist samurai must allow for a variety of motives that nonetheless coalesce into a situationally transcendent impulse. Some samurai turned old grudges into the stuff of new power relations. Some sought simple self-gratification. Others sympathized with the plight of the poor commoners, whereas still others championed the cause of Japan against the ravages of foreign intervention in Japanese internal affairs. The motives of all these samurai fed the stream that flooded the political ground of the mid-1860s, and they were finally channeled into a disposition not only to overthrow the bakufu, but also to make a new Japan, a country that would be better able to meet its domestic and international problems. Not all of the loyalists were simplifiers, but they shared a sense of adventure which animated them to try every kind of change, from political coup to more tedious if novel attempts to grasp the power of the realm.

What characterizes all imperial loyalists is their unwillingness to wait. There lay the source of their fundamental dissatisfaction with the old regime. The loyalists aimed to disperse all the other forces in order to attain their own ends. Needing the cachet of a new movement to propel them, they sought to mobilize the ancient Japanese myths on their side. As they appropriated the historical mythology, they let loose powerful levers for change, more powerful than any of the underlying institutional patterns of change that can be charted and measured through the long duration of the Tokugawa period. When it fell to the loyalists in their hour of triumph to keep the realm intact, they found it hard to do. The genie rarely goes back into the bottle.

Early in the fall of 1866, just when the bakufu was about to abort its expedition to punish Chōshū, two samurai surreptitiously left a stunning (and strictly proscribed) indictment of the old regime outside a bakufu office in the teeming Edo subcenter of Koishikawa. Although the writers, using pseudonyms, called the Chōshū armies "traitors" and referred to the bakufu armies as "official" ("*kangun*"), their object was to reveal the faults of the existing system. The text also makes it plain that the authors had devised a broad spectrum of reforms designed to redeem Japan in its own eyes and those of the wider world. Chōshū's people right down to the most ordinary folk, states the text, were willing to sacrifice everything for the sake of the domain. Were the people of Edo so dedicated? What the bakufu needed was an "army of righteousness" ("*jingi no hei*") to carry out a twelve-point program of national redemption. Here are the principal planks in the program:

To assure employment for all, and eliminate poverty.
To build hospitals, and institutions for the aged and handicapped.
To lower food and commodity prices.
To rehabilitate rather than execute criminals (except for murder).
To eliminate starvation, thievery, and indolence.
To educate the citizenry in proper schools.
To promote talent and merit irrespective of social status.

If these and other measures were taken, presumably by the bakufu but in principle by any national leadership, Japan could become a "natural good government" ("*shizen no jinsei*"), make foreign trade flourish, and "enrich the country and strengthen the military." Ultimately Japan ("Nihonkoku") would become "the world's foremost good country" ("*sekai daiichi no zenkoku*").[39] Even the use of the word "Nihonkoku" for Japan in relation to "the world" ("*sekai*") suggests a foretaste of nationalistic thinking rare for 1866 among samurai of modest means. This is clearly a use meant to extend beyond the governing elites and embrace the people of the country. In short, it was intended to construe them all as one nation.[40]

The impact of so sweeping a statement as this Koishikawa manifesto could not be lost on a contemporary reader. Bakufu officials who saw it probably laid it to visionary folly and shrugged, or quietly resented their own inability to implement its proposals. The manifesto was traditional in that the Confucian phrases for order and good government appear, but it was revolutionary, too, in its insistence on a utopian transformation that would redeem a desperate situation at home as well as abroad.[41] The two worried authors, who called themselves Ōkawabe Chikara and Takeda Shūunsai, wanted more than anyone could then achieve. Neither the old nor the new regime could fulfill such hopes immediately. The demands expressed in the text resemble the dreams of millenarian commoners who would later be discouraged by the new government. The quest-romance symbolized by these two Koishikawa writers never reached fruition. Yet some of their ambitions for Japan finally did become the grandest achievements of the Meiji oligarchs, such as the expansion of overseas trade, termination of the unequal treaties, and especially "the enrichment of the country and strengthening of the military" (*fukoku kyōhei*). Probably the makers of the manifesto never survived the turmoil of 1866–69; certainly no one ever came forward claiming to be Ōkawabe or Takeda. And even if they did indicate an allegiance to the bakufu in their words, their sentiments put them in the camp of the simplifiers and sloganeers who sought Japan's redemption in the emperor's name.

The struggle that culminated in the Meiji Restoration consumed many of these loyalists, victims of bakufu or daimyo justice, or targets of the oversimplifying zealots known as *shishi* within their own loyalist ranks. Yet those who lasted out the struggles were the ones who inherited the realm. It was not easy, however, to reimpose order amid such chaos.

Although the survivors did manage to restore order, they paid a high price to do so. They mortgaged the future of Japan to their own ability to imagine a reconstruction program. As simplifiers themselves, even the best of them were disinclined to be generous. They came down hard on internal dissent, because they distrusted the diversity that they themselves had helped to sow, and they feared proposed solutions that were mutually conflicting. The situation they transcended was also one they overcame – by destroying it – and they were left holding the empty bag. It was up to these loyalist survivors to fill that bag, and they did not long countenance the menacing residues of other situationally transcendent forces, such as the followers of Tenrikyō or the makers of rural uprisings.

It is the common people that other treatments of the Meiji Restoration have often overlooked. Their rebellions, cult behavior, pilgrimages, and carnivals do not lend themselves to the kind of neat causal explanation that most historians normally seek. Documentation is scanty and incomplete, much of it nontraditional in nature. The letters, memoranda, and state papers prepared by the well-educated leaders of this era do not accord much space to the doings of the masses, whose foibles and expressions of concern must have gone substantially unrecorded. We cannot establish connections among revivalist and millenarian movements, and it is hard to insert the manifestations of popular distress into a straightforward narrative focusing on the politics of Japanese reform, exclusion, and imperial loyalism. That these various popular phenomena did erupt at a time when rural riots were on the increase in the middle 1860s is undeniable, but it appears coincidental, or simply epiphenomenal, as if the troubled times would naturally spawn public fears and anxieties and produce an outbreak of symptoms of social unrest.

Of course, coincidence on its face is neither a result nor a byproduct of anything. The public outcry over the state of the world and the yearning for *yonaoshi* represent constituent elements of the history of bakumatsu Japan. We ignore the appearance of these manifestations at the risk of constructing an inadequate account of what happened, for the masses who took some part in the turmoil of life in the 1860s make up a sizeable portion of the Japanese population at the time. Whether their expressions of concern should be treated as "meaningful coincidences" – instances of *synchronicity*, without cause-and-effect attribution – or just as markers on the known historical terrain is a matter that cannot be decided by appeal to evidence alone.[42] But theirs were powerful expressions that color the period's history and give it depth. It follows that in the arrangement of historical actors for this essay "the people" occupy an important place.

* * *

To conclude the essay requires drawing up a balance sheet of sorts. What are the advantages of the method outlined here? Are there disadvantages that offset or invalidate the method? Lack of voluminous supporting evidence weakens the force of any argument that bases itself on the motives of the actors, but this offsetting condition does not render the claims of the argument invalid. Such claims will remain, perhaps indefinitely, hypothetical, or abductively logical, in the term preferred by Charles Sanders Peirce.[43] On the other hand, among the advantages of this method are its freshness and feel of authenticity. The motivational approach to bakumatsu history leads right past tired controversies that have locked scholars in combat without resolution. Marxists and modernization theorists have no place here. They both posit evolutionary schemes that assume a progression from darkness to light, from barbarity to some kind of utopia. But the punctuated disequilibria of bakumatsu times defy evolutionary theory of whatever ideological stripe.

By contrast, the object of motivational history is to study the groups of actors themselves so as to discern their purposes and what they seem to have thought was happening. This kind of analysis depends on the historian's ability to fathom the perceptions and motives of the actors. It is obligatory to forsake the conventional realm of cause-and-effect explanation; instead, we need to confront and give paramountcy to the disruptions and upheavals that shook the people who were there when the Meiji Restoration was gestating.

From such a perspective it is possible to see how unlikely any particular outcome was. The actors were continually surprised by every turn of events. Plans and blueprints had no practical worth. These people were obliged to act on an ad hoc basis, and their improvisations followed no fixed program, but only the deeper cultural and subcultural inclinations that prefigured their attitudes and perhaps guided their actions. Recognizing this diversity of perception and motive, the method proposed in this article requires taking the history of Japan from the late 1850s to about 1870 and bringing it toward a new interpretation. Such an interpretation must acknowledge the place of all sorts of impulses that historians usually relegate to epiphenomenal status. Examples include the abrupt rise of new religious followings, the outbreak of angry riots in cities and villages, but also the sudden release of energy through carnivals in the streets. Normally wary of myth, historians moving toward such a new interpretation must also recognize claims of inspiration from mythical sources such as the ones that arose from the timely rediscovery of the Japanese imperial institution and its liminal utility in politics. These sweeping trends all assume importance because of the application to historical problems and data of concepts developed by ethnography, religious studies, literary criticism, and other intellectual disciplines. The integration of these trends into a set of four overlapping stories goes farther than do the usual political accounts to explain the rapidity of the changes that followed the Meiji Restoration. The new leaders not only needed to build a central government, they also felt obliged to suppress potential challenges to their authority in the form of irregular and antinomian trends. Their government could thereby be perpetuated through maintaining social stability.[44]

Negative and cautionary problems remain. The high degree of formalism in this explanatory scheme bespeaks my lack of confidence in what historians normally applaud, namely, the diversity of history. So diverse is history that ultimately it may prove wiser to admit the need to impose order on its data than to suffer with the effort to construct a narrative that insists too stridently upon "objectivity." More directly, I have assumed a cross-cultural similarity of motives, and this assumption may be unwarranted. Even though allowance can be made for ideological variables different from those of Western Europe or the United States, is it possible to posit a universal human set of cognitive attitudes? This whole scheme rests conceptually on Hayden White's Eurocentric doctrine of formal rhetorical determinism with its assertion of linguistic deep structures, or poetics, as prefiguring forces in deciding how history will be perceived and how language will be deployed in order to convey historical narratives and interpretations.[45] Even if White is correct in his ambitious assessment of the European mind, how can anyone begin from the presumption of a similar Japanese psychology? It would be nice to do so, if only because it would help give the lie to Western conceits about the uniqueness of the modern *mentalité* and the alleged inscrutability of the Oriental mind. But this presumption of similarity is a hypothesis, and one that can be tarnished to the extent that linguistic theory does succeed in indicating a correspondence between linguistic protocols and cognitive attitudes toward the perceived world. As languages differ, in other words, so may knowledge and perception.

Still this may be a worthy effort. For too long, a kind of acquired historicism (it is not innate) has directed scholars toward writing smooth, almost homogenized narratives and painting conveniently well ordered and congruous pictures of events in the past. Looking back to the principals for evidence of their conflicts should facilitate mirroring the *present* they faced, rather than our own *past*, as they lived through dilemmas that we can only reconstruct, not relive. This historiographical refinement carries the potential for making the past more like the present, in which we see multiple causes and multiple avenues of future action because we cannot yet benefit by hindsight. Like scientists who specialize in elementary particle physics, historians can focus on the interactions among the occupants of the field instead of emphasizing the activities of just one single sort of occupant. Winners and losers appear in the shifting context of their interactions and interrelations.

The method staked out here is "structuralist" in some sense or other, and the implications of structuralism – however the term may be defined – will carry the investigator toward a holistic view of the problem. If the narrative divides to accommodate the motives of four separate groups of actors, it reunites in the holism of the structuralist perspective.[46] The transdisciplinary potential of this method can allow historians to examine the face of bakumatsu Japan and the Meiji Restoration as a whole – as a configuration or gestalt. The negative side of this totalization process is that no scheme or intellectual system can comprehend all of the transformations that the system is capable of generating. The wily Kurt Gödel, engaging the *Principia*

Mathematica of Alfred North Whitehead and Bertrand Russell, demonstrated by using the terms of their own brilliant system that its axioms could not yield all of the theorems and propositions that are compatible with it.[47]

A like conclusion applies to history, that inexact discipline, where accident and circumstance play a necessarily more prominent role than they do in the mathematical sciences. No deductive scheme can, by the use of logic alone, produce all of the truths or suggest all of the action permutations that may arise from its principles. Nor can the method proposed in this essay – to view the watershed years of bakumatsu Japan through the stories of four groups of protagonists – succeed in revealing all the plots and motives that contributed to the history of the Meiji Restoration, its prelude, or the novel coda that followed it. But the method can provide a new perspective on the interactions between the chief historical agents on the scene at the time. And it can help to illuminate some of their seemingly confused acts and purposes.

NOTES

1 G. B. Sansom, *The Western World and Japan* (New York: Alfred A. Knopf, 1950), 281.

2 Claude Lévi-Strauss, *The Savage Mind* (Chicago: University of Chicago Press, 1966), 259.

3 Victor W. Turner, "Myth and Symbol," *International Encyclopedia of the Social Sciences* (New York: Macmillan–Free Press, 1968), X, 576.

4 Ibid.

5 For paradigmatic examples in English of these opposing appraisals of the Meiji Restoration, see Barrington Moore, *Social Origins of Dictatorship and Democracy: Lord and Peasant in the Making of the Modern World* (Boston: Beacon Press, 1966), ch. 5; and John Whitney Hall, *Japan: From Prehistory to Modern Times* (New York: Delacorte Press, 1970), chs 11–14. In English, the most comprehensive treatment of Japan during the mid-nineteenth century is that of W. G. Beasley, *The Meiji Restoration* (Stanford: Stanford University Press, 1972). But see also the meticulous study of the bakufu's last years by Conrad D. Totman, *The Collapse of the Tokugawa Bakufu, 1862–1868* (Honolulu: University Press of Hawaii, 1980).

6 R. G. Collingwood, *The Idea of History* (Oxford: Clarendon Press, 1946), 213.

7 Kenneth Burke, *A Grammar of Motives* (Berkeley: University of California Press, 1969), xv–xvi.

8 H. W. Fowler, *A Dictionary of Modern English Usage* (New York: Oxford University Press, 1944), 470–71.

9 Joan Didion, *The White Album* (New York: Simon and Schuster, 1979), 11.

10 Lévi-Strauss, *Savage Mind*, 258. Lévi-Strauss regards perceived and recorded history as a batch of "fraudulent outlines" whose only peculiar characteristic is chronology, i.e., the temporal order or sequence in which events occur (pp. 258–62). "Dates may not be the whole of history . . . but they are its *sine qua non*, for history's entire originality and distinctive nature lie in apprehending the relation between *before* and *after*, which would perforce dissolve if its terms could not . . . be dated." Therefore no history of the French Revolution can give an accurate impression of what happened, but only a chronologically correct (yet contextually truncated) account of events (p. 258).

11 Totman, of course, is an exception to the general tendency to write the history of

the winners. His *Collapse of the Tokugawa Bakufu* chronicles the dismal if enlightening human tragedy that befell the managers of the Tokugawa system despite their best intentions and efforts.

12 Turner, "Myth and Symbol," 576–77.

13 The quaternary scheme presented here derives from Hayden V. White's 1973 article, "Interpretation in History," in his *Tropics of Discourse* (Baltimore: The Johns Hopkins University Press, 1978), 51–80.

14 Clifford Geertz, *The Interpretation of Cultures* (New York: Basic Books, 1973), 6–10.

15 Northrop Frye, *Anatomy of Criticism* (Princeton: Princeton University Press, 1957), 158–239; for a succinct statement of the four "narrative categories of literature" as "generic plots" or *mythoi*, see page 162.

16 The definitions of *cognition* and *perception* are at issue here, but I am using them in a nontechnical manner outside the field of professional psychology. Both cognition and perception signify awareness or discernment as well as the process by which someone becomes aware or discerning; knowledge and its acquisition are involved.

17 Geertz, *Interpretation of Cultures*, 89–90, 126–27. In his formulation of the complementary concepts of ethos and world view, Geertz defines ethos as "the tone, character, and quality of . . . life, its moral and aesthetic style and mood"; he defines world view as a people's "picture of the way things in sheer reality are, their concept of nature, of self, of society" (p. 127).

18 For an elaboration of this typology of explanatory strategies, see Stephen C. Pepper, *World Hypotheses: A Study in Evidence* (Berkeley: University of California Press, 1942), ch. 7. Integrative world hypotheses, writes Pepper, are inadequate in scope, whereas dispersive ones are inadequately precise (pp. 142–46).

19 On the Richardson affair and its aftermath, see Beasley, *Meiji Restoration*, 183, 199–200.

20 The French *démarche* toward the bakufu is covered in English by Meron Medzini, *French Policy in Japan during the Closing Years of the Tokugawa Bakufu*, Harvard East Asian Monographs, no. 41 (Cambridge: Harvard University, 1971), chs 8–15.

21 On situational congruence and situational transcendence as incompatible attitudes toward existing social reality, see Karl Mannheim, *Ideology and Utopia: An Introduction to the Sociology of Knowledge*, Louis Wirth and Edward Shils, trans. (1936; rpt. New York: Harcourt Brace Jovanovich, n.d.), 192–204.

22 Quoted in Beasley, *Meiji Restoration*, 256.

23 William Irwin Thompson, *The Imagination of an Insurrection: Dublin, Easter 1916* (New York: Oxford University Press, 1967), 242.

24 Murakami Shigeyoshi, *Kindai minshū shūkyō shi no kenkyū*, rev. ed. (Tokyo: Hōzōkan, 1963), 91.

25 Murakami Shigeyoshi, "Bakumatsu ishin ki no minshū shūkyo ni tsuite," in *Minshū shūkyō no shisō*, Murakami Shigeyoshi and Yasumaru Yoshio, eds., Vol. 67 of *Nihon shisō taikei* (Tokyo: Iwanami Shoten, 1971), 568–69.

26 *Ibid.*, 565.

27 Murakami, *Kindai minshū shūkyō shi no kenkyū*, 124–25.

28 Kishimoto Hideo, ed., *Japanese Religion in the Meiji Era*, John F. Howes, trans. (Tokyo: Ōbunsha, 1956), 329.

29 *Ibid.*, 332.

30 Joseph Kitagawa, *Religion in Japanese History* (New York: Columbia University Press, 1966), 221, and n. 85.

31 For *ee ja nai ka* in general, see Takagi Shunsuke, *Ee ja nai ka* (Tokyo: Kyōikusha, 1979).

32 *Ibid.*, 210–13. I know of no postwar historian who regards *ee ja nai ka* as the result of a conspiracy. While the prewar scholar Tsuchiya Takao in 1931 called *ee ja nai*

ka "the nonsense in Restoration history," even a critic like Tōyama Shigeki, who plays down the significance of *ee ja nai ka*, admits that it was a popular and widespread phenomenon. See Nishigaki Seiji, *Ee ja nai ka: minshū undō no keifu* (Tokyo: Shinjinbutsu Ōraisha, 1973), 252; and Tōyama Shigeki, *Meiji ishin to gendai* (Tokyo: Iwanami Shoten, 1968), 103.

33 Itō Tadao, "Ee ja nai ka," in *Yonaoshi*, Sasaki Junnosuke, ed., Vol. 5 of *Nihon minshū no rekishi* (Tokyo: Sanseidō, 1974), 312–13, 327–28. A table of the frequency of rural uprisings appears on page 328.

34 *Ishin no gekidō*, Vol. 7 of *Kyōto no rekishi* (Tokyo: Gakugei Shorin, 1974), 172.

35 *Ibid.*, 186.

36 *Ibid.*, 360.

37 Geertz, *Interpretation of Cultures*, 89–90, holds that the relation between the two concepts of ethos and world view is one of mutual confirmation: "In religious belief and practice a group's ethos is rendered intellectually reasonable by being shown to represent a way of life ideally adapted to the actual state of affairs the world view describes, while the world view is rendered emotionally convincing by being presented as an image of an actual state of affairs peculiarly well-arranged to accommodate such a way of life."

38 Itō, "Ee ja nai ka," 324–31.

39 "Tora hachigatsu Koishikawa," in *Bakumatsu hishi shinbun kaisō*, Meiji Bunka Kenkyūkai, ed. (1934; rpt. Tokyo: Meicho Kankōkai, 1968), 269–71.

40 Tanaka Akira, *Meiji ishin*, Vol. 24 of *Nihon no rekishi* (Tokyo: Shōgakkan, 1976), 28.

41 "Tanaka Akira, "Bakufu no tōkai," in *Kinsei 5*, Vol. 13 of *Iwanami kōza nihon rekishi* (Tokyo: Iwanami Shoten, 1977), 344.

42 Carl Gustav Jung, "Synchronicity: An Acausal Connecting Principle," in *The Structure and Dynamics of the Psyche*, Vol. 8 of *The Collected Works of C. G. Jung*, R. F. C. Hull, trans., Bollingen Series, no. 20 (Princeton: Princeton University Press, 1969), 417–531.

43 Peirce mentions abductive reasoning in several places. He regarded it as an alternative to inductive reasoning and deductive reasoning (from the particular to the general, from the general to the particular). He said that we can know only the facts we can observe (perceive), and if they are insufficient to allow inference we must add "guess-work," which leads to "the first starting of a hypothesis": this step itself is what he called *abduction*. Even if we cannot prove X, for example, if Y were provable then X would also be provable; hence, abductive reasoning, which Peirce thought characterizes most of our inferences anyway. See Charles Sanders Peirce, *Philosophical Writings of Peirce*, Justus Buchler, ed. (New York: Dover, 1955), 150–52.

44 The imperial loyalists were adventurous romantics who expended immense efforts to build an empire. It would therefore be interesting to apply Martin Green's method of linking adolescent reading habits with adult political activities in the British Empire to the data of Meiji Japan. See Martin Green, *Dreams of Adventure, Deeds of Empire* (New York: Basic Books, 1979).

45 Hayden V. White, *Metahistory: The Historical Imagination in Nineteenth-Century Europe* (Baltimore: The Johns Hopkins University Press, 1973). White employs Frye's scheme of plot structures (*mythoi*), Pepper's typology of explanatory strategies, and Mannheim's dichotomy of situational congruence and situational transcendence. White's articles convey his method as effectively as the larger book does. Several of his best "essays in cultural criticism" are collected in his *Tropics of Discourse*.

46 My sense of structuralism generally follows the summary by Jean Piaget more than that of Peter Caws. Both are clear expositions of a movement whose "movers" refuse to acknowledge their likenesses, and both are prescient about the

intellectual development of structuralism across many disciplines during the 1970s. Both identify linguistics as the source of inspiration for structuralism. But Piaget stresses the holism of structuralist systems in their synchronic approach to problems, whereas Caws emphasizes the patterns of binary opposites, polarities, and complementarities that are often employed to explicate structuralist arguments. See Jean Piaget, *Structuralism*, Chaninah Maschler, trans. (New York: Basic Books, 1970); Peter Caws, "Structuralism," *Dictionary of the History of Ideas* (New York: Charles Scribner's Sons, 1973), IV, 322–30.

47 See Ernest Nagel and James R. Newman, *Gödel's Proof* (New York: New York University Press, 1958), 3–6, 98–99.

4 The Meiji Restoration*

M. B. Jansen

*Source: *Cambridge History of Japan*, Vol. 5 (Cambridge: Cambridge University Press, 1989), Ch. 5, pp. 308–66. Cross-references citing chapters etc. relate to the original publication.

The Meiji Restoration stands as one of the turning points of Japanese history. Although the actual events of 1868 constituted little more than a shift of power within the old ruling class, the larger process referred to as the Meiji Restoration brought an end to the ascendancy of the warrior class and replaced the decentralized structure of early modern feudalism with a central state under the aegis of the traditional sovereign, now transformed into a modern monarch. The Restoration leaders undertook a series of vigorous steps to build national strength under capitalist institutions and rapidly propelled their country on the road to regional and world power. Thus the Restoration constituted a major event for Japanese, East Asian, and world history. The process whereby this came about has inevitably become a central issue in Japanese historiography, for verdicts on its content and nature condition all appraisals of the modern state to which it led. The work of historians has been undergirded by a vast apparatus of sources preserved by a history-minded government concerned with its own origins, and the scholarship that has been produced illuminates the intellectual history of Japan's most recent century.

TROUBLES WITHIN, DISASTER FROM WITHOUT

Japan's political crisis of the 1860s was preceded by serious internal difficulties and foreign danger that brought to mind formulations of Chinese historians who habitually coupled internal decline with border incursions made possible by that decline: "troubles within, disaster from without" (*naiyū gaikan*). A great deal of historical inquiry has been directed to the questions of how severe the first would have been in the absence of the second. Once the ports had been opened, there was no mistaking the complementary vibration between internal and external problems, but in the absence of foreign aggravation, the possibility of an internal upheaval sufficient to bring about the collapse of the feudal order remains uncertain. What is clear, however, is that the almost total isolation of Japan before its "opening" by the West served to magnify the consequence of the foreign impact in the public imagination.

The regime's internal difficulties came into striking focus during the years of the Tempō period (1830–44), which receive detailed treatment in Chapter 2. During those years Japan was devastated by crop failures that caused ruinous famines in central and northern areas. These combined with governmental inefficiency and unresponsiveness to encourage or provoke popular resistance. The most spectacular revolt of this period was one led by a model Confucian samurai official in Osaka, Ōshio Heihachirō, whose emotional call to insurrection made him a hero for later historians who sometimes dated the loyalist revolts from his manifesto. Ōshio's uprising resulted in little more than the burning of large areas of Osaka, but the striking incompetence shown by bakufu officials in its suppression contrasted with his own courageous (though equally maladroit) performance to symbolize what was wrong with the regime. Ōshio's revolt, led by samurai and centered in the second most important city of the land, provided a national shock,[1] but it was only one of many risings in that period. Peasant insurrections and urban "smashings" had tended to grow in size with the interrelationships of Japan's increasingly close-knit economy, and popular risings often moved rapidly along lines of communication. An added phenomenon of the period was the increase of chiliastic and millenarian movements. The world renewal (*yonaoshi*) uprisings were frequently led by a self-sacrificing individual who willingly martyred himself for the eventual good of his fellows. Ōshio, too, came to take on such an appearance in popular thought.[2]

Nevertheless, the insurrections of the period proposed few alternatives to the social and economic system that gave them birth. Manifestoes and petitions usually focused on recent or threatened violations of what had come to seem as acceptable, though admittedly burdensome, government demands. Communication routes were natural conductors for such protest, as the villages along the right of way were expected to provide the *sukegō* porter service that moved travelers and transport on human and animal backs. Needs for such services increased in late Tokugawa times.

Rural order was also reinforced by an interesting group of nonofficial rural reformers whose teachings of sobriety, thrift, mutual cooperation, and agricultural improvement were designed to give farmers a better livelihood. The agricultural technologist Ōkura Nagatsune (1768–1856), the rural reformers Ninomiya Sontoku (1787–1856), with his plans for mutual cooperatives, and Ōhara Yūgaku (1798–1858) all worked to restore the health of the rural areas. Significantly, all three focused on the reclamation of land left fallow, whether by bad government or famine or migration. Their teachings were usually moralistic and pietistic, stressing the maintenance and care of land as an essential part of filial piety and ancestral obligation. Such efforts, though surely helpful to the government, were also evidence of the government's inability to fulfill the paternal role it had long ago set for itself. Equally important, the appearance of genuine rural leaders of this sort testified to a rising level of scholarship and leadership among the commoner elite throughout the Japanese countryside.[3]

The bakufu's response to these troubled times took the form of the Tempō reforms launched by the *rōjū* Mizuno Tadakuni in 1841. As Harold Bolitho points out in Chapter 2, the reforms, which included edicts against migration from country to city, provided relief for bakufu retainers' debts, abolished merchant guilds, and attempted to rationalize and concentrate bakufu landholdings within a set radius of Edo and Osaka, struck at vested interests of townsmen and vassals, and ended in failure. Simultaneous reforms in some of the larger domains, notably Satsuma and Chōshū, were somewhat more successful, but none fully met its goals. The bakufu's failure was particularly important, for its inability to raise its revenues augured ill for the greater crises that lay ahead. Nevertheless the ambitious, though abortive, plans for more intensive bureaucratic control of society have provided the basis for some historians' interpretations of the Tempō years as inaugurating late-feudal nineteenth-century "absolutism." Although judgments of these issues differ sharply, undoubtedly the future Meiji leaders, "men of Tempō" who experienced that turmoil in their early years, built on those lessons to their loss or gain.

The bakufu that had to deal with these problems was in many ways a less flexible and less adequate instrument of government than it had been. Although the eighteenth-century administrators had felt able to experiment rather widely within the pattern of the past, the language of the nineteenth-century leaders increasingly stressed the "obligations of the past" (*sono sujisuji no gohōkō*) in a rigid adherence to tradition. Central authority, as Harold Bolitho's study of the *fudai* daimyo points out, had not grown;[4] if anything, the shift from strong to weak shoguns had resulted in bureaucratic immobility. Mizuno's effort during the Tempō reforms to reclaim some vassals' holdings roused a storm of complaint, and yet his abortive efforts anticipated the measures that would be found necessary by future reformers when the crisis deepened in the 1860s. The once pragmatic bakufu had become a rather fine-tuned instrument that found it difficult to proceed without the cooperation of a number of distinct interest groups. Institutionally it remained premodern. The senior counselors (*rōjū*) served on cycles of monthly rotation, and the adoption of regular responsibilities and the abolition of the rotation system came only on the eve of the Tokugawa fall in 1867. Internal disaffection and bureaucratic rigidity may not have reached the levels that characterized contemporary China, but both regimes operated in a setting in which custom and precedent placed limitations on central power. More important, both regimes were limited by an inadequate governmental share of the nation's product. The precedents set by the ancestors and the barriers set by established and deeply routinized patterns of administration made it difficult to initiate radical change. The bakufu, though charged with the responsibility for the national defense, had access to only the income of its own lands. A shogunal procession to Kyoto in the 1860s required most of its regular cash income for that year, and the cost of restoring traditional preparedness and purchasing modern arms was soon to become prohibitive.[5]

The crisis in foreign affairs that followed the Tempō years is treated by

William Beasley in Chapter 4. As he points out, it was a crisis that had been developing for decades. A growing consciousness of the foreign danger had been one of the unsettling elements in the nineteenth-century climate of opinion among informed intellectuals. The defeat of China in the Opium War of 1838–42 brought this consciousness home to a far larger public. The Japanese had ready knowledge of that disaster through the messages brought by Dutch and Chinese merchants to Nagasaki, and Chinese accounts of the problem, notably Wei Yüan's *Hai-kuo t'u-chih*, went through many editions in Japan, where they were immediately accessible to all who had received formal education. In a secluded island country whose great metropolises were collection points for the literate elite of all sectors, speculation inevitably led to uneasy fears that imperialist flotillas would next come to Japan.[6]

Such consciousness had also been advanced by changes in the world of thought, which are treated by Harry Harootunian in Chapter 3. The nativist thought of national scholarship (*kokugaku*) moved in increasingly extreme directions in the nineteenth century. In the teachings of Hirata Atsutane and his disciples, it combined an increasingly assimilative and syncretic utilization of non-Japanese thought with a religious fervor focusing on the sun goddess Amaterasu as a national deity. A new and compulsive ethnicity was in formulation. Still premodern and perhaps only protonationalistic, this thought lay at hand as a potent incitation to alarm and indignation when once the sacred soil and sparkling waters of Japan might be sullied by foreign boots and hulls.

Knowledge about the West, and consequently informed awareness of its capability, was also available through the rise of Western learning (*rangaku*). A practice of translating Western books, launched in 1771 with the discovery by several doctors that the human anatomy conformed more closely to Dutch than to Chinese anatomical charts, grew so rapidly that at the time of his death in 1817 Sugita Gempaku, one of the doctors involved, compared it with the translation movement from Chinese a millennium earlier. The bakufu did its best to channel such learning and also to appropriate that part of it that seemed useful, but restless minds and figures soon carried it beyond the bound of the permissible. In the *Morrison* incident of 1837 a group of "Dutch scholars" concluded that the rude rejection of an English emissary would subject Japan to great danger. The ship in question had in fact already been repulsed successfully, but political criticism of this sort provided the impetus for political repression of the scholars in the purge of 1839.

A third, and ultimately the most important, development in the thought world of the nineteenth century was a growing concern with the imperial institution, which was the product of the *kokugaku* tradition. This cut across all groups, but it found its most forceful and powerful formulation in a blend of ethnic and Confucian teaching that associated loyalism with morality and justified – and even required – participation in the political process under its imperative. In the slogan "revere the emperor, drive out the barbarian!" (*sonnō-jōi*), loyalism wedded to antiforeignism became the most powerful emotion of mid-century Japan.

Historical scholarship has often limited its consideration of emperor-centered thought to treat it as a political tactic without considering its substance, in good measure as a result of and in reaction to the use made of the institution by the modern state.[7] In fact, however, it can be demonstrated that the development of loyalist thought had a long continuity in Tokugawa intellectual history and was not without its roots in Chinese thought as well. The dominant stream of Tokugawa Confucianism drew on the Neo-Confucian thought of Sung China, which developed at a time when the foreign danger in the form of northern barbarians was at the forefront of scholars' consciousness. The antiforeign thrust of Chu Hsi Neo-Confucianism became blunted in a China ruled by Manchus, but in Japan the nonfunctioning throne became idealized, and it ended as the focus of ethnic nationalism. In samurai minds the identification of "country" with "virtue" tended to make absolutes of duty and action. "Loyalty" (*chūgi*) became a "great duty" (*taigi*) and the supreme test of the moral individual. This primacy of political values became the more powerful because, as Maruyama Masao has pointed out, it carried with it the implication that it was the vassal's responsibility to "correct" or "admonish" as well as to "obey" his superior.[8] In the nineteenth century, Tokugawa Confucian scholarship stressed a hierarchical scheme of obligations in which sovereign came to stand above shogun. Chinese civilization gradually came to seem distinct from the country of its birth, particularly after the fall of the Ming to the Manchus in the seventeenth century. Indeed, many nineteenth-century writers referred to Japan as the central country.

There were also trends in Tokugawa policy that gave impetus to this trend of imperial loyalism. In the eighteenth century, the bakufu, increasingly responsive to Confucian morality, demonstrated its respect for the court by protecting and maintaining the imperial tombs and by increasing the miserly stipends that the early shoguns had provided for the court and courtiers. Whereas Ieyasu and his immediate successors had taken care to sever the ties the court had had with the military class up to that time,[9] awards of imperial rank and title to the Tokugawa cadet houses now became expected. Gradually extended to other leading daimyo, such titles became a matter of prestige and pride and helped lead to daimyo–court connections against which the early shoguns had guarded. Gradually and almost imperceptibly, the bakufu's "virtue" came to be identified with its ability to protect and insulate the court and country from outside contact. *Sakoku*, begun as a measure to ward off domestic dissidence in the mid-seventeenth century, ended by becoming a criterion of shogunal loyalty and performance.

Intellectually this package of patterns and ideals found its most persuasive setting in the writings of a group of scholars in Tokugawa Nariaki's domain of Mito. Aizawa Seishisai's *Shinron* (1825) provided in particularly compelling form a warning of the power of the West, insistence on the sacred nature of Japan and its imperial polity, and reminders that that superiority was based on the benefits of the imperial family. Mito thought, and especially Aizawa's book, became widely read in the 1840s and 1850s, at a time when the Mito daimyo began to take a vigorous part in urging measures of moral and material rearmament and in extending his political contacts to the Kyoto court.

THE HARRIS TREATY AND ITS AFTERMATH

The opening of Japan to international contact, described by Professor Beasley in Chapter 4, produced problems that were made more difficult by these strains. Economic difficulties and military unpreparedness made it important for Japan to avoid military conflict until preparations had been advanced. This required information (gathered by the Bansho shirabesho, the new Institute for Western Learning established in 1855), money (collected through new taxes, forced loans, and government economies), and political consensus to provide a time of quiet during which plans could be prepared. The search for that consensus brought efforts to consult, and thereby to educate, the daimyo and the Kyoto court. That consultation had the effect of activating first them and then their vassals and subordinates. A broadening circle of concern among people who were often poorly informed about foreign affairs but who were anxious to use those issues for internal affairs came close to paralyzing government processes.

The bakufu's first response to the news of the Opium War was to relax its standing orders for the prompt repulse of foreign vessels and to order that supplies be provided for them when they requested them. This order, issued in 1842, brought a reminder from Emperor Kōmei four years later to be careful about coastal defense. However mild its wording, it was an early indication that the court would consider itself involved in matters of foreign policy and defense. A letter of warning from the king of Holland in 1844 and the Biddle mission of 1846 were successfully turned aside, but no one doubted that more such would follow. Bakufu orders to daimyo to be vigilant about coastal defenses were issued in 1849, but because of the general financial stringency of the times, no real advances had been made when the Perry mission arrived in 1853.

Abe Masahiro, an able conciliator who had been *rōjū* since 1845, sent the Perry letter to the court for information and to the Tokugawa vassals with requests for advice. Abe was aware of the need for change; he had promoted a number of low-ranking officers to key posts. He also had a keen awareness of Japan's military weakness and had established an office of coastal defense over which he himself presided and which he manned with his own followers. Abe tried to outmaneuver the leading exponent of exclusion, Tokugawa Nariaki of Mito, by appointing him to a key defense post. The opinions that the bakufu received from daimyo and lesser vassals revealed a wide range of views on the American request, but for the most part they agreed that conflict should be avoided. The bakufu made its decision without a great deal of reference to the views that came in; it was a full year before it sent the text of the Shimoda treaty that its negotiators had worked out with

Perry to the daimyo and the court. At the same time its orders to the daimyo had sharp reminders of the importance of coastal defense, and police officials (*metsuke*) were given sharp warnings about the importance of quick and ruthless action to prevent contacts between foreigners and ordinary Japanese. Abe seemed to have resolved the first step, but even his political agility could not conceal the change that was to come. In 1854 the court issued an order to melt down temple bells for guns, the first time in the entire Edo period that Kyoto had taken it upon itself to issue a national directive. Matsudaira Shungaku (Yoshinaga, Keiei), the collateral house (*shimpan*) daimyo of Fukui, Abe's father-in-law, and a leading figure in national politics from then on, wrote to remind Abe that daimyo respect for the bakufu was contingent on the bakufu's respect for Kyoto. In the future, the bakufu's desire for daimyo support in difficult decisions would find it consulting them more frequently, and the court itself developed the tactic of suggesting that daimyo, or at least leading Tokugawa vassals like the *gosanke*, should be consulted again.[10]

The Commercial Treaty of 1858 negotiated by Townsend Harris marked the real opening of Japan to trade and residence. Harris drew his most effective arguments from the disasters that China met in the second round of warfare (the *Arrow* war) that ended with the Tientsin treaties in 1858. Oddly enough, the bakufu's fear of following the course of China into foreign subjection led it to accept treaties almost identical to those inflicted on China.[11]

The debates about the Harris treaty next became inextricably interwoven with the problem of shogunal succession. Tokugawa Iesada, who died in the summer of 1858, had no successor, and so adoption procedures had to be set in motion. The leading candidates were Hitotsubashi Yoshinobu (Keiki), an able young man who was in fact one of the many sons of Tokugawa Nariaki of Mito, and a still-immature descendant of the Tokugawa house of Kii (Wakayama), the future Tokugawa Iemochi. Iemochi's selection would be the more conventional, and in the maneuvering that took place, reference to an "able" heir was code language for choosing Hitotsubashi (later Tokugawa) Yoshinobu.

Hotta Masayoshi, who had succeeded Abe Masahiro as chief bakufu official, informed Townsend Harris that the regime would need the formality of court approval of the new treaty before signing it, and he arrived in Kyoto to secure that approval in the spring of 1858. To his astonishment, the court instructions he received a half-month later instructed the bakufu that because this was of utmost importance to the country, it should take up the matter once more with the three cadet houses (*gosanke*) and the daimyo. This marked the first time in the Tokugawa years that the court had presumed to disagree publicly with bakufu policy. What had happened was that a number of leading daimyo, among them Tokugawa Nariaki, had recognized in the commercial treaty an issue on which they could use the court's xenophobic instincts to influence bakufu policy in the matter of shogunal succession. Henceforth they would propose that the court couple reluctant approval of the treaty with the condition of selecting an "able" and mature heir to the shogun.

When Hotta addressed his second request for approval to the court, he was close to having his way when eighty-eight Kyoto nobles joined to protest. As a result, instructions to consult the vassals were handed down a second time. With this the lines were drawn for a showdown. House succession went to the heart of Tokugawa policy and was an internal Tokugawa matter. As the *fudai* daimyo of Hikone, Ii Naosuke, put it in a letter, selection according to ability might be the "Chinese way," but it was not the way things were done in Japan. Last-minute bakufu lobbying blocked a court plan to call for an able shogun.[12]

The court's second rebuff came in a context of growing exasperation with Kyoto xenophobia and obstruction, and it brought hard-liners to the fore in Edo. Shortly after Hotta's return from Kyoto, Ii Naosuke of Hikone became regent (*tairō*) and took over the leadership role in the Edo councils. He now began a period of personal leadership that had no real precedent in the history of shogunal ministers. It seemed to him that the reassertion of bakufu control over dissidents was a matter of the highest priority and that other issues were secondary.

On June 25, Harris was promised that the treaty would be signed by September 4. Once again letters were sent off to the daimyo in apparent conformity with imperial instructions. But when Townsend Harris brought word of the Treaty of Tientsin and speculated that the British and French warships would probably proceed to Japan next, the treaty was hastily signed on July 29 before the results of the new survey were in hand and without court approval. Ten days later the bakufu announced that shogunal succession had gone to the young Iemochi of Kii. Thus Ii Naosuke had decided the two burning questions of the period within ten days, and quite on his own authority.

Ii now moved against the opposition. Bakufu moderates and foreign affairs specialists who had come to office under Abe and who had favored a cooperative and conciliatory policy toward the daimyo were dismissed, demoted, or moved to less important posts. The great daimyo who had lobbied through their agents in Kyoto for the succession of Yoshinobu as heir were driven into retirement and, usually, house arrest. Matsudaira Shungaku of Fukui, Tokugawa Nariaki of Mito, Tokugawa Yoshikumi of Owari, and Yamauchi Yōdō of Tosa were only the most eminent of those punished.

Emperor Kōmei was furious at this flouting of his sentiment and even considered abdication to demonstrate his frustration. He ordered that the head of one of the three cadet houses (*gosanke*), or the *tairō* himself, come to Kyoto, only to receive the response that the house heads were being punished and that the *tairō* was too busy with national affairs to absent himself from Edo. A lesser *rōjū*, Manabe Akikatsu, was designated as emissary, and even that worthy delayed almost two months before setting out for Kyoto. The court struck back; its directive to the bakufu, in a totally unprecedented breach of channels and security, was transmitted to the Kyoto representative of Mito and sent on to Edo by him to the consternation of the bakufu, which forbade Mito to divulge its contents to other quarters. At Kyoto, low-ranking agents of the daimyo who had favored the Hitotsubashi cause urged on inexperienced courtiers in misguided efforts to have the court insist on a reversal of bakufu policy, the dismissal of Ii, and a reversal of the Harris treaty. Ii Naosuke had his own agent in Kyoto, one Nagano Shuzen, who reported all this activity to Edo and helped provoke the counterstrokes that followed.

By October, bakufu arrests of those agents began. Umeda Umpin, Mito agents, and others were arrested in Kyoto. Hashimoto Sanai, Matsudaira Shungaku's chief emissary, was arrested in Edo. The men arrested in Kyoto were transported to Edo in cages and under heavy guard, and once there they were severely interrogated by a judicial board of five that sat for only the most serious offenses. The sentences handed down were unexpectedly severe and made this one of the largest crackdowns in the history of the bakufu. Over one hundred men were sentenced. Eight were condemned to death, and six of them were beheaded like ordinary criminals.

While all this was in progress, *rōjū* Manabe was working to wring approval from a sullen and reluctant court for the treaty that had already been signed. His hand was strengthened as bakufu punishments approached the court itself, with a round of changes and retirements in courtier positions there. In the end the reluctant sovereign agreed that because the treaties had been signed, it was too late to stop them.

Ii Naosuke has had harsh treatment at the hands of historians, especially those who wrote before 1945. His personal rigidity and harshness were untypical of bakufu procedure and, indeed, of most of Japanese administrative history with its preferences for collegial decision making. Moreover, his victims included some of the ideal types revered by the future Meiji state. The Fukui counselor Hashimoto Sanai, trusted assistant of Matsudaira Shungaku, was clearly carrying out instructions from his lord. In character and attainments he had won universal respect and admiration. Despite this, his sentence read: He "should have remonstrated with his lord that this was a serious matter . . . and he acted without respect for Bakufu will."[13]

Even more serious and tragic in popular imagination was the fate of the Chōshū scholar-teacher Yoshida Shōin. Yoshida began as a low-ranking but brilliant student of military science. After traveling to Nagasaki and elsewhere he concluded that these places would not suffice to protect Japan. He came under the influence of the modernizer Sakuma Shōzan and tried to persuade Perry to take him back to America with him for a period of study in 1854. After Perry maintained his commitments to the shogunate and refused this request as illegal, Yoshida was discovered, arrested, and sent back to Chōshū. There he was given partial freedom to teach in a village academy that came to number among its students many of the future Meiji leaders. Furious at what he considered bakufu disrespect to Kyoto and the servility to foreigners shown in signing the Harris treaty, Yoshida schemed with Umeda

Umpin to engineer the assassination of Manabe on his way to Kyoto. Arrested and extradited to Edo, Yoshida was executed after his fellow inmate Hashimoto Sanai. He became posthumously exalted as a martyr for emperor and country.

Postwar historians, however, have been kinder to Ii Naosuke. Freed from the compulsion of earlier historiography to side with those who fell in the "Ansei purge" and able to see courage and intelligence on both sides of the struggle that was to rend the political fabric of mid-century Japan, later writers have softened their denunciations. Yet in any case, Ii Naosuke did not long survive his triumph. On a snowy day in March 1860, as his entourage approached the Sakurada gate of the great Edo Chiyoda Castle, a group of swordsmen, seventeen from Mito and one from Satsuma, cut through his guards, whose swords were covered to protect them from the late winter snow, and took the *tairō*'s head. The assassins' manifesto attacked the regent personally rather than the government he had headed, but it made it very clear that Ii's crime had been that of indifference to the imperial will, and it urged all Tokugawa retainers to turn with shame to the sun goddess of Ise in penitence. The loyalist years had begun.

THE LOYALISTS

The purge that Ii Naosuke carried out had resulted in his murder; the persecuted loyalists had retaliated by assassinating the chief bakufu minister. These events ushered in a period of violence and terror that transformed the setting of late Tokugawa politics. The loyalists, known to their contemporaries and to history as *shishi* – men of high purpose – became an explosive element in local and national affairs and ended by serving as ideal ethical types for the ideology of the modern imperial state and also as models for young radicals in future periods of instability.

Shishi tended to be of modest rank, status, and income. Lack of status meant that they were little encumbered by official duty and office, which were reserved for higher samurai rank. They lived in a world that was less structured by ritual than was that of their superiors, and communication with men from other domains was also easier for them than it was for their superiors. Because the *shishi* were at the outer circumference of the ruling class, frustrations of limited opportunity and ritual humility often made them suspicious and critical of their cautious superiors. Poorly informed about the context of national diplomatic and political issues, they were inclined to the simplistic solutions of direct action. Calls for preparedness that accompanied the opening of Japan produced a lively expectation of war and led to a setting that was alive with rumor and that put new emphasis on the importance of the martial arts. Swordsmanship academies were crowded as never before with students, and together with tournaments they became settings for political bravado and self-assertion. The *shishi* were men of the sword.

The lower samurai's frustrations often meshed with the discontent of the rural samurai and village leaders. In the countryside, pseudo-samurai pretensions were symbolized by swords, surnames, and rudimentary scholarship. These could combine with the experience of administrative responsibility to encourage critical attitudes toward urban-based but underemployed samurai, sometimes with the conclusion that it was the leadership of the farm villages that really mattered. In Tosa, for example, a Shōya League of the 1840s produced complaints that summed up many of the frustrations and that harked back to a past order in which village leaders had carried out the court's commands without interference from castle town samurai. Tosa *shishi* included sons of rural leaders as well as lower samurai.[14]

Shishi learning varied widely, but it tended to include assertion of the primacy of sincerity demonstrated through action. The Satsuma hero Saigō Takamori was steeped in the views of Wang Yang-ming Confucianism which stressed the identity of knowledge and action. Others drew on popularized teachings of Chu Hsi and Mencius to emphasize the meaning of sincerity and a well-ordered polity and to draw quick conclusions from bakufu concessions to the imperialist powers and its apparent disregard of the wishes of the court. Although they were drilled in the virtue of loyalty and subordination (*meibun*) as the highest duty (*taigi*) of all, the *shishi* also accepted the retainer's obligation to correct his superiors when convinced of their errors. The bakufu itself accepted this in its death verdict against Hashimoto Sanai. He "should have remonstrated with his lord" instead of blindly carrying out his instructions in Kyoto. By the same logic, the *shishi* were ready to condemn bakufu officials for carrying out shogunal instructions in defiance of the sovereign's wishes. A popular history of Japan that was written from the standpoint of Confucian loyalism, Rai San'yō's *Nihon gaishi* (Unofficial history of Japan) circulated in increasing volume, first in its Chinese original and then in Japanese translation, to spread the praise of loyal servants of the court in former days. Rai Mikisaburō, a younger son of the historian, was executed in 1859, one of the victims of Ii Naosuke's purge.

The *shishi* began as loyal retainers, convinced of the identity of their lord's wishes and the desires of the court. Ii Naosuke's punishment of the daimyo who had advocated the Hitotsubashi cause and did their best to block the Harris treaty turned them against the bakufu minister in the name of loyalty to their lord. In the southwestern domain of Tosa, for instance, an oath signed in blood committed a group of young swordsmen to a loyalist party in the fall of 1861 with a statement that combined indignation at the humiliation of Japan by the barbarians and the punishment of "our former lord . . . who, instead of securing action, was accused and punished." "We swear by the gods," the statement concluded, "that if the Imperial Flag is once raised we will go through fire and water to ease the Emperor's mind, carry out the will of our former lord, and purge this evil from our people."[15]

At the outset, ethnic nationalism, retainer loyalty, and imperial reverence could be combined in a devotion that was relatively free of moral dilemma. But once feudal loyalty seemed at variance with imperial reverence – when the daimyo chose the path of caution and pulled back from the loyalist cause – the *shishi* faced a difficult personal choice. Large numbers resisted renewed subordination to their superiors through flight from the domain jurisdiction, seeking protection and employment under the aegis of a domain perceived as more committed to the imperial cause (Chōshū long served as a protector of men from all over the country) or entering the employment of court nobles in Kyoto who had need for bodyguards, agents, and messengers as the political cauldron heated up. Participation in politics in this way was dangerous and often tragic for men who gave up the security of family, home, and safety, but it also proved stimulating and ennobling for many who contrasted the excitement of their new life with the tedium of the ritualized subordination that they had known at home. The Tosa activist Sakamoto Ryōma wrote his sister to contrast the importance of his activities with this old life at home, "where you have to waste your time like an idiot"; at another time he asserted that "the idea that in times like these it is a violation of your proper duty to put your relatives second, your domain second, to leave your mother, wife, and children – this is certainly a notion that comes from our stupid officials. . . . [But] you must know that one should hold the Imperial Court more dear than country, and more dear than parents."[16]

The loyalists did not have a structured view or program toward which they were working. They had slogans (of which the most important was *sonnō-jōi* – revere the emperor! drive out the barbarians!) but not programs. They were opposed to their authorities but not to authority; they were full of ethnic nationalism but only dimly aware of the possibilities of a true nation-state in which the two-sworded class would not stride forth as a special repository of virtue and privilege.

This point requires further comment. E. H. Norman's pioneering study of the Restoration[17] perceived a coalition of "lower samurai" and "merchants" at the center of the political movement, with implications for future social change, but more recent writers have differed sharply over the utility of this as an analytical distinction. The "merchant" participation has proved even more difficult to examine, much less establish. W. G. Beasley's masterly summary of Restoration politics examined the evidence in a number of the most important domains to conclude:

> There is, therefore, a valid connection between low-rank – rank below that of hirazamurai, which qualified a man for domain offices of some responsibility – and rebellion, terrorism, or the threat of violence. The rōnin who were the placard-posters, the demonstrators, the conspirators, the assassins were characteristically men of lower standing than the "politicians."

The same argument extends, Beasley wrote, to others whose "claim to samurai status was tenuous or even nonexistent: the village headmen, rich farmers, and merchants who had perhaps bought the right to use a family name and wear a sword."[18] Tokugawa status divisions had no provision for the political participation of such individuals, and to participate at all was to set aside authority and to ally oneself with kindred spirits who had at least some claim to status. Thus the Tosa loyalists included a goodly number of rural samurai (*gōshi*) (including Sakamoto) and village heads or their sons whose normal horizons of political awareness would have been expected to be limited to the valley within which their acreage lay.

Albert Craig, who restricted his focus to Chōshū, found the "lower samurai" phrase imprecise and without analytical value. "Almost any large movement of samurai would by necessity be a lower samurai movement," he wrote, and the conventional definition of "upper" would fit only seventy or eighty (out of five thousand, or counting rear vassals, ten thousand) Chōshū samurai families. Moreover, in Chōshū there were high-ranking loyalists and low-ranking conservatives. "The samurai class," Craig concluded, given its disparity, "could not act as a class, a gentry class, with common class interests."[19] Thomas Huber, who also studied Chōshū but limited his attention to the students of Yoshida Shōin's academy, defined "lower" as an income of two hundred *koku* or less to conclude that the Chōshū movement, which included commoner village administrators, represented the interests – or at least the discontents – of the "service intelligentsia," thus refining and improving Norman's argument and position.[20]

Even when one grants the frustration and occasional fury of low-ranking members of the Tokugawa military elite and grants the importance of their enthusiasm and violence in energizing a political situation theretofore torpid and somnolent, one is reminded that the story that unfolded after the loyalist years was one of action and decisions taken by domains. Loyalists *as such* were brought under control after 1864 and required the cooperation of men who held power. *Han* policy was set by men of rank with access to the narrow elite that monopolized the highest offices. That elite seldom moved until it was convinced that the perils of inaction outweighed the risks of participation. At the last, the danger of failing to join a common front was that of exclusion from a new political order and structure. Regional and family self-interest had to be calculated with the greatest precision by men who inherited status, authority, and wealth. The *shishi* helped create an atmosphere in which movement was possible. Many, perhaps most, of them, perished in that work. Those who inherited the fruits of their labors were for the most part middle- and upper-ranking samurai who moved their *han* into positions in the years that followed.

Han policy and the logic of events seemed to enroll most samurai in some domains, notably Chōshū, under the loyalist banner before the Tokugawa fall. But in 1867 Chōshū had the most to lose and the most to gain. In other areas the scales were balanced differently. But just as many – indeed, far more – similarly placed samurai in other domains responded differently in other contexts, remaining aloof or following other banners. The bakufu responded to disorder and terror in Kyoto and Edo by recruiting and organizing *shishi* or *rōnin* who, seeing the Chōshū–Satsuma force as regional and "selfish," proved potent instruments of counterviolence. Lower samurai of the Tokugawa domain of Aizu, who served to keep the peace in Kyoto through the final Tokugawa years, were subject to the same class interests and frustrations as were their Chōshū counterparts and probably included as many advocates of exclusion and imperial loyalism among their number. But they responded to different regional and historical affiliations, and their domain provided the single most effective counter to Satsuma and Chōshū military strength until the Aizu castle was put to the torch in the desperate siege of Wakamatsu in 1868 that ended the Aizu presence in the national scene.

COURT AND CAMP, DAIMYO STYLE

The domains of Satsuma, Chōshū, Tosa, and Hizen furnished the early Restoration leadership. With the notable exception of Mito, which destroyed its strength in a civil war, remarkably few other *han* achieved a clear-cut presence or identity in the Restoration movement. Among these, Saga was a latecomer and was co-opted only after 1867. It may have joined the charmed circle chiefly because its proximity to the port of Nagasaki, which it was required to defend, helped bring some able and experienced leaders to the fore. Consideration of the sources of Restoration leadership therefore leads immediately to inquiry into the special characteristics of a very small number of domains. If samurai constraints and frustration were roughly comparable in all parts of Japan, what additional factors distinguished those southwestern domains and the few others that counted in the late Tokugawa years?

Factors of size and location come to mind immediately. Satsuma was second, Chōshū ninth, Saga tenth, Mito eleventh, and Tosa nineteenth in assessed productivity among the feudal domains. Distance and tradition helped create pride and autonomy. Large-scale resources were necessary for mounting a significant military force through the purchase of Western ships and guns in the 1860s. Satsuma, Chōshū, and Tosa also had disproportionately large numbers of samurai. Satsuma and Chōshū had been on the losing side in the struggles that brought the Tokugawa to power in the early seventeenth century; they suffered a loss of territory and had compressed a large military force into a reduced area. Also, the three domains were integrated territorial units with defensible borders along land communication routes that permitted vigilance over contacts with contiguous areas. Satsuma, at the extremity of southern Japan, was particularly famous for its own exclusion system. Each was a *tozama* domain, although Tosa's status was special because the Tokugawa founder had installed a man of his own selection after expelling his predecessor. Consequently, the Tosa lord sought some way of combining gratitude with warning and worked out the suggestion for shogunal resignation. Elsewhere, compunctions of loyalty were weaker. The entire samurai class of Satsuma and Chōshū and the lower ranks in Tosa, many of them rear vassals who had served the previous daimyo, harbored a centuries-old resentment of Tokugawa rule.

Remoteness and secure borders made for a greater degree of autonomy and of self-consciousness. "Han nationalism," to use Albert Craig's term, guaranteed that strong competitive urges operated to drive men on and to exacerbate fears of being left behind or out of whatever new political order might eventuate. Remoteness also made for a smaller role and presence in Edo, for higher costs and greater inconvenience attached to the central bakufu control mechanism of *sankin-kōtai*, and for reliance upon the Osaka market over that of the shogunal capital. Distance and size made possible relatively autonomous responses to bakufu and imperialist demands, as when Satsuma refused to make amends for the murder by its retainers of an English trader who happened along its line of march on horseback (the Richardson, or Namamugi incident), and when Chōshū tried to expel the foreigners by shelling ships along its shores without bakufu authorization. These incidents brought both domains face to face with the superiority of Western military technology, demonstrated by the British fleet against Kagoshima in 1863 and a foreign flotilla against the Chōshū Shimonoseki batteries the following year.

Remoteness had other consequences. At a time when money economy, economic change, and social dissolution were making the domains along the main-traveled parts of the Osaka and Edo plains, most of them held by Tokugawa houses, less feudal, social and economic relationships in southwestern Japan were still backward and traditional. The higher ratio of samurai to commoners in southwestern Japan could also be used to inhibit commoner complaint or participation; this was particularly so in Satsuma. Traditional authority structures provided an effective base for efforts to bolster the domain economy, tap more of its surplus for the regime, and speed military reforms. The Tempō reforms failed in bakufu territory, but Tempō fiscal and economic reforms in Satsuma and Chōshū left those domains in a much stronger position for the competition that lay ahead. In Saga, too, the mid-century decades witnessed a successful campaign to redistribute land equally once again on the lines of the old Heian *kinden* system, a "land reform" program that spoke volumes for the ability of the feudal administration to control its most important resource.[21]

At mid-century the great fiefs of the southwest also enjoyed strong and able leadership. Throughout Japan able daimyo were few and far between in the late Tokugawa years, and in Edo itself shogunal power was entirely in the hands of surrogate bureaucrats during the reigns of Iesada and Iemochi. In Satsuma and Tosa, however, a fortunate accession to power of able men, products of the adoption system, introduced strong direction at the center. Saga too had an able daimyo, though the Chōshū lord was a cypher. What counted was the presence of a generous number of unusually able and adroit subordinates in each fief, men who did not hesitate to speak their minds.

This combination of historical, geographical, and economic circumstances helps to account for the few domains that took leading roles. But it does not explain why so few other domains, some more or less comparably endowed, took vigorous part in national politics. In Mito, where the loyalist teachings of the Confucianists and the personal prestige of Tokugawa Nariaki made for a leading role in the 1850s, an internal power struggle that destroyed domain unity combined with a Tokugawa affiliation to remove the *han* once Tokugawa Yoshinobu became a bakufu leader. In Fukui, also a related Tokugawa house (*shimpan*), Matsudaira Shungaku's early leadership gave way to watchful waiting and hoping for the moment when political conciliation would again be possible. But most daimyo – and indeed most upper samurai – witnessing the dangers that could accompany wrong judgments, preferred to conserve their resources and keep their counsel until the situation was clarified. There was no "anti-imperial" party, but there was a good deal of suspicion, much of it well founded, that those who professed loyalty to Kyoto were chiefly interested in their own advantage. For Tokugawa adherents, on the other hand, the twists and turns of bakufu policy made it both difficult and dangerous to follow a consistent and active line.[22]

The assassination of Ii Naosuke was followed by a series of efforts to bring court and bakufu together in a new and more cooperative structure. It did not succeed. For Edo, as Beasley points out, it meant "a bolstering of bakufu authority by the use of the imperial prestige," while to the great lords involved "it implied a renewed possibility of intervening in politics in the Emperor's name so as to achieve, among other things, an increase in baronial privilege."[23] Yet these efforts were important, for they led to the Bunkyū reforms of 1862, reforms which so changed the political balance of power that a recent study begins its consideration of the Tokugawa fall at that point. Meanwhile for others the hopes they engendered returned at the last to inspire the Tosa proposal under which the last shogun agreed to surrender his power in 1867.

The proposals are usually grouped under the slogan *kōbu-gattai*, for reconciliation of court (*kō*) and camp (*bu*). The first of these to be proposed was put forward by Chōshu, where the official Nagai Uta persuaded his daimyo to urge that a new agreement make it clear that the shogunate ruled "in accordance with the orders of the court," which would thus set policy while the bakufu carried it out. Having secured agreement with this in Kyoto, Nagai proceeded to Edo for negotiation. But there he was soon overtaken by a Satsuma proposal and mission that seemed to promise Kyoto a good deal more. This proposed pardon for all those who had been punished by Ii Naosuke in 1858 and dismissal of the principal bakufu leaders who had held office since then. More important, the court would designate certain daimyo to represent its interests in Edo; the two principal figures of the succession quarrel, Matsudaira Shungaku, daimyo of Echizen (whose vassal Hashimoto Sanai had been executed for advancing the candidacy of Tokugawa Yoshinobu), and Tokugawa Yoshinobu (Keiki) himself were to be appointed to newly created offices. Yoshinobu, who had been denied the shogunate, would serve as guardian (*kōken*) for young Iemochi, while Shungaku would be Supreme Councillor (*seiji sōsai*). This set of proposals was brought to Edo by the court noble Ōhara Shigetomi, and the escort was provided by a large Satsuma military force headed by the regent Shimazu Hisamitsu.

These plans had antecedents in thinking that began in the years following the arrival of Townsend Harris under the urgency of military reform. The great lords who had lobbied for the succession of Tokugawa Yoshinobu wanted cooperation to replace the costly control measures of the Tokugawa system. Yamauchi Yodo, the Tosa daimyo, had proposed a seven-year moratorium on *sankin-kōtai* duty for daimyo at that time, and many large domains had developed steps for financial reform to make military spending possible. Saga had pushed the implementation of its land division program, and Tosa and Satsuma had developed programs for central merchandising of regional specialties to increase domain income – Satsuma with sugar from its southern islands and Tosa with its camphor and indigo. Modification of the ritualized alternate attendance at Edo would be the best possible economy measure.

Unfortunately the strains generated by Ii Naosuke's purge and the enforced absence through punishment of several of the daimyo who were most important to the Ansei reforms had changed this pattern of planned cooperation into one of competitive assertion and rivalry. The Ōhara–Satsuma mission itself was soon followed by a third, this time accompanied by troops from Tosa.

While Yamauchi Yōdō was still in forced retirement, his chief minister had been assassinated by loyalists, who promptly moved to the center of the decision structure that surrounded the young successor daimyo. Takechi Zuizan, the leader and founder of the Tosa Loyalist Party, now proposed in his young lord's name that the court nobles Sanjō Sanetomi and Anegakōji Kintomo proceed to Edo with orders from the court that the bakufu prepare to expel the foreigners immediately. These plans went on to propose establishing the Osaka–Kyoto (Kinai) plain as the private realm of the court, granting the court clear political primacy, ending *sankin-kōtai* so that the daimyo could spend their money for defense, establishing seven or eight of the daimyo of southwestern Japan in Kyoto as support for the court, and establishing a private defense force of courageous *rōnin* from all parts of the country to defend the court. Costs of all this would be met by ordering wealthy merchants in the Osaka area to put up the money. This proposal was one of the most sweeping the loyalists put forward, and it serves to illustrate the way thinking became radicalized. But it did not get much farther, for much to Takechi's surprise his former daimyo, Yamauchi Yōdō, moved skilfully to oust the Tosa loyalists after he was released from house arrest. After lengthy interrogation Takechi was ordered to commit suicide in 1865 for insubordination.[24]

The Chōshū and Satsuma initiatives, however, produced results before the Sanjō–Tosa procession had reached Edo, and the changes that came are known as the reforms of the Bunkyū era. These changed the political setting so basically that a recent study of the Tokugawa fall begins with the assertion that "the Tokugawa bakufu's time of troubles began early in 1862 . . . [when]

a series of political changes . . . reduced the bakufu to a secondary role in national politics."[25] In terms of politics, the most important changes were the implementation of the Ōhara mission proposals: Matsudaira Shungaku of Fukui was appointed *seiji sōsai* (Supreme Councillor) and Hitotsubashi (Tokugawa) Yoshinobu *kōken* (guardian), the latter appointment specifically announced as made at "imperial request." Japan's problems with the imperialist powers, the extent of court disaffection, the insecurity of top-level bakufu officials, several of whom had been assassin's targets, and the appearance of the strong Satsuma military force in Edo to accompany Ōhara had combined to suggest to bakufu officials the wisdom of retreating from Ii's insistence on traditional bureaucratic direction of bakufu and national affairs. Shungaku and Hitotsubashi were in any event from Tokugawa houses, and the appointments did not at first seem an undue participation by outsiders in bakufu and national affairs.

Unfortunately for those who thought in these terms, Shungaku saw his appointment as a first step in a sharing of power by the great lords who had been his allies in the succession dispute a few years earlier. He began by insisting on a general pardon for those who had been punished by Ii; having carried his point he went on to demand punishment for the bakufu officials who had helped direct the purge. There followed a stream of demotions. The house of Ii lost its mandate as protector of Kyoto, and Ii's retainer and adviser Nagano Shuzen was ordered to commit suicide. Soon additional pressures represented by the Sanjō–Tosa mission persuaded bakufu officials of the need to show good faith with the court by extending the punishments to almost all officials who had worked with the successor governments that followed the murder of Ii and to the men who had negotiated the treaties with the foreigners. In considering the remarkable equanimity with which most Tokugawa fudai saw the bakufu collapse a few years later, it is well to keep in mind the demoralizing effect that turnabouts of this sort must have had on vassals' loyalty and resolution.

The 1862 reforms went on to a series of steps that were cumulatively disastrous to bakufu primacy. The first of these was the moderation and virtual abolition of the system of *sankin kōtai*, undertaken in order to permit economies to facilitate domain military preparedness. The period of daimyo residence at Edo was reduced to one hundred days in three years. Many of the lords, freed from duty at Edo, now transferred their attention to Kyoto, which thereafter competed with Edo as center of a national politics. Within a year bakufu officials were trying to undo the effects of this; two years later the bakufu asked all daimyo to send their families to Edo as before. Some lesser lords complied, but the more important domains showed no interest in returning to the restrictions of earlier times. By 1865–6 the great lords hardly granted the bakufu the courtesy of a reply to its summons, and a bakufu survey of Edo mansions turned up the fact that some of the lesser lords had gone so far as to rent their residences to commoners.[26]

Another step that was undertaken to repair relations with Kyoto involved a visit to the imperial court by the young shogun Iemochi. No shogun had visited Kyoto since the third shogun Tokugawa Iemitsu had traveled south with a mighty retinue in 1634 to demonstrate his power. Iemochi's trip to Kyoto was a dramatic contrast to that of his ancestor. Iemitsu had gone to Kyoto to show his might; he had acted to sever daimyo connections with the court, and redirected daimyo residence and attendance from Kyoto to Edo.[27] Iemochi, however, went to Kyoto as part of an attempt to gain strength from reconciliation at a time when daimyo attention was shifting from Edo back to Kyoto. In one point the visits were comparable. Iemitsu had taken an imperial princess as consort, and the same course was now suggested to Iemochi. In an effort to further cement relations with the court an imperial princess (Kazu no Miya) was proposed as consort for the young shogun. The arrangements were made in apparent disregard of her own reluctance and that of the Emperor Kōmei, and the matter served to inflame loyalist indignation further as a demonstration of shogunal disrespect.

Iemochi's trip was planned to be a short one for reasons of economy and politics; bakufu optimists hoped that his presence would serve to reestablish the awareness of bakufu primacy in Kyoto. It worked out quite differently; before the young shogun could be extricated from the intrigues at the imperial capital four months had gone by. He was obliged to show ritual humility in processions to imperial shrines, and his ceremonial deference to the emperor left little doubt of his subordinate position. In 1634, in contrast, it was the emperor who had called at the shogun's Nijō castle. The shogun's position had always depended in the last analysis on force; it was therefore significant that bakufu ministers now thought it desirable to secure specific court authorization of shogunal authority. Unfortunately, that commission included orders to drive out the barbarians. Further instructions reminded Iemochi to consult with daimyo on major questions and to respect "lord and vassals" relations. "Not since the Muromachi period," Totman observes, "had a shogun been given such a patently empty title of authority."[28]

The shogun's visit was an important step in the growing transfer of political centrality to Kyoto. Within months of his return to Edo proposals for a second visit were under way; he was to die at Osaka, still a youth, on his third visit in 1866. More and more daimyo now established headquarters in the ancient capital. Kyoto became a prime object of political and military planning for the southwestern domains. It was preeminently the preserve, at least until 1864, of the radical loyalists and *shishi* who made its streets unsafe for suspected enemies. In one celebrated instance of symbolic rebellion, they lopped the heads off statues of the Ashikaga shoguns. In order to retain control of the capital the bakufu appointed Matsudaira Katamori, young lord of Aizu, protector (*shugo*) of the city in 1862, and as a result he became an important actor in the politics of the next decade. So important did Kyoto become to Edo policy that the fifteenth and last shogun, Tokugawa Yoshinobu, spent his entire period in office in the Kyoto area and never once felt free to take time for a return to Edo. All this added urgency to the bakufu's economic problems. The Kyoto visits of Iemochi were ruinous for bakufu finances, and the necessity of maintaining an ever larger force and presence three hundred miles from the Tokugawa heartland worsened an already difficult situation.

A fourth product of the Bunkyū reforms was cooperation with the great daimyo. This had indeed been at the very heart of the program of proposals grouped as *kōbu-gattai* from the first, and it constituted the platform on which the last shogun based his resignation in 1867. The great lords that mattered included, in addition to Matsudaira Shungaku and Tokugawa Yoshinobu, a number of leading lords: Yamauchi Yōdō of Tosa, Shimazu Hisamitsu of Satsuma, Date Munenari of Uwajima, Mōri Yoshichika of Chōshū, and Matsudaira Katamori of Aizu. They were intermittently drawn into conference to discuss court–bakufu relations and diplomatic problems. In theory this was supposed to prevent unilateral, "selfish" bakufu direction. But the meetings, which began in 1862 and continued sporadically thereafter, produced no real results. There was no agreed-upon program of procedure, and the lords themselves were at least as "selfish" as the bakufu, usually retiring to their domains when things did not go well. The Tokugawa members, meanwhile, inherited the suspicion of bureaucratic "regulars" in Edo. The first attempt ended particularly badly when Matsudaira Shungaku, Supreme Councillor who had brought the whole program into being, resigned and returned to Fukui, followed by a bakufu order that he place himself under house arrest. He was pardoned by the summer of 1863 and remained a major figure, but then and later his program of conciliar cooperation had no real basis in regional interest and bureaucratic politics. As far as bakufu leaders in Edo were concerned, Shungaku and the others were outsiders whose interest in and loyalty to the Tokugawa cause was quite different from their own. In addition, haughty daimyo had great difficulty in controlling irritation and overcoming disagreement. Confrontation was not a congenial mode of resolution for them. A system without provisions for retreat and conciliation found them bargaining by absence and boycotting meetings. Most important of all, however, was the fact that the Western pressure left no slack for the resolution of differences. The insistence of court xenophobes on undoing the treaties clashed directly with the deadlines that had been agreed upon with the Western powers.

The Bunkyū program foundered most importantly on the issue of foreign policy. Throughout most of the negotiation about restructuring power between Edo and Kyoto, Japan was facing diplomatic problems and military threats that required more effective central-government decision making at the very time that power was becoming more diffuse. Important figures at the Kyoto court never wavered in their distaste for the treaties that had been signed with the Western powers, and an inevitable effect of the increased attention to court wishes in the rhetoric of 1862 and 1863 was subscription to promises, however ambiguously worded, to get rid of the foreign plague.

The Ansei treaties opened to foreign trade Yokohama (Kanagawa),

Nagasaki, and Hakodate; within four years (by January 1863) Osaka, Hyōgo (Kobe), Niigata, and Edo were to be opened. Hakodate proved of little importance, and foreigners soon lost interest in Niigata, but Osaka was a national center and located, together with Hyōgo, close to the imperial court at Kyoto. In the spring of 1862 the bakufu sent a mission to Europe to ask for delay in the opening of additional ports, and an attack on the life of Andō Nobumasa, just after the mission had sailed, underscored its assertions about domestic difficulties as grounds for the request. Trade had not yet assumed major proportions, and even Rutherford Alcock, British consul general and later minister, thought the request reasonable. A protocol delaying further openings until 1868 was worked out as a result.[29]

The agreement unfortunately unraveled quickly. Within Japan competitive jockeying for favor at court produced more extreme demands for exclusion of foreigners, while on the spot "exclusion" in the form of samurai and *rōnin* terrorist attacks on foreigners (and, in 1863, on the British legation itself) produced a negative response on the part of the imperialist powers. At Kyoto demands for exclusion were set in motion to embarrass the bakufu, which then confounded its critics by agreeing to exclusion even after many great lords had backed away from the prospect of unsuccessful war.

The Satsuma regent, Shimazu Hisamitsu, emerged as a force for moderation. On his way into Kyoto in 1862 his men crushed a *rōnin* conspiracy in which his retainers had taken a leading role, and upon his return from Edo (whither he had conducted the court noble Ōhara) he warned of the impossibility of exclusion. Unfortunately his samurai had also taken a major step in strengthening English policy by their murder of Richardson on the way back to Kyoto. Thereafter Hisamitsu was preoccupied with the impending threat of British reprisal (which took the form of shelling and burning of his castle town of Kagoshima), and he helped destroy the hopes for a successful council of great lords by leaving Kyoto for Satsuma.

In Chōshū during this same period the pendulum swung from conservatism to radicalism. The initial Chōshū initiative represented by the proposals of Nagai Uta had failed before the more sweeping counter initiative of Satsuma; Nagai was disgraced, retired, and ultimately ordered to commit suicide. By summer of 1862 Chōshū stood as the principal protector and instigator of radical *shishi* and *rōnin* activities at Kyoto. In the latter part of 1862 Chōshū strength was joined by that of Tosa after the loyalists had taken control of that domain.

Thus it happened that, as has been described, the Tosa–Sanjō mission to Edo carried with it the clearest call yet for immediate and unconditional exclusion of foreigners from Japan. The chief bakufu representatives in Kyoto, Matsudaira Katamori (guardian of Kyoto) and Tokugawa Yoshinobu (shogunal guardian), were inclined to the view that the bakufu would have to announce agreement with this demand to show sincerity, and meanwhile look for some way of delaying its implementation, but the regular bakufu officials at Edo were aghast at the dangers involved in even a verbal pledge of exclusion. Edo leaders were operating under the guns of foreign warships in Edo bay and in fear of an English bombardment of their city when they hurriedly agreed to pay over to Great Britain an indemnity for the murder (by Satsuma men, it will be remembered) of Richardson in the spring of 1863, just as Tokugawa Yoshinobu was returning from Kyoto where he had agreed to a court demand for a promise of expulsion. It seems probable that Yoshinobu and other officials hoped they could avoid a clear deadline for action, and that even when they accepted, reluctantly, the court-imposed date (June 25, 1863) they thought of it as a date on which negotiations would commence (and inevitably fail). In any event they passed it along to the daimyo but with instructions to avoid hostilities. In Chōshū, however, the extremist-dominated administration seized the opportunity for full compliance and opened fire on an American merchant ship at anchor in the Shimonoseki straits and later on French and Dutch vessels as well. Thus the *kobū-gattai* program ended in a shambles: the Satsuma lord in Kagoshima vainly trying to prepare for a British attack on his city; Matsudaira Shungaku, author of the program, in retreat in his domain in Fukui; the bakufu verbally committed to exclusion at the same time that it was paying damages to Great Britain for actions it had not committed; and a defiant Chōshū determined to carry out exclusion on its own.

THE TREATY PORTS AND FOREIGN INFLUENCE

The Western powers had created the bakufu's political problems, and they remained to complicate them by their presence in the ports that had been opened. From the time that Yokohama, Nagasaki, and Hakodate were opened to trade in 1859, the bakufu found itself faced with insoluble dilemmas in having to yield to foreign pressures at the same time that it was being pressured to end the foreign threat. The foreign presence, however, also contained elements of hope for the bakufu: Tariffs provided a new source of central income, and the purchase of foreign weapons and foreign assistance in training soldiers and sailors was more easily available to the bakufu than to other governments in Japan. But arrangements for capitalizing on these opportunities were slow in being planned and worked out, and long before they might have helped restore Tokugawa political and military primacy, the negative aspects of the foreign presence had dealt mortal blows to some of the institutional aspects of Tokugawa power.

In some ways, however, the Tokugawa political institutions proved surprisingly resilient in their capacity to accommodate the problems that the mid-nineteenth century brought, for the tradition of seclusion contained few of the expectations of international hierarchy and national centrality that bedeviled contemporary Chinese efforts to accommodate institutions to international society.[30]

From the first, Abe Masahiro entrusted negotiation with the Americans to men he had selected for their ability. By the summer of 1858 a new magistracy was set up to specialize in foreign affairs, the *gaikoku bugyō*; with the appointment of five men to serve in a collegial capacity. From then until 1867, when a more streamlined and responsible structure was worked out, a total of seventy-four officials served in it. This also demonstrates a difficulty: Institutional flexibility was there, but political instability and uncertainty made the post hazardous to occupy. Policy shifts required new teams, and the magistracy changed its occupants like a revolving door. The individual and career patterns of virtually all late-Tokugawa high officials show the political hazards. The board of *rōjū* showed a 100 percent turnover with the substitution of Ii for Hotta. Ambassadors sent to the United States in 1860 to ratify the Harris treaty disappeared into a (probably well deserved) obscurity upon their return to Japan. Lower-level interpreters and "technicians" like Fukuzawa Yukichi and Fukuchi Gen'ichirō, on the other hand, survived to travel again and become the commentators and pundits of the future.[31]

The bakufu sent a series of missions to the West in the 1860s. They became more frequent, more professional, and more serious. The first, in 1860, included seventy-seven men. The discovery that life was possible in the West without mountains of straw sandals and the full panoply of ritual that accompanied Tokugawa society made it possible to be more selective with future missions. In 1862, thirty-eight men went, the interpreters for a second time; this group stayed longer, worked harder, and learned more. Mission followed mission, and a sixth was abroad at the time of the shogun's fall in 1867. By then a number of leading domains, including Satsuma and Chōshū, had smuggled students abroad to study. It will be remembered that Yoshida Shōin, the Chōshū martyr, had himself wanted to sail with Perry to learn about the West. The shogunate too sent students to Leiden to study. Upon his return, one, Nishi Amane, was charged with drawing up a modern charter for the shogunal regime. Japan had an exhibit at the Paris Exposition of 1867, as did Satsuma, which sent its own exhibit and tried to work out independent status as ruler of the Ryūkyū Islands. The bakufu rescinded its ban on the construction of oceangoing ships as early as 1853: It permitted Japanese exhibitors to go to Paris and buried the last of the seclusion provisions in June 1866 with a tariff convention that removed all restrictions on Japanese trading at the open ports, on Japanese purchase of foreign ships and employment of foreigners, and on Japanese travel abroad. In legal and institutional terms, in other words, the bakufu was able to move speedily to dismantle the barriers it had established between Japan and the outer world.

Politically it was another matter. The readiness of the bakufu officials to build bridges with Kyoto at the cost of the careers of the officials who had negotiated and approved the early stages of the opening meant that foreign affairs specialists' careers showed a dizzying, roller-coaster sequence. Obscurantism and xenophobia among the two-sworded men who cursed the foreign presence meant that it was dangerous to be known as an expert in the new specializations associated with the West. Fukuzawa Yukichi found himself in fear of his life when he returned from Europe and America with the material that he made into his best-selling book, *Siyō jijō* (Conditions in the West). Prominent consultants like Sakuma Shōzan and Yokoi Shōnan who had the ear of decision makers were murdered on suspicion of being pro-Western and even, in Yokoi's case, pro-Christian. The most trusted retainer could find himself ordered into suicide when the wind changed for his lord.

Yet for those who had access to foreign travel or, in time, the products of such travel in books like Fukuzawa's, the power of Japan's overseas adversaries provided convincing proof of the need to open Japan in order to strengthen its institutions and arms. Nor was the evidence all baleful. Fukuzawa found much in the West to praise: George Washington was almost a culture hero in late Tokugawa Japan; so, too, was Peter the Great. The West offered attraction as well as repulsion. Repulsion was close to hand on the Shanghai coast. Japanese who traveled to Shanghai on missions to buy ships and arms for their domains saw in the conditions at Shanghai a glaring example of humiliation and insult they were determined to avoid for their own country. Others recognized power: Inoue Kaoru, a Chōshū loyalist and future Meiji leader, recognized in the "forest of masts" in the Shanghai harbor sure evidence that exclusion could never succeed, and Takasugi Shinsaku, his superior in that movement, was shocked by the incidence of Western arrogance and superiority he encountered in Shanghai.

Nevertheless few Japanese made that trip, and none were more consistent in xenophobic instincts than the court nobles and their loyalist allies. Iwakura Tomomi, who had worked for the success of a reconciliation with the bakufu and helped arrange the shogun's marriage with Kazu no Miya, found himself out of office and forced into hiding to protect himself from angry *shishi*.

The representatives of the Western powers were quick to credit the erratic course of Japanese politics to dishonesty and deception. Rutherford Alcock, who initially favored accommodating the bakufu's requests to delay the openings of additional ports, changed from an advocate of accommodation to one of retribution. Japan's inability to protect foreigners was seen as bakufu unwillingness to do so, and security was sought in the presence of foreign detachments – Britain's came to number fifteen hundred men, and French units added several hundred more. These inevitably brought new problems and resentments with them. In 1864 the arrival of Harry Parkes as British minister brought to Japan one of the most vigorous and choleric of the China-coast specialists in gunboat diplomacy. Parkes soon developed contempt for the bakufu's inability to control the daimyo and domestic violence, and before long he added doubts about the bakufu's *de jure* authority to the clear evidence of its deficiencies in de facto authority. Leon Roches, the French minister who preceded Parkes by a few months, on the other hand, never showed the slightest doubt about bakufu legitimacy and detected an opportunity for French leadership in providing military assistance, economic advice, and institutional suggestions to the Tokugawa leaders. Yet even Roches was quick to join his colleagues in joint demands for bakufu concessions, and he warned Tokugawa officials that it would be folly for them to try to stand against the foreigners' wishes. The foreign presence thus provoked antiforeign incidents, which in turn brought demands for additional concessions, with the result that the imperialist presence became a one-way ratchet opening Japan. It was a process that wounded the bakufu more than it did the daimyo, for it was the bakufu that claimed, but could not exercise, full authority. Meanwhile, the evidence of foreign influence and the fears of more to come stimulated and fed a sense of danger and crisis among the Japanese elite. This was only natural. In addition to the background information about the fate of China, there were stories closer at hand. There was a Russian "occupation" of Tsushima for several months in 1861, and the possibility of future danger in a contest between Great Britain and France for leadership, the one favoring the great lords and the other helping the bakufu.

The economic impact of the opening of the ports on the social unease and political turbulence of mid-century Japan requires particular attention. Japan entered the world trade system at its point of greatest growth and at a time when the English Industrial Revolution was the chief locomotive of the trade expansion. The nineteenth century saw an exponential growth in the rate of world trade: Beginning with the 1820s, the growth rates for the successive decades were roughly 33 percent, 50 percent, 50 percent, 80 percent (for the 1850s), and 44 percent for the 1860s, when the Civil War in the United States slowed trade. Exports constituted an ever-larger part of England's product, surpassing 60 percent in the 1850s. The unequal treaties with non-Western countries were important instruments of that advance. Persia (in 1836 and 1857), Turkey (in 1838 and 1861), Siam (in 1855), China (in 1842 and 1858), and Japan (in 1858), entered that system in quick succession. Commercial arrangements that had been worked out for other areas were easily and speedily applied to Japan. The Peninsula and Oriental Steamship Company (founded in 1840) steamers added Yokohama to their calls. At Yokohama and, secondarily, at Nagasaki, the trading houses, agencies, and banks that had been set up along the China coast extended their networks and assigned their men to the newly opened ports of Japan.

From the first the Japan trade exceeded the modest expectations that had been held of it. In 1860, imports stood at 1.66 million and exports at 4.7 million Mexican dollars, respectively; five years later, exports had quadrupled, and imports were up ninefold. At a time when world trade was complicated by the American Civil War and the China trade was disturbed by the Taiping Rebellion, the unexpected growth of Japan drew pleased surprise from British consular and trading representatives and doomed any hopes that bakufu optimists might have had of Western willingness to accept reduction or forgo the planned opening of additional ports.[32]

Japan's trade grew rapidly because of the integration and efficiency of the national market. Goods flowed naturally and easily to the new markets at the new ports. The same flow complicated and ultimately defeated bakufu efforts to control the course of trade and channel its profits into politically desirable hands. Indeed, foreign trade in open ports served to accelerate a shift from metropolitan commerce, channeled through authorized guilds, to regional centers of production. This shift was long in process, and it had long been a subject of contention and dispute.[33] Unfortunately for the bakufu, the metropolitan guilds were important to its control of the economy and to the profits of the merchant houses whose forced loans (*goyōkin*) it called on to meet the rising need for cash. An effort was made to channel trade through Edo in 1860, when "five products" (thread, cloth, wax, hair and lamp oil, and grains) were to be shipped through Edo. But as the trade grew, its largest items were raw silk and tea. In 1863, at a time when the bakufu was ostensibly committed to closing Yokohama, the silk thread guild sought relief from taxes levied on its products that did not move through Edo, and for a time it virtually managed to close Yokohama by boycotting shipments. A year later the bakufu tried to reassert its authority by banning the planting of additional mulberry trees on lands under its control. Such efforts drew quick protests from the representatives of the foreign powers, so much so that some historians suggest that the naval demonstration against Chōshū in 1864 had as a secondary aim the intimidation of the bakufu's efforts to channel trade. The foreigners' demand coincided with that expedition and brought abandonment of the ruling that products move through Edo channels. The following year the powers succeeded in getting tax and tariff agreements against the imposition of internal transit taxes on goods bound for the ports. Foreign trade thus had the effect of weakening the bakufu's ability to control domestic commerce and opened Japan to the ports as well as opening the ports to the foreigners.[34]

The market for Japanese silk was made larger by the European silkworm blight that resulted in large exports of cards of silkworm eggs in 1865 and 1866. The consequence was a dramatic rise in the price of eggs and thread for the Nishijin weavers of Kyoto, whose raw material prices doubled almost overnight. The unemployment that resulted became an element in several urban riots. Urban handicraft laborers and fixed-income groups were the chief victims of price instability in products that had long seemed stable.

Foreign trade was, however, only one element in a wild inflation that sent the prices of all essentials spiraling upward in the early 1860s. The major element in this instability was the bakufu's need to recoin. A closed country had been able to maintain a 1:5 gold-to-silver ratio as long as neither could be exported. But the open ports brought in a flood of Mexican silver dollars from nearby Shanghai, where the international rate of 1 to 15 prevailed. The disruption that followed, in what one author called the "great gold rush," was countered by the bakufu in a basic recoinage program that was punctuated by charge and countercharge between foreigners and Japanese officials. Gold, silver, and copper coinage all were devalued. At the same time the hard-pressed bakufu grew more liberal with its permission to the daimyo to mint their own coin and to print paper currency. Currencies of this sort were not supposed to circulate beyond domain borders, but the integration of Japan's commercial economy guaranteed their spread. Satsuma, for instance, minted millions of copper coins and profited hugely from them. Counterfeit coinage added to the problem. At the time of the Restoration there were sixteen hundred issues of paper money in addition to the multiple varieties of coinage in circulation.[35] An economy that had always known a multiplicity of issues – the bakufu had first debased its coinage in the late seventeenth century and did so fairly periodically thereafter – in the short space of a decade now enormously increased the number, variety, and quality of its issues. Regular requirements of large payments to the foreign powers – for equipment, military needs, and indemnities – worsened the problem by skimming off a significant fraction of the gold and silver bullion available; such payments were assayed with the greatest care and exactness.

The consequence of all this was a galloping inflation that drove up the price of essentials, particularly rice. For the daimyo and upper samurai who measured their income in *koku*, this posed no discomfort, but the vast majority of the warrior class had long since had their incomes commuted to money. Emergency levies in the form of stipend reductions added to the injury. City dwellers were equally distressed. As early as 1862 the Edo city magistrate reported that inflation had raised commoners' living costs by 50 percent. Placards denouncing merchants and foreigners contributed to the tension and growing level of violence. During one month in 1863, "some twenty people were murdered in the city (Edo), and uncounted others were attacked and threatened. . . . One worrisome aspect of the situation was the extent to which the keepers of the peace were becoming the breakers of the peace."[36] In addition to undisciplined members of *rōnin* units, the bakufu had coopted to cope with policing problems, "members of the new Bakufu infantry units were suffering from demoralization, and some of them also became engaged in brawls and abuse of city folk." Open ports also brought disease. A major cholera epidemic coincided with the opening of the ports. Nationwide, births in 1861 were 12 percent fewer than the year before, and in some central provinces they were as much as 80 percent lower.[37] If one adds the earthquakes in Edo in 1854 and 1855 and the severe crop failures in 1866 and 1869, it becomes clear that the last years of Tokugawa rule were difficult for most Japanese.

Finally, mention must be made of the monetary payments that the bakufu had to make to the foreign powers. The Richardson indemnity, paid for Satsuma violence, came to £100,000. The Shimonoseki indemnity was set at an astounding 3 million Mexican dollars. "During the early days of the seventh month of 1865," Conrad Totman noted, "officials at Edo secretly transported to Yokohama some 30,000 to 40,000 *ryō* per day for delivery to the foreigners as another $500,000 payment on the indemnity."[38] Even this was only part of the very large sums that were shipped to the ports to pay for costs involved in new shipyards, guns, batteries and missions abroad in the next few years. National politics, the visits of the shogun to Edo, support to needy daimyo, rebuilding the Kyoto palace (destroyed by fire in 1854) and Edo castle (destroyed by fire in 1863), and the movement of troops to the Kyoto area – all, or most such expenses, could be described as direct or indirect consequences of the opening of the ports. As the inflation worsened, all impoverished the city dwellers and also those on fixed incomes, and all weakened the political posture of the bakufu. Confidence can hardly have been raised by the series of impressive drives for special loans from merchants that were launched between 1862 and 1867; some specified numbers and amounts expected, and others established classes of contributions, for a total of 2.5 million *ryō* of gold, or three times the bakufu's regular annual income in specie.

BAKUFU RALLY

In 1863, loyalists at Kyoto and in the domains overplayed their hand. Satsuma recalcitrance against the English brought on the bombardment of Kagoshima, and Chōshū insistence on implementing exclusion without waiting for bakufu instructions resulted in the four-power naval demonstration at Shimonoseki and doomed the bakufu's efforts to stave off the opening of additional ports and to take up the closing of Yokohama. The Tosa loyalists' efforts to seize the initiative in the name of their former lord resulted in their punishment and elimination on grounds of insubordination after Yōdō was free to turn his attention again to the direction of domain affairs.

This series of miscalculations enabled the bakufu leaders in Kyoto to claim to be more effective implementers of the imperial orders for exclusion programs and to oust the loyalists from Kyoto. Their colleagues at Edo took heart from these developments and tried to reassert Tokugawa control more broadly. The latter part of 1863 and most of 1864 saw the bakufu leaders advocating reconciliation with the court, but this time to their own, and not to the great lords', advantage.

The loyalist military and political setbacks came in quick succession. In September 1863, Aizu troops staged a successful coup with the assistance of Satsuma to drive Chōshū units out of Kyoto and thereby make it impossible for Chōshū loyalist leaders to communicate with and claim the authorization of the court. In the Kyoto area two loyalist risings, one led by a Tosa figure and the other by a Fukuoka *shishi*, were crushed by bakufu units when they tried to rally rural leaders to the loyalist cause and set up a regional political base. Nearer to Edo, in the summer of 1864, a loyalist movement led by elements of the Mito samurai class that began as the product of confusion over bakufu purposes was exacerbated by obtuse leaders and erupted into full-scale civil war. When it was finally crushed five months later, the domain of Mito was for all practical purposes eliminated as an effective political force. Over one thousand men died in the fighting, and hundreds of the holdouts who had been taken prisoner were executed the next year. Also during the summer of 1864, Chōshū loyalist units tried to avenge their setback by staging a military invasion of Kyoto that was driven back, though at immense loss of property in the fighting and fires that swept through the ancient capital. Leading loyalist court nobles fled to Chōshū with the defeated loyalists, thus ridding the court of some of its most troublesome elements.[39] Though discomfited by the way that suppression efforts had revealed its military ineptness, the bakufu stood to gain from this new evidence of loyalist rashness and insubordination, and it now tried to demonstrate its own loyalty to the court's instructions. During the shogun's first visit to Kyoto, the bakufu had accepted the imperial order for exclusion, and Tokugawa Yoshinobu had been named supreme commander of Imperial Defense. Yoshinobu now assumed a steadily larger role in Kyoto, though not without incurring the suspicions of Edo bureaucrats that his apparent acceptance of expulsion was wrongheaded and impractical.

For a few months after the shogun's return to Edo in the summer of 1863, the bakufu basked in the discomfiture of its Chōshū critics. Unfortunately, however, Kyoto's approval still hinged on the implementation of promises of expulsion that were clearly impossible to keep. Within months the shogun was in receipt of an imperial order directing him to return to Kyoto to report on the progress he was making in closing Yokohama. Edo bureaucrats put off compliance as long as they could, citing the pressure of diplomatic efforts and national politics. Their arguments had a good deal of substance, for the early stages of the unrest that would result in the Mito rising were evident, and a disastrous fire had reduced much of the shogunal castle complex to ashes. But by early 1864 the shogun was back in Kyoto, now in much higher favor, privileged with a number of audiences with Emperor Kōmei and able, through his appointment of Matsudaira Katamori of Aizu as guardian of the capital and the exclusion of Chōshū, to exert exclusive authority over access to the court.

Unfortunately these "gains" were still premised on promises of expulsion. When the bakufu informed the daimyo that it had been decided to work toward the closing of Yokohama, it encouraged some to press for stronger measures at the same time that it convinced the foreign emissaries of its mendacity. And when bakufu bureaucrats tried to extend their reassertion of control over Kyoto with steps to move toward a return of daimyo residence at Edo, they received lame excuses that should have told them that their old political primacy could not be restored.

The high point of the new bakufu enthusiasm for *kobū-gattai* – on its own terms – came in 1864 after the impetuous attack of the Chōshū loyalists had resulted in a devastated Kyoto and an indignant court purged of its most extremist nobles. Ironically, the bakufu's decision to punish Chōshū, which was demanded by the court in late summer, was made more attractive because of the prior demands of the foreign powers, who wanted retribution for the shelling of their vessels. At first the bakufu tried to tie that punishment to the closing of Yokohama, only to have the imperialist powers respond that they would then undertake it themselves at bakufu expense. They did so in late summer, before the bakufu expedition got under way, and submitted as their bill the demand for the indemnity of three million Mexican dollars, which they offered to waive in return for immediate opening of an additional port. Bakufu administrators, committed by their promises to the court to have fewer and not more ports, saw no alternative but to agree to pay the indemnity, although doing that also strained their understanding with the court.

The court now insisted that the bakufu go ahead with its own punishment of Chōshū, thereby adding further expenses to the heavily burdened regime. A ponderous allied force commanded by the Tokugawa daimyo of Owari, with Saigō Takamori of Satsuma as his chief of staff, got under way and seemed for a brief moment to represent the return of the kind of Tokugawa-led coalitions that had been formed in earlier centuries. Yet the conditions were very different; it was not in the interest of allied daimyo to deplete their own forces for bakufu purposes or to provide precedents for the future by crushing the Chōshū dissidents. Consequently, a compromise, one that disappointed both court hard-liners and Edo traditionalists, was worked out. The expedition was declared a success, and the armies were disbanded before Edo had given its full approval. Under the terms, Chōshū was to offer a formal apology, suppress the irregular militia companies that had attacked Kyoto, turn over the loyalist court nobles who had fled to Chōshū to Fukuoka for custody, and order the suicide of the three domain elders (*karō*) who had been responsible for the mistaken loyalist attacks. The nobles were duly transferred and the apology delivered, together with the heads of the three *karō*.

This settlement was acceptable to the bakufu leaders in Kyoto, but men in Edo anxious to reassert full Tokugawa primacy did not find it punishment enough. They wanted the terms strengthened to include the bringing of the Chōshū daimyo and his heir to Edo, as a symbol of submission and as a prelude to the return of other major daimyo to residence there. In short, the squelching of loyalist dissidence in the Kyoto and Edo areas and the encouraging evidence of ascendancy over Chōshū had brought personnel shifts that saw the hard-liners again take over bakufu policy positions. Some were seasoned specialists in foreign affairs, wanted an end to the charade of exclusion, and thought the time had come for closer coordination of policy planning and implementation. *Fudai* traditionalists in Edo were fully supportive of this and desirous that the influence of the "outsiders" who represented the Tokugawa cause in Kyoto be lessened. This medley of purposes produced a consensus that led to the preparation of a second Chōshū expedition, the death of young Iemochi in Osaka where he had gone to "lead" his armies, and the disasters of the second Chōshū campaign of 1866. By then daimyo awareness of Tokugawa purposes had also produced a very different political climate, one that made all such plans depend on a convincing military victory.

REGIONAL REFORM

With central power diminishing, the future of Japan was to be decided by a contest among regional powers, and the chief contestants were the great domains of southwest Japan and the bakufu itself. Preparation for the struggle was primarily military and secondarily administrative. What counted was the ability to marshal resources and to use them effectively within a social context of obsolescent status distinctions.

Military reforms had been anticipated in some of the frantic preparations for possible war that followed the coming of Commodore Perry. In the domain of Tosa in the 1850s, for instance, desperate efforts were mounted to procure and produce better weapons. Officials were sent to Satsuma to study efforts that had been made to build a reverbatory furnace for arms production. The most important Tosa innovation was probably the decision to form a people's corps (*mimpeitai*) made up of commoner formations commanded by rural samurai (*gōshi*). But these efforts were abandoned after a few years' experience; war with the West had not eventuated; and Yoshida Tōyō, the administrator who had sponsored these efforts, was assassinated by the loyalists. The loyalists who succeeded him in control of domain fortunes were men of the sword and not of the gun.

In Chōshū, however, loyalist extremism accommodated Western arms and methods. In that domain, military reforms began in the 1860s, and as extremism drove the *han* into solitary opposition to the bakufu and its allies, the sense of crisis served to speed up military reform. The innovation for which Chōshū was to become best known was the recruitment of militia companies (*shotai*) with complements drawn from both samurai and nonsamurai; of these the Kiheitai are the most famous. Some of these companies were set up by government action, and others collected around extremist samurai who lived away from the castle town. All the companies were made up of samurai and commoners. The commoners showed a wide range of origin (hunters, mountain priests, townsmen, and fishermen), but the largest category seems to have been sons of village headmen. Thus the leaders of these companies were the sort of men who exercised effective, as opposed to formal, authority in the countryside. The companies also included *rōnin* from other areas. In the fighting that followed in 1866 and 1868, these units fought with tenacity and even ferocity. They must have known that if they failed, neither the bakufu victors nor the highly placed Chōshū conservatives would have shown much compassion. More than any other domain, Chōshū was becoming a small-scale "nation in arms" of the sort that the Meiji modernizers wanted.

The capitulation of the Chōshū government to the first expedition mounted by the bakufu displeased loyalists of many sorts in Chōshū, but none more so than the military units that were to be disbanded by the terms of the settlement. One of these, led by Takasugi Shinsaku, revolted and seized a government office in Shimonoseki before the ink was even dry on the agreements, thereby producing an offer from the bakufu negotiators to provide a body of troops to help the domain regulars suppress them. The Chōshū administration, confident in its own ability to subdue the militia, declined, but its confidence proved misplaced. Within a short time, additional *shotai* victories had produced an advance on the castle town itself and a strong sentiment of criticism against the domain administration that had let the civil war come about. This situation was resolved by the emergence of a new domain administration in the early spring of 1865 that represented a coalition of extremist and moderate samurai. This group led the domain on its collision course with the bakufu and into the early Restoration government.

The Chōshū violence had elements of class or at least of status conflict, and yet it was not a contest between upper and lower in any simple sense. The new administration produced a commitment to the loyalist cause, yet it was also staunchly Chōshū centered in values and objectives. It was nominally antiforeign and exclusionist in its goals, and yet places of influence were beginning to be found for individuals who knew the West. Itō Hirobumi, one of the future leaders of the Meiji state, symbolized the course of a leadership generation in the shifts of his career: a student of Yoshida Shōin, then a student in England, an interpreter and translator in the concluding stages of the foreign bombardment of Shimonoseki, next a commander of a militia company, and finally a protégé and trusted lieutenant of Kido Takayoshi, probably the single most important figure in the new Chōshū administration. Itō was of modest rank and origin. Responsibility and opportunity sobered judgment, and information about the outer world gradually moderated the extremism of the young warriors. Yet what seemed to their elders reckless "extremism" had brought them to power within Chōshū, and their pursuit of the bakufu was not likely to be more conciliatory.

Satsuma, unlike Chōshū, experienced no internal violence or political upset. Its samurai numbers were large and needed no supplement of commoners; distinctions of rank and income within its samurai ranks were so large that rifle-bearing companies could be mounted with little of the status compunctions that hampered the bakufu levies. Most importantly, however, the Satsuma regent Shimazu Hisamitsu was able to maintain political control and enlisted the talents of Saigō Takamori and Ōkubo Toshimichi, men who had been tempered by danger and punishment in 1858. They helped suppress Satsuma extremists at the beginning of the *kobū-gattai* movement in 1862, and by 1865–6 they recognized and acted on the need for the domain to know more about the West. Fourteen students were selected and sent to London under the guidance of domain officials. Once in Europe the students were set to studying a variety of technological and military specialties. Before long they were joined by a second group. Satsuma officials in Europe tried to secure for their domain status as an independent country for the Paris Exposition of 1867, citing as reason the domain's control of Okinawa. They negotiated a number of agreements for industrial and mining operations, and although little came of most of these, the purchase of five thousand rifles added important strength to the Satsuma military. Thus, whereas Chōshū, under great military pressure from without, underwent a political upset that placed power in the hands of "extremists" who had use for the advice of the Western-experienced Itō and Inoue Kaoru, Satsuma, without the goad that military crisis provided for administrative change in Chōshū, was, thanks to the English bombardment of Kagoshima, no less alert to the need for Western equipment. Expulsion, one may conclude, was now a dead letter (though it remained a useful slogan) after the shellings of Kagoshima and Chōshū. The overthrow of the bakufu, which was not a practical proposition before the reforms of 1862, had become a goal of many men by 1865.

The changes of the early 1860s had made the bakufu itself a regional power. No set of reforms was more impressive and more extensive than the changes that the Tokugawa leaders initiated in their Kinai and Kantō territories. The Osaka and Edo plains were under full foreign and Japanese observation and hence subject to all the interference that national and international politics could provide. These territories were also divided between those under direct bakufu administration and the lands of minor daimyo and *hatamoto* who administered their holdings independently. Cumulatively the largest holdings of any daimyo in the Tokugawa structure, the Tokugawa *tenryō* was also the most affected by urban and national commerce and communications, the most "modern" in economic developments, and the most lightly invested by resident samurai. In Tokugawa lands, samurai as a percentage of domain population were relatively few and highly urbanized. The bakufu thus faced particular problems in its military modernization.

The bakufu's Bunkyū reforms of 1862 included administrative and military changes as well as the relaxation of daimyo controls that have already been discussed. On the whole, the administrative changes were more successful than the political changes. New procedures were developed for the rapid promotion of able men. Unessential jobs were eliminated; so many, in fact, that the unemployment that resulted required special programs of aid and relief for the newly unfortunate.

Military reforms found the bakufu (and its rivals) struggling to acquire the most lethal weapons at a time when firearms were undergoing rapid change in the Western world. A second problem was to transform the corps of house retainers (*hatamoto* and *gokenin*) into rifle companies. This last was easier to do in theory than in practice, for the urbanized samurai, who were essentially an army of occupation that had spent many generations in peace and quiet, often resisted drill.[40]

Extensive plans were worked out for a modern army and navy within the confines of the troop strength that retainers were expected to be able to provide. Efforts were made to correlate income to the rank structure of the modern forces, and planners set the goal of drawing one-half of those forces from the bakufu's house retainers. Thus it was assumed from the outset that it would be necessary to augment samurai with commoner strength.

Naval training got its start when a small Dutch training contingent came to Nagasaki in the 1850s; in the early 1860s Katsu Kaishū was assigned the responsibility of organizing a naval training school at Hyōgo. Katsu's tendency to recruit his men from many areas alarmed bakufu conservatives, who saw the institution becoming a nest of loyalists, and so Katsu was replaced in 1864. The point is significant: Bakufu reformers tended to draw on men of many areas, but the great southwestern *han* could be exclusive and probably had more esprit de corps. Sustained efforts were devoted to the land arm of the new military structure. By 1864 some ten thousand weapons had been imported through Yokohama, and from then to the end of the bakufu, gunrunning to Yokohama and to Nagasaki (for the southwestern domains) proved one of the most lucrative aspects of trade at the ports. As the second expedition against Chōshū drew near in 1865, bakufu leaders were beginning to realize that their reliance on their retainers (and especially the landholding *hatamoto*) would have to change. First they tried to get them to provide conscripts as part of their feudal military service requirement, but before long it became clear that a better system of recruiting commoners was needed. As the forces took shape, the composition of the principal rifle-bearing units gradually became commoner based. By degrees, *hatamoto* military service requirements were becoming commuted to a money tax that was used to cover the costs of conscripting and training peasants. All of this affected only part of the Tokugawa vassal armies, but it was that part that indicated future trends.[41]

The Tokugawa military reforms required extensive foreign cooperation, but as the nominal government of the entire country, the bakufu had the best access to foreign assistance. Its first moves were by way of the traditional link with Holland, and in the fall of 1864 three navy officers were sent to the Netherlands to study shipyards and other Western military developments. Negotiations for a shipyard were begun with the Dutch and also for a warship; talks also began for the building of a warship (the future *Stonewall*) in the United States.

But the most important channel of foreign assistance was that with France. Minister Leon Roches, who arrived in Japan in April 1864, worked unceasingly to consolidate for his country the role of principal source for military – and, he hoped, political – reform in Japan. Those plans developed gradually; they represented Roches' enthusiasm and not that of his government. Foreign aid never assumed the dimensions that the bakufu's domestic rivals feared it would, because neither Tokugawa nor French leaders were prepared to take risks. Yet the plans were extensive and stand as reminders of the possible impact that imperialist competition could have had on a developing Japan.[42]

Roches began with specific goals: The French silk industry was in dire need of help from Japan because of a silkworm blight, and that made him the bakufu's most importunate customer. But he was free with additional suggestions. Before long he had secured the appointment of Kurimoto Joun as special liaison officer between himself and the *rōjū*, and by the end of 1864, bakufu officials had requested his help in planning for the construction of a naval yard and arsenal at Yokosuka. Gradually confidence in Roches' intentions developed. In 1865 a mission was sent to Europe to seek military assistance as well as machinery and equipment for Yokosuka. Arrangements for a mint and a military training mission took shape, and bakufu officials began to develop hopes of a special source of access to the technology and training they knew they needed.

These experiments gathered momentum with proposals for an officially sponsored trading company that would generate funds for bakufu purchases abroad. The banker Fleury-Herard was invested as the bakufu representative in Paris and put in charge of purchasing equipment for a foundry and mint. French advice (though not, it should be noted, French money), began to pour into Tokugawa circles about ways to restructure Japan's economy and administration in order to speed modernization and build up power. Long before much could come of this, however, the Tokugawa forces were gathering in Osaka to carry out the second punitive expedition against Chōshū. When hostilities broke out in the summer of 1866, it was still a largely traditional congeries of bakufu vassal forces that tried to contest the issue with the more highly motivated Chōshū units.

The second war with Chōshū proved a disaster. Although elements of the bakufu's new units were employed, they were fielded together with old-style units from other *han*. The bakufu army was a coalition of vassals' armies, as had always been the case, enabling the Chōshū warriors to select their target and attack the Tokugawa forces where they were weakest. Bakufu efforts to attack Chōshū at each of its borders were poorly coordinated, and the forces were poorly led. While all this was in progress, the young shogun Iemochi died at Osaka.

When the full scale of the military disasters became clear, Tokugawa Yoshinobu, now the ranking figure on the bakufu side, reluctantly decided that the battle would have to be broken off and seized upon the shogun's death as a face-saving reason for a cease-fire. Yet the cease-fire left Chōshū troops occupying areas of bakufu and *fudai* land, and it dealt the shogunate a blow in prestige from which it never fully recovered.

The defeat of the bakufu armies by Chōshū gave the Tokugawa modernization movement new urgency. The last year of the Tokugawa shogunate saw sweeping changes that portended centralization, rationalization, and bureaucratization. Once Yoshinobu was fully invested as shogun, with full honors and titles, the reconstruction of the bakufu began in earnest. Foreign relations were regularized. Permanent missions were set up in capitals. Yoshinobu's younger brother Akitake was sent to France as the bakufu representative at the Paris Exposition of 1867, and plans called for him to spend years of study there to prepare him for future leadership. Appointive changes brought to office some of the most effective of the modernizing officials of the recent half-decade. The entire foreign diplomatic corps was invited to Osaka for an audience with the new shogun, who entertained them at a dinner prepared by a newly employed French chef. Western dress replaced Japanese at the shogunal court for that occasion.

Numerous requests for advice were addressed to Roches, and he answered during long sessions with senior officials and a private audience with the shogun Yoshinobu himself. The list of questions covered administrative changes, taxes, military development, mineral resource development, economic growth, queries about Switzerland and Prussia, and questions about the abolition of feudalism by European countries.[43] Administrative reforms followed; these set up a sort of cabinet system with specialized responsibilities replacing the monthly rotation of all-purpose generalists that had been the pattern. New personnel practices were designed to facilitate the selection of competent officials, with a regularized salary system for government departments. A great deal of time went into the preparation of diagrams laying out specific administrative responsibilities and procedures, and initial steps working toward the commutation of vassal lands and stipends developed. Shogunal power in the Edo area was strengthened by measures to call in small nearby fiefs in order to rationalize and centralize administrative procedures. Military reforms were pushed particularly rapidly. A French military mission arrived in January 1867. Western uniforms were adopted; obsolete forces were disbanded; and steps were taken toward the substitution of a monetized tax on house vassals as the basis for a peasant conscription system. Nishi Amane, newly returned from study in Holland, was ordered to draw up a more modern scheme of government and produced a parliamentary draft that envisioned a division of power among the court, an executive branch, and a bicameral legislature with an upper house of daimyo empowered to dissolve the lower house.

As a result, it can be asserted that the bakufu leaders were launching a modernization program – perhaps a "Tokugawa restoration" – that would in time have emulated at many points the programs adopted by their successors in the Meiji government. Seen in this light, it can be said that the civil war of 1868 was fought over the issue not of whether Tokugawa feudalism would survive but whether its demise would be presided over by Tokugawa or anti-Tokugawa leaders. It was no longer a matter of saving the bakufu system but of replacing it, now that it was collapsing. As Totman said of the period immediately before the summer war, "there was no longer in Japan an authority symbol capable of moving the feudal lords. There was no national polity; the *bakuhan* system no longer existed."[44] Ironically, however, these needs were probably seen more clearly by the bakufu leaders than by the southwestern lords who opposed them.

RESTORATION

The changes launched in Edo are difficult to evaluate, for they did not mature in time to help the bakufu; it is always easier to sketch reforms than to carry them out. Nevertheless, the fear that they would result in a greatly strengthened shogunate was an important factor in impelling leaders in Satsuma and Chōshū to try to anticipate such success with efforts of their own to overthrow it. What they particularly feared was that the administration of Yoshinobu would use French military and administrative assistance to build a central government capable of destroying the daimyo, with the shogun serving as its chief executive officer.

In 1867, the death of Emperor Kōmei of smallpox brought changes at the court as well. Though consistently antiforeign, Kōmei had usually been well disposed toward the bakufu as represented by Tokugawa Yoshinobu, with whom he had established relations of considerable trust. With the succession of the boy Mutsuhito, the future Meiji emperor, court nobles had a new field for political maneuver. The most able and important of those courtiers was now Iwakura Tomomi, a shrewd judge of events and possibilities. By the fall of 1866 Iwakura was writing that the court had the choice of siding with the bakufu against Chōshū and, possibly, Satsuma, or maneuvering to make itself the center of a new united polity. Because bakufu prestige and power were in decline, he suggested that "the Emperor should issue orders to the Bakufu that from now on it must set aside its selfish ways, acting in accordance with public principle; that imperial rule must be restored; and that thereafter the Tokugawa house must work in concert with the great domains in the Emperor's service." To restore national prestige and handle the foreigners, the country would have to be united, and "for policy and administration to have a single source, the Court must be made the center of national government." In additional documents Iwakura sounded more and more like the Satsuma leaders with whom he communicated, as when he wrote: "In the heavens there are not two suns. On earth there are not two monarchs. Surely no country can survive unless government edicts stem from a single source. . . . Hence it is my desire that we should act vigorously to abolish the Bakufu" and relegate the Tokugawa house to the ranks of the great domains.[45] Some of this language was echoed in future proposals, as in a Satsuma–Tosa document worked out in the summer of 1867:

> There cannot be two rulers in a land, or two heads in a house, and it is most reasonable to return administration and justice to one ruler. . . . It is evident that we must reform our regulations, return political power to the court, form a council of feudal lords and conduct affairs in line with the desires of the people . . . only then can we face all nations without shame and establish our national polity.[46]

These notes of national danger, international prestige, and the need for an effective, single center of government recur in many pronouncements of late Tokugawa days. In fact Japan now had not only two governments but even two bakufus, given the presence of Yoshinobu in Osaka/Kyoto and the more Tokugawa-centered world of the bureaucrats at Edo.

Although such divisions of power seemed impossible to men like Iwakura and many others, they also made it troublesome for foreign representatives who wanted firm guarantees of their privileges and a clear understanding as to the channels of power. Roches accepted the bakufu as a legitimate national government and devoted his efforts to help it become a more effective one. His British counterpart Harry Parkes was not sure and suspected that Japan would not have a real government until basic changes in Edo–Kyoto relations took place. Though junior to Roches in time of residence, Parkes proved a ruthless competitor, on one occasion forcing his way into a private meeting between Roches and Yoshinobu to insist on equal treatment as Her Majesty's representative. When the bakufu requested postponement of the second installment of the enormous indemnity exacted for Shimonoseki because of the costs that had been incurred in the preparation of the second campaign against Chōshū, Parkes demanded an accounting of those costs. When the bakufu argued court opposition as grounds for delay on Hyōgo, Parkes demanded – and secured – explicit court approval of the treaties by staging a demarche at Osaka in November 1865. When he saw the bakufu's difficulties with its recalcitrant daimyo, Parkes concluded that England, in a spirit of neutrality, should cultivate those daimyo as possible future power holders, and he alarmed bakufu officials by visiting several castle towns in the southwestern domains, including Kagoshima. Parkes's interpreter Ernest Satow, probably the best informed foreigner in late Tokugawa Japan, maintained close friendships with the leaders of the southwestern *han* and wrote a pamphlet (which was immediately translated into Japanese) arguing that English policy should work toward the creation of a council of great lords, of whom the Tokugawa head would be one, under the emperor, in order to secure binding guarantees of foreign privileges and rights. This private opinion was widely taken to represent English policy and seemed to be in the process of implementation by the actions of Harry Parkes. Thus foreign as well as court and daimyo opinion was working to exacerbate unstable national politics.

As the great domains shook off their subordination to bakufu leadership, they began to negotiate private agreements among themselves. These were no longer the personal discussions of daimyo, as in the early years, but policy decisions reached by the bureaucratic leaders who staffed *han* administrations. The most important of these was an agreement between Satsuma and Chōshū that was worked out early in 1866 to lessen the possible dangers for Chōshū in the approaching second bakufu punitive campaign. The agreement was made possible by the efforts of Sakamoto Ryōma and Nakaoka Shintarō of Tosa who provided their good offices. In February 1866, Kido Takayoshi, for Chōshū, and Saigō Takamori, for Satsuma, agreed that Satsuma would provide its help in mediating for Chōshū at court; it would do its best to prevent the bakufu from crushing Chōshū; it would secure Kyoto if necessary; and it would join with Chōshū, once that domain had been pardoned, in working for "the glory of the Imperial country."

After the defeat of the bakufu armies at the hands of Chōshū, the Satsuma–Tosa agreement that has been mentioned added another agreement. The two domains agreed on a program for politics: The court should have full authority, and a council with two houses would be established in Kyoto, one chamber staffed with daimyo and the other made up of "retainers and even commoners." The shogunate as such would be abolished. New treaties would be drawn up with the foreign powers "on the basis of reason and justice"; institutions would be revised and brought up-to-date; and self-interest was everywhere to take second place to the consciousness of the larger national good.

This optimistic view of an unselfish future, clearly a legacy of the *kōbu-gattai* persuasion, represented a Tosa plan to secure a peaceful solution to Japan's political crises. Chōshū, flushed with its victories in the summer war, was still technically under the ban of both court and bakufu and determined to exploit its military advantage in further violence. Simultaneously, the treaty powers were demanding action on the opening of Hyōgo, which was scheduled for the summer of 1867. Once again the great lords assembled to discuss the crisis. Matsudaira Shungaku, Shimazu Hisamitsu, Yamauchi Yōdō, and Date Munenari proposed to Yoshinobu that the bakufu combine a solution to the two and proposed to the court a pardon of Chōshū together with court approval for the opening of Hyōgo. Yoshinobu, however, was inclined to hold out for the impossible condition of an apology from Chōshū, but because Hyōgo could not wait, he preceeded to wrest approval from the court for that opening on grounds of pressing national danger.

This stance confirmed Satsuma's discouragement with even a reformed bakufu and helped produce a new Satsuma–Chōshū agreement for a military coup against the shogunate in the summer of 1867. The Tosa leaders, holding a median position, still tried to head this off with a peaceful solution. Tosa's size made it fearful of losing out in a military showdown. Its relationship to the bakufu, which had treated the Yamauchi house favorably, was also one of obligation and loyalty. All this reinforced hopes of a negotiated settlement by which the shogun would agree to step down and become one of the great lords in a new conciliar structure under the aegis of the throne. Similar hopes had been at the heart of the *kōbu-gattai* movement since 1862. Matsudaira Shungaku reappeared on the scene once again. Sakamoto Ryōma, once a Tosa loyalist and then an associate of the bakufu official Katsu Kaishū, subsequently sheltered by Satsuma and central to the Satsuma–Chōshū agreement of 1866, now worked out an eight-point program that contained Tosa hopes for a negotiated settlement. The Satsuma leaders who willingly subscribed to this program in endorsing the Satsuma–Tosa compact in the summer of 1867 were quite willing to help propose the bakufu's voluntary dissolution and were prepared to use force if a peaceful settlement should fail.

These currents converged in November 1867. While Edo modernizers were pushing reforms to produce a more effective bakufu and Chōshū and Satsuma leaders were readying their troops for a military showdown, Tosa representatives in Kyoto presented Yoshinobu with Yamauchi Yōdō's proposal that he resign his office and titles. The proposal contained eight parts: The court would rule, but a two-house council, made up of daimyo and court nobles, would be established; new treaties would be worked out; an imperial army and navy would be established;[47] "errors of the past" in procedure and institutions would be abolished; "wrong customs" in the court would be reformed; and once again, self-interest would be put aside.

Yoshinobu accepted the proposal. He did so without consulting the Edo government leaders and after almost no consultation in Kyoto. Clearly he saw it as a way of escaping his predicament of responsibility without power and retaining the power base that his reforms were building at Edo. Once the court accepted his resignation as shogun, the Tokugawa polity of 267 years formally came to an end.

But there was still nothing to replace it. The council of daimyo did not materialize, for uncertainty was so widespread that only sixteen daimyo arrived in Kyoto in response to a court request for attendance. *Kobū-gattai* proved no more viable in 1867 than it had been in 1862. Soon large contingents of samurai were being sent to Kyoto; parts of the Chōshū domain army, still unpardoned, were nearing the city. The Satsuma–Chōshū plans for a military coup were still intact, and tension grew steadily. On January 2 and 3, 1868, an assembly at the court was convened, dominated by Iwakura and Satsuma men. Yoshinobu and his closest supporters, suspicious of what was planned, declined to attend. The meeting resolved to transfer the palace guard from bakufu to non-Tokugawa hands, to abolish old offices, and to demand the surrender of Tokugawa domains to the "court." Yoshinobu, in doubt as to his next step, withdrew to Osaka.

For over three weeks, things were at a standstill. Court representatives ordered Yoshinobu to appear in formal contrition and surrender, only to have him propose that all daimyo dedicate a comparable fraction of their income and land to the court. Roches offered Yoshinobu such French aid as he could muster, an offer that was not accepted, but neither was the advice of bakufu leaders who wanted to fight. A powerful document from Yoshinobu to the court calling attention to Satsuma's duplicity and his own exemplary behavior was kept from the young emperor. The former shogun's indecision began to cost him the support of even Tokugawa houses Finally, in late January 1868, Yoshinobu decided to return to Kyoto with a body of troops to remonstrate. His commanders did not expect to have to fight their way back; their formations and composition represented an unlikely mixture of modern and premodern companies. To their misfortune they were opposed and ambushed by modern Satsuma and Chōshū units that stopped them and drove them back. The civil war had begun; force would decide the issue.

Fighting at Fushimi-Toba went on for four days and produced a casualty count of five hundred dead and one thousand to fifteen hundred wounded. On both sides, units fought well, but the leadership and determination of forces committed to the Kyoto cause was superior to that on the bakufu side. The bakufu commanders seem to have let a fear of popular disorder keep them from using all their Western-trained and armed troops at the front, whereas their adversaries had their best units at the right places. The bakufu units, trying to advance along two narrow roads, one on either side of the Yodo River, had the harder task to carry out. In some units, morale was a problem, but others, notably those of Aizu, fought with dash and courage.

When the dimensions of this new disaster were apparent, Tokugawa Yoshinobu and his bakufu army headed north for Edo. Within two weeks the former shogun had decided against further resistance to his enemies, despite Roches' encouragement and advice that he try again. The bakufu army was dismantled as the daimyo took their units to their own domains, some to join and others to apologize and submit to the "imperial" armies that advanced from the south. In the spring of 1868 Edo itself was surrendered by the bakufu official Katsu Kaishū to an imperial army commanded by Saigō Takamori.

But the war was not over, for the fighting known as the Boshin conflict went on until May 1869, when the Tokugawa naval units that had sailed to Hokkaido and held out there under the command of Enomoto Takeaki surrendered. The war in the northeast had been carried on by a daimyo alliance headed by the Sendai domain. Its cause was really not that of the Tokugawa, which was clearly doomed, but, rather, that of its region against the distrusted southerners from Satsuma and Chōshū. This "Northeastern League," in fact, claimed that its members were more loyal to the emperor than were the "selfish and self-serving" southerners. The most fierce battle of the campaign came at Aizu castle in Wakamatsu, where the men of Matsudaira Katamori, former *shugo* of Kyoto and long a thorn in the side of Satsuma and Chōshū, fought desperately. The castle was put to the torch, and Aizu lost almost three thousand samurai in the war, more than the combined total of the opposition. After its defeat, the domain was broken up, and its ruling family was moved to a niggardly and inhospitable plot of ground unable to support the remnants of its former retainer force. Katamori himself was made a Shinto priest, guardian of the Tokugawa burial shrines. No other domain was treated as harshly, though a number of recalcitrant daimyo were forced into retirement and others into house arrest. Tokugawa Yoshinobu himself was ordered to retire as house head and withdrew to Numazu in Shizuoka where he did his best to maintain his retainers. By the 1890s he had been received by the emperor and restored to honor. His successor, Iesato, was first head of the House of Peers.

The regime that replaced the bakufu, as Chapter 10 makes clear, underwent many changes before becoming the Meiji government.[48] Its first institutional probings came in the January meetings that maneuvered Yoshinobu into opposition. The same meeting that declared bakufu offices abolished established a new three-tier structure of *sōsai*, *gijō* (councilors), and *san'yo* (junior councilors) and named Prince Arisugawa *sōsai* in order to make the greatest possible use of imperial legitimacy. Gradually, however, status and office filtered downward to the samurai leaders of the southwestern *han* whose lords dominated the original table of organization, and as that process matured, the Meiji government took form.

In a basic sense, the program of the new government was enunciated as early as the spring of 1868, at a time when the regime was still seeking to reassure the doubtful and to enlist the wavering. In April, one day after Katsu and Saigō negotiated the surrender of Edo, the young emperor was presented with what became known as the "Charter Oath," five articles that bridged the transition from the Tosa proposals of 1867 to the constitutional order of the modern Japanese state. These articles promised the creation of "deliberative councils" and the determination of policies on the basis of "general opinion," the cooperation of all classes in carrying out the administration of affairs of state, full opportunity for commoners as well as for officials, and the abolition of "evil customs of the past." They also proposed basing everything on the "just laws of nature." Finally, a search for knowledge "throughout the world" would follow in order to "strengthen the foundation of imperial rule." This was a document couched in terms sufficiently general to conform to the social structure of its day, but it also held out the possibility of changes so basic that it could still be cited as authorization for the democratic institutional changes that followed World War II.

THE RESTORATION IN HISTORY AND HISTORIOGRAPHY

If the definition of the Meiji Restoration is limited to the events of 1867 and 1868, it constituted little more than a coup that shifted rule from one sector of the ruling class to another. But when it is considered as a larger process, one that began before mid-century and that culminated in the modern state at the century's end, it can be seen to have brought revolutionary changes in Japanese society. Studies of these events during the century that followed them have inevitably been intertwined with the climate of opinion within which they were carried on. The nature of the nineteenth-century historical process, and the motive forces involved, have provided basic problems of classification and analysis.

The orthodox view of Japanese history before 1945, and one that is by no means dead, was based on interpretations that emphasized the maturization of currents of imperial loyalism through the Tokugawa period. With the coming of Perry and the foreign danger, the textbooks explained, selfless patriots – the *shishi* – fought to reverse their *han* policies and to defeat the bakufu by wakening long-slumbering imperial and national consciousness. Saigō, Ōkubo, Iwakura, Kido, and all the heirs of Yoshida Shōin were portrayed as though foretold by anguished loyalists of earlier times. Laudatory biographies told their stories as they themselves would have wished to be remembered. Official historiographical institutes provided proportional representation for the southwestern *han* to make certain that the praise would be allocated equitably. These views were spread by a modern education system that was centered on patriotism and loyalty, reinforced by the popular press, and fortified by scholarly compilations. So brief a summary risks distortion. There was enough of substance in the commitment of Restoration figures, enough romance and color in what they did, and enough national pride in what they produced to retain for the loyalist leaders a secure place in any historiography. But the identification of their success with morality and patriotism also introduced a strong bias in much that was written in a highly nationalistic setting.

Yet the nationalist emphasis of prewar history had developed in a context of much more critical writing. By the 1880s, historians had begun to fit Japan's experience into international models of liberal and capitalist societies, and some were becoming troubled by the disparities they sensed between the "deliberative councils" that had been promised and the reality of the Imperial Diet they saw approaching. Japan seemed to be eclipsing the timetable of other countries in modernization, but the reforms granted "from above" were somehow different from the reforms won from below. By late Meiji times the conservative and pragmatic government leaders in power also seemed quite unlike the hotheaded, two-sworded idealists of romantic memory. To some, they were becoming Japan's new problem, and judgments of the bakufu softened as a result. By the early twentieth century a new generation of writers had begun to separate the leaders from what they had brought about, to minimize the conflicts, and to explain the Restoration and modernization programs by showing the material advances that had taken place in Japanese society under Tokugawa rule. Tokutomi Sohō argued that it was not the Meiji leaders but inexorable trends that had created the new Japan. He and others stressed the fragility of feudal society, and the growing independence of stouthearted rural leaders, as the critical factors in the overthrow of Tokugawa feudalism. In turn, such interpretations were usually related to political advocacy and the desire to find legitimacy for liberalism and to advance social reform in Japan.[49] By the 1890s, however, the flush of victory over China, soon to be followed by the conquest of Russia, the maturation of the ideology of the imperial state, and the completion of the network of national schools all combined to reinforce the official orthodoxy with its sanctification of the modern state. Tokugawa Yoshinobu himself, in his memoirs (1915) and in an authorized biography (1918), became a loyalist.

After World War I, Marxist analysis provided a new and powerful teleological expectation of what the Restoration should or could have produced. Economic instability culminating in the world depression, increased political and intellectual surveillance consequent to the formation of the Japan Communist Party in the form of the Peace Preservation Act of 1925, and the aggressive course of Japanese foreign policy all combined to encourage new evaluations of Japan's recent past. Marxist historians divided into the Labor–Farmer (*rōnō*) group, which was prepared to describe the Restoration as a basically bourgeois movement that had ended feudalism in Japan, and the gloomier Lectures (*kōza*) group which held that feudal relationships had lived on in the countryside through noneconomic and non-contractual restraints on tenants as the basis of a new "absolutism" built around the "emperor system," a term that was utilized in the Japan Communist Party theses of 1932. Like their Meiji predecessors, these historians were directing and relating their views to problems of political advocacy.[50]

Japan's surrender in 1945 freed the air of "emperor system" orthodoxy (although it replaced it with equally compulsive derogation for a time) and produced immensely important work that retained some of the Marxist categories without repeating the simplistic formulas of much of the earlier writing. Nevertheless, the presentist orientation of historical evaluation continued, and many writers' concerns were to identify and eliminate feudal remnants and advance democracy.[51]

When the focus of research is brought closer to the decade in which the bakufu was toppled, problems still outnumber answers. The principal actors among the leaders have been clearly delineated, but the source of their backing remains a matter of dispute. Shibahara Takuji, after summarizing movements of popular discontent and disorder in Restoration times, did not hesitate to term agrarianists the "moving force" of the Restoration and saw popular antifeudal sentiments as the key historical ingredient in the events of the decade. On the other hand, Conrad Totman's analysis of the bakufu's fall, though recognizing commoners' antifeudal attitudes, concludes:

> This anti-feudal mentality did not become an anti-Bakufu mentality, however, and the reason seems to be that the political contest of the 1860s was pitting some parts of the ruling or feudal elite against others. . . . In consequence one finds commoners in all camps and on all sides of major disputes . . .[52]

One statistical examination of the incidence of popular revolts between 1865 and 1871 (a total of 545) found that they were least prevalent in future "Restoration-led" areas and most common in Tokugawa-ruled or related areas and related this to the relative prosperity and productivity of the Tokugawa areas and the relatively depressed and suppressed state of the antibakufu domains. Effective anti-Tokugawa *political* action cannot be related to such popular discontent, but Tokugawa efforts to maintain control and counter nonsamurai resistance were, presumably, hampered by the relatively less stable social base of the Tokugawa territories.[53]

No one can doubt the evidences of commoner restlessness and movement. Recent studies of a bizarre movement that swept the principal communications routes of central Japan during the final months of Tokugawa rule provide fascinating evidence of a widespread and rather joyous spirit of revelry and mischief that was so troublesome for Tokugawa forces of order that some were prepared to blame the outbreaks on loyalist suggestion and stimulation. Yet the mood of the crowds was overwhelmingly optimistic, more appropriate to festival than to fury, and more social than political. The wealthy, who were expected to provide food and entertainment because the gods had favored them with talismans of good fortune, paid the bills.[54] Nonetheless, it is clear that the bakufu leaders interpreted such movements as threatening their control of society. Spontaneous, large-scale febrile movements like this also related to the rising trend of popular pilgrimage to Ise in the nineteenth century. Occasionally they became associated, at least briefly, with sentimental homage to loyalist *shishi* killed in the Restoration violence.[55] There was much political satire in occasional wall writings and shrine placards, but these phenomena do not seem to have been sufficiently focused to grant them a very significant role. The search for an independent merchant interest and role has also been unprofitable. Some merchants did assist the *shishi*: Shiraishi Shōichirō, a Shimonoseki shipping guild merchant, was a man of culture and means whose diary includes the names of four hundred *shishi*, to whom he was generous with food, drink, and lodging. But even more merchants, whether or not by choice, assisted the bakufu, which based a good deal of its emergency financing on massive loans. It seems logical to conclude that in a setting of widespread disaffection with the state of political and social order, many commoners favored those who promised change. But it is also true that regional loyalty – and distrust – affected commoners as well as samurai.

Another series of debates centers on the foreign threat. The increasing intimacy of Leon Roches with the bakufu leaders in the closing years of their regime and the bluster with which Harry Parkes obstructed that contact have led many to emphasize the danger of imperialist competition for influence in Japan. There was at one point negotiation for a French loan that would be predicated on Hokkaido's resources, and Roches apparently offered Yoshinobu the services of the small French military mission after the Fushimi–Toba disaster in January 1868. But the danger of foreign intervention has probably been exaggerated. Satow's influential pamphlet on English policy was written, as his memoirs make clear, without the knowledge of his short-tempered chief, and Roches seems consistently to have extended his personal diplomacy, as he called it, beyond the authorization of his government, which had all the imperialist problems it could handle in Mexico and in Southeast Asia during those years. Even if the bakufu leaders had decided to commit themselves to French assistance, they would have found that there was very little to be had: Far from being able to negotiate loans, they had to pay for everything in advance and in cash. Yet it has also to be granted that none of this lessens the perceptions of foreign danger that the Japanese held in the 1860s. That impression itself was a fact impelling men to action, and the fear of entangling loans and foreign leverage lasted throughout the decades of nation building in the Meiji period.

The importance of the imperial institution and the role of the court present further problems for historical analysis. The policy of the Meiji government to keep that court area sacrosanct and to accept it as a basic element in national character and history produced an understandable reaction in post-World War II days when authors minimized its substance and stressed its use as a tactic and artifice of the Meiji planners. Yet clearly there was more than tactic involved. Although the Restoration leaders frequently lamented popular indifference to the existence of the court, they themselves clearly kept it uppermost as the quintessential center of national identity, and that emphasis was later diffused among the people through centralization, mobilization, and education. The emotion generated among the *shishi* by charges that the bakufu had somehow allowed the emperor to be disturbed – heightened at court, where nobles knew that the emperor was in fact indignant – was a powerful solvent of ordinary discipline and restraint. Yet the court itself, after the loyalist frenzy of the early 1860s, was much less a factor than it had been at the beginning of the process. As Totman put it: "It was *shishi* who gave effective voice and real content to this *sonnō-jōi* rhetoric, and so the prominence of the imperial role is primarily attributable to *shishi* success in making their views heard."[56]

The historian turns finally to the Restoration leaders, men of modest rank but immodest self-assurance, who gloried in the opportunity to establish for themselves, their friends, and their domain a visibility that had been denied them under the constraints of feudal discipline and status, and who saw their cause as pure and selfless because it held out the hope of winning for their emperor and country the place they felt they deserved among the nations. Those hopes were great and almost the reverse of the circumstances of their time. For a country humiliated by Western powers, they wanted a leading role in the world; for a sovereign restricted to secluded impotence, they demanded full authority over a country his ancestors had once ruled; for their domain, they wanted a full share in national politics instead of second-class vassalage and, for themselves, honored status as imperial servitors instead of vassals' rear vassals.[57]

Yet in the final analysis, most of this concerned the locus of leadership and not its goals. Most Tokugawa partisans wanted much the same thing. One is struck by the convergence of planning between bakufu and Restoration leaders in the last decade of Tokugawa history. Indeed, the bakufu leaders, charged with responsibility, approached the steps that their adversaries worked out later. Discussion of shogunal resignation and substitution of a council of great lords began in Edo quarters, found its way into Tosa councils by that route, and came to fruition in the Charter Oath's promise of "deliberative councils"; later it was integrated into Meiji political institutions. Military reforms found the bakufu, like its southwestern vassals, discovering that samurai hauteur went poorly with the discipline and drill required for infantry companies and substituting, by steps, a personnel and then a money tax as a basis for a conscription system that would displace the samurai altogether. The bakufu planners who worked this out were, like their adversaries from the southwestern *han*, of middle rank within their status hierarchy, *hatamoto* or petty daimyo who set about disestablishing their fellows. Needs of administrative retrenchment and rationalization produced programs for integrating the vassal domains nearest to the metropolitan centers, leading to rumors that a system of postfeudal, effective centralization was being prepared. The Meiji government, which used the Tokugawa lands as its own without parceling them out to daimyo after the civil war of 1868–9, kept them as the core for the centralization that was consummated by the return of feudal registers in 1869 and the establishment of prefectures in 1871. In brief, the pressures posed by opening and reconstruction revealed to friend and foe alike the impossibility of long continuing with the institutional structure of the *bakuhan* system and the need to replace it with the structure of a central state.

NOTES

1 Tetsuo Najita, "Ōshio Heihachirō (1793–1837)," in Albert M. Craig and Donald Shively, eds., *Personality in Japanese History* (Berkeley and Los Angeles: University of California Press, 1970), pp. 155–79; and Ivan Morris, *The Nobility of Failure: Tragic Heroes in the History of Japan* (New York: Holt, Rinehart and Winston, 1975), pp. 180–216, provide the best coverage in English of the man and his revolt.

2 Two essays that suggest the dimensions of the problems in such uprisings are Irwin Scheiner, "Benevolent Lords and Honorable Peasants: Rebellion and Peasant Consciousness in Tokugawa Japan," in Tetsuo Najita and Irwin Scheiner, eds., *Japanese Thought in the Tokugawa Period: Methods and Metaphors* (Chicago: University of Chicago Press, 1978), pp. 39–62; and Sasaki Junnosuke, "Bakumatsu no shakai jōsei to yonaoshi," in *Iwanami kōza Nihon rekishi*, vol. 13 (*kinsei* 5) (Tokyo: Iwanami shoten, 1977), pp. 247–308.

3 Thomas C. Smith, "Ōkura Nagatsune and the Technologists," in Craig and Shively, eds., *Personality in Japanese History*, pp. 127–54; and Miyata Noboru, "Nōson no fukkō undō to minshū shūkyō no tenkai," in *Iwanami kōza Nihon rekishi*, vol. 13 (*kinsei* 5), pp. 209–45.

4 Harold Bolitho, *Treasures Among Men: The Fudai Daimyo in Tokugawa Japan* (New Haven, Conn.: Yale University Press, 1974).

5 Conrad Totman, *The Collapse of the Tokugawa Bakufu, 1862–1868* (Honolulu: University of Hawaii Press, 1980), provides excellent brief discussions of bakufu finances in the 1860s, pp. 190ff.

6 Ōba Osamu, *Edo jidai ni okeru Chūgoku bunka juyō no kenkyū* (Tokyo: Dōhōsha, 1984), pp. 388ff., for bakufu orders of Wei Yüan's work.

7 Nagahara Keiji, "Zenkindai no tennō," *Rekishigaku kenkyū* 467 (April 1979): 37–47; and Bitō Masahide, "Sonnō-jōi shisō," *Iwanami kōza Nihon rekishi*, vol. 13 (*kinsei* 5), pp. 41–86. See also Hershel Webb, *The Japanese Imperial Institution in the Tokugawa Period* (New York: Columbia University Press, 1968).

8 Maruyama Masao, "Chūsei to hangyaku," in *Kindai Nihon shisōshi kōza* (Tokyo: Chikuma shobō, 1960), vol. 6.

9 See Asao Naohiro with Marius B. Jansen, "Shogun and Tennō," in John W. Hall et al., eds., *Japan Before Tokugawa* (Princeton, N.J.: Princeton University Press, 1980), pp. 248–70.

10 Abe's tactics and ability have received poor marks from most historians, but more appreciative verdicts are rendered by Conrad Totman, "Political Reconciliation in the Tokugawa Bakufu: Abe Masahiro and Tokugawa Nariaki, 1844–1852," in Craig and Shively, eds., *Personality in Japanese History*, pp. 180–208; and Bitō Masahide, "*Bushi* and the Meiji Restoration," *Acta Asiatica*, 49 (Tokyo, Tōhō Gakkai, 1985): 78–96.

11 The point is Ono Masao's in "Kaikoku," *Iwanami kōza Nihon rekishi*, vol. 13 (*kinsei* 5), pp. 1–39. Nakamura Tetsu, "Kaikokugo no bōeki to sekai shijo," however, points out that the Ansei treaties were superior to the Tientsin treaties because they did not legalize opium or permit missionaries and provided better tariff arrangements, pp. 108–9.

12 George Wilson, "The Bakumatsu Intellectual in Action: Hashimoto Sanai and the Political Crisis of 1858," in Craig and Shively, eds., *Personality in Japanese History*, pp. 234–63, quotes Ii's retainer Nagano: "To nominate a lord because of his intelligence is to have inferiors choose their superior and is entirely the Chinese style . . . the custom of our empire must be to respect the direct line of descent," p. 260. But Nagano was too dogmatic in this; the adoption system permitted great flexibility in succession to secure ability.

13 Wilson, "Bakumatsu Intellectual: Hashimoto Sanai." The Japanese text charges Hashimoto with disrespect for the *kōgi*.

14 Marius B. Jansen, "Tosa During the Last Century of Tokugawa Rule," in John W. Hall and Marius B. Jansen, eds., *Studies in the Institutional History of Early Modern Japan* (Princeton, N.J.: Princeton University Press, 1968), pp. 340–1.

15 Marius B. Jansen, *Sakamoto Ryōma and the Meiji Restoration* (Princeton, N.J.: Princeton University Press, 1961), pp. 108–9.

16 Jansen, *Sakamoto*, pp. 174–5.

17 E. Herbert Norman, *Japan's Emergence As a Modern State: Political and Economic Problems of the Meiji Period* (New York: Institute of Pacific Relations, 1940 and later printings).

18 W. G. Beasley, *The Meiji Restoration* (Stanford, Calif.: Stanford University Press, 1972), p. 171.

19 Albert B. Craig, *Chōshū in the Meiji Restoration* (Cambridge, Mass.: Harvard University Press, 1961), pp. 112–13; and "The Restoration Movement in Chōshū," in Hall and Jansen, eds., *Studies in the Institutional History of Early Modern Japan*, pp. 363–73.

20 Thomas M. Huber, *The Revolutionary Origins of Modern Japan* (Stanford, Calif.: Stanford University Press, 1981).

21 See, for Chōshū, A. M. Craig, *Chōshū in the Meiji Restoration*; for Tosa, M. B. Jansen, *Sakamoto Ryōma*; and for Satsuma and other *han*, Ikeda Yoshimasa, "Bakufu shohan no dōyō to kaikaku," in *Iwanami kōza Nihon rekishi*, vol. 13 (*kinsei* 5), 174–207.

22 Totman, "Fudai Daimyo and the Collapse of the Tokugawa Bakufu," *Journal of Asian Studies* 34 (May 1975): 581–91.

23 Beasley, *Meiji Restoration*, p. 177.

24 Jansen, *Sakamoto Ryōma*, pp. 131–7, and Ikeda, "Bakufu shohan," pp. 184–6.

25 Totman, *Collapse of the Tokugawa Bakufu*, p. 3.

26 Ibid., p. 141.

27 Asao Naohiro, "Shogun seiji no kenryoku kōzō, in *Iwanami kōza Nihon rekishi*, vol. 10 (*kinsei* 2), pp. 13ff.

28 Totman, *Collapse*, p. 58.

29 Beasley, *Select Documents on Japanese Foreign Policy 1853–1868* (London: Oxford University Press, 1955), pp. 1–93, provides the most incisive account.

30 See, for China, Immanuel C. Y. Hsu, *China's Entrance into the Family of Nations: The Diplomatic Phase, 1858–1880* (Cambridge, Mass.: Harvard University Press, 1968); and Masataka Banno, *China and the West: 1858–1861, The Origins of the Tsungli Yamen* (Cambridge, Mass.: Harvard University Press, 1964).

31 For figures of officials, *Dokushi sōran* (Tokyo: Jimbutsu ōraisha, 1966), pp. 648–51. Eiichi Kiyooka, trans., *The Autobiography of Fukuzawa Yukichi* (Tokyo: Hokuseidō Press, 1948), and many other studies. For Fukuchi, James L. Huffman, *Fukuchi Gen'ichirō* (Honolulu: University of Hawaii Press, 1979).

32 Nakamura Tetsu, "Kaikokugo no bōeki to sekai shijo," in *Iwanami kōza Nihon rekishi*, vol. 13 (*kinsei* 5), pp. 95–6, 111.

33 For a dispute of 1823 in which 1,007 villages resisted the jurisdiction of Osaka guilds, see William B. Hauser, *Economic Institutional Change in Tokugawa Japan:*

Osaka and the Kinai Cotton Trade (New York: Cambridge University Press, 1974), pp. 97ff.

34 Ishii Takashi, *Bakumatsu bōeki shi no kenkyū* (Tokyo: Nihon hyōronsha, 1943).

35 This astounding count of currencies reflects the fact that none was ever fully withdrawn or retired, so that the money chargers had a constantly changing ratio to work out. See John McMaster, "The Japanese Gold Rush of 1859," *Journal of Asian Studies* 19 (May 1960): 273–87; and Peter Frost, *The Bakumatsu Currency Crisis*, Harvard East Asian Monographs, no. 36 (Cambridge, Mass.: Harvard University Press, 1970).

36 Totman, *Collapse*, p. 94.

37 Akira Hayami, "Population Movements," in M. B. Jansen and G. Rozman, eds., *Japan in Transition: From Tokugawa to Meiji* (Princeton, N.J.: Princeton University Press, 1986).

38 Totman, *Collapse*, p. 193.

39 The fullest account of the Mito rebellion in English can be found in Totman, *Collapse*, pp. 108–21. Chōshū loyalist reverses can be followed in Craig, *Chōshū in the Meiji Restoration*, pp. 208–46; Tosa in Jansen, *Sakamoto*, pp. 145–52; and loyalist reverses more generally in Beasley, *Meiji Restoration*, pp. 197–240.

40 For Satsuma, Beasley, *Meiji Restoration*, p. 246; for bakufu military reforms, Totman, *Collapse*, pp. 25–7: (for Bunkyū), p. 182 (for 1864), and p. 199 (for 1865). Totman's discussion of technological changes involved in muzzle loaders, Minie rifles, breech-loading rifles, and multishot pistols, p. 25, is particularly useful.

41 Totman, *Collapse*, p. 182. For purposes of brevity, this discussion telescopes changes that came at different speeds in different periods and areas.

42 Mark David Ericson, "The Tokugawa *Bakufu* and Leon Roches," Ph.D. diss., University of Hawaii, 1978, p. 243, improves on the earlier work of Meron Medzini, *French Policy in Japan During the Closing Years of the Tokugawa Regime* (Cambridge, Mass.: Harvard University Press, 1971).

43 Ericson, "The Tokugawa *Bakufu* and Leon Roches," pp. 238ff.

44 Totman, *Collapse*, p. 291.

45 Beasley, *Meiji Restoration*, pp. 261, 266–7.

46 Jansen, *Sakamoto Ryōma*, p. 300.

47 The proposal read: "We must have a force which will have no equal in the world."

48 See Albert Craig, "The Central Government," Marius B. Jansen, "The Ruling Class," and Michio Umegaki, "From Domain to Prefecture," chaps. 2, 3, and 4 in Jansen and Rozman, eds., *Japan in Transition*.

49 See Jiro Numata, "Shigeno Yasutsugu and the Modern Tokyo Tradition of Historical Writing," in W. G. Beasley and E. G. Pulleybank, eds., *Historians of China and Japan* (London: Oxford University Press, 1961), pp. 264–87, for the evolution of Meiji historiography within inherited, Chinese tradition; and Peter Duus, "Whig History, Japanese Style: The Min'yūsha Historians and the Meiji Restoration," *Journal of Asian Studies* 33 (May 1974): 415–36.

50 The immediate prewar years saw publication of authoritative summaries of the positions mentioned here: Tokutomi Iichirō, *Kinsei Nihon kokuminshi* for Duus's "Whig History"; the monument of government historiography, *Ishin shi*, 6 vols. (Tokyo: Meiji shoin, 1941); and the definitive statement of the *kōza* position that gave the school its name, *Nihon shihonshugi hattatsu shi kōza,* 7 vols. (Tokyo: Iwanami shoten, 1932–3). For a recent and cogent analysis of the Marxist struggle, see Yasukichi Yasuba, "Anatomy of the Debate on Japanese Capitalism," *Journal of Japanese Studies* 2 (Autumn 1975): 63–82. See also Germain A. Hoston, *Marxism and the Crisis of Development in Prewar Japan* (Princeton, N.J.: Princeton University Press, 1986), for its analysis of prewar Marxist writing.

51 See, for a brief comment on the contributions of Maruyama Masao, Ōtsuka Hisao, and Kawashima Takeyoshi in the postwar climate, Nagahara Keiji,

Rekishigaku josetsu (Tokyo: Tokyo daigaku shuppankai, 1978), pp. 51ff. The most influential postwar summary of Restoration scholarship was Tōyama Shigeki, *Meiji ishin* (Tokyo: Iwanami shoten, 1951), which argued the "absolutist" thesis. Most recent and influential is a "people's history" that emphasizes the indigenous and internal development of Japanese history, focusing (as did Tokutomi to some extent) on rural elites at mid-century. Carol Gluck, "The People in History: Recent Trends in Japanese Historiography," *Journal of Asian Studies* 38 (November 1978): 25–50. An important statement of this school, Irokawa Daikichi's *Meiji no bunka* (Tokyo: Iwanami shoten, 1970), has appeared in translation as *The Culture of the Meiji Period*, ed. Marius B. Jansen (Princeton, N.J.: Princeton University Press, 1985).

52 Totman, *Collapse*, p. 458; Shibahara Takuji, "Hanbaku shoseiryoku no seikaku," in *Iwanami kōza Nihon rekishi*, vol. 14 (*kinsai* 1) (Tokyo: Iwanami shoten, 1962), pp. 169–212.

53 Yoshio Sugimoto, "Structural Sources of Popular Revolts and the Tōbaku Movement at the Time of the Meiji Restoration," *Journal of Asian Studies* 34 (August 1975): 875–89.

54 Takagi Shunsuke, *Eejanaika* (Tokyo: Kyōikusha rekishi shinsho, 1979), pp. 209–34.

55 Onodera Toshiya, "Zannen san kō: Bakumatsu Kinai no ichi minshū undō o megutte," *Chiikishi kenkyū* 2 (June 1972): 46–67, discusses pilgrimages to the tombs of Yoshimura Toratarō and Yamamoto Bunnosuke around the time of the Restoration.

56 Totman, *Collapse*, p. 462.

57 Hopes and expectations of course changed dramatically with the intensification of political conflict and the revelation of bakufu incapacity during the 1860s. See Yoshio Sakata and John W. Hall, "The Motivation of Political Leadership in the Meiji Restoration," *Journal of Asian Studies* 16 (November 1956): 31–50; and Sakata Yoshio, *Meiji ishinshi* (Tokyo: Miraisha, 1960).

5 The imperial oath of April 1868

Ritual, politics, and power in the Restoration*

J. Breen†

*Source: *Monumenta Nipponica* 51 (1996): 407–29.

By the beginning of April 1868, the leaders of the new Restoration government were close to surmounting two of three major challenges to the legitimacy that they so desperately sought. The first challenge was military and came from the Tokugawa and their allies. After scoring a decisive victory over the Tokugawa at Toba Fushimi at the end of January 1868, the 'imperial' forces quickly pacified the western provinces and by early March they had begun their eastern advance on the Tokugawa stronghold of Edo. The end of March saw the imperial army camped in Suruga, 160 kilometers from Edo, with the Chief of Staff, Saigō Takamori, planning the final assault. Edo Castle would have been stormed within two weeks had not former shogun Tokugawa Yoshinobu sent to Suruga on 1 April to sue for peace. Saigō's conditions proved acceptable to the Tokugawa and bloodshed was averted.[1] The swift conclusion to this eastern campaign did not, as it turned out, mark an end to the civil war, but it did provide an immense boost to the Restoration government in its search for legitimacy.

The second challenge came from the foreign presence, but it too, at least in one of its many manifestations, had been successfully met by the beginning of April. By declaring neutrality in the civil war in mid-February, the powers signaled that they no longer regarded the Tokugawa as Japan's legitimate rulers. The special satisfaction that this caused the new leadership, coming just two weeks after a murderous attack on unarmed foreigners in Kobe, was almost immediately undermined by another attack, this time on French sailors in Hyōgo; two weeks later, on 23 March, a British delegation under Sir Harry Parkes was ambushed en route for an audience with the emperor at the Kyoto palace.

The potential of these episodes to provoke foreign involvement in the civil wars or, at the least, to delay foreign recognition of the transfer of power did not finally materialize: the leadership adroitly seized the opportunity provided to demonstrate 'the reality of imperial rule'.[2] Indeed, the decisiveness, speed, and severity of the government's response on each occasion delighted and fully satisfied Parkes. By the beginning of April, he and other diplomats no longer regarded the three incidents as an impediment to good relations.[3]

It was to deal with a third and quite different dimension to the problem of authority, namely, opposition from within, that the imperial oath event was staged in the Kyoto palace on 6 April. Two specific groups, ensconced within the highest echelons of government, had throughout this first phase of the civil war, indeed ever since the Restoration on 3 January, consistently challenged the Satsuma–Chōshū leadership, questioning their right to rule: the conservative courtiers, whose tactics and influence were of special concern to the Satsuma leader Ōkubo Toshimichi, and the introverted daimyo, who similarly engaged the concern of Kido Kōin from Chōshū.[4] A temporary respite from anxieties about the civil war and foreign intentions now freed the leadership to address the problem of obstructionist courtiers and daimyo within government ranks.

From the seminal work on the imperial oath by Ōkubo Toshiaki and Inada Masatsugu, we know that the five articles of the oath assumed their final form during the brief respite in the first week of April, and that Kido's influence was decisive.[5] It is less often noted, but of equal importance, that the event at which the articles were to be made public was conceived, designed, and approved during this same time. Again Kido's role was critical. It was he who insisted that the emperor personally lead the assembled nobles and lords in taking an oath to the enshrined deities of heaven and earth.[6]

In their preoccupation with the text of the five articles, its progress from earlier drafts by samurai from Tosa and Echizen, and the historical significance of Kido's amendments, Ōkubo, Inada, and other scholars, Japanese and Western alike, have overlooked the critical importance of the oath as event. It is this oversight that the present article seeks to correct. In doing so, it is informed by J. L. Austin's observation that an oath is a 'performative', that it is never *simply* a text, a statement, or series of statements to be analyzed.[7] An oath is, by definition, a performance and, given certain conditions – notably its use of symbols and its intimate proximity to the sacred – that performance becomes ritual.

Since the imperial oath as state event, as ritual, is little known, I begin with a straightforward ethnographical reconstruction based on *Meiji Tennōki* and *Fukkoki*.[8] The second part of the present article employs recent anthropological insights into the meaning of political ritual, and suggests a possible way of 'reading' the oath as ritual. The third section then addresses the five articles themselves and considers whether, in light of the ritual context in which they are embedded, there is not some scope for a revision of received wisdom.

Two further comments are in order here. In recent scholarship, both Japanese and Western, confusion regularly arises from the practice of referring to the five articles themselves as 'the oath'. In fact, the oath and the five articles are not synonymous. As a result, in what follows, 'oath' refers exclusively to the ritual performance; by contrast, the five articles setting out the broad outline of Restoration government policy are referred to as 'the five articles'. Secondly, I have avoided use of the now current term 'Charter Oath'. I do so partly to de-emphasize the importance of text as against ritual; principally, however, because, whatever the five articles' import, it must be at least questionable whether they were really ever 'destined to play a part in the constitutional development of Japan similar to that of the Magna Carta.'[9]

THE RITUAL PERFORMANCE

Shortly before 4.00 p.m. on Tuesday, 6 April 1868, the incumbents of the most senior posts in government, the *gijō*, or Senior Councilors, and *san'yo*, or Junior Councilors, took their places in the Shishiiden Hall of the imperial palace in Kyoto. In preparation for the emperor's solemn entry, government ritualists conducted purification rites and recited a 'deity-summoning prayer' (*kami oroshi shinka*): they then marked the deities' descent to the Shishiiden shrine with offerings of sakaki branches.

At 4.00 p.m. precisely, the sixteen-year-old emperor entered the hall through a sliding panel in the northern wall, accompanied by Sanjō Sanetomi and Iwakura Tomomi, the *sōsai*, or Chief Executives.[10] The emperor sat down on the low *hirashiki* mat, enclosed within a three-sided screen, halfway along the length of the hall. Looking to his right, some twelve meters away at the western end of the hall, he could see the shrine and, in front of it, tables set with bowls of salt and rice used in the purification rites, as well as sakaki branches that he himself would proffer to the enshrined deities. Closer to the emperor, in the center of the hall, was set a low writing-table with documents and writing brushes. At the eastern end, to his left, were seated the courtiers and daimyo of *gijō* rank; seated behind them were assorted courtiers and, accommodated in the corridors behind them, sword-bearing ministry officials.[11]

Sanjō arose and moved to center stage before kneeling in front of the shrine to address the deities on the emperor's behalf. He declared the emperor's intent to assume the reins of power, beseeching their help in bringing order out of chaos and in punishing any who infringed the pledge that they were about to make.[12] Sanjō then returned to his place, and the emperor now arose. He proceeded to the center of the hall, turned toward the shrine, where he bowed and placed his offering of sakaki; he then retraced his steps and sat motionless. Sanjō again arose, this time to recite to the enshrined deities each of the famous 'five articles':

> Item. We shall determine all matters of state by public discussion, after assemblies have been convoked far and wide.
>
> Item. We shall unite the hearts and minds of people high and low, the better to pursue with vigor the rule of the realm.
>
> Item. We are duty bound to ensure that all people, nobility, military, and commoners too, may fulfill their aspirations and not yield to despair.
>
> Item. We shall break through the shackles of former evil practice and base our actions on the principles of international law.

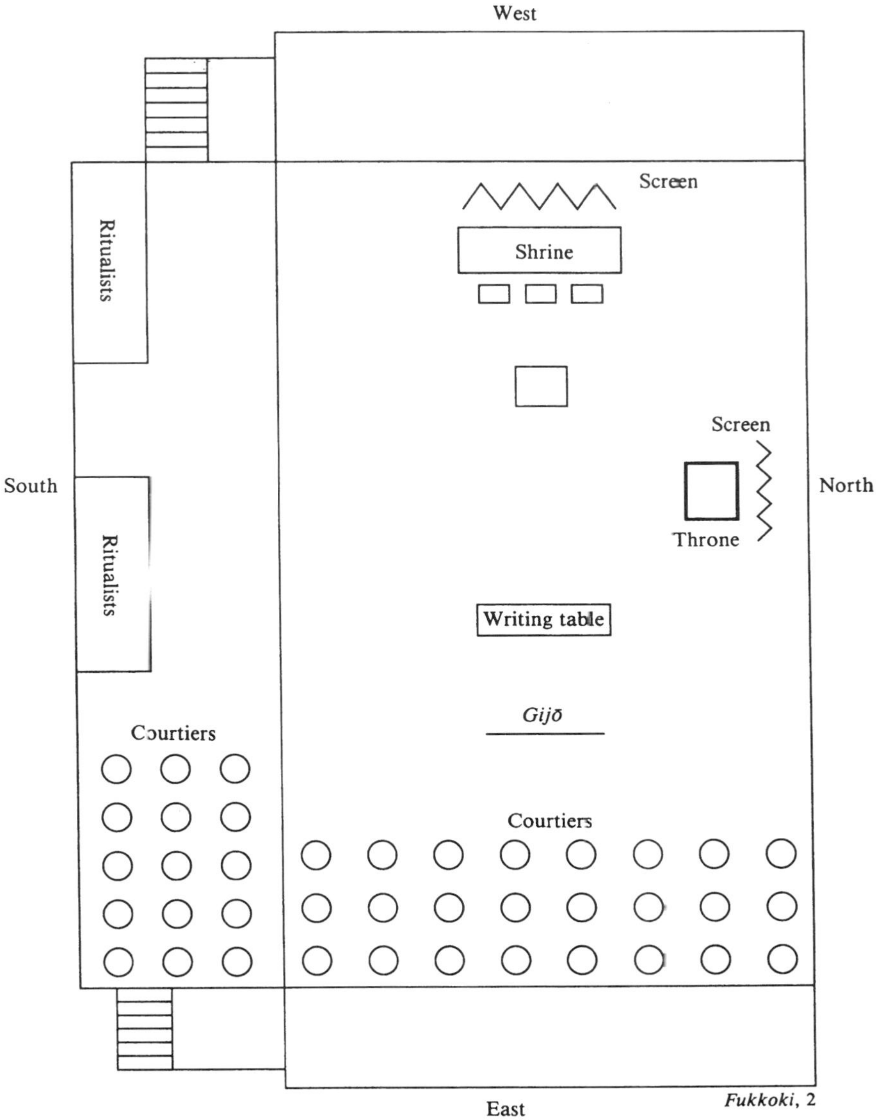

The imperial oath ritual in the Shishiiden

> Item. We shall seek knowledge throughout the world and thus invigorate the foundations of this imperial nation.[13]

On behalf of the emperor, Sanjō concluded,

> My intention is to implement reform the likes of which have never before been seen. I have, therefore, seized the initiative; I have sworn an oath before the gods of heaven and earth; I have set forth our national goals, and I hope, thus, to establish a path of safety for all my subjects. May you be inspired by this initiative. Unite your hearts and be unsparing in your efforts. . . .[14]

Next it was the turn of the *gijō* to rise. One at a time, they stepped forward to bow to deities and emperor, before kneeling at the writing-table to sign their names beneath that of the emperor, to a pledge that read:

> We are truly overawed by the boundless nature of the imperial will. May the crisis of the day make way for the establishment of these eternal principles [of governance]. We, your subjects, humbly submit to your will. We pledge our lives to you and shall spare no efforts in our devotion to duty. May we put His Majesty's mind at ease.[15]

Once the thirty *gijō* had finished signing, the emperor stood and led Sanjō and Iwakura out through the sliding door in the northern wall. It took four hours altogether for the assembled nobles, daimyo, and officials, 411 men in all, to venerate the shrine and then sign their names to the pledge. At around 8.00 p.m. the oath ritual came to an end. The ritualists removed the offerings of sakaki from the shrine, the 'deity dismissing verse' (*kami age shinka*) was recited, and the assembly dispersed.

RITUAL AND POLITICAL POWER

It is clear from the foregoing that the five articles of the imperial oath constitute a ritual symbol of paramount importance, but it is equally clear that they are one ritual symbol among many. The enshrined deities, the emperor himself, the men of *sōsai* and *gijō* rank, too, are all key 'symbols', for a symbol can be an active human player as well as a static material object. And each is accorded a significant role in the performance of the oath. The imperial oath as ritual is about much more, therefore, than the well-known text of the five articles. Like all political rituals, it is first and foremost about political power.

In a recent review of anthropological writings on ritual, Kelly and Kaplan have suggested that rituals constitute 'acts of power in the fashioning of structures'.[16] This is an observation of much value in directing our attention to two salient features of political ritual. First, it points up the fact that a ritual's dominant symbols are typically to be found arranged in hierarchical fashion and not haphazardly – the 'structures' referred to are created out of ritual's symbols. The imperial oath is a clear example of such structuring: the deities occupy the most elevated position above the emperor, who in turn is super-ordinate to the *sōsai*, the *gijō*, and other ranks. This hierarchy of power is 'activated', as it were, by the ritual actions and words of the participants: by the emperor through his presentation of offerings to the deities and his pledge to adhere to the five articles; in the conveying of the five articles as imperial command by the *sōsai* to the *gijō*; and in the *gijō*'s rising to venerate the emperor and pledge to him in turn their loyalty.

By talking of structures fashioned, however, Kelly and Kaplan highlight a second dimension of great importance, namely, that the structures, the hierarchies, are ones that ritual itself is creating. These structures do not, that is, reflect society as it presently exists beyond the boundaries of the ritual stage; rather, they are a projection of an ideal. To borrow Clifford Geertz's categories, the structures in this political ritual do not constitute a model *of* society so much as a model *for* society.[17] Here in the imperial oath, the model constructed for Japanese society, the ideal projected, is one in which the emperor, mandated by his ancestors, the deities in heaven, rules directly over a nation harmonious, loyal, and obedient. Nothing, of course, could have been further removed from the political or social reality of Japan in spring 1868.

The imperial oath, then, is on one 'level' a statement about the power relationships between the emperor and the participating daimyo and courtiers. But power operates here at a much deeper and more discreet level too, namely, in the relationship between those who constituted the axis of power – Kido from Chōshū, Ōkubo from Satsuma, and the court noble Iwakura – on the one hand, and those ritual participants who staffed the imperial government on the other. In brief, the April oath was conceived, designed, and staged to enable Kido, Ōkubo, and Iwakura to manipulate the emperor, the better to bolster their own authority within the fledgling government; only in this way could a government unified in intent be forged, and only thus could they hope to assert the authority of that government over the conflict-ridden nation. Here it will suffice to note that the ritual was focused above all at the *gijō*, in whose ranks were to be found the most obstructive of the court nobles and daimyo. Four hundred and eleven men in all signed the pledge of loyalty to the emperor on 6 April, but the *gijō* alone were scripted an active role within the ritual; they alone were 'privileged' to pledge their loyalty in person to the emperor.

Before we consider further the part written for these men, it will be instructive to look critically at the emperor and his role. For the imperial oath, it emerges, can be read as a sort of rite of passage for the new emperor. The *gijō* and others present in the Shishiiden on 6 April were witnesses to nothing less than the making of the modern Japanese monarch. This is a significant claim and it requires a suitable measure of justification.

THE MEIJI EMPEROR

In the days and weeks following the January Restoration, the emperor was to be found engaged in two distinct realms of activity; the first of these was political, while the second was ritual or sacerdotal. The political had its beginnings in the emperor's enforced attendance at the conference in the Kogosho Hall of the palace on 3 January. The 'Kogosho conference', as it is usually called, was convened to mark the successful prosecution of the court coup and the inauguration of the new era of imperial government. On this occasion, the emperor was a passive presence, hidden from view behind a jeweled screen and excluded from participation, as contending factions disputed bitterly over the future course of government.[18]

A month later, however, pressure from Ōkubo resulted in a dramatic expansion of the emperor's political role. In a famous petition in February urging the creation of a new capital in Osaka, Ōkubo had demanded the emperor assume the ways of Western sovereigns, that he 'come down from the clouds', appear before the common people, and assume such a presence as might, by turns, move people to tears and shock them into silence with a single command.[19] The proposal for a new capital was rejected, but a matter of days after the petition the emperor left the palace for the first time ever, and embarked on a historic and highly symbolic progress to the former Tokugawa base, Nijō Castle, some 200 meters away. There he attended a 'cabinet' meeting, reviewed cavalry displays, and shared refreshments with a select number of the domain lords now gathered in the capital.[20] In March, in a striking new development, the emperor famously gave audiences to a string of foreign diplomats at the Shishiiden Hall of the imperial palace.[21] On 2 April, he then presided over what a British diplomat called 'the first parliament of Japan', again in Nijō Castle, a conference of *sōsai*, *gijō*, and *san'yo,* at which the development of Hokkaido was discussed.[22]

There were two striking ways in which the April oath marked a further definition to the increasingly active political dimension to the imperial office. First was the manifestation of political 'will' in both the emperor's ritual words and actions. The emperor, it will be recalled, had begun the ritual by beseeching the heavenly deities to chastise any who breached the pledge of loyalty that they were about to sign. Next, in a reference to the five articles, he declared himself poised to implement reforms 'the likes of which have never before been seen'. This authoritarian resonance to the emperor's ritual words was clearly echoed in the closing passage of an imperial missive handed to the *gijō* as they left the Shishiiden. In it, the emperor admonished all who expressed dismay when 'I do nothing so much as raise my foot off the ground', so preventing 'me from exercising my will.' They threatened to 'have me lose not only the way of the sovereign but this sacred land itself.'[23] The emperor's ritual actions – significantly they required him to raise both feet off the ground – underscored his new-found political initiative. He had led the *sōsai*, the government's Chief Executives, into the Shishiiden at the start of the proceedings and then led them out; even when seated passively, he was evidently in command. His single action of arising and proceeding to offer sakaki to the deities at the shrine acquired immense political significance when it was replicated by each of the *gijō* in turn. The emperor was no longer *attendant* in the political center, as he had been in January, February, and March; he was now cast as a political leader possessed of will and authority.

This politicizing of the emperor is underscored by an important adjustment to the role of the *sōsai* disclosed by the ritual. Under successive rounds of administrative restructuring in February, the political brief of the *sōsai* had been defined as 'passing judgment on all things'.[24] No reference was made to the emperor in these reforms, no political function was accorded him, and his relationship to the political center remained without legal underpinning. The imperial oath makes it clear, however, that the *sōsai*'s role had been transformed. The *sōsai* was no longer in the business of 'passing judgment on all things'. His actions and words were now all emperor-led and emperor-centered; he did nothing more than 'represent' and 'assist'. The new, politically subordinate relationship of *sōsai* to emperor was shortly confirmed by the 'June Constitution', which abolished the *sōsai* post and replaced it with an office styled *hoshō*, or Imperial Attendant. The special function of the *hoshō* was precisely that forecast by the ritual: to 'assist' and 'report to' the emperor; the emperor himself was henceforth to 'determine all matters of state'.[25]

The second sense in which the imperial oath marked an 'embellishment' in the political dimension to the imperial office was no less significant. For, now for the first time, the emperor's political function was embedded in a sacred, ritual context. Prior to the April oath, he had been engaged in all manner of ritual activity, it is true. In February, for example, he had celebrated his coming-of-age ritual in the Shishiiden and New Year rites for the Ise and Kamo shrines in the Kogosho;[26] in March he had attended a ritual in commemoration of his ancestor, the first emperor, Jimmu, again in the Shishiiden.[27] These and other court rituals shared in common the following characteristics: they were (1) 'passive' in the sense that the emperor attended, but did not actively celebrate; imperial offerings were made by proxy and not in person; (2) 'exclusivist', since ritual participation was restricted to the emperor, ritualists, princes of the blood, and select courtiers; and (3), most important of all, they were entirely 'apolitical' rituals, occupying a privileged realm entirely distinct from the political.

With the imperial oath of April, the private ritual of the premodern court was transformed by a single stroke into a public, state ritual with a dominant political meaning; by the same token, the emperor's political role now acquired a new ritual context and with it a sacred authority. This politicization of the imperial office and the ritualization of imperial politics implied a dramatic development in the nature of the imperial institution. It was in this sense that I suggested earlier that participants in the imperial oath ceremony were witness to the 'making of an emperor'. We can be more precise and say that they were witness to the making of an emperor in the image of Jimmu. This degree of precision is permissible because of an historical declaration, the *saisei itchi no gofukoku*, issued on 5 April, the day before the imperial oath. In it, the leadership had declared the inseparable quality of politics and ritual, citing the precedent of Jimmu: 'Following the example set by Emperor Jimmu, ritual shall hereafter once again be united with politics.'[28] Jimmu was the mythical first emperor who, according to the classical account in *Nihon Shoki*, combined prototypically the political with the ritual. He was the great hero whose military and political vision helped lay the historical foundations of Japan, yet never did he lose sight of the need to 'make sacrifice to his ancestors, the deities in heaven, in order to demonstrate his filial piety.'[29] The new incumbent of the imperial line, too, was now in similar fashion laying the foundations for a new Japan; his act of sacrifice demonstrated his filial virtue to be no less than Jimmu's.

By locating Jimmu as the archetype for the Meiji emperor, Kido, Ōkubo, and Iwakura were quite simply claiming for him (and so for themselves who manipulated him) the legitimacy that comes to all those who, in the words of Mircea Eliade, 'return to original forms'.[30]

THE EMPEROR'S GOVERNMENT

It is not difficult to imagine that the emotional impact of this event upon the participants was considerable. This originated partly in the sensory nature of the ritual experience: the sight of the ritual symbols; the sounds of the ritual language; the sense of sacred place imparted by the Shishiiden Hall; and, above all, perhaps, the knowledge of privileged participation in an event that was at one with Jimmu's primordial sacrifice. The impact derived, too, from the transformed, enhanced nature of imperial power that all of this implied.

Back in January, the emperor had been but a silent presence at the Kogosho conference. At one stage in the proceedings, the daimyo from Tosa had accused Iwakura and others of 'stealing the emperor', no less. Iwakura had retorted that the emperor was a man of incomparable vision and had carried out the Restoration himself. The events of the day, he said, were the results of the imperial will. 'What impudence to suggest that the emperor was seized!'[31] This, of course, was a fiction, and none was present who did not know it; yet it was enough for Iwakura to impute political will to the emperor for the Tosa daimyo to be shamed into silence. Three months on, the fiction is fleshed out: the emperor is no longer a hidden, passive observer; no longer is he spoken for; it is rather he who, legitimized by his Jimmu-like act of 'sacrifice', now visibly dictates, threatens, demands.

The emotional, psychological dimension of all ritual events is important since somewhere in the realm of emotions, of the psyche is to be explained the otherwise unexplainable: why political ritual has the ability to induce participants to accept the unacceptable, and endure the unendurable; and how, in ritual, the obligatory is rendered desirable. That ritual possesses such 'mystifying' qualities as was apparent to the nineteenth-century designers of the oath as it is to contemporary anthropologists.[32] These qualities no doubt derive to some extent from ritual's ability to 'empower' participants even as it disempowers them. The fact that many of the participants at the Shishiiden event were actually being divested of power and influence – this we must shortly confirm – was somehow compensated for by their privileged, and thus empowering, access to this momentous event.

This analysis of the oath ritual began with the assertion that it was, first and foremost, about power and power relationships; the emperor was one key player in the newly fashioned structure of power, and we must now turn our attention to the second: namely, the *gijō,* those Senior Councilors who were in nominal charge of all the departments within the government and wielded potentially destructive influence outside government. They had to be disempowered and, equally, for a government whose authority was being questioned from within, they had to be seen to be disempowered. For the *san'yo* and other officials present in the corridors of the Shishiiden on 6 April, the drama played out before them was in one of its many dimensions that of fractious *gijō* courtiers and daimyo submitting meekly to the imperial will.[33]

In all, there were some thirty *gijō* divided about evenly between court nobility and daimyo.[34] The *gijō* separated out naturally between two major and mutually hostile factions: the Tosa–Echizen group of daimyo centered around the 'conciliatory' leaders of these domains, Yamanouchi Yōdō and Matsudaira Yoshinaga respectively, and the 'Nakayama group' of courtiers comprising the emperor's maternal grandfather, Nakayama Tadayasu, Ōgimachi Sanjō, and Nakamikado Tsuneyuki, who had all played a critical role in the events leading up to 3 January.[35] If the two groups, the former in many ways progressive, the latter highly conservative, shared one thing in common, it was a profound suspicion of Kido, Ōkubo, and Iwakura. The intensity of antagonism toward the ruling elite surfaced with violence at the Kogosho conference on 3 January. We have already seen that Iwakura had shamed Yamanouchi into silence by 'reminding' him that the emperor himself had carried out the Restoration. At the heart of the matter here was which group – Ōkubo and Iwakura or the conciliatory daimyo represented by Yamanouchi and Matsudaira – had the right of access to the emperor.

There was still more at stake: notably the fate of the last Tokugawa shogun, Yoshinobu, presently ensconced just a few hundred meters distant in Nijō Castle. Why was he not admitted to the proceedings? Why should he be forced to resign his office and relinquish his land-holdings?[36] Inseparable from the Tokugawa question for the Tosa–Echizen group was their advocacy of government by a permanent daimyo council: Tokugawa Yoshinobu was to have a decisive political role. If, owing to the machinations of Satsuma and Chōshū, such a council never materialized, what political future would remain for them?

There was also at this conference on 3 January a highly revealing exchange between Iwakura and Nakayama Tadayasu. Nakayama's cooperation with Iwakura had been essential to the success of the coup d'état. He was the emperor's grandfather and thus controlled access to the emperor. Such was Nakayama's influence that he was the natural choice to assume the chair at this inaugural session of the Restoration government. Nakayama remained in the chair until the language between the anti-Tokugawa and pro-Tokugawa factions became violent. Having lost control of the proceedings, he rose to his feet in despair and wandered off to utter complaints to other courtiers, prompting Iwakura to snap: 'You are in the emperor's presence! His Majesty is here to listen to the debate on policy, not to your idle chatter!'[37] Subsequent days and weeks gave little opportunity for these various differences to heal. As Senda Minoru has pointed out, the Restoration government was defined by a constant process of conflict and forced accommodation between the ruling axis, the conciliatory daimyo, and the nobility.[38] For our present purposes, it is important to confirm the intensity and tenacity of these tensions since they form the backdrop to the April oath.

The three offices of *sōsai*, *gijō*, and *san'yo*, and the regular convening of the *sanshoku kaigi*, or 'conference of the three offices', served to give an important voice in decision-making to the Tosa–Echizen group. But the conferences fell far short of the exclusive daimyo conference ideal embraced by Tosa and Echizen, and the frustration of Yamanouchi and Matsudaira grew as key decisions, mostly those concerning the pursuit of the Tokugawa, were being implemented without *sanshoku* consultation .[39]

Hostilities began at Toba Fushimi on 29 January, for example, without *gijō* consultation, and Matsudaira and Yamanouchi immediately tendered their resignations. The resignations were not accepted, but both men refused appointments as Assistant Chiefs-of-Staff for the 'imperial forces'[40] At issue here was both lack of consultation and the fact of war against the Tokugawa. In March, as the imperial forces prepared to launch their expedition to pacify the east and take Edo, Matsudaira once again led *gijō* opposition, but again in vain.[41] He continued to move vigorously for the abandonment of the campaign. On 12 March, for example, he petitioned for the expedition to be halted, but this was dismissed with a *sōsai* order that he abstain henceforth from interceding on behalf of the Tokugawa. Communication with the enemy was the unique prerogative, he was told, of the Commander-in-Chief of the imperial forces.[42] With the imperial forces camped in Suruga preparing to attack Edo Castle, Matsudaira once again demanded an immediate halt.[43] That peace was soon thereafter negotiated owed nothing, however, to his intervention.[44]

Elsewhere the Tosa–Echizen group and their allies used to greater effect their voice in the *sanshoku kaigi*. The most important example of their obstructionism emerged over Iwakura's memorial for an imperial 'expedition' to Osaka, put to the *gijō* on 21 February. The memorial, a revision of Ōkubo's petition for relocating the capital to Osaka that the Tosa–Echizen group, in uncomfortable alliance with Nakayama, had successfully rejected, was regarded by Ōkubo himself, Iwakura, and Kido as essential to the assertion of their authority within government.[45] That it was resisted so stubbornly by Matsudaira and Yamanouchi was partly on the grounds of its anti-Tokugawa symbolism; partly because it had not 'first been debated by a conference of daimyo', but partly too as an anti-Ōkubo–Kido gesture.[46] The *gijō* debated the Osaka expedition again at Nijō Castle on 25 February, the historical occasion of the emperor's first progress from the imperial palace. After the discussion – to the details of which we are not privy – the *sōsai* were 'summoned into the emperor's presence and received notification' of his imminent departure for Osaka.[47] The decision had once more been made without *gijō* approval, and the *gijō* were not won over by a party hosted for them by the emperor later in the afternoon.[48] Such indeed was *gijō* resistance that a postponement of the expedition had to be announced on 2 March. On 19 March, the date was set back again to 28 March. 'The dissemination of all manners of rumors and the disturbed state of people's minds' was the official explanation.[49] On 25 March, a further postponement was announced. It was, significantly, not until the day after the imperial oath, on 7 April, that the leadership felt sufficiently confident to set a date that they could keep – a week after the ritual on 14 April.[50]

The Nakayama group presented the leadership with a challenge of a different sort. Haraguchi Kiyoshi points out that they were by no means opposed to reform in principle.[51] Nakayama, Ōgimachi Sanjō, and Nakamikado had been quick to support the creation of the *sōsai*, *gijō*, and *san'yo* offices, thus abolishing the traditional court hierarchy of *sesshō* and *kampaku*, from which they had always been excluded. They had even acknowledged the need to employ 'men of talent'. Nor were they, apparently, irreconcilable to some form of government by discussion Nakayama was prepared, for example, to allow the creation of an upper and lower debating chamber with government. Nonetheless, it remains that they were incapable of conceiving of any form of administration in which they and their views were not dominant, and those views, when held up for closer inspection, proved dangerously conservative.

In the weeks after the Restoration, increasingly bitter at its alienation from the center, the Nakayama group's antagonism toward the Kido–Ōkubo power axis deepened. Nakayama was, for instance, quite as vociferous as Matsudaira had been in opposing the proposals for both capital relocation and the imperial expedition to Osaka.[52] The grounds for his opposition were similar: such proposals, he argued, were none other than a ruse on the part of Satsuma and Chōshū to 'snatch away the emperor' in an effort to shore up their own authority.[53] Nakayama and his circle no doubt had an inkling, too, of the reality, namely, that the intention was, in Ōkubo's words, to sweep from the emperor's entourage 'the stench and decay of ultra-conservatism.'[54]

It was on the foreign question, however, that the Nakayama group proved most intransigent. In a famous petition made at the end of February, Matsudaira, Yamanouchi, and other *gijō* daimyo had proposed that Japan engage 'without a second thought' in foreign intercourse, abide by international law, and demonstrate its good will by having the emperor receive foreign delegations in audience.[55] 'The *gijō* nobles', noted *Meiji Tennōki,* 'were profoundly disturbed' at the prospect of imperial audiences being granted.[56] So upset was Nakayama Tadayasu, in fact, that as the date approached – it was set for 23 March – he became involved in a hapless plot to have the emperor declared unfit for duty. Shocked to learn from Nakayama of the emperor's sudden and most serious illness, Iwakura had his health checked independently, only to discover that he was, in fact, perfectly well.[57] As Sir Harry Parkes and the British delegation made their way to the palace on the morning of the 23rd, they were attacked by two sword-wielding samurai. While there is no suggestion that Nakayama's group was behind the assault, they were certainly sympathetic. Successive delays in the government's response to Parkes's insistence that notices be displayed nationwide condemning attacks on foreigners were almost certainly the result of the tactics of Nakayama and his group. As Algernon Mitford was told by two of the more 'enlightened' members of the government, it was the fault of 'the old conservative spirit of the capital'.[58] The resistance was indeed considerable: the notices were promised on 2 April, on the 6th, the 14th, but were only finally issued a month later on 2 May.

The daimyo and courtiers of *gijō* rank were the cause, then, of disunity at the heart of government and they had to be brought to heel. This is precisely what Kido, Ōkubo, and Iwakura sought, through the emperor's role in the imperial oath, to effect. The entire oath can be read, on one of its many levels, as a dialogue between emperor and *gijō*. But the salient point is that it was a one-way dialogue: the emperor did not present policy to the *gijō* for their consideration or approval. The ritual format, upon which the *gijō* had exerted no influence whatsoever, rendered discussion, criticism, and rejection, too, out of the question. It was the emperor who moved, spoke, threatened, promising reforms 'the likes of which have never before been seen' and demanding obedience. The ritual deprived the *gijō* of any response other than acquiescence, and it was in this sense that the ritual 'disempowered' them.

THE FIVE ARTICLES

The one-way ritual dialogue was designed to engage the *gijō* group to the emperor in a new relationship: to prize the daimyo away from their own agendas and obsessions, to dislodge the courtiers from the premodern, conservative court, and bind both to the emperor as his loyal subjects. The oath sought at the same time to bind the *gijō* to a new imperial 'ideology'; generally, to the idea that ultimate authority derived from the emperor; more specifically, however, to that cluster of ideas encapsulated within the five articles. It is to these that we must now turn our attention.

In early February, the Echizen samurai Yuri Kimimasa had produced five broad principles for government policy, which he sought, in vain, to have published immediately. Government legitimacy depended, he had suggested, on a swift declaration of the broad direction in which the government was heading.[59] These items were amended a few days later by the Tosa samurai, Fukuoka Takachika, whose major contribution was to the first article. Where

Yuri had advocated 'all matters of government' being decided by 'public discussion', Fukuoka proposed 'the creation of daimyo assemblies' to determine 'all matters of government'. But no doubt because daimyo assemblies were anathema to Kido, Ōkubo, and Iwakura, the document never saw the light of day. It was not until the first week of April, as we have seen, that Kido acquired a copy of Fukuoka's document and began his own editorial work.[60] He made two textual changes: he removed the 'daimyo assemblies' of the first article, substituting the less obviously restrictive 'widely convoked assemblies'. He rejected Article Five on the appointment of domain representatives in favor of an item abandoning 'former evil practice'. Kido placed this fourth. He retained without change, except in their sequence, Fukuoka's three other items on 'uniting the hearts and minds of all people', 'the fulfillment of popular aspirations', and 'the seeking of knowledge throughout the world'.

Japanese scholars have identified in these five articles a whole range of meanings, from the fountainhead of Japan's tradition of liberal thinking at one extreme, to 'the founding declaration of the absolutist Meiji state' at the other.[61] By contrast, Western scholars of the Restoration have tended to be more skeptical of the articles' long-term importance, regarding their significance as much more immediate. The immediate term is of greater concern to us here, and it will be useful to review critically the classic interpretations of the articles offered by William Beasley and Marius Jansen, the outstanding interpreters of the Restoration outside Japan.

Beasley and Jansen both see the five articles first and foremost as an exercise in reassurance. For Beasley, they set out to 'reassure the domains about the attitudes and objectives of those who had carried out the Restoration.' For Jansen they 'reassure[d] the daimyo that all would have a place in the new order that was to come.'[62] Jansen develops this line further. The articles were evidence of the 'cautious and uncertain' approach of the leadership, of their anxiety to 'avoid any confrontation that might antagonize or alarm the privileged strata.' 'Any suggestion of radical change received short shrift,' he adds.[63] A close reading of the articles, in light of Kido's amendments and of their full ritual context explored above, must surely raise questions about the validity of these interpretations.

The imperial oath was, as we have seen, about political power and, on one level at least, about the power relationship between the ruling clique, via the emperor, and the fractious *gijō*. The articles were directed in the first instance, then, not exclusively at the class of daimyo, but at the *gijō* in whose ranks both the most influential daimyo and the most senior court nobility were represented. The *gijō* was a group at once broader and narrower than that identified by Beasley and Jansen. More problematic, though, is the question of a leadership anxious to 'reassure'. Neither author offers any textual or other evidence that reassurance was at the heart of the matter, and the fact is that neither Kido, whose idea the ritual was, nor, Ōkubo speak anywhere in their published petitions, diaries, or correspondence of 'reassurance'. What little evidence there is – memorials by Ōkubo and Kido, Kido's revision of Fukuoka's articles, and above all the symbolism of the ritual – suggests that the contrary was the case.

Ōkubo's petition of mid-February had idealized an emperor capable of 'shocking people into silence with a single command'. The missive handed to the *gijō* as they left the Shishiiden after the ritual was obviously inspired by Ōkubo's memorial and severely admonished any who stood athwart the imperial will. Kido's petition, in which he promised the staging of an event in which the emperor would swear an oath before the deities, spoke only of the need to 'demonstrate to the realm the extent of the court's authority', not of conciliation. His ritual design cast the emperor in authoritarian mode, denying to ritual participants all possibility of debate and dispute of the sort, for example, that had disrupted the Kogosho conference in January. The emperor had determined policy and now demanded *gijō* compliance with it.

We should note here that the April mise en scène was itself strikingly different from the one that Fukuoka Takachika had been promoting in February. Fukuoka wanted his five articles made public in an exclusive daimyo conference; the emperor would attend as a passive witness to a pledge of loyalty that all the daimyo would sign; the pledge would be exchanged among the daimyo and not directed to the emperor. There would be no courtier representation.[64] Undoubtedly such a ceremony would have offered reassurance to the daimyo, but this was rejected by Kido and, with it, the entire 'daimyo conference' idea, which the Tosa and Echizen camp continued to champion. What further light, though, does a closer reading of Kido's final version of the articles shed on the leadership's approach to government?

Kido's Article 1 advocates convoking assemblies far and wide, and idealizes some ill-defined form of government by public discussion. If this appears to be a prime example of reassuring Tosa and Echizen, and others besides, we should recall that Kido had inserted the item in place of Fukuoka's 'conference of daimyo'. Kido's 'widely convoked assemblies' was different in scope and can have only been regarded by the Tosa–Echizen camp as a clear rejection of the daimyo conference idea. It is highly questionable whether Kido's Article 1 can have been any more comforting for the court nobility than it was for the conciliatory daimyo. For the nobility, it was perhaps a marginal improvement since it did not deny them all access to power, but it remained worrying, especially in combination with articles 2 and 3. These placed emphasis on 'uniting the hearts and minds of people high and low', and ensuring that commoners, too, might be able to 'fulfill their aspirations and not yield to despair'. Taken together, these first three items served as a warning that in the new era the old elite would have to make way for men of other social classes. Notwithstanding some assertions that the articles left 'room for the perpetuation of the early modern elite structure',[65] precisely the opposite appears to have been threatened in articles 1, 2 & 3.

If there is a degree of vagueness, possibly intentionally so, about the first three, there is too about the 'evil customs' of Article 4, although what effects the vagueness may have had are difficult to estimate. Inada has suggested that the evil customs were meant and taken as a threat directed specifically at the court nobility and their conservative ways.[66] Indeed, an early Meiji commentator explained, and it was no doubt rumored at the time, that the 'evil customs' to be abandoned was precisely the premodern court itself.[67] Again, how many of the court nobility can there have been to whom the obligation of conforming to 'the principles of international law' was acceptable? There was certainly none in the circle of Nakayama Tadayasu, whose bitter opposition to the leadership's pro-foreign thrust we have already seen above. Article 5's assertion of the need to 'seek knowledge throughout the world to invigorate the foundations of the imperial polity' would likewise have been unpalatable. Both 4 and 5, though, would have met with little opposition from at least some of the daimyo contingent in the *gijō* ranks.

In short, the famous five articles constituted a striking declaration of the onset of a new era of radical change by a leadership emboldened by initial success in the war against the Tokugawa and by the respite that it had obtained in its fraught relationship with the foreign powers. In the ritual context in which they were embedded, these articles represented a decisive assertion of authority over the *gijō* and all in government whose loyalty was suspect. The message was direct and simple: the emperor has now determined a broad direction of policy, and you, as imperial subjects, abide by it or suffer the consequences.

CONCLUSION

How, then, may we assess the historical importance of the imperial oath? Its significance needs to be weighed in three different dimensions. First, there is the question of the five articles themselves; second, that of the *gijō* and their relationship to power; and finally, that of the emperor and the imperial institution.

The prewar scholar Osatake Takeki famously suggested that no understanding of the Restoration was possible without a thorough familiarity with the five articles.[68] There are good reasons, however, for a rather more qualified appraisal of their importance to government in both the short and long terms. That the articles implied a widening of the political base and a commitment to creating national wealth and strength involving Western techniques and the abandonment of expulsion is not in doubt.[69] But we should not lose sight of the tension between the first of the articles, justly the most famous, and the dominant symbolism of the imperial oath ritual. The former spoke optimistically of 'determin[ing] all matters of state by public discussion, after assemblies have been convoked far and wide,' but the latter idealized an authoritarian approach to government in which the emperor threatened punishment and demanded obedience. Kido, Ōkubo, and Iwakura remained forever alert to the danger to their own authority of too rapid and too great a sharing of political power, and the political history of the early and mid-Meiji period was, in one sense, a struggle between these two contradictory and incompatible approaches to government.

Second, there is a curious anomaly to be accounted for. Just four years later, in 1872, Kido Kōin was in Washington, D.C., as a member of the Iwakura mission, 'seeking knowledge throughout the world'. He wrote in his diary how, in conversation with a fellow ambassador, he had mentioned that Japan really needed a document such as the U.S. Constitution. His colleague had reminded him of the five articles, and it is quite clear that their existence had completely slipped Kido's mind. Asukai Masamichi would have us believe that Kido had been anxious to forget the 'reactionary' context – the sacred ritual and its symbols – in which the articles were made public, and he naturally dismissed from his mind the 'progressive' articles themselves as well.[70]

It is surely more plausible, however, that the five articles were simply of less importance to their author than is usually assumed. We should recall that Kido's memorial that led to the staging of the oath argued for a 'display of authority', but made no mention at all of the five articles. It is well to reiterate, too, that the pledge signed by the *gijō*, and eventually by all courtiers and lords as well, was not a pledge to abide by the articles; it was rather a personal pledge of loyalty to the emperor. It was to the statement, 'We, your subjects, humbly submit to your will. We pledge our lives to you and shall spare no efforts in our devotion to duty' that they signed their names. I believe that for Kido, at least, the articles were secondary in importance to the pressing political need for order and unity within government ranks.

A final point to make is that if Kido quickly forgot the existence of the articles, others did not. Emura Eiichi's research on the freedom and popular rights movement reveals that in the decade 1871–1881 a total of 130 petitions were submitted to the government demanding some form of popular representation. Of the ninety-six whose content can now be verified, fifty-one cited in justification the government's promise in the five articles to allow for the creation of popular assemblies.[71] In short, far from serving as a guide to the leadership in their implementation of social policy, the five articles rapidly became a stick – a highly effective one – with which those out of power castigated the government.

What, then, of the importance of the oath – as opposed to the five articles – for government, specifically for the *gijō* ranks in government? A week after the oath, Kido wrote of his despair that there appeared to be no sign of change. The constant carping of the court nobility, he told a colleague, remained for him 'a source of the gravest concern'.[72] It was not long before his fears about daimyo localism and samurai extremism resurfaced. Kido's expectations that his ritual 'display of authority' would have a lasting effect were clearly not fulfilled. His concerns endured, without respite, until the abolition of the domains and the implementation of a more centralized administration in early autumn 1871. Nonetheless, the oath was a major turning point in the consolidation of government. On the one hand, it marked the first of several stages in the process of reforming the 'evils' of the imperial court, and the emperor's month-long 'Osaka expedition', announced on the day after the imperial oath and implemented a week later, was a second key stage.[73]

On the other hand, it marked the final and irreversible tilt of power toward Kido, Ōkubo, and Iwakura: the *gijō* daimyo in this, their first pledge of loyalty to the emperor, were relinquishing the idea of a daimyo conference. They were, at the same time, anticipating the summer of 1869 and their surrender of domain registers to the emperor. In its political dimension, this event (*hanseki hōkan*, as it is known) was calculated to sever the bonds of loyalty between domain lord and vassal, and, in so doing, bind all men to emperor and nation in a new relationship.[74] This trend reached fulfillment with the abolition of domains in 1871, but it traces its origins to the imperial oath of spring 1868.

A third and final legacy of the oath relates to emperor and imperial institution. We have seen that the oath achieved at a single stroke the 'politicization' of imperial ritual and the 'ritualization' of imperial politics. In the process, it effected a lasting transformation of the imperial office. It defined the new emperor as a monarch in the mold of Emperor Jimmu, as one who combined in his single person the qualities of political sovereign and celebrant of state ritual. A detailed exposition cannot be attempted here, and it must suffice finally to note how this principle was not abandoned but rather given clearer definition in the reforms that followed the abolition of the domains in 1871.

These reforms, insofar as they related to the imperial institution, sought to establish 'the principle of a Dajōkan emperor', that is, a sovereign who 'presided' over the Dajōkan, 'passing judgment on all things', 'assisted' in this task by the Dajō Daijin or prime minister.[75] This was none other than the institutionalization of the political principle that we saw established in the imperial oath. The fact that the emperor was rarely seen to assume this privilege is of less importance for our immediate purposes than certain developments in ritual that were now implemented.

In October 1871, a new ritual structure, known as the *sanshinden*, was constructed in the imperial palace to house the three imperial shrines side by side. The *kashikodokoro*, dedicated to Amaterasu, the imperial ancestress, had always been in the palace and was now joined by shrines to the eight protecter deities and the deities of heaven and earth. The short-lived *Jingikan* in which both had resided thus far was now abolished.[76] The creation of the *sanshinden* (which, excepting its occasional destruction by fire, has remained the site for modern imperial ritual to the present day) was marked by a solemn state procession led by the emperor from the site of the old *Jingikan* to the palace; all senior government officials participated. The same occasion saw the publication of an imperial rescript in which the emperor declared that it was 'by venerating the deities here [at the new *sanshinden* shrine within the palace] that We shall be enabled to oversee the governance of all things.'[77] In the wake of the rescript came the publication of a new program of imperial ritual, the *shiji saiten*. The twenty rituals contained within this program, a mixture of genuine and invented tradition, remained the framework of state imperial ritual until the postwar period.[78] Thus the Jimmu ideal of imperial rule, established by the imperial oath in April 1868, was perpetrated into the modern era.

NOTES

† For helpful comments on earlier drafts, the author wishes to thank William Beasley, Richard Bowring, Albert Craig, Mark Elvin, Roger Goodman, Peter Kornicki, Naitō Kōko, and Richard Sims.

1 The one unacceptable condition was that Yoshinobu should be placed in confinement in Bizen domain; it was later arranged that he retire to Mito. On the progress of the civil war, see Charles Sheldon, 'The Politics of the Civil War in 1858', in William Beasley, ed., *Modern Japan: Aspects of History, Literature and Society*, University of California Press, 1975.
2 W. G. Beasley, *The Meiji Restoration*, Oxford U.P., 1972, p. 314.
3 Foreign Office [FO], London, 46–93, Parkes to Stanley, 8 April 1868. See also Beasley, *Meiji Restoration*, p. 315.
4 Beasley, *Meiji Restoration*, p. 316.
5 For Kido's decisive role, see Ōkubo Toshiaki, *'Gokajō no Seimon ni kansuru Ichikōsatsu'* in *Ōkubo Toshiaki Rekishi Chosakusha*, 1, *Meiji Ishin no Seiji Katei*, Yoshikawa, 1986; and Inada Masatsugu, '*Gokajō no Goseimon to Seitaisho no Happu*', in Inada Masatsugu, *Meiji Kempō Seiritsu Shi*, Yūhikaku, 1960–1962, 1, pp. 9–15.
6 Kido's memorial to this effect is given in Kunaichō, ed., *Meiji Tennōki*, Yoshikawa, 1968, 1, p. 654. By insisting on this format, Kido himself was influenced by Fukuba Bisei, a Shinto scholar from Tsuwano. The latter's precise role is unclear, but Sakazaki Bin wrote in his memoirs that Fukuba 'exerted a decisive influence in determining the manner of the ritual'. Sakazaki Bin, '*Gokajō Goseimon*', in Shidankai, ed., *Shidankai Sokkiroku*, Hara, 1973, 30, p. 230. On Fukuba and his relationship to Kido, see Takeda Hideaki, 'Kindai Tennō Saishi Keiseikatei no Ichikōsatsu', in Inoue Nobutaka & Sakamoto Koremaru, ed., *Nihongata Seikyō Kankei no Tanjō,* Daiichi, 1987, pp. 94–95, and John Breen, 'Shintoists in Restoration Japan', in *Modern Asian Studies*, 24:3 (1990), pp. 579–84.
7 J. L. Austin, *How to Do Things with Words*, Oxford U.P., 1962, p. 6.
8 *Meiji Tennōki*, 1, pp. 647–50, and *Fukkoki*, Naigai, 1929, 2, pp. 830–35.
9 Such is the justification offered by Uyehara for his use of the term 'Charter Oath'. He was, I believe, the first to employ the term in non-Japanese scholarship. George Uyehara, *The Political Development of Japan: 1867–1909*, Constable, London, 1910, p. 57.
10 Strictly speaking, Sanjō and Iwakura occupied the office of *fukusōsai*, or Deputy Chief Executive. The *sōsai* himself, the courtier Arisugawa no Miya, was absent from Kyoto on 6 April, commanding the imperial forces in Suruga. *Meiji Tennōki*, 1, pp. 615–16. Since Iwakura and Sanjō effectively dominated the *sōsai* office, I use this title when referring to them.
11 For the plan of the Shishiiden, see the diagram *Saijō Ryakuzu*, in the Shimazu family archives (reproduced from *Fukkoki*, 2, p. 832), on page 109.
12 *Meiji Tennōki*, 1, p. 648.
13 *Meiji Tennōki*, 1, pp. 648–49. Earlier renditions of the five articles into English employ the passive voice; the Japanese original text, however, is in the active voice.
14 *Meiji Tennōki*, 1, p. 649.
15 *Meiji Tennōki*, 1, p. 649.

16 Raymond Kelly & Temma Kaplan, 'History, Structure and Ritual', in *Annual Review of Anthropology*, 19 (1990), p. 140.
17 Clifford Geertz, 'Religion as a Cultural System', in Clifford Geertz, *The Interpretation of Cultures*, Harper Collins, New York, 1973, Chapter 4. Models *of* society more typically occur at times when stability prevails. See also Christel Lane, *The Rites of Rulers*, Cambridge U.P., 1981, pp. 39–40.
18 *Iwakura-kō Jikki*, Iwakura-kō Kyūseki Hozonkai, Kyoto, 1927, 2, pp. 157–61.
19 The petition is in *Ōkubo Toshimichi Monjo*, Nihon Shiseki Kyōkai, 1927, pp. 191–96.
20 *Meiji Tennōki*, 1, pp. 611, 617, 619 & 634–35.
21 *Meiji Tennōki*, 1, pp. 638–39.
22 *Meiji Tennōki*, 1, p. 644; Mitford to Parkes, 9 April 1868, FO 46–93 (132). 'The Mikado made a gracious speech from the throne [in which he] complimented members of the government for their labours. . . .[He then] called for wine and a loving cup was drunk all round.'
23 *Meiji Tennōki*, 1, pp. 649–52.
24 Shinobu Seizaburō, *Nihon Seijishi, Meiji Ishin*, 2, Nansōsha, 1976, pp. 194–95.
25 Shinobu, p. 206.
26 Regrettably little is known about these rituals. They are described only cursorily in *Meiji Tennōki*, 1, pp. 593–94 & 599–600.
27 *Meiji Tennōki*, 1, pp. 641–42.
28 Naikaku Kempōkyoku, ed., *Hōrei Zensho*, Hara, 1965, 1, p. 63. This is the second citation of Jimmu's achievement in a state document of the new era. The first was in *Ōsei Fukko no Daigōrei*, 3 January, which spoke of the new emperor's desire to be 'guided by the example of Jimmu' in implementing all manner of reforms of court and government. *Fukkoki*, 1, p. 1.
29 W. G. Aston, tr., *Nihongi: Chronicles of Japan from the Earliest Times to* A.D . 697, Tuttle, 1972, pp. 133–35.
30 Mircea Eliade, *The Myth of the Eternal Return: Cosmos and History*, Arkana, London, 1989, p. 21.
31 *Iwakura-kō Jikki*, 2, pp. 158–59.
32 On Japan's tradition of ritual writing, see Bob Tadashi Wakabayashi, *Anti-foreignism and Western Learning in Early Modern Japan: The New Theses of 1825*, Harvard U.P., 1986, pp. 116–23.
33 It should be stressed that the oath ritual was not obviously targeted at any wider social group than the *gijō*. The foreign diplomatic community, for example, appears to have remained entirely ignorant of the event; similarly ignorant of the ritual was the general public.
34 In their ranks were also two retired daimyo and one Shinto priest. A complete list of *gijō* incumbents is set out conveniently in Takayanagi Mitsutoshi et al., ed., *Kadokawa Nihonshi Jiten*, Kadokawa, 1976, pp. 1249–50.
35 On the contributions of these men to the Restoration, see Ōkubo Toshiaki, *Ishin Zen'ya no Gunzō*, 7, *Iwakura Tomomi*, Chūkō Shinsho, 1990, pp. 175–209 passim.
36 *Iwakura-kō Jikki*, 2, p. 159.
37 *Iwakura-kō Jikki*, 2, p. 160.
38 Senda Minoru, *Ishin Seiken no Chitsuroku Shobun*, Kaimei, 1975, p. 34.
39 The *sōsai* office was advised directly by Kido and Ōkubo, and, as Shimoyama Saburō points out, it was within the powers of the *sōsai* to take decisions and issue edicts without referring to the *gijō* or *san'yo*. Excessive use of this power would make a nonsense of the *sanshoku kaigi* and so it was used sparingly. Shimoyama Saburō, *Kindai Tennōsei Kenkyū Josetsu*, Iwanami, 1976, p. 47.
40 Shimoyama, p. 40.
41 Matsuo Masahito, *Ishin Seiken*, Yoshikawa, 1995, pp. 38–39.
42 *Meiji Tennōki*, 1, p. 632, and Iwasaki Eiju, ed., *Boshin Nikki*, Nihon Shiseki

Kyōkai, 1925, pp. 207–08. *Boshin Nikki* is Matsudaira's 'Restoration diary' and the briefest perusal leaves the reader in no doubt about the depth of his commitment to Tokugawa Yoshinobu and a peaceful, favorable settlement for the Tokugawa.

43 *Boshin Nikki*, pp. 253–54.

44 It owed everything to Saigō's negotiations with Katsu Kaishū, Shimoyama, pp. 74–76.

45 Shimoyama, p. 80.

46 *Boshin Nikki*, p. 129. The earlier Ōkubo memorial had been rejected on precisely the same grounds (Matsuo, p. 46). One of the daimyo shortly to become a *gijō*, Hachisuka Mochiaki of Awa, objected to the imperial expedition on the grounds that the traditional and proper place for the emperor was in confinement within the inner recesses of the palace – out of reach, presumably, of Satsuma and Chōshū. His memorial is contained in *Fukkoki*, 2, p. 356.

47 *Meiji Tennōki*, 1, pp. 611–12.

48 *Meiji Tennōki*, 1, pp. 611–112. It was just at this time that the British minister, Sir Harry Parkes, was writing to London of the threat to the survival of 'the Mikado's party' by the 'want of cohesion or of unity among the daimios who compose it.' FO 46–91, Parkes to Stanley, 25 February 1868.

49 *Meiji Tennōki*, 1, p. 633.

50 *Meiji Tennōki*, 1, p. 655.

51 Haraguchi Kiyoshi, '*Meiji Dajōkansei Seiritsu no Seijiteki Haikei*', in *Myōjō Shogaku*, 38:1 (1990), pp. 138–39. The author also points up the severe limitations to the reformist tendencies of this group.

52 *Meiji Tennōki*, 1, p. 603.

53 Shimoyama, pp. 80–81.

54 *Ōkubo Toshimichi Monjo*, 2, p. 219.

55 *Meiji Tennōki*, 1, pp. 624–26.

56 *Meiji Tennōki*, 1, p. 627.

57 It appears that Nakayama's daughter was the instigator of the scheme. *Meiji Tennōki*, 1, p. 638.

58 FO 46–93, Mitford to Parkes, 5 April 1868. Mitford was reporting comments made to him by Date Munenari of Uwajima and the one pro-foreign courtier, Higashikuze Michitomi. Mitford reported, 'They were frank in their confession of the difficult position in which they are placed.' Parkes's audience with the emperor finally took place on 26 March.

59 Inada, p. 7.

60 The classic studies of the progress of the five articles from their conception through to completion are Osatake Takeki, *Ishin Zengo ni okeru Rikken Shisō*, Hōkōsha, 1939, 1, Ōkubo Toshiaki, '*Gokajō no Seimon ni Kansuru Ichikōsatsu*'; and Inada, '*Gokajō no Goseimon*'.

61 Osatake, '*Ishin Zengo ni okeru Rikken Shisō*', and Inada, '*Gokajō no Goseimon*' are typical examples of the former. Haraguchi is the most vociferous advocate of the latter and has reiterated his view in several places: '*Meiji Ishin Seifu no Seiritsu*', in *Rekishigaku Kenkyū*, 258 (1961), pp. 18–21; *Nihon Kindai Kokka no Keisei*, Iwanami, 1968, pp. 41–43; and '*Meiji Ishin no Kokka Kenryoku*', in Hara Hidesaburō et al., ed., *Taikei Nihon Kokkashi*, 4, *Kindai 1,* Tōkyō Daigaku Shuppankai, 1975, pp. 68–84. Classical and more recent scholarship on the oath is surveyed in John Breen, '"The Charter Oath": Some Historiographical Reflections', in *Current Issues in the Social Sciences and Humanities: Occasional Papers*, Hōsei University, 1994, 12.

62 Beasley, *The Meiji Restoration*, p. 322, and Jansen, 'Meiji Ishin: The Political Context', in Nagai Michio & Miguel Urutia, ed., *Meiji Ishin: Restoration and Revolution*, United Nations University, Tokyo, 1985, p. 13.

63 'The Ruling Class', in Marius Jansen & Gilbert Rozman, ed., *Japan in Transition: From Tokugawa to Meiji*, Princeton U.P., 1986, p. 76.
64 Inada, p. 11.
65 Jansen, 'The Ruling Class', p. 76.
66 Inada, p. 19.
67 The commentator was Sakazaki Bin; see his *'Gokajō no Goseimon'*, pp. 228–29. James Ketelaar has proposed in a provocative and important study of Meiji Buddhism that the 'evil customs' were 'explicitly associated with Buddhism's defiling presence'. James Ketelaar, *Of Heretics and Martyrs in Meiji Japan: Buddhism and Its Persecution*, Princeton U.P., 1990, p. 62. But the author presents no evidence to support this view and overlooks the fact that Kido, whose influence on the articles was decisive, was by no means anti-Buddhist. See my review of Ketelaar's book in MN 46:2 (1991), pp. 272–73.
68 Osatake, 1, p. 244.
69 Beasley, *The Meiji Restoration*, p. 324.
70 Asukai Masamichi, *Bunmei Kaika*, Iwanami, 1985, p. 18.
71 These figures are derived from the statistics provided by Emura Eiichi, *Jiyū Minken Undō no Kenkyū*, Hōsei Daigaku Shuppankyoku, 1984, pp. 66–91.
72 *Kido Kōin Monjo*, 2, p. 123.
73 Haraguchi, pp. 76–78.
74 Matsuo Masahito, *Haihan Chiken: Kindai Tōitsu Kokka e no Kumon*, Chūkō Shinsho, 1986, p. 50.
75 Haraguchi, p. 56.
76 On the Meiji Jingikan, see Haga Shōji, *Meiji Ishin no Shūkyō*, Chikuma, 1994, Chapter 1; Takeda, passim; and Breen, 'Shintoists in Restoration Japan', pp. 582–84.
77 *Meiji Tenrōki*, 2, p. 545.
78 The details of the new program are conveniently set out in Haga, p. 129.

6 Shintoists in Restoration Japan (1868–1872): Towards a reassessment*

J. Breen†

*Source: *Modern Asian Studies* 24 (1990): 579–602.

INTRODUCTION

In April of 1868, the Restoration government issued an anti-Christian proscription – 'a fixed law for all ages' it was styled.[1] Christianity was declared a pernicious sect; rewards were offered for information leading to the discovery of Christians. In the name of the proscription, the government carried out a persecution which, in the first four years of the new era, resulted in the deaths of as many as 500 native Christians. These men, women and children died from torture, starvation or from sickness induced by the conditions in which they were kept. The native Christians were, of course, from the recently discovered hidden Christian communities around Nagasaki. The Nagasaki Christian affair is a fascinating one to which I shall return, but I mention it at the outset since it serves usefully to stress the climate of the times as far as Christianity was concerned. Given this climate, it is remarkable that there emerged by 1871, or thereabouts, a small number of enlightened intellectuals who criticized government policy on Christianity and went so far as to advocate religious freedom. The most famous of the few were Mori Arinori, Nakamura Keiu, Fukuzawa Yukichi and Nishi Amane – names known to anyone familiar with early Meiji intellectual history. There is, however, one other name that needs to be added to this short list. That is Fukuba Bisei. The little known Fukuba Bisei was, perhaps, the most remarkable of these men since he was an early Meiji Shintoist. He was a disciple of the *Kokugakusha* Ōkuni Takamasa, himself a disciple of the chauvinistic Hirata Atsutane. It was Fukuba, moreover, who ran the early Meiji *Jingikan* ('Shinto Council') and Fukuba, too, who formulated the Restoration government's *saisei itchi* ('religious ritual and government are one') policy.[2]

In the latter half of 1871, the Shintoist Fukuba, in his capacity as *Jingi Shōfuku*, argued as follows: 'Although it is true that Buddhism and Confucianism came to Japan from abroad, they do not contravene the will of the gods . . . The people should be free to select and to follow the religion they wish'.[3] It is clear from the following that no exception was being made here for Christianity: 'The Western religion (teaches) nothing other than punishment for evil actions and reward for good deeds. It is no longer as it was in the age when the Portuguese subjugated the East . . . Should people wish to follow this religion, they should be spared our wrath and allowed to make a free choice.'[4] To be sure, Fukuba saw this 'freedom of conscience' as being in the context of people revering 'the Imperial lineage which is eternal as heaven and earth itself'.[5] But this of course was not unique to Shintoists like Fukuba. Nishi Amane, for example, for all his alleged progressiveness, demanded 'absolute reverence for the Emperor and his unique and eternal lineage.'[6]

Fukuba's views on religious freedom appear to disprove at a stroke persistent assertions that *saisei itchi* inevitably meant Christian suppression and Buddhist annihilation (*haibutsu kishaku*),[7] since it was Fukuba who devised the *saisei itchi* policy. They similarly disprove the assertions that all early Meiji Shintoists were 'xenophobic, and intellectually narrow-minded'[8] whose aim was the 'promotion of an absolutely intolerant Shinto religion'.[9]

Attitudes to foreign creeds is the first area of major misunderstanding about early Mejji Shintoists. There are, I suggest, at least two others. One concerns attitudes to antiquity; one scholar recently alleged that all early Meiji Shintoists were obsessed with the 'vision of antiquity'.[10] He refers, of course, to the Shintoist-led 'return to antiquity' movement of the late Tokugawa period whose participants sought to resurrect in the present the institutions – especially the *Jingikan* – and the customs of the utopian *Ritsuryō* age. The second misunderstanding relates to the substance of late Tokugawa/early Meiji Shinto. It was, we are invited to believe, characterized by a very strong '*religious*' quality, in contrast to the more purely *ethical* nature of late Meiji 'State Shinto' – a difference suggested by the universal application of the terms *Shintō Kokkyō* for the former, and *Kokka Shintō* for the latter.[11]

The misunderstandings have arisen, it seems to me, because scholars have overlooked a number of more or less obvious facts: the first is that in the early Meiji period there were *two* Shinto factions in the government. One was the Hirata faction; the other was the Ōkuni faction. The second is that it was the Ōkuni faction who ran early Meiji Shinto affairs and not the Hirata faction – who by comparison were powerless. The third is that there were fundamental differences between the thought of Ōkuni Takamasa and Hirata Atsutane. In short, the allegations regarding obsession with antiquity, the religious nature of early Meiji Shinto and exclusivism towards other creeds all apply to a greater or lesser extent to the Hirata faction, but not, as I shall demonstrate, to the Ōkuni faction.[12] Given the importance of the Ōkuni faction in early Meiji Shinto affairs, the key to an understanding of early Meiji Shinto must be an analysis of Ōkuni Takamasa's thought and not that of Hirata Atsutane and his disciples. My own analysis will be structured around the three problem areas identified above: attitudes to antiquity, the 'religious' nature of Shinto thought, and attitudes to other creeds.

ANTIQUITY VERSUS THE FUTURE – ŌKUNI'S 'BANKOKU SŌTEI' THEORY

For the Hirata faction, a 'return to antiquity' seems to have been an ethical imperative. Yano Gendō the most active Hirata disciple at the Restoration, presented to the government in January 1868 a lengthy memorial outlining his response to the challenge of the new era.[13] In fact, the memorial was little more than a detailed analysis of the institutions and customs of the ancient *Ritsuryō* state. For example, he discusses at length the niceties of ancient court dress, and asserts that the Empress should cultivate her own silk worms, sweep out the silk worm chamber and and weave her own cloth. All this and much else is justified and necessitated for Yano entirely by the fact of their existence in the utopian *Ritsuryō* age – the question of political or social relevance to the new era is not raised. The *Ritsuryō* age was, of course, the age in which worship of the deities was institutionalized in the form of the *Jingikan*, and that institution's revival was perhaps the Hirata faction's most urgent goal. It was Yano, in fact, who spearheaded the late Tokugawa movement for the revival of that office, and he, too, who campaigned most vigorously – though vainly – for the revival of every ritual that had taken place in that ancient, sacred institution.[14]

Brief though it is, the foregoing has perhaps conveyed some idea of the Hirata faction's views of antiquity. 'Obsession' may not be too strong a word. Turning now to Ōkuni's views of antiquity, the first thing to note is this general statement: 'There are those *Kokugakusha*', he writes, 'who take the period from the time of the Age of the Gods up to the 14th Emperor as the age when Shinto flourished – since foreign ways had yet to reach Japan – and would have us return to that era; likewise others take the age from Emperor Ōjin up to Tenji and Temmu as the time of Shinto's thriving . . . but they are all wrong. It is the present age alone that will really thrive. It will thrive like no age before in either Japan or China or any nation on earth.'[15] It is not, then, too surprising to learn that Ōkuni Takamasa played absolutely no part in the 'return to antiquity' movement, and at no time advocated the revival of the *Jingikan*. It remains that the Ōkuni faction did run the Meiji *Jingikan*, but we find that they ran it and viewed its existence in a very different way to the Hirata idea. Two examples will serve to underline this important point. The first concerns a specific ritual; the second concerns the *Jingikan* institution.

In summer 1868, Iwakura Tomomi asked Fukuba Bisei to devise a new ceremony for the Meiji enthronement. In his reply of acceptance, Fukuba wrote: 'The age we live in is a new and open one. The enthronement ceremony must be a suitable reflection of this.'[16] Fukuba's innovations were three-fold. Firstly, he had the political leadership in attendance and not, as had formerly been the case, the non-political court nobility. Secondly, he had a globe placed on the dais to represent Ōkuni Takamasa's idea – to which we shall return – of the Emperor as 'Global Super-Emperor'. Thirdly, there was the coronation verse that Fukuba devised for the ceremony. Traditional verse had reminded the courtly audience of the great achievements of the Emperor Tenji who had seen through the Taika reforms and instituted the system of nobility. Fukuba's verse, however, omitted all reference to Tenji, the Taika age and the nobility, and recalled, instead, that Amaterasu Ōmikami had instituted the Imperial Line in Japan and had, thereby, bequeathed the modern world to Japan. This was, indeed, a ceremony for the modern age.[17]

The second example concerns the Ōkuni faction's approach to the *Jingikan* itself. In the ancient *Jingikan* there had been a shrine to the Eight Deities, the *Hasshinden*, before which ceremony had been performed, and which had given to the *Jingikan* its character as a sacred site of state ritual, distinct from other merely administrative organs. In 1868 the *Jingikan* was resurrected, but the shrine had yet to be installed and, until it was, resurrection was obviously rather less than complete. Certain Hirata followers, like Tokoyo Nagatane, who occupied subordinate positions within the *Jingikan*, campaigned vigorously for the shrine's installation, and finally, almost two years after the Restoration, and for reasons which do concern us here, it was in fact installed.[18] What is of interest, however, is Tokoyo's very brief comment on Fukuba's attitude to the whole affair. He writes: 'Fukuba and his followers are *obsessed with the present*; their concern is exclusively with the mood of the moment; they do not revere the Eight Deities nor do they appear interested in constructing even a temporary shrine for them [within the *Jingikan*].'[19] (emphasis added)

The different reactions of the Ōkuni and Hirata factions to the dissolution of the *Jingikan* in 1871 are also worth noting briefly. Tokoyo wrote that its dissolution meant 'the start of the decline of the nation's Way', and then he recorded Fukuba's very different reaction: '[Fukuba said that] many people will sigh for a while, but in fact [the abolition of the *Jingikan*] has provided us with the basis from which the nation's Way may truly flourish'.[20] Indeed, it is beyond doubt that Fukuba himself played the leading role in the dissolution of the Council.[21]

The differences between the two factions in attitudes towards antiquity – as well as the tensions they created – should be obvious from these examples. We need now to say something positive about the Ōkuni faction's response to the challenge of the new age. The best starting point is probably Ōkuni's *Bankoku Sōtei* theory. *Bankoku Sōtei*, which means something like 'Global Super-Emperor', is an idea to which he constantly returns in his writings. So central is it that all his Shinto thought seems to be structured and restructured around it. The theory is a simple one: namely, that the Emperor of Japan will one day be acknowledged by all peoples of the world as their ruler, and that Japan will one day, too, be acknowledged as the Founding Nation of the earth. In short, Ōkuni believed that Japan had a sort of 'manifest destiny', if you like, a god given role to play in what he understood to be a newly emerging world order. Ōkuni apparently arrived at his grand conclusions regarding the Emperor's future world role through a reading of the myths which he regarded as 'the source of all learning'.[22] Ōkuni's reading of the myths was as follows: 'When the creator deity Amenominakanushi no kami created heaven and earth, he made the sun the centre of the heavens; [in like fashion] he made our great nation of Japan the centre of the world and gave to us an Imperial Line coeval with heaven and earth, whose Emperors he made the centre of all peoples.'[23]

This is the basic theory which he embellishes and rephrases on countless occasions. The eternal nature of the Imperial line, he writes, is due to the fact that in the Age of the Gods, the deities were unanimous that Amaterasu's descendants should become the master of the globe. 'Of all the matters determined by the deities, none was as far-reaching, as great, as firm or as righteous as this.'[24] 'Our Emperor is an Emperor [whose lineage] remains unchanged from the Age of the Gods. This means that he is to be the Super-Emperor of all Nations. He is not to be spoken of in the same breath as the Kings of, say, China or Russia. He is a Great Lord, far superior to them.'[25] 'Foreign nations have their kings, but in no case are they intimate with the deities; Japan's Emperor is the descendant of the gods and their relationship is therefore intimate.'[26]

It is important to realize that much of Ōkuni's writing was composed with a Western audience in mind. 'Diplomacy' indeed he saw as a principal function of *Kokugaku*. '*Kokugakusha* must always bear in mind meetings with foreigners; they should know how to reply when asked this question; and what to say when asked that question.'[27] This 'calling' to communicate with foreigners was undoubtedly one of the major impetuses behind his own keen exploration of Western learning. That is, in order to convince foreigners that the Emperor had really been appointed at the time of creation to play a special role in world history, he knew he had to account for Western theories of creation as well. They had to be examined and explained in such a way as did not compromise the central truth of the myths. So it was that he argued, for example, that the Japanese creator deity Amenominakanushi no kami, who gave to Japan the Imperial Line, was none other than that deity to which Westerners refer as *Tenshu* (or the Christian Lord of Heaven). 'Proof' of this, he demonstrated, lay in the philological fact that within the word Amenominakanushi are found the *Ten* (read as *Ame*), and the *Shu* (read as *Nushi*) of *Tenshu*.[28] Adam and Eve, too, found a place within his system. He disputed that they were in reality Izanagi and Izanami, the male and female deities ordered by Amenominakanushi to give birth to the myriad nations of the world. Instead, Adam and his wife deity Eve, he understood to have been among the holy beings (*shinsen*) who 'sped through the air creating foreign nations in the Age of the Gods'.[29] In this fashion, Ōkuni believed he was able to account for foreign theories in a way that left the Emperor's unique position beyond the inevitable foreign challenge.

Ōkuni's application of Western learning is perhaps best illustrated in his writings on International Law.[30] He came across International Law, probably in Nishi Amane's translation, sometime in 1866 or 1867. He was fascinated to discover that International Law had been set up in the West precisely to compensate for the fact that there existed no one divinely appointed and universally acknowledged ruler of the world. He looked forward to pointing out to Westerners that there was such a ruler after all – the Emperor of Japan. Foreigners' claims about the truth of international law were based on foreigners' ignorance, he believed, of the fact that the Christian God was in reality the deity who had appointed Japan's Emperor to rule the globe. It followed from this that what the foreigners regarded as international law was false. True International Law was nothing other than the commands of Japan's divinely appointed Emperor.

It is important to add that Ōkuni's use of foreign learning was not confined to such cases as the above. He was widely read and appears to have had a genuine interest in all matters foreign; he was well aware that Japan could not afford to ignore the more practical benefits of Western knowledge, the seeds of which he anyway regarded as having been sprinkled in foreign minds by Sukunahikona no kami in the Age of the Gods.[31] His frequent warnings that the myths were to be regarded as the source of all knowledge were meant to ensure that scholars did not lose sight of Japan's divine endowment; they were not intended to warn people away from Western learning: 'Though foreign learning may come to Japan from abroad it is not to be despised. It is to be used. To fail to use it, indeed, would be to ignore the command of the deities in heaven.'[32]

As can be imagined, Ōkuni's *Bankoku Sōtei* theory, which lies at the heart of his Shinto thought, had profound implications for his attitudes towards diplomatic and other relations with the West. In fact, we find in his work none of the raw xenophobia that marks the writings of Hirata Atsutane and his followers, or, say, the late Mito school. Ōkuni was, for example, no advocate of the late Tokugawa *jōi* or 'expel the barbarian' movement – not anyway in the accepted sense. Ōkuni dubbed this violent anti-foreign movement *shōjōi* or 'little *jōi*'. He advocated, instead, what he called *daijōi* or 'great *jōi*'. This he defined as 'stirring love of the Emperor in foreign hearts'.[33] Ōkuni's position was quite simply that if the Japanese Emperor was to fulfil his god-given role as a ruler among rulers in the new world order, then it could not be the wish of Amaterasu Ōmikami for Japan to shun contact with the West,[34] or retreat into some utopian antiquity.

As early as 1818, when Ōkuni was on a study trip to Nagasaki, we find him looking forward to the day when rulers of other nations would come to pay tribute to Japan's Emperor.[35] Several years later, in 1854, Ōkuni found himself in Edo when Commodore Perry was back for the second time. His reaction is striking. 'I heard about the treaty articles that were to be signed. People loathed Perry for his violence. I, however, thought otherwise. I wished to congratulate him. He is a very great man. It is people like Perry that have made America a great nation.'[36] A year later in 1855 he gave a more considered view of the new international situation facing Japan: 'Recently foreign vessels have become frequent visitors to our shores. When I think on the cause, it seems to me it is to be found in the year being the 2,500th since the reign of the Emperor Jimmu. It is a sign that all is to change . . . The arrival of the foreigners is a sign of the flourishing of a new age of wisdom. It is a cause for joy. Many bewail [their advent]; many are enraged by it, and all try to drive them off. This is because they do not understand the will of the gods.'[37] It was Amaterasu's will to bring all nations to Japan and so have them pay homage'.[38] Ōkuni was understandably overjoyed, then, on hearing of the court's formal recognition of the trade treaties in 1865, since it was by trade, of course, that all nations could be drawn to Japan.[39]

What helped Ōkuni to confront the new age with such apparent calm and poise was, in part at least, his belief that all was developing in accordance with the will of Amaterasu. Amaterasu, he believed, was working to a plan, one aspect of which consisted in overseeing major changes in the human world every 1,250 years, or multiples or fractions thereof – hence the reference above to 2,500 years after Jimmu's accession. He calculated that it was 5,000 years after Niniginomikoto came down to earth that the first Emperor Jimmu came to the throne. It was near enough 1,250 years after that Buddhism came to Japan and 1,250 years after that was the Bakumatsu period.[40] For Ōkuni this was proof enough that great change was in the offing. Japan was in the charge of Amaterasu; the Japanese Emperor was soon to assume his central role in world history. It goes without saying that, in view of all this, it would be erroneous to suggest that Ōkuni Takamasa shared the Hirata faction's obsession with antiquity. He and his faction were looking, instead, to Japan's future.

'RELIGIOUS SHINTO' AND 'ETHICAL SHINTO'

We must now consider the second of our three problem areas – that relating to the allegedly 'religious' nature of early Meiji Shinto. Here 'religious' is obviously meant in a very narrow sense, and refers specifically to a preoccupation with the other world, with judgement, with eternal happiness or eternal damnation and with a central, transcendental creator deity. None of these were given especial prominence in the myths or the writings of, say, Motoori Norinaga. All, however, acquire a special prominence in the Shinto thought of Hirata Atsutane and his disciples, enabling us to define it as 'religious Shinto'. In order to sharpen the contrast with the Ōkuni faction's position, we can usefully take a closer look at these religious features of Hirata Shinto.

In a sense, the essence of Hirata Shinto is summed up in this statement of Hirata's regarding the greater importance of the other world: 'The present world is not the real world. The reason why the gods created man in this world was to purify his heart and determine and test the degree of his virtuous actions; for this reason they caused him to lodge here but temporarily.'[41] Again he writes 'Ōkuninushi no kami, the deity of the Hidden Realm, knows well the good and evil that men commit in this life . . . For those sins men commit against the commandments of the creator [Amenominakanushi] men will be punished; those who do his will shall be rewarded for their virtue.'[42]

The political ramifications of thus emphasizing other-worldly priorities are what concern us, because it is with the deities Amenominakanushi and Ōkuninushi, and not with the temporal authorities that ultimate authority is seen to lie. It was for this reason that Hirata demanded that men of politics should 'first serve the deities in heaven, and only then deliberate on matters of government'.[43] Indeed, when Hirata spoke of *saisei itchi* or 'the unification of religious ritual with government', he seems to have had in mind a sort of theocracy in which politics were subordinate to religion, and this world subordinate to the claims of the next.[44]

Hirata's establishment of Amenominakanushi as the central deity is one of his most striking theological innovations. In the myths, the deity is portrayed as just one of many who came into being *after* the creation of the universe, but Hirata rewrites the relevant passage to read: 'In ancient times, *before* either heaven or earth came into being, there was one god who existed, and his name was Amenominakanushi no kami.'[45] 'It is the God Amenominakanushi who, from eternity, has sat in the heavens and masterminded the creation of the universe; this god is the creator god – his virtue is boundless.'[46] The important point about recentering the Shinto pantheon around Amenominakanushi is that it served, in the eyes of Hiratas critics, to relativize the importance of Amaterasu, the founder of the Imperial Line, and so relativize the position of the Imperial Institution. The Mito school, for example, were swift to condemn his 'wondrous theories' for 'obscuring the [ethical] Way of the divine realm'.[47] All of these religious ideas developed by Hirata continued to feature prominently in the writings of Yano Gendō and other Hirata disciples at the time of the Restoration.[48]

Were one to assess the nature of early Meiji Shinto on the basis of their writings, then, the 'religious' label would stick. As I have repeated, however, this would be an error. We cannot assess the qualities of early Meiji Shinto without considering the Ōkuni faction's position. It was, needless to say, very different. Basically, Ōkuni fully shared the Mito criticism of this Hirata tendency to emphasize the next world and thereby relativize the absolute importance of the Emperor. Ōkuni writes: The scholars of the Hirata school [of *Kokugaku*] know that there is an after-world, but they fail to make a distinction between the after-world and this world.'[49] The afterworld is the afterworld; and this world is this world. While we are in this world, let us obey the laws of this world and pay not a moments heed to the next.[50] On other occasions, too, he returns to the matter, but only to record his scorn for those who try to understand the next world. On the matter of judgement in the next life, Ōkuni confesses his confusion and simply says that the matter is 'of extraordinary complexity'.[51]

In Ōkuni Shinto, Amaterasu Ōmikami is re-established as the central Shinto deity since she is the divine ancestor of the Emperor, and founder of the Imperial Line. However, Ōkuni did not deny the importance of

Amenominakanushi – we have already seen how he identified that deity with the Christian God. But he successfully avoids a compromise of Amaterasu's – and hence the Emperor's – position by pretending to see a mystical identity between the two deities: 'Amenominakanushi and Amaterasu are', he writes, 'one god, two spirits'.[52] Amaterasu is the manifestation in time of Amenominakanushi who existed before time'.[53] And again: 'Amenominakanushi is the origin; Amaterasu is the manifestation'.[54] The greater emphasis on the latter is beyond doubt, for 'Amenominakanushi has now receded without trace'.[55] This reasserting of the importance of Amaterasu, and the placing of Amenominakanushi backstage, as it were, achieves the greater emphasis on the Emperor and this-worldly political concerns.

We have encountered Ōkuni's belief that it was Amaterasu who had guided foreigners to Japan's shores in order to establish a new world order in which the Japanese Emperor would assume his position as 'Global Super-Emperor'. Behind Amaterasu's method, Ōkuni espied a metaphysical principle. The principle is one he calls *moto/sue*. Essentially, *moto* means 'origin' or 'source'; *sue* meaning 'end' or perhaps 'periphery'. Amaterasu has established the Japanese Emperor, Japan and the Japanese people as *moto*, while foreign rulers, foreign nations and foreign people are *sue*. Most importantly, however, Ōkuni understood that essential to Amaterasu's role was the application of this same strictly hierarchical *moto/sue* principle to the restructuring of human society. 'Lord, father and husband – these are the *moto*. The Way consists in obeying the *moto*; in having those who are *sue* (vassal, son and wife) obey the *moto*.'[56] Time and again he stressed that Shinto for him consists primarily in these ethical, strictly hierarchical principles: 'My principle teachings are the Way of Lord and Vassal, Father and Son, Husband and Wife.'[57] It is the great principle of Shinto that its essence should consist in *chūkōtei* (loyalty, piety and chastity).[58] These three principles he sees as divinely bestowed on Japan to ensure the continuity of the Imperial Line: 'The three maxims of *chūkō* and *tei* are the greatest practical ethical maxims in the human world – in Japan, these are correctly observed and that is why the Imperial Line has remained unchanged since distant antiquity.'[59] Obeying the *moto* is the essence of the Way. Chinese and Indians lose their Kings precisely because they do not have the spirit of obedience to the *moto*.'[60]

What Ōkuni demanded was reverence for and obedience to the Imperial Line. His brand of Shinto – 'Amaterasu Shinto' as he often called it – was certainly not 'religious' in the narrow sense. Heaven, hell and the other realm were issues of no importance; the only deity of any consequence to him was Amaterasu, a 'political' deity engaged in political, ethical work; and the essence of his Shinto teaching consisted in little more than the one-directional submission of vassal to lord, son to father and wife to husband.[61]

It is here that we can usefully return to the issue of ritual. In the early Meiji period after the *Jingikan* had been revived, we find the Ōkuni faction for the first time advocating the adoption of a policy of *saisei itchi*, one which was, however, rather different from that of the Hirata faction. For Ōkuni, ritual (*sai*) appears to have had two principal functions, both of them political. Firstly, it served to inculcate those ethical norms at the core of his Shinto thought. For this reason, all of the ritual devised by the Ōkuni faction involved the Emperors personal reverence not to the myriad deities, but almost exclusively to either Amaterasu or the spirits of deceased Emperors (*kōrei*).[62] His personal performance of ritual in either case became the ultimate display of loyalty and filial piety. Secondly, of course, imperial ritual served to proclaim the divine origins of the Imperial Line and so serve as the ultimate stamp of legitimacy. In either case, however, it is essential to note that religious ritual was seen as serving government. For Yano Gendō and other Hirata disciples, however, religious ritual (*sai*) had a rather different meaning: it was a religious communion with the deities; it was more a celebration of the greater truth of the other world than a legitimizer of the Emperor's absolute role in this; and, finally – incidentally almost – it was served to inculcate ethical norms.[63]

I do not wish to overstate my case. The contention here is not that ethical qualities were entirely absent from mainstream Hirata Shinto, nor, either, that religious elements were entirely lacking in Ōkuni Shinto. However, for the Hirata school, the claims of the other world were dominant; for the Ōkuni school this world was the real world, and obedience to the temporal authorities the primary consideration. In Hirata Shinto, the religious emphasis is much greater, and its political and ethical value, therefore, correspondingly less.

It seems only correct to suppose, then, that when Ōkuni Takamasa advocated in 1868 the dissemination of what he called 'restoration Shinto' (*Ishin no Shintō*),[64] he did not have in mind the institution of a Hirata-type theocracy, nor the conversion of the entire populace to a 'religious Shinto' substitute for Buddhism. His interest, as we have seen, was in inspiring loyalty and reverence towards the Emperor and the Imperial family. Some scholars claim to see further evidence of 'religious' Shinto in the Imperial pronouncement – possibly penned by Fukuba – of February 1871 to mark the launching of the Great Propaganda Campaign.[65] Why, is far from clear. This Imperial Pronouncement, the *Daikyō Senpu no Mikotonori*, announces the launch of the nation-wide propaganda campaign, but then does nothing more or less than proclaim the government's intention to 'clarify ethical teachings' (*chikyō*) in order that 'the attitudes of the people may be exemplary'. The clarification of these 'ethical teachings', it says, is the essence of the 'Great Way of the Gods'.[66] These views are entirely consistent with the predominantly politically-useful, ethical qualities we have already seen in Ōkuni Takamasa's Shinto.

In the next and final section, we must consider the third of the assumptions about early Meiji Shinto. This will involve a discussion of the Ōkuni factions attitudes to foreign creeds.

ON FOREIGN CREEDS

(i) Buddhism

In his pre-Restoration writings, it is true, Ōkuni Takamasa was not beyond the occasional fulmination at Buddhists, but, on balance, his was a far more accommodating position than that of the ferociously anti-Buddhist Hirata Atsutane. Ōkuni dismisses Buddhism as 'a stupid old custom'.[67] He condemns it for its devotion to 'the preaching of heaven and hell', which leads astray the common people. At the same time, though, he says that 'its harm is a shallow one',[68] and he is ready, too, to give it credit. In a passage on the evils of Christianity, he writes that it was only Buddhism arriving in Japan before Christianity that saved Japan from succumbing to the perniciousness of that sect.[69] The explanation for this attitude, as for so much, is to be found in his conviction that Buddhism's advent accorded with 'the will of the gods'. 'Recent scholars of no repute [see the arrival of Buddhism as a catastrophy]; but this is not so. This too was part of the plan of the gods in heaven'.[70] Ōkuni does predict that Buddhism will one day die out,[71] but he stresses it 'would not be a good thing forcibly to rid the hearts of the lower classes of Buddhism'.[72]

Ōkuni's main concern appears to have been establishing the correct relationship between Shinto and Buddhism, firstly in the theological terms: 'Buddhists talk of *honji* and *suijaku.* They say that the deities in our ancient records were sent by Buddha, the Absolute Deity (*honji)*, as helper-gods made manifest (*suijaku*) to assist in the work of salvation. From the Shinto point of view, however, it is Buddha who is a mere manifestation (*sakimitama*) of the [Shinto] gods.' It is the conclusion Ōkuni draws from this that is noteworthy: 'This comes to mean, of course, that Buddhism is one aspect of the truth of the Great Way.'[73] This reversal of the *honji suijaku* theory, which is of course by no means unique to Ōkuni, is nevertheless indicative of the fact that what he sought was the 'relativization' of the Buddhist pantheon and not its denial.

In institutional terms, too, it is the relativization of Buddhism that he appears to have sought. There is no suggestion that he advocated the wanton destruction of Buddhist institutions. Some scholars have asserted that the Bakumatsu reforms implemented by the Ōkuni faction in Tsuwano fief were calculated to achieve the 'obliteration of Buddhism',[74] but there is no hard evidence for this. The above discussion suggests this interpretation may be off the mark, and there are important economical factors, too, worthy of consideration. A fief directive in 1867 bewailed the huge increase in temple numbers in recent years lamenting: 'They use up valuable land . . . , and so put a strain on the fief.' 'They place intolerable financial burdens on the people. Buddhists priests neglect their religious duties and devote themselves exclusively to the financial affairs of their temples. Surely this is against the true meaning of the Buddha's way?'[75] In such terms were justified the Tsuwano reforms, which involved merging recently built Buddhist chapels with the main temple of the sect; and offering financial incentives to Buddhist priests to return to the laity. Shrines, too, were similarly affected. 'With these reforms', the people were told, 'all things will go well and you will be able to lead worshipful lives'.[76] Here again the possibilities for social upheaval were keenly perceived: 'These reforms are not to be carried out at once, but gradually over time.'[77]

The first Ōkuna faction statement on Buddhism in the new era surely supports the view that denial of Buddhist deities and destruction of Buddhist property was not on their agenda. The document in question is a policy proposal submitted by Kamei Koremi, the Lord of Tsuwano, to the Grand Council of State in April 1868.[78] Articles 1 and 2 between them recommend that all shrines using incorrect terms such as 'Hachiman Buddha' should cease forthwith and use, instead, the 'correct' term 'Hachiman, the Shinto Deity'; that shrines using Buddhist statues to represent Shinto deities should abandon the practice forthwith; and that all Buddhist priests serving at Shinto shrines should return to lay life or, alternatively, become Shinto priests.[79] Articles 3 and 4 go on to recommend (a) that all people should be made to register at their local shrine and swear oaths there to prove they are not affiliated to pernicious sects; and (b) that there be a reform of burial customs 'based on the Sacred Classics'. It adds, however, that 'this reform is not to be forced upon people'. The final clause is of especial interest since it stipulates that while Shinto is to be hereafter officially established in Japan, 'adherents of Buddhism are not to be obstructed from practising on a private basis'.[80]

What Kamei proposes here is that there be an official clarification of what, historically, is and is not Shinto, and what is and is not Buddhist. This is followed by recommendations which clearly aim at putting an end to the state's recognition of Buddhism as state religion. The Tokugawa system of compulsory registration at Buddhist temples it recommends be abolished, as well as the Buddhist monopoly on checking religionists. Finally, there is a proposed reform of the state system of Buddhist funerals. Buddhist funerals were also compulsory, of course, under the Tokugawa, and here Kamei proposes that a choice be given. All of which most certainly does amount to a plan for religious reformation and the demotion of Buddhists and their religion, but hardly their denial or destruction.

The zealous attacks on Buddhist institutions and the wanton destruction of Buddhist property in the early Meiji period undoubtedly had support amongst the Hirata faction. Indeed, the vandalistic activities of the Hirata disciple, Juge Shigekuni, junior official in the Shinto Office and confidant of Iwakura Tomomi, are well documented,[81] and Yano Gendō, too, is on record as demanding summary execution for Buddhists who preach their evil to the populace.[82] The objective of the politically aware Ōkuni Shintoists lay elsewhere, however. It lay in the official promotion of their brand of ethical, political Shinto and the demotion – not destruction – of Buddhism.

This, then, is something of the historical background against which Fukuba's proposals for religious freedom for Buddhists, noted at the outset of this paper, are to be seen. There we saw Fukuba argue that Buddhists should be free to practise Buddhism as they pleased, with the proviso, which we also noted, that their loyalty to the 'divinely instituted' Imperial Line was absolute. In fact, Fukuba went further still and suggested that Buddhist institutions had a positive role to play in the new era. 'Has not Buddhism been widely believed in by the people of Japan for more than a thousand years?' he asked in 1871. 'Its assistance (in strengthening the nation) should be sought.'[83] In a public speech a year later in 1872, we are hardly surprised to find him praising the Buddhist saints Kukai and Dengyo for having taught the Japanese to lead 'useful and good lives'.[84]

(ii) Christianity

That Christianity was for long a source of very grave concern for Ōkuni Takamasa is beyond doubt. With scholars of the Mito school like Aizawa Seishisai, he shared a profound fear of the Western religion.[85] The inevitability of Christianity's advent alone seems seriously to have qualified his anticipation of the Wests coming. Passages such as the following suggest the difficulty he had in regarding Christianity's coming as being in accord with the 'will of Amaterasu': The frequent arrival of the foreigners in recent years is in order to introduce the Way of Friendship of the Christian God. It is a most frightful thing. Their aim is to destroy the true way of loyalty, piety and chastity (*chūkōtei*).[86] And again: 'People will be intoxicated with [the Christians'] talk of friendship and love. They help the sick and seek no reward. They comfort the lonely. It appears a good way, but in reality it is evil. When they form bands neither lord nor father can have any control over them. It is not the Japanese way of loyalty and justice.' [87] However, it becomes obvious that admiration for the foreign religion was not far behind Ōkuni's view of the religion as pernicious.

It is in Ōkuni's writings of 1862 that, for the first time, the true measure of his admiration for Christianity surfaces. (Interestingly 1862 marks a high point in the anti-foreign movement.) It surfaces first in a remarkable political and social study of the West called *Kyūjō Ichiran* ('Scanning the Globe') which he wrote in that year.[88] He starts with a discussion of England because 'England is the most powerful nation in the world'. What concerns us is his understanding of the source of English strength: 'In very few years, England was able to become incomparably the strongest and most vigorous nation in the whole world. And the reason is the Reformation. At first they had Catholicism (*Tenshukyō*), but then they changed it for the religion that Luther set up. He was a brilliant religious leader and, together with the King and his ministers, they contrived to make the nation wealthy.' I think there is little doubt that Ōkuni saw a function for Shinto in Japan somewhat analogous to that of Protestantism after the Reformation in England.

Anyway, in the section just quoted, he is unspecific as to the precise contribution of Protestantism to England's strength, but it is clearly connected with what he calls Christianity's 'Way of Friendship and Love'. Here the reference is brief, but in subsequent works[89] he often returns to the matter. 'Friendship and love' refers to the fact that in England Christians built children's homes, and looked after poor children; caring for them and educating them; they built hospitals and cared for the sick. '[But in all this] they do not take money from the people; instead, they get money from the King for these good works as well as from the followers of the religion.'[90] In all probability, Ōkuni saw Christianity's friendship and love as contributing to England's social cohesion and hence to its strength.

For Ōkuni the Christian way of friendship and love goes beyond this. He understands the same way as explaining what his contemporaries thought of as Western rapacity: 'Western nations wish to engage in friendly relations and give aid to other nations – that is why they regard countries such as China and Japan who refuse to sign treaties with them as contravening the wishes of heaven.'[91] He speaks with approval, for example, of those Western nations which, in the name of Christian friendship and love, topple the cruel regimes of other nations. His remarkable conclusion is: 'Foreign nations do not indiscriminately (*midari ni*) steal the territory of other nations'[92]

Ōkuni's obvious recognition of the power of Christian friendship and love, in all its various guises, may well explain the centrality that Ōkuni gives to what he calls *aitasukuru koto* in his own Shinto.[93] It goes without saying, however, that great though his admiration of Christianity's contribution strength was, Ōkuni was *not* advocating the adoption of Christianity in Japan. Christians would, he believed, preach disloyalty to the Emperor. For Christians, the source or *moto* was not the Emperor, and not the father or husband. Jesus, the founder of their religion, was the *moto*.[94] In other words, whatever benefits Christianity may have brought the West, it was quite incompatible with the ethical, social order that Ōkuni understood Amaterasu to be realizing based on the *moto sue* metaphysical principle. So, the identity Ōkuni had early on discovered between Japanese deities and the Christian *Tenshu* did not appear to soften his opposition to Christianity's acceptance in Japan. The opposition, and the ethical reasons for it, he shared with all Japan's anti-Christian polemicists of the late Tokugawa period. What ultimately distinguishes Ōkuni Takamasa from these others is that, by 1868, he appears to have worked out a framework for Christianity's acceptance. The evidence for this is in a memorial Ōkuni wrote in early 1868 in response to the eruption of the Nagasaki Christian affair which I briefly touched upon at the start of this paper.

The occasion for the memorial was the summoning of an Imperial Conference in May 1868 to debate the disposal of the thousands of recently discovered 'hidden Christians'.[95] The proposal before the conference, composed by Kido Koin and Inoue Kaoru, recommended the execution of the Christian ringleaders in Nagasaki and the internal exile of the remainder.[96] Ōkuni Takamasa's reaction to the whole episode is recorded in a number of places, the most articulate being a short memorial called *Tenshukyō ni kansuru iken-sho* ('Christianity: My Views in Writing').[97]

The document begins with a brief historical survey in which he distinguishes between the Christianity propagated in China by the Jesuits Matteo Ricci, Guiglio Aleni and others on the one hand, and that propagated in Japan by the Spanish and Portuguese on the other. Ignorant, perhaps, that the Portuguese in Japan were Jesuits as well, he notes that their brand of Christianity was known even in the West as a 'pernicious religion', while the Christianity propagated in China was known by the Chinese as 'Western Confucianism'. Establishing this fundamental distinction between an apparently acceptable and an obviously unacceptable Christianity serves to soften the ground for his comments on the events reported from Nagasaki. 'The Christianity set up in Nagasaki recently', he writes, 'is vastly different from the *Kirishitan* religion of former times. It is the religion worshipped in England, in France and in America as the Orthodox Religion of Jesus (*Yaso Seikyō*). Loyalty, filial piety and chastity (*chūkōtei*) are its universal values. It devotes itself exclusively to charity and to good works.[98] The references to charity and good works we have had before, but here, for the first time, he writes that Christianity shares the values of loyalty, piety and chastity with Shinto. For the first time, too, Ōkuni notes an equivalence between the Christian Lord of Heaven and Amaterasu: 'The Christian God is', he writes enigmatically, 'a shadow of Amaterasu'.[99] The significance of Ōkuni's passing reference to Christianity in China as 'Western Confucianism' is now clearer. For surely he is arguing that just as Chinese Confucianists regarded Christianity as acceptable, as a Westernized form of their own ethical system, so in Japan too could Christianity be regarded as a sort of 'Western Shinto'. If this is a correct judgement, then the implication of this must be that in 1868 Ōkuni Takamasa was seeking some form of accommodation with Christianity – and not the absolute rejection that scholars persistently attribute to early Meiji Shintoists.

It is one thing to note the change in Ōkuni's thought. It is quite another to account for it satisfactorily. One can point of course to the fact that Ōkuni's often reiterated belief in the 'will of the gods' had long provided him with a rationale for accepting Christianity, as had his early identification of Shinto deities with the Christian God. Ōkuni himself cites the influence of his reading of Grotius's 'International Law' and Martin's *Tendo Sogen*,[100] and these may well have been the catalyst. The former, it will be recalled, argued that it was possession of Christianity alone that made a nation worthy of the epithet 'civilized'. Martin was a 19th century Protestant missionary in China and he argued, like Ricci before him, that Confucian and Christian ethics were not incompatible. Whatever the reason, however, the fact is Ōkuni's views on Christianity's acceptability had changed. His views were inherited by his disciples such as Fukuba Bisei and Kamei Koremi, and this is clear from the official reactions of these men to the same Nagasaki Christian affair.

Not only do both men avoid referring to Christianity as a pernicious or evil religion, they evidently deplored the Meiji leadership's proposals for execution of the Christians. Kamei Koremi wrote that it would be 'the most pitiful thing' to execute any of the Nagasaki Christians.[101] Fukuba likewise protested that 'it would be a disgrace to the gods to execute the Christians for believing in the foreign religion. Let bygones be bygones.'[102] Subsequently also: 'Shinto is the great Way of the Universe. Why treat Christians cruelly?'[103] The Ōkuni faction alone, of all the seventy or more who sent memorials to the government on the Nagasaki incident, advocated humane treatment for the Christian villagers.

However, the politically aware Ōkuni faction did not propose the new government adopt a *laissez faire* policy on Christianity. They recommended, in fact, a two-fold response consisting, firstly, of proscribing Christianity. In view of the preceding examination of Ōkuni's views on Christianity and Fukuba's earlier noted arguments that those wishing to follow Christianity should be allowed to do so, it seems conceivable that the Christian proscription was not proposed as a 'fixed law for all ages',[104] so much as a temporary political measure. That the proscription was advocated at all may well simply reflect the Ōkuni factions anxiety to conform to the expectations of their political masters. Secondly, their response involved, in Fukuba's words, 'clarifying the Great Way of this Imperial Nation'[105] and 'impressing upon the people the uniqueness of the imperial line, divinely instituted and eternal'.[106] The dynamics of this are unfortunately not expanded upon, but for our present purposes, it is sufficient to note that the eradication of Christianity, and the apostasy of Christians were not called for. After all, Christians' ethics were essentially the same as Ōkuni's own.

CONCLUSION

The aim of the foregoing analysis has been to re-examine early Meiji Shinto and Shintoists, and thereby to dispel some common misconceptions. My concentration on the thought of Ōkuni Takamasa and his faction to the exclusion of the Hirata and other factions is justified by the fact noted at the outset, namely, that it was the disciples of Ōkuni Takamasa, and not the Hirata faction, who ran early Meiji Shinto affairs.

To sum up, then, we have seen that, unlike the Hirata faction, the Ōkuni Shintoists were not obsessed with 'the vision of antiquity'. They were not advocates of a retreat into antiquity or even of the revival of ancient institutions such as the *Jingikan*. Their concerns were clearly with the international age and the Emperor's destined role in it. The nature of their Shinto reflects this concern. Ōkuni Takamasa's Shinto did not concern itself with the other world nor with the promise of eternal rewards for good deeds; rather his 'Amaterasu Shinto', his concept of the Way, consisted, as he stressed time and again, in nothing other than the ethical maxims established by Amaterasu of loyalty, piety and chastity (*chūkōtei*). The reassertion in Ōkuni

Shinto of the supremacy of Amaterasu, founder of the Imperial Line and controller of the new world order is a reflection of this greater concern with this-worldly, politico-ethical concerns. Shinto, for Ōkuni, was the servant of the state. As far as other creeds were concerned, the Ōkuni faction's proposals evidently did not involve socially, politically disruptive attacks on Buddhist property or the prohibition of Buddhist practice, nor did they involve the annihilation of Christianity or even its permanent proscription. Aware no doubt of the political folly of attempting to wipe out Buddhism and annihilate Christianity and equally aware that both had some political contribution to make, the Ōkuni faction proposed instead 'accommodation' for these religions and their followers, conditional upon their conformity to the ethics of *chūkōtei*.

The current misconceptions about early Meiji Shintoists have, heretofore, served to provide scholars with a ready explanation for the abolition in 1871 of the *Jingikan* and the reforms which followed in its wake. In other words, it is asserted that the political leadership abandoned any support given the *Jingikan* and its 'narrow-minded, xenophobic' leaders in the immediate aftermath of the Restoration, precisely because of the Shintoists' continued preoccupation with antiquity and not with present political realities; with religion rather than ethics useful to the state and with the elimination of foreign creeds rather than their accommodation. It should now be obvious that this is too simplistic an explanation for the change in religious policy after 1871. An investigation of the real reasons is beyond the scope of this present paper; suffice to say, however, that the policy change was, in fact, proposed and implemented by the Ōkuni faction itself as a fulfilment of their Shinto ideals.

NOTES

† Research for this article was supported by the Japan Foundation. The author is greatly indebted to Professor Sakamoto Koremaru of Kokugakuin University, and Takeda Hideaki, one time graduate student of Kokugakuin, for their invaluable assistance, encouragement and friendship.

1 Naikaku Kanbōchō (ed) *Hōrei Zensho* (Tōkyō, Hara Shobō, 1974), vol. 1, p. 6.
2 On the leading role of Fukuba and the Ōkuni Takamasa faction see the recent research by Takeda Hideaki: 'Kindai Tennōsaishi Keisei Katei no Ichikōsatsu' in Inoue Nobutaka and Sakamoto Koremaru (eds.), *Nihongata Seikyō Kankei no Tanjō* (Tōkyō, Daiichi Shobō, 1987).
3 *Jingishō – gokaikaku shorui gairyaku basshō* in Nihon Shiseki Kyōkai (ed.), *Iwakura Tomomi Kankei Monjo* (Tōkyō, 1927), vol. 7, pp. 439–40.
4 *Ibid.*, pp. 440–1.
5 *Ibid.*, pp. 439.
6 Yasumaru Yoshio, *Kamigami no Meiji Ishin* (Tōkyō, Iwanami Shinsho, 1979), p. 206.
7 The most recent assertion is by Miyaji Masato in his otherwise very useful *Nihontsūshi 3 – Kokusai Seijika no Kindai Nihon – Kingendai* (Tōkyō, Yamagawa Shuppansha, 1987), p. 42.

8 Haga Shōji, 'Meiji Jingikan no Seiritsu to Kokkasaishi no Saihen' (ge), *Jinbungakuhō*, 51, p. 74.
9 Haga Shōji, 'Shintō Kokkyōsei no Keisei', *Nihonshi Kenkyū*, 264, pp. 2 and 30.
10 Yasumaru, *op. cit.*, p. 48.
11 The religious nature of 'restoration Shinto' is dwelt on especially in Haga Shōji, 'Shintō Kokkyōsei no keisei', *passim*, and Nishida Nagao, 'Meiji Shintōshijosetsu'; 'Meiji Shinseifu no Shūkyō Kaikaku' in *Nihon Shintōshi Kenkyū*, vol. 7, *Kinseihen* (*ge*) (Tōkyō, Kodansha, 1978).
12 One reason for the confusion may be that Ōkuni went to considerable trouble on occasions to argue his claims to the position vacated by Hirata Atsutane in the *Kokugaku* lineage. He wrote his *Gakutō Benron* (*Ōkuni Takamasa Zenshū* (hereafter *Zenshū*)) (Tōkyō, Yūkōsha, 1939, vol. 4) for this purpose.
13 The memorial, *Kenkin Sengo* ('Humble Ramblings'), is published in Haga Noboru, Matsumoto Sannosuke *et al.* (eds), *Nihon Shisō Taikei, 51: Kokugaku Undō no Shisō* (hereafter *Kokugaku Undō*) (Tōkyō, Iwanami Shoten, 1971), pp. 548–85.
14 On the *Jingikan* revival see Haga Shōji, 'Meiji Jingikan no Seiritsu to Kokkasaishi no Saihen' (jō), *Jinbungakuhō*, 49.
15 *Hongaku Kyoyō, Zenshū*, 1, p. 20.
16 Takeda, *op. cit.*, p. 117. For the coronation plans, see *ibid.*, pp.117–21.
17 Fukuba's handling of the Meiji *Daijōsai* is another example. His innovative approach was attacked by Yanō and others, and Fukuba responded by accusing them of being *kaika no bōgai* or 'obstacles to enlightenment' (Ehimeken Ōzu Chūgakkō Yōshōkai, *Yano Gendō Sensei Ryakuden* (Ehime, 1915), p. 45). On the Meiji *Daijōsai* see Takagi Hiroshi, 'Meiji Ishin to Daijōsai', *Nihonshi Kenkyū*, 300.
18 For a contemporary account of the *Hasshinden* controversy see Tokoyo Nagatane, *Shinkyō Soshiki Monogatari* in *Kokugakuin Daigaku Nihon Bunka Kenkyūjo Kiyō*, vol. 52, pp. 184–5. See also Yasumaru, *op. cit.*, pp. 120–1.
19 *Shinkyō Soshiki Monogatari*, p. 185.
20 Tokyo Nagatane, *Jingikan Senkaku Monogatari*, in *Kōkoku*, 355, 6, pp. 88–9.
21 Takeda, *op. cit.*, pp. 139–41.
22 See, for example, *Hongaku Kyoyō*, p. 60.
23 *Ibid.*, p. 3.
24 *Amatsu Norito Futonoritoko*, in *Zenshū*, vol. 7, pp. 227–8.
25 *Bunbu Kyojitsuron*, in *ibid.*, vol. 1, pp. 156–7.
26 *Shinshin Kōhōron*, in Tahara Tsuguo *et al.* (eds), *Nihon Shisō Taikei, 50: Hirata Atsutane, Ban Nobutomo, Ōkuni Takamasa* (hereafter *Ōkuni Takamasa*) (Tōkyō, Iwanami Shoten, 1973), p. 501.
27 *Gyoju Mondō*, in *Zenshū*, vol. 1, p. 79. Ōkuni writes that Norinaga and Hirata Shinto 'may be enough to convince Japanese people, but to convince foreigners they are insufficient.' (*ibid.*, p. 119).
28 *Ibid.*, p. 112. See also *Shinshin Kōhōron*, pp. 495–6 for a variation.
29 *Bunbu Kyojitsuron*, p. 128.
30 The following is based on his 'New True International Law' (*Shinshin Kōhōron*) in *Ōkuni Takamasa*, pp. 493–511.
31 *Gakuunron*, in *Zenshū*, vol. 4, pp. 79–80.
32 *Sonnōjōi Shinsakuben*, in *Zenshū*, vol. 3, p. 390.
33 *Sonnōjōi Isetsuben* in *Zenshū*, vol. 2, p. 362. On *shōjōi* and *daijōi* see also his *Shinshin Kōhōron*, pp. 504–5.
34 *Sonnōjōi Isetsuben*, p. 358.
35 Quoted in *Ōkuni Takamasa*, p. 646.
36 *Kyūjō Ichiran*, not paginated (I have used the Kokugakuin Daigaku manuscript copy).
37 *Gyoju Mondō*, p. 75. See also p. 97.

38 *Sonnōjōi Isetsuben*, p. 358.
39 *Shinshin Kōhōron*, p. 504.
40 See Tamagake Hiroyuki, 'Bakumatsu ni okeru "Shūkyō" to "Rekishi" – Ōkuni Takamasa ni okeru shūkyōron to rekishiron to no kankei o megutte', *Tōhoku Daigaku Bungakubu Kenkyu Nenpō*, 31, p. 90.
41 This translation of a passage in Hirata Atsutane's *Honkyō Gaihen* is by Donald Keene, who points out that Hirata lifted the passage almost verbatim from a work by Matteo Ricci. See Donald Keene, 'Hirata Atsutane and Western Learning', *T'oung Pao*, 42, p. 308.
42 *Koshiden*, quoted in *Kokugaku Undō*, p. 529.
43 E. Satow, 'The Revival of Pure Shintau', *Transactions of the Asiatic Society of Japan*, vol. 2, p. 72.
44 On this point see Harootunian's stimulating study of Tokugawa *Kokugaku: Things Seen and Unseen: Discourse and Ideology in Tokugawa Nativism* (Chicago, The University of Chicago Press, 1988), pp. 32 and 167.
45 Nagata Hiroshi, 'Fukko Shintō no Tokushitsu' in *Nihon Hōkensei no Ideorogï* (Tōkyō, Hakuyōsha, 1960), pp. 276–7.
46 *Ibid.* Nagata questions whether these religious aspects of Hirata Shinto are really attributable to Christian influence, as many scholars have suggested.
47 Mitoshi Kyōikukai (ed.), *Tōko Sensei no Hanmen* (Tōkyō, 1909), p. 72, and Fujita Toko, *Kōdōkanki Jutsugi*, in Imai Usaburō *et al.* (eds.), *Nihon Shisō Taikei, 53: Mitogaku* (Tōkyō, Iwanami shoten), 1973, p. 322. Interestingly, Fujita saw the influence of Christianity in Hirata's *Kokugaku, ibid.*, p. 265 and note.
48 In addition to the introductory section of Yano's *Kenkin Sengo*, see also his *Zen'aku Ōhōron* quoted in Nishida, *op. cit.*, pp. 338–9. Yano's biographer informs us that in the early Meiji period his Shinto ideas led to his being branded as a Christian (Yano Tarō, *Yano Gendō Okina Ryakuden* (Matsuyama, Matsuyamadō shoten, 1933), p. 140).
49 *Hongaku Kyoyō*, p. 451.
50 *Shintō Michishirube*, in *Zenshū*, vol. 1, p. 333. This statement is highly reminiscent of Confucius' 'You are born into this world, so devote yourself to it' (also quoted by the Mito scholar Fujita Toko (*Kōdōkanki Jutsugi*, p. 331).
51 *Shigo Anshinroku*, in *Zenshū*, vol. 5, p. 335.
52 *Naobi no Tama Hochū*, in *Zenshū*, vol. *2*, p. 126.
53 *Ibid.*, pp. 100–1.
54 *Ibid.*
55 *Ibid.*, p. 117. The best piece on Amaterasu in Ōkuni Shinto is Tamagake, *op. cit.*, pp. 102–10.
56 *Koden Tsūkai*, in *Zenshū*, vol. 6, p. 91.
57 *Yamatogokoro Ihon I*, in *Zenshū*, vol. 2, p. 127.
58 *Jingikan Hongi*, in Inoue Zuishi (ed.), *Ishin Zengo Tsuwanohanshi Hōkō Jiseki* (Tōkyō, Aoyama Kiyokichi, 1900), p. 38.
59 *Hongaku Kyoyō*, vol. 1, pp. 4–5
60 Quoted in *Ōkuni Takamasa*, p. 550.
61 My interpretation of Ōkuni Shinto differs fundamentally from that of Professor Harootunian who writes, for example (*op. cit.*, p. 346), that Ōkuni 'eliminated the sharp differentiation between ruler and ruled; . . . [and] had manoeuvred to displace the perceived differences between social classes necessitated by politics, and their consequences for order.' My understanding, however, is that his ethical Shinto aimed precisely at reinforcing the traditional social structure. He does not consider Ōkuni's own definition of Shinto as consisting essentially in the hierarchical principles of *chūkōtei.* Again he writes: 'Ōkuni saw the Imperial Office as secondary in significance to the creation deities and the community.' (*op. cit.*, p. 356). While this judgement applies to Hirata *Kokugaku*, it does not do so to Ōkuni

Kokugaku, Professor Harootunian arrives at his understanding here, without considering Ōkuni's *Bankoku Sōtei* theory in which the Imperial Office is primary.

62 See Takeda, *op. cit.*, pp. 131–8.
63 See above n. 48.
64 *Gokui Zonnensho, in Kansaikō Hōmu Yōsho Zanpen* (not paginated) (Iwanami Shoten copy).
65 See for example Haga Shōji, 'Shintō Kokkyōsei no keisei', pp. 11–12.
66 The pronouncement is translated in full in Kōno Shōzō, 'Kannagara no Michi', *Monumenta Nipponica*, vol. 3, no. 2.
67 *Sonnōjōi Isetsuben*, p. 348.
68 *Gyoju Mondō*, p. 112.
69 *Sekijubutsu*, in *Zenshū*, vol. 4, p. 164
70 *Yamatogokoro*, in *Zenshū*, vol. 3, p. 90.
71 *Sandōsanyoku Shōkuzusetsu*, in *Zenshū*, vol. 2, p. 299
72 *Sonnōjōi Isetsuben*, p. 347.
73 *Sekijubutsu*, pp. 166–7.
74 Yasumaru, *op. cit.*, p. 86.
75 *Shaji Onkaisei Onshuigaki*, in Kabe Iwao (ed.), *Otoroganaka* (Tōkyō, 1908), pp. 464–5.
76 *Satoshigaki*, in *ibid.*, p. 474.
77 *Shaji Onkaisei Onshuigaki*, p. 464.
78 *Kansaikō Hōmu Yōsho Zanpen.*
79 *Ibid.*
80 *Ibid.*
81 See for example Yasumaru, *op. cit.*, pp. 52–4. For further evidence of Hirata followers' involvement in local *haibutsu* activities see Yasumaru *op. cit.*, pp. 98–100, and Itō Tasaburō, *Kinseishi no Kenkyū*, vol. 1 (Tōkyō, Yoshikawa Kōbunkan, 1982), p. 59.
82 *Kenkinsengo*, in *Kokugaku Undō*, p. 582.
83 See above n. 3.
84 Muraoka Tsunetugu, 'Meiji Ishin no kyōkatosei to Hirata Shintō', in Ishikawa Ken (ed.), *Hatano Sensei Kentei Ronbunshū – Tetugaku oyobi Shūkyō to Sono Rekishi* (Tōkyō, Iwanami Shoten, 1938), p. 582.
85 For Aizawa's views of Christianity, echoed closely by Ōkuni, see Bob Tadashi Wakabayashi, *Anti-Foreignism and Western Learning in Early Modern Japan: The New Theses of 1825* (Harvard East Asian Monographs 126, Cambridge, Mass., Harvard University Press, 1986), esp. pp. 68–76.
86 *Bunbu Kyojitsuron*, p. 400.
87 *Ibid.*
88 *Kyūjō Ichiran* (not paginated).
89 *Shinri Shōgen* is one example. I have again used the Kokugakuin Daigaku manuscript copy (not paginated) of this work.
90 *Shinri Shōgen.*
91 *Ibid.*
92 *Ibid.*
93 On this see, for example, *Hongaku Kyoyō*, p. 15.
94 *Ibid.*, p. 30.
95 See my 'The Restoration Government's Anti-Christian Measures: The Question of Motive' (paper presented to the European Association of Japanese Studies Conference (Durham 1988)). The standard account of the Nagasaki affair is Urakawa Wasaburō, *Urakami Kirishitanshi* (Tōkyō, Zenkoku Shobō, 1943).
96 See *Dajōruiten*, 1, 21, 28.
97 In *Kansaikō Hōmu Yōsho Zanpen.*
98 *Ibid.*

99 *Ibid.* We have seen Ōkuni equate Amenominakanushi with *Tenshu* (the Christian God), but despite his identification of Amenominakanushi with Amaterasu, Amaterasu and *Tenshu* are here equated for the first time.

100 *Ibid.*

101 *Kamei Koremi Kaki* (Shiryō Hensanjo, Tōkyō Daigaku).

102 *Ōkuma Monjo* A4151, 15 (Waseda University).

103 Kabe Iwao (ed.), *Mokuen Fukub a Bisei Shoden.* (Tōkyō, Yōrōbunko, 1908), p. 73.

104 The Restoration government had declared the Christian proscription to be such a law (*eisei no teihō*) in the *Gobō no Keiji* published on April 7th 1868. See above n. 1.

105 See above n. 3.

106 *Ibid.*

7 The Korean Crisis of 1873 and early Meiji foreign policy*

M. J. Mayo†

*Source: *Journal of Asian Studies* 31 (1972): 793–819.

The clash in the Council of State, October 1873, over whether or not Japan should take military action against Korea (*seikan ronsō*), was crucial in the making of the early Meiji state – even more so than generally assumed. Viewed in the abstract, it posed the question of order and violence in the Meiji Restoration – how fast and how far Japan should go in radical change and with what risk in disruption and violence. It brought to the surface major differences among the Meiji leaders, not only over timing and tactics but in goals and policies. Beyond that, conservative and extreme reformers were more deeply divided than most of them cared to admit in their vision of Japan as an enlightened, prosperous, and independent nation. Their quarrel over principles was furthermore intertwined with a struggle for power – which ideas and which cliques would control the politics of Japan's renovation. All parties to the dispute experienced considerable anguish, but when it was all over a number of basic principles had been formulated which would guide domestic reconstruction and foreign policy through the next two decades.[1]

Although the emphasis here will be primarily on diplomatic matters, it is necessary to keep in mind – as did the Japanese – the broader questions of modernization and the interrelationship between domestic and foreign policies. The Korean crisis erupted shortly after the return of the Iwakura mission from its tour of the Western treaty countries and pitted the ambassadors (Iwakura Tomomi, Kido Takayoshi, Ōkubo Toshimichi, and Itō Hirobumi) against several prominent members of the caretaker government of 1871–1873 (Saigō Takamori, Itagaki Taisuke, Soejima Taneomi, Etō Shimpei and Gotō Shōjirō). Their confrontation began with the Korean issue but quickly turned into a substitute for the grand debate on policies and priorities envisaged by the planners of the mission back in 1871.[2] Theoretically, major reforms and new political appointments were to be held to a minimum in the mission's absence. Iwakura and his colleagues, although travelling abroad as envoys of the Emperor, considered themselves still very much a part of the home government, In December 1871, on the eve of the mission's departure, the ambassadors and the caretakers had signed a pledge to communicate regularly with each other and refrain as much as possible from drastic departures in policy. Both sides realized, of course, that problems requiring some independence of action would arise, particularly in connection with efforts by the central government to extend its authority into the newly designated prefectures (*haihan chiken*), but basic changes, for which there had been no provision, were to be avoided or postponed until the mission returned with its reports and recommendations.[3]

As it turned out, the caretakers did much more than merely guard the house or mind the store. Major laws were enacted in 1871–73: compulsory education, military conscription, and a revised land tax.[4] All of these measures, however, were well along in the discussion and even planning stage before the mission left and elicited few serious objections from the ambassadors.[5] But a host of lesser laws touching upon everything from hairstyles, clothing fashions, and the calendar struck them as rash or unwise. Kido often lamented in his letters home that much of such legislation was merely superficial enlightenment.[6] Also in the mission's absence, certain initiatives were taken in diplomacy which extended the frontiers of Japan and reflected expansionist sentiment. All of this, as agreed in the pledge, was reported to the ambassadors in a variety of ways, either by official correspondence, copies of the government gazette, or clippings from newspapers.[7] Other sources of information were personal messengers and an informant or two. Iwakura, for example, had a friend in the lower ranks of the Foreign Ministry, Ōhara Shigezane, who wrote every month with news about everything, including the latest palace gossip.[8] Twice at least, after receiving such reports, the mission flexed its political muscles, once to stop the Council of State from announcing reductions in *shizoku* or ex-samurai stipends and on another occasion to discourage the foreign minister from granting permission to foreigners to trade and travel outside the treaty settlements.

The most glaring violations of the pledge were the appointments of new *sangi* or councilors in the spring of 1873, and the reorganized Council's subsequent decision in mid-August to accredit Saigō Takamori as ambassador to Korea with the full understanding that his mission would very likely provoke hostilities and lead to war. However, Saigō was asked to delay his departure until Iwakura's return. And the new appointments to the Council were less a power ploy than a desperate effort by Chief Minister Sanjō Sanetomi, a dedicated but not forceful chief executive, to keep the government functioning.[9] Heads of the various executive departments were competing to expand their powers and acquire a larger share of the budget, or threatening to resign when they failed to get exactly what they wanted. To increase the tension, there was throughout the spring and summer of 1873 a rapid rise in the number of agrarian riots and general disturbances. Japan was probably closer to social revolution than at any other time in the early years of the Meiji era.[10] Sanjō's panic over all of these problems and not specifically over the Korean question had prompted him to press Iwakura for the early release of Ōkubo and Kido from the mission. The two men did return before the others, in late May and late June respectively, in answer not only to Sanjō's pleas but also to an urgent summons from the Council of State.[11] Once back, however, they stayed away from meetings of the now enlarged Council, although Kido as a *sangi* was entitled to participate and Ōkubo, still the minister of finance, was offered a promotion and invited to join the deliberations. Apparently, neither wished to be identified with any momentous decisions until Iwakura and the others were home, but they did begin to maneuver behind the scenes and to formulate their positions.[12]

All of this Iwakura learned in greater detail when he returned in September. He received a steady flow of visitors, read numerous reports and memorials, and became increasingly furious at the condition in which he found the country and the government. The caretakers, he believed, had unduly antagonized the populace with restrictive and incessant domestic legislation. Their foreign policy was dangerous and ill-inconceived. To Samejima Hisanobu, the young Japanese chargé d'affaires in Paris, he wrote in disgust that the changes undertaken in his absence were in fact superficial, contrary to the glowing accounts he had been receiving during the trip of steady progress at home.[13] To the British minister, Sir Harry Parkes, with whom Iwakura was usually truthful if discreet, he admitted that

> the changes are not to my mind satisfactory. Much is said about progress but I find our progress is more superficial than real and that our recent administration is wanting in earnestness and permanence. Our measures must be better adapted to the actual condition of our people. It is a mistake to think that Japan is at present fitted to take rank with the nations of England and America. We have not yet acquired the requisite wealth nor the necessary degree of knowledge. And even in domestic matters the government though apparently successful in Yedo has caused great discontent in the provinces, and it is there that the efficiency of the Government is chiefly tested.[14]

Parkes thought such remarks were indeed sage, but Iwakura had more in mind than a humble confession of inadequacy to the British envoy. What he told Parkes would be in substance his position during the Council of State's debate in October. As a result of his journey to the West, he was extremely anxious to move Japan ahead but at an appropriate pace, or as he later said to change Japan drastically but without seeming to make changes. Widespread unrest, whether among the farming populace or the former samurai, he believed, could seriously weaken the Restoration government and frustrate its enlightenment program. Somehow conservatives would have to be won over to the support of radical reform and extremists persuaded to reflect more deeply upon the implications of basic change. Iwakura had found in the United States and Western Europe, or thought he had, much evidence to prove the wisdom of a rational, systematic, and gradual program of progress.[15]

Instead of turning directly to comprehensive planning or indulging for a time in abstract theories as to the best course for Japan to pursue, the ambassadors were forced to confront the immediate question of Saigō's proposed mission to Korea. Saigō had considerable backing within the government and from ex-samurai, particularly in the southern prefectures, who were enraged by stories of Korean insults to Japan and eager to combine adventure with employment at a time when their stipends were in question and a conscript army was being recruited.[16]

It is tempting to reduce the complicated arguments and politics of the Korean debate to a contest between Saigō and Ōkubo, two boyhood chums and *ishin* colleagues from Satsuma who now come to a final parting of the way and who symbolize the conservative and radical wings in the Restoration movement.[17] This does make the tale much simpler to relate and far more dramatic. However, Saigō was in league with persons who had far more to do with foreign policy in 1871–73 than he, foremost among them the foreign minister, Soejima Taneomi. On the opposite side, Iwakura and Kido were as important as Ōkubo in achieving the final victory. Itō Hirobumi and the Iwakura mission's allies within the caretaker government (Ōkuma Shigenobu, Inoue Kaoru, Yamagata Aritomo, and Kuroda Kiyotaka) played important supporting roles. Kido, in particular, has been unfairly criticized for fleeing from the fight, but he was in fact seriously ill. From mid-September to early December, he was bedridden with a variety of ailments, including partial paralysis of his legs. At times, he could not stand or even sit up. It was Kido, however, who had launched the counterattack even before Iwakura's return with advice to Sanjō to be cautious in foreign affairs and with the submission to high officials in August of a memorial warning against military ventures in either Korea or Taiwan.[18] In October 1873, Itō acted as his liaison man while Iwakura and Ōkubo assumed the burden of politics and debate.

Ōkubo's position was cogently expressed in his well-known seven point memorial (probably circulated among Council members in early October), answering Saigō argument for argument and raising far more profound questions on economic, political, and military matters than the advocates of the Korean venture seemed capable of.[19] Ōkubo, like Iwakura and Kido, had been much changed by his experience abroad and had come home even more deeply committed than before to economic modernization and considerably more sophisticated in his understanding of the measures to be taken.[20] Iwakura, a man of stronger will and fewer scruples than Sanjō, took over as acting senior councilor when Sanjō collapsed with "convulsive fits"[21] after a long night of useless pleading for a compromise with a stubborn Saigō and an equally adamant Iwakura. Thus it was Iwakura who made the final summation of arguments, on October 23, in the presence of the young Emperor. The documents do not say exactly how Iwakura persuaded the Emperor to reverse the previous decision, but presumably there was far more to it than the force of logic.[22] The backers of the Korean expedition resigned, leaving most of the basic decisions of the next few years and the implementation of the major reforms to the victors. The crisis and its settlement marked the beginning of the process by which Hizen and Tosa – never as fully committed as Satsuma and Chōshū in 1867–68 to the restoration of the Emperor by force or the elimination of the shogun from political life – would lose out in national power but become, as the critics and opposition, equally important in the modernization of Japan. Saigō returned to Satsuma and local politics only to emerge in 1877 as the reluctant leader of a full-scale rebellion against the Meiji leaders and their renovation policies.

I would like to summarize here the major arguments of both sides, first those of the caretakers and then of the ambassadors, and also the background of events leading to the controversy; for much was at stake in 1873 and Japan did come close to war. There were in fact not one but three foreign policy issues in dispute: Korea, Taiwan, and Sakhalin. By the time Iwakura returned, plans for a show of force were well advanced. Saigō and Soejima already had in mind an expedition of considerable size to Korea – as many as 50,000 men – and had earlier been thinking about still another one of smaller size to Taiwan – approximately 10,000 soldiers. For example, they proposed to land two armies of 25,000 on the northeast and northwest coasts of Korea, leave 10,000 in garrison to cut off support from Russia or China and march the rest of the troops south to the capital. They did not expect the Koreans to hold out for more than a hundred days and surmised that Korea, being rich in mines and silk, could thereafter support many Japanese soldiers.[23] In 1872–73, Saigō and Soejima had commissioned a few students, private agents, and military officers to gather intelligence on the continent and also in Taiwan where aborigines had killed Ryukyuan castaways.[24] Reports in the summer of 1873 of the latest in a series of Russian attacks on Japanese settlements in Sakhalin led to demands that troops be sent up north as well.[25] But it was the Korean question which in the end aroused the greatest emotion and passion and provoked the confrontation of October.

The Korean problem was hardly a surprise to the returning ambassadors, though the advanced stage of the war plans probably were. By 1873, resentment of Korea's treatment of Japanese envoys and merchants was deep and widespread. There had been much pressure both within the government and from outside, 1868–73, to punish the Koreans for refusing to accept the official greetings of the Emperor and to acknowledge the change from shogunal to imperial rule. Most of the militant talk centered on glory and prestige rather than security or trade, although the Japanese were indignant at the Deshima-like conditions in which Korea forced the small Japanese merchant community at Tōrai to live.[26] One of the last gatherings of the Council of State before the Iwakura mission's departure was devoted to a discussion of the latest Korean outrages.[27] When Commodore John Rodgers, commander of the American Asiatic Fleet, sailed from Japan in December 1871, he was convinced that the government was seriously considering war. "The Japanese," he wrote to his wife, "are anxious to invade Korea and I think may do it – but I am not sure. I know however that I did not talk on the side of peace between the countries."[28] The British chargé d'affaires, Francis O. Adams, a veteran of several years in Japan, had also heard from confidential sources that the Japanese might pick a quarrel with Korea and send a military expedition. He made a point of seeking out Iwakura and in words prophetic of the ambassador's own stand two years later, Adams warned against such measures, "for I could not but view such a policy as most dangerous in the present transition state of Japan, whilst vast reforms were still only in process of accomplishment, and at a moment when her whole attention should be devoted to internal affairs." Iwakura, he thought, seemed a little hesitant to talk about the problem but did give him positive assurance that the Japanese government had no intention of making war on Korea; all it had in mind was the dispatch of another mission in an attempt to establish direct diplomatic relations between Tokyo and Seoul and end the previous practice of relying upon intermediaries from the island of Tsushima.[29]

In April 1872, in much the same vein, Soejima reassured Adams that war with Korea would be a calamity to Japan "at a moment when she should concentrate all her energies upon internal affairs."[30] As foreign minister, Soejima's inclinations were at first quite in line with Iwakura's, and he sent one of his subordinates, Hanabusa Yoshimoto, to Korea in September on a steam transport convoyed by a war vessel to repatriate Korean castaways, end Tsushima's management of the trading post at Tōrai and evacuate some of the merchants and former officers, adjust claims in the Korea–Tsushima trade, discontinue any practices that might be regarded as tributary, forbid the use of the Korean king's seal on official Japanese documents, and reconfirm traditional rights under the old treaty of 1609. Hanabusa, however, was ordered not to provoke hostilities. He did have some difficulties with local Korean authorities, and word got around in the winter of 1872–73 that he was treated with discourtesy. Rumors of an impending invasion of Korea were circulating in Japan as early as February and March, 1873, reinforced by sensational items in the newspapers but not by warlike activities in the Army and Navy Ministries. *Shizoku* pressures upon the government to make an issue out of this mounted. Within the government, Soejima agreed that Japanese–Korean relations could not continue in this fashion, but instead of backing an expedition, he sent agents to Korea in early 1873 to gather more information about internal politics.[31]

Soejima, along with Saigō, may have had bigger plans for Korea ultimately, but his initial caution grew out of other anxieties weighing upon him in 1872–73. He had begun talks in the summer of 1872 with the newly appointed Russian representative in Japan, chargé d'affaires Eugene Butzov, on the Sakhalin question, continuing his predecessor Iwakura's policy of exploring ways to end joint occupation of the island. There was concern that strife between the Japanese and Russian settlers might entangle the two governments in war. Though its case was weak, Japan was still laying claim to at least half of Sakhalin as part of its Ezo territory and asking for division of the island along a north–south boundary line. Privately, Japan realized that Russia probably would never agree, for it already had many more settlers there and used the island as a penal colony. Japan could therefore try to settle for an equivalent in money or an exchange of territorial claims in Sakhalin for the Kurile Islands and thereby free itself to concentrate on the development of Hokkaido to which it had more right. In earlier exploratory talks, Iwakura had let it be known that he thought it wrong or dishonorable to sell territory for money, but probably he was much more worried about the domestic repercussions of seeming to give up Japanese territory or neglect national interests. And so was Soejima, who already had considerable diplomatic experience with the northern question when he became foreign minister.[32] If Japan were to relinquish the whole island, Russia would have to give ample compensation. On and off for several months, Soejima and Butzov discussed the obvious options – purchase, exchange of territory, protection of fishing and mining rights. There is also some evidence that Soejima went for higher stakes and requested Russian neutrality or even support should Japan find it necessary to take military action against Korea.[33]

Even more militant than all of the angry talk about Korea in the winter of 1872–73 was the movement generated in Satsuma to send an expedition to Taiwan and avenge the massacre of fifty-four shipwrecked Ryukyuans in a particularly horrible incident of December 1871. For a time, the Taiwan issue eclipsed the Korean problem. The Ryukyuans were now being spoken of as Japanese subjects even though for centuries their kings had been paying dual homage to the Chinese Emperor and the *daimyō* of Satsuma.[34] The Meiji government had been puzzling over a proper policy for the islands even since August 1871, when the domains were converted into prefectures and the *daimyō* ordered to live in Tokyo. Foreign Ministry officials were sent to the Ryukyus to inquire into the islands' relations with China and Satsuma. Soejima first heard about the murders from Satsuma officials and from Yanagihara Sakimitsu, whom he had sent to China early in 1872 to attempt revision of the Sino-Japanese treaty before ratifications were exchanged. The news so enraged Satsuma *shizoku* that several of them made the rounds of the Foreign Ministry and Army Ministry from September to November urging Soejima, Yamagata, and the Saigō brothers to organize a punitive expedition. Soejima responded by sending three agents to China, disguised as merchants, to gather information on political, economic, and military conditions; and soon Major Kabayama Sukenori of the Army Ministry was on his way to Taiwan to conduct a first hand investigation of the incident. In October, Japan unilaterally asserted exclusive sovereignty over the Ryukyus by incorporating them as a *gaihan* or outer domain of the central government, thus ending Satsuma's authority and theoretically China's as well. The Foreign Ministry assumed control of Ryukyuan foreign relations on October 30. (Soejima was incidentally also advancing Japan's claim to the Bonins.) In late October, therefore, when the American minister to Japan, Charles E. DeLong, introduced Soejima to General Charles W. LeGendre, the American consul-general at Amoy (1867–72), who was passing through Japan on his way back to Washington to lobby for a higher post, the Japanese were already talking about sending as many as 10,000 soldiers to Taiwan to punish the aborigines and seek redress.[35]

LeGendre's impressive knowledge of Taiwan, his previous success in negotiating a pact with the aborigines (1869), and his advice on overall foreign policy so impressed Soejima that he recommended the general's appointment as adviser to the Foreign Ministry with a high title and generous salary. In numerous memoranda, written between November and February, LeGendre gave extensive practical advice on an expedition to Taiwan and even encouraged the Japanese to colonize the aboriginal areas before one of the great powers grabbed the island. As he warmed to the subject, he included the Chinese settlements in Taiwan, the Chinese coastal city of Amoy, and Korea as regions into which Japan should expand and spread civilization.[36] The Foreign Ministry and Council of State, after much bickering, had already independently concluded that Japan must make a show of force in Taiwan against the Botans,[37] and LeGendre supported that decision as wise and humanitarian, adding that Japan should also seek ways to end these savage attacks on castaways. But first, he suggested, Japan should clarify China's relationship to the aboriginal territories. If China claimed it was the sovereign power, then it must, in accordance with the standard tests of international law, accept the responsibilities of such authority. If it refused to act or delayed, as LeGendre thought likely, then Japan would be justified in taking measures on its own. The American minister, DeLong, also spoke of Taiwan as a no-man's land and without authorization from the State Department led the Japanese to believe that the United States would be glad to see Japan, rather than another Western power or China, possess it.[38] More cautious advice was given by another American recently hired by the Foreign Ministry, E. Peshine Smith, graduate of Columbia College, holder of a law degree from Harvard, and a former legal claims adviser in the Department of State. Smith was deeply enamoured of Japan and took great pains to protect its interests and show no favoritism to the United States. In this instance, he urged the Japanese to consult first with China.[39]

In accordance with these suggestions, the Council of State in December 1872, authorized a mission to Peking with Soejima as the ambassador.[40] About this time, Saigō, who held concurrently the titles of Councilor, Field Marshal of the Army, and General of the Imperial Guards, left Tokyo to mend fences with Shimazu Hisamitsu, father of the ex-*daimyō* of Satsuma and still a powerful figure in the prefecture, and to report the news in Satsuma of the government's willingness to take action in Taiwan. Hisamitsu had not yet taken up residence in the capital as he had promised Iwakura in 1871 and was sharply critical of the new political system and military reforms. The conscription act had just been announced a few days before, and Saigō knew he would have to answer *shizoku* critics. He and Soejima also may have been worried about the consequences of an unauthorized expedition. Saigō too had seen the LeGendre memoranda and may have found reinforcement for his own inclinations. A contemporary account declares that all of Satsuma rejoiced at the prospect of a military show in Taiwan.[41]

The Soejima Foreign Ministry was taking strong action on long-standing and complicated diplomatic issues. But did this prospective mission to China and the separate decisions on Korea, the Ryukyus, Taiwan, and Sakhalin signify the adoption of a policy of aggressive expansionism in East Asia? Or were they, first, an elaborate effort to coordinate foreign policy and give Japan greater security and, second, to check domestic dissensions? Although there is a tendency to identify Saigō as the leader of the militants, Soejima had a much broader grasp of foreign relations and of domestic requirements. Before he was appointed foreign minister, he had handled capably a variety of diplomatic and political assignments, and although his tenure at the Foreign Ministry was relatively brief, he enjoys a reputation as one of the most outstanding foreign ministers of the Meiji era. The label generally given to his policies is not "expansionism" or "imperialism" but rather "national rights diplomacy."[42] Like Iwakura, but more aggressively, Soejima worked for Japan's acceptance as an equal by the Western nations and also by China and adopted a deliberate policy of protecting the nation's interests, prestige, and security. In addition to the measures already mentioned, Soejima in 1871–73 attempted to induce foreigners to accept Japanese jurisdiction in return for permission to travel in the interior. When the Peruvian ship, *Maria Luz*, docked in Tokyo Bay, Soejima at the urging of the British chargé, came to the defense of Chinese coolies on board and freed them not only to show Japan's friendly feelings for China but to make a show of humanitarianism and thereby proclaim Japan's moral equality with the West. Although his emissary to China in 1872 was unable to persuade the Chinese to make drastic revisions in the Sino-Japanese treaty, at least there was provision for mutual extraterritoriality. On his 1873 mission to China, he was quite aware of the prerogatives of an ambassador over ministers and chargés (as determined at the Congress of Vienna, 1815), and so insisted and eventually won appropriate recognition from both the Western envoys and the Manchu court. The Western diplomats had been working for thirteen years to solve the audience question (personal reception by the Chinese Emperor on a basis of equality and without performing the elaborate series of bows and kneelings known as the *kowtow*), but it was Soejima as the ranking diplomat who was received first in a separate ceremony.[43]

Later in his career and when he was out of office, Soejima did become a vigorous spokesman for continental expansionists, but there were signs in 1872–73 that he already supported a policy of limited aggression and colonization for reasons of security and glory. There was rather little talk at that time of so-called peaceful expansionist pursuits, such as trade and immigration.[44] Much more visionary than Soejima in this early period was the government's new adviser, General LeGendre. He did not put expansionist ideas into Soejima's mind so much as articulate them better and clothe them in the language of Western power politics. He helped to reinforce and further develop Soejima's ideas. LeGendre was one of those who taught the Japanese to see the world as many Westerners did, an arena of sovereign nation states in competition to extend power and promote profits. He also taught Soejima and other Foreign Ministry officials much more about the coordination of force and diplomacy, specifically the rules and concepts of Western international law, and thus rendered valuable assistance in the modernization of Japan's diplomacy. His advice was carefully supported with arguments and citations from such standard Western legal texts as Bluntschli, Vattel, Wheaton, and Phillmore. He helped Soejima anticipate the responses of his opponents and to prepare counter-arguments. The national rights diplomacy was almost as much Western-inspired as Japanese. The Foreign Ministry was well aware of the usefulness of Western rules and clearly had decided to accept and apply them in order better to protect and promote Japan's sovereignty.

The Soejima mission to China, March–July, 1873, and the subsequent debate over Korea, taken together, are the best evidence we have for assessing the strength and sophistication of expansionist sentiment in early Meiji Japan and for uncovering those ulterior designs to dominate Asia so repeatedly attributed to the Japanese. A great deal hung on the China mission, and it is important to sort it out as accurately as possible for the sake of the historical record and to gain more insight into international power relations in East Asia. The official and announced purpose, as stated in Soejima's letter to the Chinese government in December 1872, was to exchange ratification of the Sino-Japanese treaty and to secure an audience with the Chinese Emperor (Soejima had been briefed on the audience question and did intend to press the point of being personally received). After a delay of several months, probably because of the negotiations with Butzov over Sakhalin, threats from Peru over the *Maria Luz* affair, money problems, and some continued opposition in the Council of State, Soejima finally left for China in March, 1873, taking General LeGendre with him as an adviser on protocol and diplomacy and stopping in Kagoshima for a final check with Saigō.[45] He sailed at a time when *shizoku* sentiment in southern Japan was running high for a demonstration of power in Taiwan. Shortly before his departure, Soejima was in addition officially authorized by the Emperor and the Council of State to assert Japan's sovereignty over the Ryukyu Islands, ascertain the extent of China's control over aboriginal Taiwan, demand satisfaction for the murders of the Ryukyuans, and urge China to use its influence in improving Japanese–Korean relations.[46]

The aims of Soejima's trip were reported in full to Iwakura by the Foreign Ministry, Sanjō, and Iwakura's friend, Ōhara. Their official communications and letters left no doubt but that bold and possibly dangerous moves were under contemplation. As Sanjō wrote in January 1873, the Council had secretly agreed to take the necessary measures in Taiwan if China either neglected or refused to act against the aborigines. "This is a very serious step, but we have to do it. We can't lose the opportunity."[47] Ōhara sent a much more detailed account to Iwakura a few days later.[48] The international status of the Ryukyus, he said, was still vague, and Soejima was to establish clearly that the islands had come under Japanese jurisdiction. On current maps, Taiwan was labeled as China's possession, but the peninsula was occupied by aborigines and it was doubtful that China's administration actually extended that far. Soejima therefore was to discuss three possibilities with the Chinese:

1. China should punish the aborigines and obtain compensation for the families of the victims.
2. China and Japan should send a joint expedition to subjugate them.
3. China should entrust Japan with the task.

"We anticipate," he continued, "that the Chinese will give us a lively debate, but our ambassador is prepared to answer their assertion that the Ryukyus belong to China and therefore Japan has no need to interfere." The American, General LeGendre, had settled a similar problem between the Chinese and Americans a few years before and had been hired to advise Soejima. The foreign minister, he observed, wished to extend Japan's prestige abroad, and Taiwan was "the throat of Asia." The land was fertile, and the products abundant. Many European countries were ready to gobble up the island. Rather than allow that, Japan should subjugate Taiwan itself. However, China might object. A battle against the aborigines would give Japanese soldiers a good workout, but a war against China was another matter. The outcome was unpredictable. Japan's army was small, and money and supplies were scarce. "We are very concerned, but Soejima says that he has taken all of this into consideration and must go ahead with the mission, whether or not Sanjō agrees. Finally, Sanjō gave in." Ōhara ended his letter with assurances that troops would not be sent until Soejima had returned from his mission to China.

> However, Councilor Saigō is already in agreement with the argument to conquer Taiwan. The governor of Kagoshima, Ōyama Kakunosuke [Tsunayoshi], has prepared a memorial supporting this. There has been much dissatisfaction ever since the conscription law was announced and intentions to reduce samurai stipends. Ways to give vent to such anger outside of the country are under consideration. Up to now, Soejima has not yielded to general opinion but has stuck to his own ideas and has had much success in carrying them out. This will be the biggest event since our invasion of Korea in the 1590's. Japan's reputation will be much affected by it. If we succeed, the Emperor's glory will shine not only in Asia but throughout the world. We will show that our military force is as great as in the past. If we fail, we will invite contempt. So this will really be important.

Ōhara's letter reveals that LeGendre's arguments had been assimilated by many within the government. The Japanese had just about convinced themselves that China, by the tests of international law, had no jurisdiction over aboriginal Taiwan, and therefore they were fully justified in planning to chastise the tribes on their own. Nevertheless, they did not want to precipitate a war with China. They were expansionists but not fully-fledged imperialists in the sense that they were more deeply concerned about security and prestige than driven by the will to power or overseas dominion. Soejima, it is true, did envision the acquisition of the entire island of Taiwan by force and diplomacy, but he did not have an elaborate plan of conquest in Asia.[49] Nor did he speak for all of the Japanese, or even for all of the expansionists.

Once in China, Soejima fulfilled his ceremonial duties with considerable finesse, committing few diplomatic blunders.[50] The foreign community called LeGendre an adventurer, a mischief maker, and an unsafe adviser, but he had in fact superbly prepared Soejima for his role as ambassador.[51] Soejima exchanged ratifications of the treaty and had a personal audience with the Emperor but did not question the Ch'ing officials as closely and openly on Taiwan and Korea as LeGendre had advised and his instructions had indicated. He did have several conversations with Li Hung-chang, Governor-General of Chihli and Superintendant of the Northern Ports; Prince Kung, head of the Tsungli Yamen, China's new office for foreign affairs; and Manchu Grand Secretary Wen-hsiang, a member of the Tsungli Yamen and, in the minds of the Western diplomats, China's real foreign minister. Their talks were limited mainly to the Sino-Japanese treaty and the audience question and touched only in a general fashion on surrounding territories. In June, during a very tense moment when the Ch'ing government was still insisting upon the West's and Japan's acceptance of a demeaning protocol during the imperial audience, Soejima threatened to leave Peking and refused even to confer with Chinese officials. He kept his lines to the Tsungli Yamen open by sending subordinates, and it was during this period, on June 21, that lower echelon officials on both sides discussed rather cursorily the important business of Korea, Taiwan, and the Ryukyu Islands. Unfortunately, the records are not complete and there were no follow-up discussions, making it possible later for both sides to charge bad faith and for historians to argue that Soejima deliberately concealed his true aims from China in order to lay groundwork for Japanese aggression in Asia.[52] I cannot say with certainty that Soejima deliberately avoided detailed talks, but enough was said and implied for the Chinese to gather that Japan was seriously contemplating punitive measures against the Botans. Perhaps Soejima had come to believe that he did not need China's permission although he did wish to know its views.

Soejima subsequently acted as though he had arrived at a satisfactory understanding with the Tsungli Yamen. The agents he detached from his entourage and sent to Taiwan were expecting Japanese troops to arrive no later than October. From Peking, he wrote Sanjō, June 29, saying China had admitted that aboriginal Taiwan was beyond the administration and culture of China.[53] This technically was true, but by Chinese reasoning this admission was not a disclaimer of jurisdiction. Even though China did not control the aboriginal territory as completely as the Chinese settlements on Taiwan, nevertheless it was the suzerain power. As the tribes became more enlightened, they would be brought under full authority in accordance with practice elsewhere in the empire. The Yamen ministers had further argued that the massacres were not really Japan's business since the Ryukyuan victims had been the subjects of a Chinese tributary country. The officials of Fukien province were the proper authorities to investigate and recommend action. Li Hung-chang, when apprised of the interview on June 21, commented simply that the Japanese had been answered satisfactorily and besides were probably not strong enough to subdue the aborigines.[54] Perhaps he thought Japan would be held in check by the mutual pledge in the first article of the Sino-Japanese treaty not to encroach upon each other's territories and lands (*p'ang t'u* in Chinese; *hō do* in Japanese). Japan, however, had never interpreted the phrase to include dependent states.[55]

After his return, Soejima claimed in a conversation with Sir Harry Parkes that Wen-hsiang had unreservedly denied responsibility for the wild tribes. Japan could do as it wished. Moreover, Li Hung-chang, he said, had expressed sympathy with Japan's plight in Korea but lamented that China was too preoccupied with the Mohammedan troubles and with Russia in Ili to help bring about an improvement. Wen-hsiang too had explained that China had no jurisdiction over Korea. It was a tributary country but independent of China's control. Korea did not always follow China's advice, nor did it permit its envoys to be obsequious at the Peking court. Korea was in fact behaving almost as rudely toward China as to Japan. Finally, Soejima implied that Russia would remain neutral if Japan should find it necessary to send an expedition to Korea.[56] Until Russian documents are examined, it is impossible to say one way or another that there was "a deal" or "an understanding." If so, it was strictly between the two ministers and not their respective governments. Soejima did spend a lot of time in Peking with General Vlangaly, the Russian minister to China, and Vlangaly later stopped in Japan on his way home in October. Since Russia had claimed all of Sakhalin, presumably it would have been happy if Japanese militants concentrated on Korea and Taiwan.

Just exactly what the Chinese and Japanese did say to each other, officially and privately, in the spring of 1873 is of considerable importance, particularly since the Japanese are so often accused of duplicity or of conscious designs to expand at China's expense. China's world order and tribute system are generally viewed as benevolent and basically pacifist, but they were in fact based as much on power as on moral suasion.[57] Recent studies have suggested the "adaptability of Ch'ing diplomacy"[58] and drawn attention to the practical, pragmatic behavior of lower-ranking Chinese officials who had to put the tribute system into operation and act out the fantasy of China as the

Universal Kingdom.[59] The Tsungli Yamen had access to foreign legal experts too, preeminent among them Dr. W. A. P. Martin, whose translation into Chinese of Henry Wheaton's text on international law was already a basic work of reference in Japan's Foreign Ministry and being used with better effect than in China. It should not have been difficult for the Chinese to divine the full implications of Soejima's mission. The diplomatic community, including the American, French, and British ministers, knew of Soejima's other business well before the meeting of June 21, partly through conversations with the ambassador and partly from LeGendre's somewhat hyperbolic talk.[60] There were rumors, although denied, that Japan planned annexation of Taiwan and had designs on Korea. The Tsungli Yamen had already realized that the tributary tie would be difficult to maintain in the modern world and had warned Korea as early as 1867 (with Japan in mind) that "her safety, like that of China herself, lay in treaties in the West."[61]

I think that it is therefore fair to conclude that the Chinese government was indeed well aware of Soejima's ostensible and real objectives but had too many other domestic and foreign worries to deal adequately with Japan. They did not officially recognize the dual tributary relationship of the Ryukyus to Japan as well as to China, but they did know about it. To counter Japanese demands for redress of the Ryukyuan murders with the argument that this was none of Japan's business might make a good point in a debate but was foolish diplomacy. The Japanese were asking some hard questions about authority and the responsibilities of power which even the most orthodox Confucian statesmen should have been able to understand. And the Japanese were asking the Chinese to take a much closer look at the advance of the West in East Asia. In 1873 (and again in 1874), Chinese diplomats and officials answered Japanese arguments with much wit and skill but also with haughty contempt, for their responses were couched in the concepts and languages of the Confucian world order. And, one should add, in the proud language of conquerors, for the memory of Manchu victories against other Asians was strong. Japan's arguments, based on Western international law and diplomacy, were annoying and irritating. In accepting Western rules, Japan was not merely abandoning traditional usages but was rejecting China's claims to cultural supremacy. Soejima was a perfect adversary, for he was not only well-versed in Western views but well-acquainted with Chinese attitudes. He could quote Wheaton, but he could also cite the *Book of Rites* and the *Spring and Autumn Annals*. When the Chinese, for example, insisted on adherence to the classical rules (such as performance of the *kowtow*), he asked which ones? How about those in the *Spring and Autumn Annals* for negotiations between independent princes? The conditions of everything under heaven changed with the passing of time. Should not etiquette therefore change to suit the occasion? Graciousness and a spirit of friendship were more important than slavish adherence to traditional ceremony. In the five Confucian categories of relationships, missions of courtesy should come under the heading of friend to friend and not servant to ruler. If the guest, as representative of his sovereign, were asked to kneel, should not the host do the same?[62]

Although Soejima's China diplomacy was dazzling and had made a good impression on the foreign community, he found upon his return that Saigō had in the meantime shifted his primary though not exclusive attention to Korea.[63] Saigō seemed to be a man obsessed with the desire to avenge Korean insults, even if it meant his own death. This was a position he arrived at apparently in June 1873, when word had arrived in Tokyo of fresh and unspeakable outrages against the Japanese community in Korea. Placards had been posted forbidding Japanese–Korean contacts, wrote Hirotsu Kōshin, chief of the trading depot at Tōrai. Monyama Shigeru, another Foreign Ministry official with much experience in Korea, had recently returned to Japan and confirmed the stories. Reports were forwarded immediately to the Council of State (by the Acting Foreign Minister, Ueno Kagenori), along with recommendations that Japan send an army and navy to protect Japanese residents at Tōrai and an imperial envoy to bypass local authorities and deal directly with the central government at Seoul.[64]

Saigō felt compelled to do something big or dramatic in retaliation but thought Japan should send a special envoy – himself – before resorting to force. Apart from this, Saigō's ultimate intentions and ambitions are not totally clear, although it is possible to venture some observations. Much, for example, has been made of an alleged death wish, but his may have been the natural bent of a samurai who had been trained in the Bushidō sentiments expounded in the popular treatise *Hagakure* and wished to confront the enemy with his passions under control and his mind calm in the face of danger. Possibly Saigō was not looking for the best place or way to die but harbored some hope of actually settling the difficulties by negotiations, for he had previously demonstrated diplomatic skills in mediating a dispute between Chōshō and the bakufu in 1865 and in arranging the peaceful surrender of Edo castle to the imperial forces in 1868. If he did wish to die (among other things, Saigō was not in the best of health), or to expiate his guilt for contributing to the early Meiji reforms, or to give the samurai a last chance for glory, he must be absolved of the charge that his maneuvers were intended to gain power for himself and convert Japan into a military state along the lines of Satsuma. At the most, all he could expect was that others, after his death, would take over the government and change the character of the renovation.

Saigō was neither ignorant nor illiterate, as some of his detractors have charged, but his contemporary, Sasaki Takayuki, may have been close to the truth when he said that Saigō had energy for high principles but little political intelligence.[65] I am inclined to believe that Saigō was acting in the tradition of the late Mito school. As the spiritual heir to Mito Nariaki and Fujita Tōko, he hoped to reinvigorate and purify the samurai spirit by military action in Korea and thus revitalize the entire nation. To his mind, *bunmei kaika*, or civilization and enlightenment, as interpreted by the Iwakura mission abroad and Ōkuma Shigenobu and his young friends in the caretaker government, had brought corruption and demoralization. Japan could remain independent only if the ex-samurai led the country and all of the people followed the way of the samurai. Japan must preserve propriety, honor, and loyalty even in the modern age. It must not shed too much of tradition. It would be unfair to label him a jingoist, but he was motivated by a larger ambition for Japan to dominate Asia. Yet his was still an inchoate imperialism, based on the assumption that military action in neighboring lands and territorial expansion would enhance Japan's security. To protect Japan, he was quoted as saying, "we must advance to Korea; and to protect Hokkaido, we must advance to Possiette Bay."[66] What kind of control he had in mind is vague.

Soejima was won over, and if he and Saigō had been the only backers of a Korean expedition, the issues might be simplified more easily; but other prominent caretakers stood with them in August and again in October 1873. Certainly Minister of Justice Etō Shimpei, a man of great talents who was elevated to *sangi* in the enlarged Council of State, hoped to further his career by identifying himself with an expedition which would be outside of regular military channels and highly popular with the disaffected *shizoku*. Etō was genuinely concerned about the decline of the samurai, but he was also an expansionist who in 1871 had presented Iwakura with an outline plan of conquest in Asia to make Japan, as he explained, the equal of the great world powers and discourage Russian aggression.[67] During the October debate, he was to argue that failure to make use of this opportunity to avenge the nation's rights would weaken Japan's prestige, make it a laughing stock, and open the door to future danger. The powers would be tempted to push Japan around. Korea had insulted the nation's honor by mistreating the Emperor's personal envoy in contrast to Sakhalin where the clashes had been strictly between private Russian and Japanese citizens.[68]

Itagaki Taisuke, whatever his original motives (perhaps to strengthen the central government by strengthening its hold on *shizoku* loyalty and to gain personal power), did retreat somewhat during the October battle. He had already been involved in political reform in Tosa, including movements for a constitution and a representative assembly, and in the end told Saigō that political reforms were more important than an expedition.[69] He took his share of responsibility, however, for the policies of the caretaker government and resigned with Saigō and Soejima.

Hambatsu rivalries were also a factor in October 1873, but not crucial. Within the various *han* cliques there were also disagreements, and alliances which cut across regional lines were often formed. The Korean debate did not neatly resolve itself into a clear-cut battle of region against region, caretakers against ambassadors, or conservatives against modernizers. But the Iwakura camp did tend to be more innovative in domestic reform and anti-expansionist abroad than Saigō's following.

The responses of Iwakura and his allies to the plans of Saigō's group showed great singleness of purpose and reflected the influence of the trip on their perception of the world and Japan's place in it. It is quite possible that without the experience abroad the anti-expansionists would have felt under great compulsion to compromise on the Korean issue. Iwakura and Ōkubo returned with a better understanding of international politics and the instability of the world order, but even before the trip these two men had been a restraining influence upon Kido.[70] Halfway through the tour, Kido too began to shed his adventurist notions. They had all seen too much in the West to think that their chief goals in diplomacy, treaty revision and security of the frontier, would come easily or cheaply. They had a greater appreciation of the gigantic dimensions of modern transformation. And they had given up any lingering Confucian biases against industrial and commercial growth, the importance of law, and extensive foreign contacts.

The arguments of these three and their supporters behind the scenes and in Council of State debates were quite similar, and, since they are well known, I will treat them very briefly.[71] To Iwakura, Kido, and Ōkubo it was axiomatic that failure to achieve true equality with the West would, in the long run, be more of a threat to Japan's security and prestige than failure to punish Korea immediately. To be strong, whether at home or abroad, and to win revision of the unequal treaties, Japan for years to come would need to concentrate on domestic reconstruction. The ambassadors were deeply concerned about foreign policy but wished to put it into proper perspective. They insisted that the northern boundary question be settled before any measures were devised for Taiwan and Korea. To invade Korea was to court intervention by Russia, Soejima's assurances notwithstanding. If Saigō was so eager to prove his courage and avenge insults to Japan, why was he not also advocating an expedition to Sakhalin where Japanese property had been destroyed and Japanese subjects murdered by Russians? The massacre of the Ryukyuans by the aborigines of Taiwan was, of course, barbaric, but why make such an important issue out of this when the Ryukyuans were merely subjects of an outer domain whereas the colonists in Sakhalin were Japanese subjects? As Ōkuma had said a few months earlier, the Koreans were behaving more like children than responsible adults. Did one slap around children but not take on bullies like the Russians?[72] Even in Russia's case, it was better to resolve the problem by negotiation.

The trio also raised questions about funds for a military venture and the capacity of the Japanese people to support such an ambitious project. To placate the *shizoku* was to impoverish the commoners and to court violence at home.[73] This could only weaken Japan, not make it more secure. How could the government fund education, local administration, industry, the colonization of Hokkaido, and legal reforms if it became entangled in war? How could the Japanese call themselves truly enlightened or equal to the West if they fought the Koreans for glory but did not become truly wealthy and strong at home? Iwakura's following was unmoved by offers from *shizoku* groups to raise funds privately, gather the weapons, and volunteer for the fighting. Such an expedition would quickly get beyond Tokyo's control.

Thus while debating foreign policy, the ambassadors also were saying that it was necessary for Japan to determine what was essential at home. Long-range plans for the nation should not be disrupted by momentary passions. The government should act or not act as its ultimate goals required. All of this sounds very sane and rational, but it should also be remembered that this particular group of Meiji leaders wanted to promote extraordinary changes and was willing to push and prod the populace and risk a certain amount of violence to get things moving.

Do the above arguments suggest that both sides were actually in agreement on the ultimate desirability of expansion and differed only on timing? The returning ambassadors, it has been argued, were in fact latent expansionists who wished to postpone action abroad only until Japan was sufficiently wealthy and powerful to take on the job.[74] Often the implication, as in the case of Soejima's mission to China, is that the Japanese already had a blueprint at most or a dream at least to dominate Asia. This, I think, would be a false reading of the debate; certainly it is an oversimplification. There were undeniably many exponents of expansionism in late Tokugawa and early Meiji Japan, but as Iriye suggests, much of such thinking was abstract and naive.[75] Even Soejima's deeper comprehension of power politics was largely derived from LeGendre and other Western advisers and not based on extensive knowledge of the world. There was also a tradition of anti-expansionism (not to be equated with closed country isolationism necessarily), and in the early Meiji era many of those who had the closest contacts with foreigners tended to be of this persuasion. It is difficult to detect in Iwakura, Ōkubo – and also in Kido after 1873 – any strong imperialist drive. What they did share was an overweening desire for Japan's acceptance as an equal by the West.

On a practical level, Iwakura recognized that to defend Japan, there must be a professional military establishment, superior weapons and ammunition, and modern transportation facilities. But it does not follow that he anticipated a program of aggressive expansion once those qualifications were met. He wished to build up Japan so that it could take whatever measures seemed necessary, whether at home or abroad. The purpose of the wealth and power program (*fukoku kyōhei*), as he viewed it, was to create an enlightened state and society and not a military juggernaut. To stop Saigō in 1873 was not to postpone expansion but to change the direction of Japan's foreign policy, for in the future Japan and the world would be a different place with different problems. As Iwakura presented the case to the Emperor on October 23:

> We will not be able to restore our national rights without first making concrete achievements and establishing real power. To accomplish this, we must consolidate political control at home and expand our wealth. Our

> work will not have lasting results if we seek rash and hasty achievements. It was my wish to present a detailed program of reform after my return, but before I could do so the cabinet was confronted with this issue of the Korean expedition.[76]

Certain statements from that time have been singled out to prove that the victors in the Korean debate were simply biding their time. There is, for example, Yamagata Aritomo's famous reply to Saigō in August 1873 that the army was not yet ready for an expedition but might be in two or three years.[77] He made very much the same observation the following year when war with China over Taiwan was the issue.

> The army is not ready to extend Japan's authority to areas outside of the country. Or to fight with China. To do so our army would have to be prepared to fight abroad, defend the borders, and take action against Russia or other Western countries. We never know who will suddenly become our enemy. Today is not the time to fight but to control our anger and think of our higher duty. It will take time to build a foundation and make progress. Furthermore, the strength of a nation depends on the knowledge and industry of its people as well as upon military power. We cannot fight unless we have professional officers, trained soldiers, modern equipment, and adequate coastal defense.[78]

In both cases, Yamagata was trying to calm his political adversaries and give a rational military assessment rather than make promises about future foreign adventures. Neither was he against expansion. His logic was simply that a nation did as the circumstances dictated. In the international order, he saw Japan responding to, rather than, shaping those circumstances.

Another seemingly incriminating remark was Kido's comment: "Let us postpone matters for now. We can decide later what to do about Korea and Taiwan. It will not be too late to act when we are properly prepared."[79] Kido until his death in 1877 was a remarkably consistent anti-expansionist. When the question of Taiwan came up again in 1874, Kido was to argue that invasion and conquest were the law of the world but that governments had the duty of determining whether or not this was appropriate, urgent, or beneficial. To expand abroad might result in gain in the short run but not permanently. Those civilized countries which did have colonies were already under control at home and could afford to expend their extra energies abroad. But Japan could not do what it had to at home, let alone annex other lands.[80] Kume Kunitake, Iwakura's private secretary on the mission, wrote in his diary of the trip that nations with enemies close at hand, as in Europe, had to maintain large standing armies, but in truly civilized countries such armies were stationed at the borders and used strictly for defense.[81]

It is true that the anti-war faction in 1873 made no idealistic or moralistic denunciation of military ventures, expansionism, or imperialism. But how significant was this, given the world of that time – the East Asia of that time?

How much more aggressive, sinister, or atavistic did this make the Meiji Japanese than any other people, including the Manchus and the Chinese? To say that the Japanese were latent imperialists in 1873 and neglect to mention the blatantly expansionist British and Americans is not to make a telling point. Although the Western powers were primarily interested in trade, a streak of militancy and self-assertion had also brought them into East Asia. There was of course no group of wilful, unprincipled, evil Japanese officials deliberately plotting aggression. To insist on this, however, would be to reduce the conspiracy argument to the absurd extreme; obviously imperialism can take place without an elaborate plan of conquest or scheme of economic penetration. There were instead expansionist and anti-expansionist Japanese. Both groups were security conscious, exceedingly patriotic, and self-righteous. And they both had some influence upon foreign policy, with anti-expansionists managing to make the basic decisions during the early Meiji years. Iwakura, for example, was cautious and restrained; he did believe in the peaceful resolution of foreign issues, but also he did not back away from assertion of national rights or acquisition of frontier areas which he considered to be Japanese. Once these not so very startling points are established, the underbrush can be cleared away for a more probing analysis of imperialism in East Asia – Western, Japanese, and Chinese.

The decision of October 1873, to be cautious abroad and bold at home, was soon followed by the adoption of a comprehensive Asian policy. The government, dominated now by Iwakura and Ōkubo, decided, after an additional three months of thinking and listening, upon priorities in East Asia (settle all difficulties with Russia first and then send an envoy to Korea); upon the relationship between overall foreign policy and strictly Asian matters (treaty revision and equality with the West must take precedence over quarrels with countries in East Asia though not to the neglect of frontier security); and upon the interrelationship of domestic and foreign affairs (internal renovation should not be jeopardized by ventures likely to impoverish the nation or invite foreign interference). The Russian and Korean problems were settled much as Japan wanted, 1874–76. In early 1874 an ambassador was appointed to St. Petersburg and issued full powers to negotiate an exchange of Sakhalin for the Kuriles and to retain, if possible, fishing and mining rights.[82] Enomoto Takeaki left on this mission in mid-March and was successful in negotiating a treaty the following year. Japan was still wary of Russia but primarily for the latter's future rather than immediate ambitions and had concluded that it was better to develop and fortify Hokkaido than persist in claims to all or part of Sakhalin. Iwakura warned the Emperor in a memorial of 1875 that Russia would bear careful watching, for it was a vast and constantly expanding country. If Russia took China, Japan's teeth would lose their lips and grow cold. The two should help each other as the wheels of a cart or the wings of a bird.[83] Iwakura was to remain a firm adherent of the "lips and teeth" relationship with China for the rest of his years in the government.

In the case of Korea, the decision was to send lower-ranking Foreign Ministry officials to make yet another survey of conditions there rather than risk a rebuff to a personal envoy of the Emperor. Moriyama Shigeru returned to Tōrai in the spring of 1874 and found the authorities a little friendlier, mainly because of political changes at the court, but he concluded that Korea would never open its door without a show of force.[84] The British were also eager to bring Korea into the treaty system in order to block Russian designs in East Asia, and the Japanese, by 1875 if not earlier, had concluded that an open and independent Korea would better serve the ends of Japan's security than a closed Korea still tributary to China.[85] In 1876, in conscious imitation of Perry's expedition, Japan browbeat Korea into negotiating a treaty of friendship and commerce after first taking care to inform China and win its blessing. There was much warlike talk at the time but mainly outside of the government. The Foreign Ministry had no intention of involving Japan in full-scale military action.

Settlement of the Taiwan issue proved to be more difficult. It turned into a nightmare and made the fine words of October 1873, seem hypocritical. Quite suddenly, in late February 1874, Ōkubo and Iwakura authorized an expedition to Taiwan. Though belatedly adopted, the plans were carefully thought out, with much emphasis on the coordination of diplomacy and force. This partial reversal of the decision of October 1873 raises the obvious question of inconsistency or ulterior motives. Upon close examination the Taiwan expedition emerges as essentially a confession of political weakness rather than an expression of imperialist ambitions. Several things happened between October 1873 and February 1874 to shake Iwakura's and Ōkubo's confidence in their control of internal politics. Saigō and many of the Satsuma police officials and imperial guardsmen had resigned and returned to their native prefecture. *Shizoku* restlessness, in Tokyo and in the provincial towns, mounted; and petitions to reconsider the Korean policy were submitted to the government. Intelligence agents confirmed the unease, which further increased after the announcement in December of a scheme for the voluntary commutation of pensions. The men whom Saigō and Soejima had sent to Taiwan and Korea now returned and sought interviews with Iwakura and Ōkubo. LeGendre, still employed by the Japanese government, edited and rewrote his previous memoranda and added new ones, along with maps, for the use of Soejima's successors, contending as before that China did not control all of Taiwan. Then on January 14, 1874, there was an attempt on Iwakura's life. Action to repair the domestic damage was swift. Ōkubo and Ōkuma were appointed to study the Korean and Taiwan problems on January 26. The first news of rebellion in Saga arrived in Tokyo by telegraph on February 3. Three days later the Korean and Sakhalin policies, previously alluded to, were adopted at a special meeting of the Council of State at the injured Iwakura's home. And shortly after that, an expedition to Taiwan was decided upon. Organization of the expedition began in mid-February while the government was simultaneously moving to crush the Saga insurrection.[86]

The Taiwan affair should not be treated as an "abortive colonial venture,"[87] though that element was certainly not lacking, but rather as older arguments would have it: a safety valve. It was not for glory, prestige, or security so much as for diversion of *shizoku* rancor. Among these men, there was great hatred of Iwakura and of all the reform measures he stood for. Very likely there would have been no expedition had there been no assassination attempt or Saga insurrection. Even at best, the expedition was of very limited size (more a gesture to the *shizoku* than a means of employment) and therefore easier to control and less expensive than full-scale action in Korea – or so the government thought. To avoid antagonizing or alarming Peking, an envoy was sent (but not soon enough) to explain that the fighting would be confined to aboriginal Taiwan. Until challenged by the Tsungli Yamen, Iwakura and Ōkubo chose to believe LeGendre's argument that China ruled only half of the island and also Soejima's report that China had admitted as much.

The troops left Nagasaki in late April and early May, with the intention of getting the job done quickly and avoiding the summer heat, although at the last minute Iwakura and Ōkubo tried to stop them when they learned of the objections of the British and American ministers to participation by their nations before China's attitude was known. Soon it was the old story. An expedition with limited ends escalated and brought Japan and China close to war. Japan's attempt to combine force and diplomacy fell apart when the Chinese objected and claimed sovereignty over aboriginal Taiwan. The Japanese army performed adequately against the aborigines, but many soldiers later died of malaria. In the autumn, Ōkubo himself set out for China in order to straighten out the mess. He played a bold game and won, managing to make the affair look like a success and to cover himself with glory. Japan got an indemnity and strengthened its claim to the Ryukyus but conceded the sovereignty of Taiwan to China. The escapade convinced Iwakura and Ōkubo that their original inclinations were right. Japan's foreign policy should, above all, be geared to treaty revision and the protection of national rights by diplomatic means and not directed toward conquest in East Asia. There could, in fact, be no successful foreign policy – no true security – unless Japan underwent thorough reconstruction at home. And that remained the essence of official thinking for the next twenty years.[88]

NOTES

† The author, wishes to thank the university's Graduate Research Board for financial assistance. Portions of this article were read at the 1970 Midwest Conference on Asian Affairs, University of Indiana, Bloomington.

1 This standard interpretation of *seikanron* has been questioned by Haraguchi Kiyoshi. He argues that there was little difference between the parties to the dispute, however dramatic the quarrel, and that "it is difficult to find qualitative differences between the character of the government before and after the political changes" of October 1873. The anti-Korean expedition people "succeeded to and developed the policies of the caretaker government and did not make any

amendments which touched upon their fundamental character." See *Nihon kindai kokka no keisei* [Formation of the Modern Japanese State] (Tokyo, 1968), p. 168. Haraguchi's account of the activities of the caretaker government (*orususeifu*, a term used both by contemporaries and by Japanese historians to designate those in charge of the central government in the absence of the Iwakura mission, 1871–1873) is excellent, but he has glossed over the problems of early Meiji foreign policy and has a very poor understanding of the aims of the Iwakura mission, its relations with the caretakers, and its contribution to evolving modernization policies before and after the trip abroad. The radical reform programs would have been jeopardized had Saigō and his chief supporters succeeded in their bid for power, October 1873. Furthermore, the earlier reforms were not simply continued but rethought, refined, and amended. Haraguchi's mistake, I think, is to confuse decrees and legislation with implementation.

2 The aims of the mission were outlined in an exchange between Sanjō Sanetomi and Iwakura Tomomi, October 1871, *Iwakura kō jikki* [Authentic Records of Prince Iwakura], ed. Iwakura kō kyūseki hozonkai (Tokyo, 1927), II, 926–938; Japanese Foreign Ministry, *Nihon gaikō bunsho* (NGB) [Japanese Diplomatic Documents] (Tokyo, 1936), IV, 62–73.

3 The pledge may be found in several sources: *Iwakura kō jikki*, II, 948–952; NGB, IV, 102–103; Tokutomi Iichirō, *Kōshaku Yamagata Aritoma den* [Biography of Yamagata Aritomo] (Tokyo, 1933), II, 274–276.

4 The best summary is in Haraguchi, *Nihon kindai kokka no keisei*, pp.104–158.

5 This is my conclusion after a survey of the genesis of the major measures, 1867–73; the letters written by Iwakura and his colleagues while abroad; and the mission's politics and policies after returning to Japan. Ōkubo and Itō, furthermore, made a quick return trip in the spring of 1872 for new credentials and were therefore on hand for discussions of the conscription act and *shizoku* stipends.

6 A typical example of such sentiments may be found in Kido to the cabinet (*naikaku*), 8th lunar month 1872 (September 3 – October 2); Kido to Inoue Kaoru, October 16, 1872, Tsumaki Chūta (ed.), *Kido Takayoshi bunsho* [Papers of Kido Takayoshi] (Tokyo, 1929–31), IV, 382–388, 397–404.

7 The original documents were destroyed in a fire at the Foreign Ministry, 1873, but fortunately there is a virtually complete set of copies, including the official reports of the mission, in the library of the Naikaku Sōridaijin Kambō (Secretariat of the Prime Minister). The numerous items in this collection, *Ō-Bei taishi zensho* (Complete Records of the Mission to Europe and the United States, as listed in the *Dajō ruiten* catalogue), testify that the ambassadors were well-informed of events back home and kept tight reins on their political power.

8 Iwakura's correspondence while abroad is in Ōtsuka Takematsu (ed.), *Iwakura Tomomi kankei bunsho* [Papers relating to Iwakura Tomomi] (Tokyo, 1927–35), V, 97–320. Some very interesting additional letters have been published in *Meiji shiryō* [Meiji Historical Materials], I, III, VI (1959–61), a series of pamphlets sponsored by the Meiji shiryō kenkyū renrakukai.

9 A conclusion borne out by evidence presented in Haraguchi, *Nihon kindai kokka no keisei*, 145–148.

10 As indicated but not explicitly stated in T. C. Smith, *Political Change and Industrial Development in Japan: Government Enterprise, 1868–1880* (Stanford, 1955), p. 30. Brief accounts of the riots may be found in the 1873 issues of the *Japan Weekly Mail* and John Black's journal *The Far East*.

11 NGB, VI, 20; *Iwakura Tomomi kankei bunsho*, V, 265–266, 280; Katsuda Magoya (ed.), *Ōkubo Toshimichi bunsho* [Papers of Ōkubo Toshimichi] (Tokyo, 1927–29), IV, 508.

12 Evidence is in the Kido and Ōkubo diaries and correspondence: *Kido Takayoshi bunsho*, VIII, 129–122; *Kido Takayoshi nikki* [Diary of Kido Takayoshi], ed. by

Tsumaki Chūta (Tokyo, 1932–33), II, 406–424; *Ōkubo Toshimichi bunsho*, IV, 521–522. See also the letter of Godai Tomoatsu to Ōkuma Shigenobu, August 5, 1873, in the Ōkuma bunsho, MSS (Special Research Room, Waseda University Library), B213.

13 *Iwakura Tomomi kankei bunsho*, V, 320–324 (letter of September 19, 1873). He also told Samejima that there had been discussions about the conquest of Korea and an expedition to Taiwan, but there had been no action yet. The information on Soejima's efforts in China was still inadequate. However, "we can't ignore the riots in Sakhalin and must begin negotiations without fail."

14 Public Record Office archives, London, Foreign Office (FO), 46/168, no. 87, October 8, 1873, Sir Harry Parkes to Lord Granville (46 is the number for the Japan file, and 168 designates the volume in the diplomatic correspondence).

15 His views may be pieced together from his letters for 1872–73 in *Meiji shiryō* and *Iwakura Tomomi kankei bunsho* and also from the observations made by his secretary on the mission, Kume Kunitake, in *Bei-Ō kairan jikki* [A True Account of America and Europe] (Tokyo, 1878), 5 vols.

16 How much the *shizoku* were animated by arguments of national security or by the hard facts of economic distress is difficult to assess. It should also be remembered that there were numerous ex-samurai who did not revolt or disagree with the renovation policies.

17 An extensive analysis of the debate will be found in Hilary Conroy, *The Japanese Seizure of Korea, 1868–1910* (Philadelphia, 1960), pp. 17–77. This supersedes the standard but now much outdated account by Nobutaka Ike, "Triumph of the Peace Party in Japan in 1873," *Far Eastern Quarterly*, II (May 1943), 286–295. In Japanese language sources, there is a good survey in *Haraguchi Nihon kindai kokka no keisei*, 158–167; and a more detailed version in Masumi Junnosuke, *Nihon seitō shi ron* [Essays on the History of Japanese Political Parties] (Tokyo, 1965–1968), I, 115–212.

18 There are several allusions to his illness in *Kido Takayoshi Nikki*, II, entries from September 15 to December 6 (424–461). His memorial on Taiwan and Korea, August, 1873, is in *Kido* Tsunoda, *et al.* (eds.), *Sources of the Japanese* to the *byōdō*, another word apparently for *naikaku* (cabinet) or *sei-in* (central board of the Council of State).

19 *Ōkubo Toshimichi bunsho*, V, 53–64. English translations of the memorial are in Conroy, *Japanese Seizure of Korea*, pp. 47–49; Ryusaku Tsunoda, *et al.* (eds.), *Sources of the Japanese Tradition* (New York, 1958), pp. 658–662; and Masakazu Iwata, *Ōkubo Toshimichi, The Bismarck of Japan* (Berkeley, 1964), pp. 168–170.

20 Two articles by Sidney Brown support these conclusions: "Ōkubo Toshimichi: His Political and Economic Policies in Early Meiji Japan," *Journal of Asian Studies*, XXI (February 1961), 183–197; and "Ōkubo Toshimichi and the First Home Ministry Bureaucracy, 1873–1878," *Modern Japanese Leadership*, ed. by Bernard Silberman and Harry Harootunian (Tucson, 1966), pp.195–232.

21 So gossip in the foreign community had it, diary of Ernest Satow, entry for October 26, 1873, MSS. Public Record Office (PRO 30/33/15/4). Conroy speaks of a "broken blood vessel" in Sanjō's brain; see *Japanese Seizure of Korea*, p. 46.

22 *Iwakura kō jikki*, II, 80–83.

23 FO 46/168, no. 91 confidential, November 3, 1873 (reporting a discussion with Iwakura on October 28 and with Soejima the following day).

24 Hsü Shih-chieh, "Taiwan jiken (1871–1874)" [The Taiwan Incident, 1871–1874], *Kokusai seiji* (1964, no. 2), 40–41; Kabayama Sukenori documents, MSS, diary for 1872–73, in the Kensei shiryō shitsu (Room for Research on Constitutional History), National Diet Library, Tokyo.

25 Kuroda Kiyotaka, head of the Kaitakushi, the Colonization Office in Hokkaido, was so angered by reports of Russian attacks on Japanese settlements in Sakhalin

that he reversed his previous moderate counsel and recommended in a letter to the central government, September 2, 1873, that Japan do something about Russian violence (Kuroda documents, MSS, Kensei shiryō shitsu, National Diet Library). I suspect, however, that Kuroda's purpose was in part diversionary – to move the Saigō faction away from its Korean fixation and to suggest a bargaining point for negotiations with Russia over the boundary problem. The northern question is surveyed in Ōyama Azusa, "Meiji shoki no hokuhō ryōdo mondai" [Some Problems concerning the Northern Territories in Early Meiji Japan], *Kokusaihō gaikō zasshi*, 60 (1960), 39–67 (Special combined issue).

26 Tōrai was a walled enclosure in the village of Ch'oryang, a short distance north of the city of Pusan, the site of the original trading post; it was named after Tongnae, the prefecture in which the village was located. Because of its earlier history and proximity to the city, the depot is also often referred to as the Pusan trading post (see George W. McCune, "The Japanese Trading Post at Pusan," *Korean Review*, I [June, 1948], 11–15). Two complementary accounts in English of Japanese–Korean difficulties, 1868–73, are: Conroy, *Japanese Seizure of Korea*, pp. 17–50; and Frederick Foo Chien, *The Opening of Korea* (Hamden, Conn., 1967), pp. 18–23. The best source from the Korean side for late Tokugawa–Korean relations and the background to *seikanron* is Ching Young Choe, "The Decade of the Taewŏngun: Reform, Seclusion, and Disaster," Ph.D. dissertation, Harvard, 1960, pp. 391–484. A convenient survey in Japanese covering the years, 1868–1871, is Kobayashi Katsumei, "Meiji shoki ni okeru tairiku gaikō; shoki seikanron o meguru Kido to Iwakura" [Continental Diplomacy in Early Meiji Japan; Kido and Iwakura on Early seikanron], *Rekishi hyōron*, no. 107 (July 1959), 68–78.

27 *Kido Takayoshi nikki*, II, 118. Tokyo had recently learned of the refusal by local Korean authorities responsible for Tōrai (the prefect of Tongnae and the commander of Pusan Fort) to treat with an envoy dispatched the previous year; Choe, "Decade of the Taiwŏngun," p.464.

28 To Anne, December 8, 1871 (Rodgers Family Collection, Manuscript Division, Library of Congress). Rodgers had been questioned on several occasions by Iwakura and other officials about conditions in Korea. In particular, the Japanese were interested in the efforts of Frederick Low, American minister to China, and Commodore Rodgers to negotiate with the Koreans in the summer of 1871. Ernest Satow, secretary of the British Legation in Japan, believed that Rodgers had recommended war against Korea as a way of consolidating Japan's internal situation (diary entry, November 26, 1871, MSS, PRO 30/33/25/4). The American secretary of state, Hamilton Fish, was at this point inclined to rely on China to persuade Korea of the wisdom of treating the shipwrecked humanely but to honor Korea's right to refuse negotiations on the establishment of commercial relations (State Department, China Dispatches, no. 77, April 22, 1871, Fish to Low; microfilm, National Archives).

29 FO 46/143, no. 121, December 25, 1871, Adams to Granville. Adams surmised that there had been considerable support for war with Korea at a recent cabinet discussion. As Iwakura had indicated, however, another mission was sent early in 1872 to ask for a new treaty with Korea. See Choe, "Decade of the Taewŏngun," pp. 465–73.

30 FO 46/153, no. 64, April 1, 1872. Soejima's dismissal of a clerk named Maruyama Sakura in March, 1872, for privately plotting a bolder Korean policy (he was collecting money for weapons and a warship) lends credence to this assertion. The Foreign Ministry had assumed sole control over Japan's relations with Korea in September, 1871, shortly after *haihan chiken*, and Sō Shigemasa, ex-*daimyō* of Tsushima (now the prefecture of Iwabara), whose family had long had the responsibility of mediating between Korea and Japan, had been given a post in the ministry.

31 Instructions, Soejima to Hanabusa, NGB, V, 345 (dated September 20, 1872). A copy of the instructions and also of Soejima's explanation to the Council of State of Hanabusa's mission were sent to. the ambassadors, thus keeping them apprised of the latest attempts at a settlement. For Hanabusa's reception, see Choe, "Decade of the Taewŏngun," pp. 473–479. Much has been made of the so-called warship on which he travelled, but according to Grace Fox the Japanese navy in 1872 consisted of seventeen vessels which for the most part "were small wooden craft, out of date and nearly useless," *Great Britain and Japan, 1858–1883* (Oxford, 1969), p. 260. American Minister DeLong's dispatches to the State Department were contradictory and ambiguous. He first wrote that Hanabusa was under orders to submit to insult and to refrain from doing anything which might provoke hostilities (no. 286, September 30, 1872). Later, he said that the mission was a success. Hanabusa had been met with politeness, and there should be no immediate complications (no. 307, November 21). The next day, he charged that Korea had been consistently rude to Japan and "its punishment had been resolved upon." Hanabusa's trip had really been "planned and executed to mislead Korea into the belief that such an adjustment had been obtained as is entirely satisfactory to this country (no. 309, November 22). He further claimed on December 7 that the Japanese were lulling the Koreans into a false sense of security. R. G. Watson, the recently arrived chargé of the British Legation, reported Hanabusa's difficulties to his government, adding that "considerable discontent seems to have been excited amongst a certain class in this country by the uncourteous treatment to which he was subjected." Nevertheless, according to Soejima, the relations between Japan and Korea "would remain on the same footing" (FO 46/156, no.162, December 16, 1872). For the subsequent moves of Saigō and Soejima, see NGB, VI, 226–247; and Tamamuro Taijō, *Saigō Takamori* (Tokyo, 1960), p.131.

32 For a résumé of the negotiations, 1870–1873, see Ōyama, "Meiji shoki no hokuho ryōdo mondai," 41–45, 66; and Peter A. Berton, "The Russo-Japanese Boundary, 1850–1875" (unpublished essay, East Asian Institute, Columbia University, 1951), pp. 55–60. Primary materials include Soejima Taneomi documents, MSS, Kensei shiryō shitsu, document 82; NGB, V, section 6; and FO 46/140, no. 133, July 11, 1871, confidential, Adams to Granville (reporting Iwakura's remarks on the northern question to Sir Harry Parkes).

33 Conversation of March 6, 1873, NGB, VII, 323–33; Berton, "The Russo-Japanese Boundary," p.57.

34 For the dual status of the Ryukyus, vassal of Satsuma and tributary of China, see Robert Sakai, "The Ryukyu (Liu-Ch'iu) Islands as a Fief of Satsuma;" pp. 112–134, and Ta-tuan Ch'en, "Investiture of Liu-Ch'iu Kings in the Ch'ing Period," 135–164, chaps. in John K. Fairbank, ed., *The Chinese World Order, Traditional China's Foreign Relations* (Cambridge, 1968).

35 Details on the background of the Taiwan problem may be found in Kabayama Sukenori, MSS, document 267; Fujisaki Seinosuke, *Taiwan shi to Kabayama Taishō* [Admiral Kabayama and the History of Taiwan] (Tokyo, 1926), pp. 220–293 (this contains portions of Kabayama's manuscript diary, but there are some discrepancies in dates); Soejima MSS, document 67; NGB, VII, 5–15; Ōyama, "Meiji shoki no hokuhō ryōdo mondai," pp. 48–50; and Hsü, "Taiwan jiken," pp. 39–42.

36 LeGendre's earlier career and employment are well-treated in two articles by Leonard H. D. Gordon, "Early American Relations with Formosa, 1849–1870," *The Historian*, XIX (May, 1957), 279–287; and "Charles W. LeGendre: A Heroic Civil War Colonel turned Adventurer in Taiwan," *Smithsonian Journal of History*, III (Winter, 1968–69), 63–76. For more details, there is the impressive multiarchival study of Sophia Su-fei Yen, *Taiwan in China's Foreign Relations, 1836–1874*

(Hamden, Conn., 1965), 125–170. The English originals of the first set of LeGendre memoranda, 1872–73, have apparently been lost, but Japanese translations have been preserved in the Japanese Army and Navy Archives (JANA, T131, Microfilm Reading Room, Library of Congress); and in the Ōkuma MSS, Waseda University, some of which have been published in *Ōkuma bunsho* [Ōkuma papers] (Tokyo, 1958–), Waseda daigaku shakai kagaku kenkyūjo (ed.), 1, 17–40. There is an English summary in Yen, pp. 175–180.

37 As of December 9, 1873, according to the Kabayama MSS, document 267. Soejima had made up his mind at least by November 22, when the Council of State had urged him to postpone his project. There was opposition from Inoue Kaoru and Shibusawa Eiichi on financial grounds and from Ōkuma, who suggested commissioning an envoy to sound out China's attitude before sending troops (Hsü, "Taiwan jiken," p. 40).

38 On November 22, DeLong wrote to Secretary of State Fish that the Japanese government in response to the restless military had decided to allow a war either with China or Korea – or to permit an expedition to Taiwan. He insisted that he and LeGendre were urging the Japanese to try diplomatic measures before resorting to force and were succeeding. However, it is likely that the two gave more aggressive advice than DeLong thought it wise to admit to the State Department.

39 Secret, undated memorandum by Smith, copies of which have turned up in Soejima MSS, document 70; Kabayama MSS, document 263 (original) and document 264 (typed copy); and in JANA (T131, R34-F45153–66). I am inclined to agree with Yen (*Taiwan in China's Foreign Relations*, p. 200) that it was written during the following spring when the rationale for a Taiwan expedition was being reexamined but would add that it seems to reflect earlier opinions. Smith argued that if China could not or would not punish the aborigines, Japan had the right to do so. But first Japan should seek China's permission, for in the eyes of the world Taiwan was Chinese territory and a Japanese invasion would be regarded as an act of hostility. Even so, such action would probably win backing in the international community, since Japan was more likely than China to extend civilization to the savages. The Kabayama version concludes with the comment (probably Kabayama's) that Japan must possess all or part of Taiwan in order to protect the Ryukyus. In subsequent advice to Soejima's successor, Smith unequivocally stated: "Aboriginal tribes are subjects, whether quiet or turbulent, of the recognized empire which has taken and held possession of the civilized portion of the island." They were domestic dependent tribes under China's jurisdiction like the Indians in the United States. To invade Taiwan without China's permission was therefore technically a hostile act (March 22, 1874, Ōkuma MSS, A4505, C781). LeGendre contradicted him at length and won the support of another foreign adviser, the French jurist Gustave Boissonade, who said that LeGendre knew more about Taiwan than Smith and agreed that Japan's expedition was legal under existing international law (Ōkuma MSS, C452; *Ōkuma bunsho*, I, 49–74). The point of this lengthy note is simply that the Japanese were on the whole being encouraged by their foreign advisers, 1872–74, to believe that an expedition would be both humane and legal. However, there was still uncertainty, even among Western powers in East Asia, about the proper application of international law, itself a shifting collection of precedents, rules, and maxims; and the Japanese in mastering it would also develop a strong measure of cynicism

40 His initial instructions were issued December 19, and the following day the Foreign Ministry sent official notification to Peking (Yen, *Taiwan in China's Foreign Relations*, p. 169).

41 Saigō left Tokyo, December 10, 1872, and returned April 5, 1873. See Kabayama MSS, document 267. Hisamitsu and Saigō were not on good terms. When the Emperor visited Satsuma in the summer of 1872 on a royal tour, Hisamitsu had

sent a strongly worded memorial denouncing the central government's slavish acceptance of Western ideas and had refused to see Saigō, one of the attendants. Saigō, as much as the progressives, was responsible for a policy which was ruining the country.

42 Two good summaries of this view of early Meiji diplomacy are Haraguchi, *Nihon kindai kokka no keisei*, pp. 154–156; and Yasuoka Akio, "Meiji ishin to gaikō" [The Meiji Restoration and Diplomacy), *Ōkurayama ronshū* (October, 1968), 241–251.

43 This honor was not won easily either from the Chinese or the foreign diplomatic community (see Public Record Office, China Correspondence, FO 17/749, no. 156, July 7, 1873, Wade to Granville; no. 159, July 19; no. 163, July 21; 228/518, no.136, confidential, May 29, 1873). On the audience question and Soejima's role in solving it, the reports from American Minister Low are much less reliable than those from the British Legation.

44 To an economic determinist, peaceful expansion of trade is a contradiction in terms, but Akira Iriye puts the question of conspiracy, ad hoc response to events, imperialist expansion, and anti-expansionism into good historical perspective in "Imperialism in East Asia," James Crowley (ed.), *Modern East Asia: Essays in Interpretation* (New York, 1970), 133–138. Much in the same vein is my introduction, *The Emergence of Imperial Japan* (Lexington, Mass.; 1970), vii–xiv.

45 Soejima may also have been waiting for Saigō to return to Tokyo (Kabayama MSS, document 267). In the Council of State, Inoue Kaoru was worried about Soejima's capacity to make mischief while in China and thought it would be better to send a lower-ranking official whose words and acts could be disavowed if necessary. It would not be wise to get involved in a war while in the midst of internal reforms; letter to Ōkuma, March 1, in Watanabe Ikujirō (ed.), *Ōkuma Shigenobu kankei bunsho* [Papers relating to Ōkuma Shigenobu] (Tokyo, 1932–35), II, 37–38.

46 Final instructions and credentials were issued February 28 and March 9, 1873, including a letter from Sanjō advising Soejima to negotiate as the occasion demanded and to observe international law and justice (Yen, *Taiwan in China's Foreign Relations*, p. 181; JANA, T131, R-34, F44854–61). The Chinese were officially informed only of Japan's desire to exchange treaty ratifications and extend congratulations to their Emperor on his accession to the throne. Soejima was given full power credentials as an Envoy Extraordinary Ambassador Plenipotentiary, but the notice to the Chinese government did not make this clear.

47 *Iwakura Tomomi kankei bunsho*, V, 299–211. In this letter, Sanjō did not single out the Korean issue as crucial. He reported simply that Hanabusa had gone to Korea, handled everything well, and returned unharmed. DeLong had told Fish (no. 320, December 7, 1872) that Japan was also planning active measures in Korea, but I have found little evidence that this was so.

48 *Iwakura Tomomi kankei bunsho*, V, 212–222. The Japanese government was also very frank in divulging the aims of the mission to the diplomatic community. Soejima, for example, told Chargé Watson that his ostensible object was to exchange ratifications of the treaty but the more special purpose was to obtain satisfaction for the massacre of Ryukyuans in 1871 by Taiwan savages. "He added that if the Chinese government admitted their jurisdiction over these savages, they would doubtless punish the offenders, and lay an indemnity, but if they declined that responsibility the Japanese government were resolved themselves to take whatever measures might be necessary in order to obtain satisfaction" (FO 46/166, no. 64, March 7, 1873). Soejima would be equally open with diplomatic representatives in China. DeLongs report to Fish is in no. 323, December 20, 1873.

49 During the period of delay between his initial appointment and departure for China, Soejima spoke of taking the southern part of Taiwan right away by

negotiation and the rest of the island either by force or diplomacy within the next four or five years (letter to Ōkuma, February 17, 1873, *Ōkuma Shigenobu kankei bunsho*, 1, 32–33).

50 The best account, by far, of Soejima's activities in China will be found in Yen, *Taiwan in China's Foreign Relations*, 175–190; additional information, largely based on the LeGendre MSS, Manuscript Division, Library of Congress, is in Sandra Caruthers, "Charles LeGendre, American Diplomacy and Expansion in Meiji Japan, 1868–1893" (unpublished Ph.D. dissertation, University of Colorado, 1966).

51 British Minister Wade was very harsh on LeGendre, but was favorably impressed by Soejima (FO 17/631, no. 148, September 4, 1871; 17/654, 131, confidential, May 25, 1873). LeGendre reciprocated Wade's feelings, describing the British minister as a man of "irrascible spells and unjustifiable transports of rage" (letter to Orville Babcock, July 2, 1873, LeGendre MSS, Library of Congress).

52 Soejima's chief assistant, Yanagihara, and his interpreter met with two Yamen ministers and the Chinese intendant of customs at Shanghai. There are Japanese versions of the interview in NGB, VI, 177–79; and *Iwakura Tomomi kankei bunsho*, VII, 491–500 (Soejima to the Central Board, August 8, 1873); but I have not yet seen a Chinese set of minutes although I assume from Li's letters and comments made by the Tsungli Yamen in May, 1874, that there was a record of some sort (Yen, *Taiwan in China's Foreign Relations*, pp. 217–218; NGB, VI, 75–77). There is a partial English translation, omitting the remarks on Macao and Korea, of the Japanese record in Yen, pp.187–189. LeGendre gave Orville Babcock, President Grant's secretary, a résumé of the interview in his letter of July 2 (LeGendre MSS, Library of Congress). Research in Chinese archives and private records on the resumption of official Sino-Japanese relations in the 1860's and 1870's has so far been disappointing, and one can draw only tentative conclusions about Chinese motivations and diplomatic flexibility. The best account I have seen is in Albert Philip Ludwig, "Li Hung Chang and Chinese Foreign Policy, 1870–1885" (unpublished Ph.D. dissertation, Berkeley, 1936), pp. 119–162. It provides more extensive coverage than the much cited survey article by T. F. Tsiang, "Sino-Japanese Diplomatic Relations, 1870–1894," *Chinese Social and Political Science Review*, XVII (April, 1933), 1–106. There is sufficient indirect evidence to indicate that the interview took place substantially as described in the Japanese minutes but that both parties drew their own conclusions for their own purposes and were guilty of a certain amount of distortion. The lack of follow-up discussions, as indicated in the text, would seem to be the real source of the trouble and subsequent recriminations. Yanagihara did indicate that the Japanese were planning punitive measures, and the Chinese did stage military displays for Japan's benefit – or so the foreign community thought. However the Japanese were sufficiently stung by accusations of bad faith in 1874 to take greater care thereafter to sound out the Chinese. And the Chinese privately admitted to themselves (Li to the Tsungli Yamen, August 26, 1874): "The local officials of Fukien never seriously investigated and managed the case [of Taiwan]. No matter how they argue about it, China is not entirely in the right. . . ." (Yen, p. 251).

53 NGB, VI, 160. China also disclaimed control of Korean affairs, he wrote.

54 Yen, *Taiwan in China's Foreign Relations*, pp. 189–190.

55 Chien, *The Opening of Korea*, pp. 9–10.

56 FO 46/167, no. 67, August 25, 1873, and enclosed memorandum, confidential, August 20. I have no evidence yet that Soejima spoke directly with Wen-hsiang about Taiwan or Korea. In this conversation with Parkes, Soejima also mentioned sending a ship or ships to aboriginal Formosa within a month. American Minister DeLong credited unofficial sources (probably LeGendre) with the information that China had disclaimed jurisdiction over aboriginal Taiwan and Korea,

"leaving Japan free to deal with the barbarous inhabitants of each of these countries." They should both be under the Japanese flag in twelve months, he predicted, and their ports open to world commerce (no. 458, August 4, 1873).

57 The classic statement on China's world order is in John K. Fairbank and S. Y. Teng, "On the Ch'ing Tributary System," *Harvard Journal of Asiatic Studies*, VI (June 1949), 135–346. There is a succinct restatement in Immanuel C. Y Hsü, China's *Entrance into the Family of Nations* (Cambridge, 1960), pp. 3–16. Although I am by no means expert in Chinese sources, it does strike me that this view is overly Sinocentric and greatly idealizes traditional China's foreign relations, much as Americans are apt to impute more benevolence to the Monroe Doctrine or manifest destiny than was there. In their treatment of the aborigines, for example (on the mainland and in Taiwan), the Chinese policy was not so much one of *laissez faire* as first grabbing what they wanted and then magnanimously deigning to live and let live. The West has been accused of not understanding the complexities of the Chinese universal state, and this is true, but the Japanese were giving the impression of being just as confused about the difference between vassal and dependency relationships in the Chinese order and protectorates in the Western system of international relations. Chien reviews this question skillfully in *The Opening of Korea*, pp. 12–17; 212–213, footnote 58. Ping-ti Ho alludes to coercive Sinicization of non-Han ethnic groups in his remarks on the extension of China's internal frontiers, in "Salient Aspects of China's Heritage," *China in Crisis*, ed. by Ping-ti Ho and Tang Tsou (Chicago, 1968), I, 4–6. See also the remarks by Ho's discussants, 42, 52.

58 Mary Wright, "The Adaptability of Ching Diplomacy, The Case of Korea," *Journal of Asian Studies*, XVII (May 1958), 363–381.

59 Fairbank, *The Chinese World Order*. The Japanese Foreign Ministry (Gaimushō), though a very recent addition to the Japanese government, was already much more professional, far-sighted, and given to careful planning than China's Tsungli Yamen, which had been created in 1860 under pressure from the Western powers.

60 There is extensive evidence on this point. In the State Department, China correspondence, there is Low to Fish, no. 264, June 13, 1873. For British Minister Wade's dispatches, see: FO 17/654, no. 111 confidential, May 1, 1873; no. 131, May 25; no. 143 confidential, June 4; 228/518, no.136 confidential, May 29; 17/749, no.163, June 21, 1873; 17/655, no. 175, August 20, 1873; and 17/673, no. 74 confidential, May 1, 1874.

61 Wright, "The Adaptability of Ching Diplomacy," p. 380. Moreover, Li had reported to the throne, early in 1871, in reference to Japan's request for a treaty: "Japan is very near to us and will always be a danger to our country. I have learned that Japan, after concluding treaties with occidental nations, has purchased machinery and gunboats, imitated and built cannons, constructed railways as well as gunboats, and also sent men to Western countries to learn all kinds of technical arts and crafts. Their purpose is really a wish to be strong in order to resist foreign aggression. After all, Japan is near to us unlike the occidental nations. If we approach Japan with friendliness, it might be serviceable to us. If we refuse Japan, it certainly will become our enemy" (adapted from Ludwig's translation, "Li Hung-chang and Chinese Foreign Policy," p. 134).

62 FO 17/749, no. 193, September 10, 1873, translations of Soejima's letters to the Yamen, June 2 and June 4, 1873. NGB, VI, 163–165.

63 Letters from Saigō in July and August to his brother and to Sanjō reveal that he still supported the Taiwan project and wanted the government to decide upon it quickly but that it was no longer the main issue with him. See *Saigō Takamori bunsho* [Papers of Saigō Takamori] (Tokyo, 1923), Hayakawa Junsaburō (ed.), pp. 94–96, 272. Neither did Soejima give up the Taiwan expedition in agreeing with Saigō's wishes on Korea.

64 NGB, VI, section 6; Chien, *The Opening of Korea*, pp. 20–21; Tamamuro, *Saigō Takamori*, pp. 131–132.

65 Tsuda Shigemaro (ed.), *Meiji Seijō to shin Takayuki* [The Meiji Emperor and his humble servant Takayuki) (Tokyo, 1928), p. 277.

66 Cited by Oka Yoshitake, "Kokuminteki kokuritsu to kokkai risei" [National Independence and the raison d'être of the State], *Kindai Nihon shisōshi kōza* [Studies in the Political Thought of Modern Japan], VIII (Tokyo, 1959–61), 13. Conroy labels Saigō's policy "pro-war, pro-conquest, pro-expansion," in *Japanese Seizure of Korea*, p. 31. Tamamuro finds nothing new in seikanron, 1871–73. It was "a diplomatic strategy to stand against the Western countries by invading Korea." It was advocated in late Tokugawa times by Yoshida Shōin, Hashimoto Sanai, and Katsu Kaishū and it was heard again in 1871 at the time of *haihan chiken*" (*Saigō Takamori*, p. 127). I think it only fair to add that Katsu Kaishū's views, like Kido's, became much more moderate. There is an interesting and persuasive discussion of Saigō's role in Haraguchi, *Nihon kindai kokka no keisei*, 159–163. Saigō's medical problems (during the time of the Satsuma rebellion) are attributed by James Buck, without citation of sources however, to large body weight, the strain of fighting, and "the progressive enlargement of a hydrocele" ("Japan Last Civil War, The Satsuma Rebellion of 1877," *Military Review*, XL [September, 1960], 25).

67 Matono Hansuke, *Etō Nampaku* [Biography of Etō Shimpei) (Tokyo, 1914), II, 289–298.

68 Etō to Iwakura, October 15. 1873, *Iwakura Tomomi kankei bunsho*, V, 341–344.

69 Haraguchi, *Nihon kindai kokka no keisei*, pp. 164–165.

70 For the pre-mission views of Iwakura, Kido, and Ōkubo on Korea, see Kobayashi, "Meiji shoki ni okeru tairiku gaikō," pp. 68–73.

71 My résumé of the debate is based on the Iwakura, Kido, and Ōkubo documents for September–October, 1873 (diaries, letters, and memorials), all of which have previously been cited. Also helpful was FO 46/168, no. 91 confidential, November 3, 1873, Parkes to Granville. The American minister to Japan, John Bingham, was in the process of learning his job, and his dispatches to the State Department were quite inaccurate on internal politics.

72 "Opinion on our Sakhalin Policy," May 1873, *Ōkuma bunsho*, I, 208–211.

73 Haraguchi suggests that an invasion of Korea for the purpose of placating the samurai could just as easily have set off peasant rebellion because of resulting economic chaos. "If this view is correct, then the antiwar faction took peasant uprisings more seriously than the spectre of samurai revolt," *Nihon kindai kokka no keisei*, p. 167.

74 See W. G. Beasley, *The Basis of Japanese Foreign Policy in the Nineteenth Century* (an inaugural lecture, School of Oriental and African Studies, University of London, 1955), pp. 20–24; George Sansom, *The Western World and Japan* (London, 1950), pp. 347–349.

75 "Imperialism in East Asia," 134–137.

76 Iwakura kō jikki, III, 83.

77 *Kōshaku Yamagata Aritomo den*, II, 308. Katsu Kaishū, minister of the navy, was also not in favor of a war (FO 46/168, no. 91 confidential, November 3, 1873).

78 Ōyama Azusa (ed.), *Yamagata Aritomo ikensho* [Memorials of Yamagata Aritomo] (Tokyo, 1966), pp. 61–64 (July, 1874).

79 *Kido Takayoshi bunsho*, VIII, 132–133.

80 *Ibid*, VIII, 149 (February 1874).

81 *Bei-Ō kairan jikki*, III, 90–93.

82 NGB, VII, 420–21; Ōyama, "Meiji shoki no hokuhō ryōdo mondai," 53–58. Having denied that China controlled aboriginal Taiwan for lack of effective administration, Japan could hardly continue to claim southern Sakhalin. For an

indication of the research and thought which went into Iwakura's formulation of a policy, see *Iwakura Tomomi kankei bunsho*, VI, 256–263; VII, 446–553 (a survey of the Taiwan, Korea, Sakhalin, and Ryukyu problems).

83 *Iwakura kō jikki*, III, 224–225. LeGendre was still writing copious memoranda in 1874–75, and he urged the Japanese to give up Sakhalin, develop Hokkaido as rapidly as possible, open up Korea without delay, and watch the British as carefully as the Russians (December 23, 1874, C480, Ōkuma MSS, Waseda University).

84 NGB, VII, 208; Conroy, *Japanese Seizure of Korea*, p. 50; Chien, *The Opening of Korea*, pp. 22–26; FO 46/190, no. 33 confidential, February 22, 1875; FO 46/195, no. 165 confidential, December 6, 1875. In his February 22 dispatch, Parkes reported a long conversation with Moriyama before the latter's departure for Korea. The envoy's orders, he learned, were pacific. Moriyama was to try, as in 1874, to see higher officials and even to bring back a Korean envoy. He revealed that he had followed Perry's example with Japan in 1853 and given the Koreans notice of his return, but he confessed that he did not feel sanguine about his chances for success. Moriyama doubted that Korea could be opened without war and criticized the Japanese government for being too cautious. It would not even send him in a ship of war. Moriyama further claimed that he had "strongly advocated" war for some time. He realized that ships alone could not do the job and estimated that 20,000 troops would be required, one division to stay at the northern border and bar the Russians and Chinese and the other to march south and capture the Korean king. "But the object of such a campaign, he added, should be the opening of the country and not permanent conquest." Moriyama questioned whether Japan could conquer and hold Korea as the British had done in India; furthermore this probably would not pay. Parkes observed to the Foreign Office that Japan's ultimate policy would probably depend upon the results of Moriyama's probe and political conditions. Korea's treatment of the Emperor's envoys had now become a national question, and the Meiji government could not let wrongs pass unnoticed, just as Britain would not at Canton after the East India Company lost its monopoly. Korea's refusal to receive Japan's official representative was not unlike China's treatment of Lord Napier in 1834. The Japanese would have to exercise much forbearance in order to avoid a war with Korea.

85 FO 46/190, no. 24 confidential, February 8, 1875; 46/195, no. 182, December 31, 1875; 46/207, no. 123, July 25, 1876; FO 46/208, no. 163 confidential, October 11, 1876. When reassuring Parkes in February 1875, that Japan's motives in sending Moriyama to Korea were peaceful, Iwakura also stated that Korean independence was of the utmost importance to Japan and should be preserved. He elaborated upon this point in several conversations, 1875–1880.

86 Hsü, "Taiwan jiken," pp. 42–45; Yen, *Taiwan in China's Foreign Relations*, 194–205 (LeGendre's second set of memoranda were more militant than the first); Masakazu Iwata, *Ōkubo Toshimichi, The Bismarck of Japan*, pp. 179–183. Japan may have been encouraged to dispatch the expedition when it did to mitigate *shizoku* anger at the loss of Sakhalin as well as the cautious Korean policy. I have no direct evidence of this, but the British minister to China conjectured that DeLong had advised the Japanese government to indemnify itself with Taiwan should it give up Sakhalin or as the American "poetically put it'," Japan "should exchange the icicle for the sunbeam" (17/673, no. 77 confidential, May 6, 1874). It is a long standing contention that the Japanese gave up the north to concentrate on the south, but security of the frontier in all directions was important to them as the Hokkaido colonization efforts testify.

87 As does Leonard H. D. Gordon very strongly in "Japan's Abortive Colonial Venture in Taiwan, 1874," *Journal of Modern History*, XXXVII (June 1965), 174–176, but less so in his "Japan's Interest in Taiwan, 1872–1895," *Orient/West*, IX

(January-February, 1964), 49–52, where he points out the varied reasons and implies that 1874 represents an aberration in early Meiji foreign policy. I agree with his observation (p. 54) that Iwakura and Ōkubo took greater risks as they went along, but I do not believe that the major reason for withdrawal after 1874 was failure but rather lack of whole-hearted commitment to begin with. It is important to distinguish between the Soejima and Iwakura policies, for the post-October, 1873, administration did not automatically inherit the Taiwan project. Soejima did want Taiwan, or part of it, as a colony, and so did many who were involved in the subsequent expedition. LeGendre in his memorandum for Ōkuma, March 13, 1874, wrote that the ostensible object of the expedition was to punish the aborigines but the real goal was to annex the island (C426, Ōkuma MSS, Waseda University). LeGendre, however influential he may have been, was not the policy maker; and his advice was heavily tinged with a desire to hold a lucrative post in a colonial government for Taiwan. Iwakura was uncertain at first about proceeding from chastisement of the aborigines to subjugation and wrote to Ōkubo that Japan could decide later whether to keep anything. The Japanese army and navy officers, on the whole, were antiwar. Ōkubo was later reconciled to a strong policy, including the risk of war but for the purpose of winning recognition of Japan's right to punish the savages and securing an indemnity and not of colonizing the island. While getting ready for war, Japan was also making plans to cede to China any territory taken by Japanese troops (Hsü, "Taiwan jiken," pp. 42, 47; Yen, *Taiwan in China's Foreign Relations*, pp. 232–235).

88 I must add – cautiously – that this conclusion is of course open to criticism, for many of the crises and incidents in Japanese–Korean relations, 1873–1894, require closer study and few scholars have as yet assessed Meiji Japan's interest in other regions of East and Southeast Asia, such as the Philippines. Beyond that, there are much larger questions about the nature of traditional and modern expansionism.

8 Saigō Takamori in the emergence of Meiji Japan*

C. L. Yates

*Source: *Modern Asian Studies* 28 (1994): 449–74.

I

According to the view current among most Japanese today, the samurai lost their last hope of surviving as a distinct social or political group when Saigō Takamori died in the autumn of 1877. In fact, the fate of the samurai class had been sealed as early as 1866, when Satsuma and Chōshū joined forces to destroy the only institutional order in which the samurai had any functional meaning. Their disappearance from the Japanese stage was brought about by forces that Saigō helped to set in motion, but over which neither he nor any other individual could possibly have exerted much control. In the end he had no significant effect on the fate of the samurai.

Most Japanese, knowing but few of the pertinent details about Saigō or his life, understand him chiefly as the hero of 1868, the leader of the Meiji Restoration movement, who in 1873 advocated a Japanese invasion of Korea as a way to prove the value of Japan's hereditary warrior class, and thus to prevent their assimilation into modern Japanese society. When that scheme was thwarted by opponents in the Council of State, so the story goes, Saigō resigned from office and returned to his home in Kagoshima, where he subsequently gave vent to his frustration in a desperate attempt to overthrow the Meiji government, in whose creation he had played such a central part. That is, Saigō thought an invasion of Korea would demonstrate the military prowess of the samurai and guarantee them a lasting place as the defenders of the Japanese polity. Deprived of that opportunity, he then attempted to destroy the existing government, so that he could replace it with one committed to the survival of the samurai.

As portrayed in this conventional view, Saigō is 'The Last Samurai' and one of the more spectacular losers in Japanese history. For this reason, as Ivan Morris has argued, the Japanese regard him as a special kind of hero, not so much because of what he attempted to do, as because he went ahead with it even though he knew perfectly well that he could not succeed.[1] There is nothing particularly remarkable about such a view. The Japanese are surely not the only people who find the failed hero appealing. However, most Japanese also view Saigō as a successful hero, one of the 'Three Heroes of the Meiji Restoration,' along with Ōkubo Toshimichi and Kido Takayoshi. In the minds of many, the Meiji Restoration of 1868 – the event that gave birth to modern Japan – could not have happened without the labors of these three men, most especially the efforts of Saigō. And so we have the interesting paradox of a Saigō who lost his life attempting to prevent the emergence of modern Japan, and a Saigō without whom modern Japan could not have emerged at all. Or, to look at it another way, we have a Saigō who is a hero because he failed, and a Saigō who is a hero because he succeeded.

As Inoue Kiyoshi, one of his most able biographers, has observed, Saigō is 'a hero steeped in contradiction.'[2] Besides 'contradiction' (*mujun*), a word Inoue is far from alone in using to describe Saigō, most accounts of him also make faithful use of the obligatory terms 'tragedy' (*higeki*) and 'mystery' (*nazo*). All three terms fit well, and much of the fascination Saigō holds for the Japanese is to be found in the irreducible enigma he appears to pose. Indeed, Saigō seems so utterly shrouded in mystery that perhaps we may suspect only the Japanese can understand him. At any rate, many of them assuredly would like to see it put that way, if only because to do so would lend some credence to their highly prized sense of uniqueness. And yet, while most Japanese have heard of Saigō, and nearly all of them have some opinion about him, I have never met one who claimed to understand him fully. Faced with such persistent ambiguity, we might ask whether there is any point at all in our trying to comprehend this elusive man.

But surely, unless we want to be fatalistic about it, we must assume that he does make sense, and that he can be understood. Certainly some of the episodes of his life are confusing, but there is a pattern to his thought, his character, and his actions. And while these things may well be contradictory, tragic, and puzzling, they are not inexplicable.

II

Most of the writing on Saigō in Japan is characterized by a special mystique. It is as though all the important questions concerning his life had been decided already, before he was dead, and to write about him at any time since then has meant little more than to assemble a selective catechism of those questions, argued from one of a limited number of established canonical positions. Original approaches to these conventional positions abound in the Saigō literature. Original positions, on the other hand, are hard to find. It is as though the Japanese, through some arcane cultural law, had been rendered incapable of looking at Saigō in new ways.

The evidence to support these venerated canonical positions, moreover, is readily available, even though some of them are so diametrically opposed in their conclusions as to be mutually exclusive. That is because most of the primary material that has survived is sometimes vague, sometimes ambiguous, and sometimes incomplete, and always on just those points that are most hotly contended. There is not enough evidence, in short, to establish any set of conclusions about Saigō as unassailably more correct than others. The evidence can be used to support incompatible interpretations; it can even be used in support of flatly contradictory ones.

For example, in one widely accepted view, Saigō was the inspiring genius behind Japanese imperialism, and is directly responsible for half a century of military oppression in Korea, Taiwan, and China. In another view, he was the last pure repository of all that is essential, noble, and true in the Japanese character. Yet another view sees him as Japan's first authentic egalitarian, champion of the common man, and a lover of peace and harmony. Japanese thinkers as different as Uchimura Kanzō, Fukuzawa Yukichi, Kita Ikki, and Mishima Yukio have all ranked Saigō among the most admirable men in Japanese history.[3] How is it possible for one man to have so many faces, to appeal to so many different tastes?

The answer to this question is that there are two Saigōs.[4] One lived from 1827 to 1877; the other, born sometime during the 1860s or 1870s, lives on today. The first one, named Saigō Takamori, was an ordinary human being who accomplished some extraordinary things in his lifetime, and whose personality and presence were such as to leave an unforgettable impression on all who knew him. The second one, known as 'The Great Saigō' (*Dai Saigō*), is a legendary figure, a mythological being who emerged out of the ambiguities surrounding the words and deeds of the mortal man even before he died. Saigō Takamori became a legend in his own time, and as a result it is now quite difficult for us to perceive him except in his legendary form.

Even a superficial survey shows that most of the literature about Saigō in Japanese concerns this latter, legendary figure. As a result, to study Saigō is to confront yet another intriguing paradox: it is difficult to find the Great Saigō in Japanese history, and it is equally difficult to find Saigō Takamori in Japanese historiography. To be sure, those who write about Saigō have studied the primary evidence carefully, and this applies as well to novelists as to historians.[5] But somewhere between the research and the writing, the pervasive Saigō mystique begins to exert its influence. What results is yet another interpretation of The Great Saigō, and once again Saigō Takamori disappears into the shadow cast by his imaginary alter ego. One cannot find the real man in what his countrymen have written about him.

The Japanese have not tired of writing about Saigō in the century and more since his death. Consequently, there is so much material on him that one cannot examine more than a fraction of it.[6] Moreover, as I have suggested, most of that material is not about Saigō Takamori, but rather about The Great Saigō, and is therefore of limited value, unless one wishes to study only the legends, and not the man behind them. In the course of the six years or so I spent studying the evidence on Saigō, it became clear that the only way to find the historical Saigō is to concentrate on his letters and other writings, and to rely on the secondary literature only with caution. Peeling away the layers of the mythology in search of the real Saigō proved to be a convoluted and fascinating process, but in the end I found that, complex though he certainly is, Saigō Takamori is not as contradictory, as tragic, or as puzzling as the biographical and interpretive traditions in Japan would have one believe.

III

The ambiguities I have outlined above make of Saigō an interesting challenge for the biographer. For much the same reasons, Saigō also poses some difficult historiographical problems. So much confusion about the meaning of the man and his life inevitably has an impact on any effort to assess his meaning in the history of his times. This is especially so because Saigō was deeply involved in some of the decisive events of nineteenth-century Japanese history. These include the plot against the Tokugawa *bakufu* between 1864 and 1868 (*tōbaku undō*) and the Meiji Restoration of 1868 (*Meiji ishin*), but the two that concern Saigō's life most directly, and that remain at the center of ongoing controversy, are the confrontation within the government over Korea in 1873 (*seikanron*) and the Satsuma rebellion of 1877 (*seinan sensō*).[7]

Because these latter two episodes are of such fundamental importance in Meiji history, and because Saigō's part in them remains a matter of debate even today, Japanese historians often have difficulty deciding how to handle him in their accounts of the period. Some attempt to minimize his role in the events listed above, in contrast to others who treat them as if their entire significance consists of Saigō's part in them. Neither approach works very well. Taking Saigō out of the picture simply makes it incomplete. Whatever the actual importance of his contributions, he made them, and so they must be taken into account. However, it is equally fruitless to take the other tack, and reduce the picture to a portrait of Saigō, even if only because it would be practically impossible to make sense of what Saigō did except by reference to the context in which he did it.

In constructing a balanced biographical account of Saigō, one must try to avoid both extremes, and to resist the temptation to devote most of one's attention to these disputed issues. Instead, one ought to tell Saigō's whole life, as a whole, and in a balanced way, giving equal weight both to the major events and to the seemingly less important passages in between them. The assumption is that one cannot render any useful interpretation of Saigō's place in either seikanron or the Satsuma rebellion except by viewing those episodes as integral parts of a larger picture. Thus, I have shaped my own view of Saigō within the framework of a set of postulates about the meaning of nineteenth-century Japanese history. It is to those postulates that we must turn now, because the argument of this essay is as much concerned with them as it is with Saigō.

IV

Three processes unfolded in Japan between 1800 and 1900 that give the century its character. The first one was the series of efforts at administrative retrenchment and fiscal recovery known as the Tenpō reforms. These reforms began as early as the last decades of the eighteenth century in some places, and continued into the 1840s in others. They all took place in response to pervasive systemic dysfunction brought on by two centuries of economic and social change. Their success in Saigō's native Satsuma and a few other domains (*han*) did not alter the basic fact that Japan's early modern institutions had evolved into something new, and were no longer amenable to traditional methods of manipulation.

The second process was the appearance, in steadily growing numbers, of Western vessels in Japanese waters, culminating in Commodore Matthew C. Perry's arrival at Edo in 1853. These incidents served notice that Japan could no longer keep itself isolated from the rest of the world. In the crisis that followed Perry's arrival, it also became apparent that the Tokugawa government (bakufu), and the institutional network of quasi-feudal domains of which it was the central part (*bakuhan seido*), had outlived their usefulness. However adequate these institutions and relationships had been as a domestic arrangement, they were incapable of performing the tasks of a national government in an international setting. The history of the last decades of the Tokugawa bakufu (*bakumatsu*) is in the largest sense a chronicle of the search for a workable alternative to the bakuhan system.

These two sets of phenomena – the breakdown of domestic institutions and the appearance of alien forces at the boundaries of the realm – comprise the classic Chinese Confucian formula of internal disorder (*naiyū*) and external threat (*gaikan*). In the Chinese view, the development of such conditions signals the impending fall of a dynasty, Japanese thinkers applied this formula to their own situation, and understood their dilemma in just this way.

The third process, which grew out of the confusion and dislocation caused by the first two, was the Meiji Restoration itself, broadly conceived as the decade of transformation through which Japan went between 1868 and 1878.[8] This process began as a new phase in the ongoing search for an alternative to the bakufu, but the model that finally emerged was the Western-style nation state, with its monopolies on international relations, the redistribution of domestic authority, and the legitimate use of force.

The popular political slogans of the bakumatsu period – *sonnō jōi* (revere the emperor, expel the barbarian), *kōbu gattai* (union of court and bakufu), *fukoku kyōhei* (rich country, strong military), and others like them – were in essence no more than provisional hypotheses in a continually evolving discourse about the nature of the Japanese polity. The referent for these slogans, unknown at the outset, eventually turned out to be the centralized oligarchic bureaucracy of the Meiji state. In other words, what bakumatsu thinkers and activists were trying to do was to formulate a new conception of Japan, and this effort led them eventually to imagine and to set about creating the Meiji state. However, until at least the later 1870s, most of these men were not so much moving toward Meiji Japan as they were trying to find a satisfying way to move away from Tokugawa Japan. That is, they knew that what they had was no longer functional, but they did not have more than the vaguest of ideas about what should replace it, and their energies went primarily into the search for a way to disconnect themselves from the restraints of the existing order, so that they could begin experimenting with alternatives. Lacking a concrete and fully articulated vision of a new Japan, they could do little more than rely on slogans that suggested some of the characteristics of what they thought they wanted.

As most of them saw more clearly with the passage of time, centralization was what Japan's government needed most, and so it was that toward which they struggled. However, they could proceed toward centralization only after removing the obstacles presented to it by traditional structures and functions of government, which were incompatible with it. Viewed in the context of this halting and uncertain progress toward centralization, both seikanron and the Satsuma rebellion have the fundamental character of symptomatic episodes in the process of dismantling traditional Japan so as to make way for the emergence of centralized government.

These three processes – the attempt to arrest the breakdown of the baku-han system, the appearance of an external threat to the Japanese polity, and the response to both between 1868 and 1878 – are worth discussing in somewhat more detail. Such a discussion will clarify what I understand these phenomena to signify, and will help to illuminate my view of how Saigō fits into them.

V

By the start of the nineteenth century, Japan had, in effect, two economies. One was the commodity economy of the provincial ruling class, the daimyō, and the other was the money economy of the urban merchant class. The daimyō had to convert their income, in the form of rice and other commodities, into cash in order to transact business outside the boundaries of their han. However, because expenses tended to outrun income, and because urban moneylenders charged very high interest rates, most daimyō by 1800 were in debt, many of them too deeply to recover.[9] The same was true of the bakufu, which was in essence nothing more than an exceptionally large and complex daimyō domain. In the early decades of the century, both the bakufu and many han attempted to regain economic control by means of administrative, fiscal, and other types of reform.

Satsuma was one of the few han whose reforms succeeded, and this was mainly because its leaders were able to convert the han into a mercantile enterprise, and to compete successfully with merchant houses in Osaka.[10]

Other han sought to increase cash flow by stepping up commodity production and taxation, enacting sumptuary and frugality legislation, and mandating a return to the putative ethical purity of early Tokugawa society. Reform following these traditional lines tended consistently to fail, and among those failures was that of the bakufu. A few other han enjoyed some success, including Tosa, Hizen, and Fukui, and all of them contributed to the overthrow of the bakufu. But the most important successful reform, aside from Satsuma's, was in Chōshū. The solvency that came with success enabled Satsuma and Chōshū to modernize militarily, and that in turn put them at a decisive advantage when the time came to challenge the bakufu's right to rule.

However, the requirements for effective reform were incompatible with those for the maintenance of traditional ways of life and thought, and success came only to those han that were willing to sacrifice enough of tradition so that realistic solutions could work. Cultural values characteristic of the sixteenth century offered little leeway for administrative techniques amenable to the problems of the nineteenth century. As a result of this conflict between tradition and change, passionate and occasionally violent collisions took place between rival reform groups in many han, including Satsuma, but even those who succeeded in gaining the upper hand and carrying out change did not realize that simple restructuring of the existing system would not be enough.

Leaders in Satsuma and elsewhere were careful to make only as many changes in the traditional order as were required to restore and maintain solvency. They consistently and intractably drew the line at the wholesale dismantling of long-standing social and political relationships. They appear not to have realized that in order to perpetuate the economic and political successes made possible by their reforms, they would sooner or later have to repudiate the spiritual, cultural, and ideological elements of their traditional way of life, together with most of the customs in which those elements were embodied. They did not realize, in other words, that the need for reform arose from the irreversible failure of traditional institutions, and that therefore it was already too late to save the way of life based on those institutions. It was not until Perry's arrival raised another whole set of questions about the Japanese polity that anyone began to suspect just how inoperable the entire bakuhan system, together with its cultural ethos, had become. Even then, those who understood the stakes clearly were few in number.

The challenge posed by the West proved lethal, both to the bakufu and to the traditional society of which it was the center. As Conrad Totman has put it, '. . . the Tokugawa regime failed because the imperialist intrusion introduced a set of demands, most immediately political, that the existing system was fundamentally unable to handle. The upshot was that the old order collapsed.'[11] It was not just the Tokugawa government that was unequal to the challenge posed by the West, however, nor was that the only challenge to be faced. The decay of the bakufu went hand in hand with that of the bakuhan system and all of its components. Thus, when the collapse came, it came both to the traditional economy throughout Japan, and to the social relationships that economy had supported.

It was this dynamic mixture of political, social, and economic decay – at first perceived but not understood by reformers at home, then highlighted and exacerbated by the coming of the West, and finally accelerated forcibly and decisively through the deliberate intervention of a new group of Japanese leaders – that provided Saigō with the context in which he was to operate for most of his life.

The combination of internal decay and external threat had prompted thoughtful Japanese to realize that reform was going to have to take place on an entirely new order of magnitude. At first, attention focused on adapting the bakufu to meet the new challenges, and no one thought seriously of replacing it altogether until the middle years of the 1860s. However, tradition and established interest proved too deeply rooted, and had to be pushed aside forcibly so that the search for a viable new form of government could proceed. The destruction of the bakufu by an impromptu coalition of court nobles and samurai in 1868 cleared the way for the creation of a new kind of state, but nobody had any precise concept of the form it ought to take. Like many others, Saigō was sophisticated enough to realize that Japan must change profoundly or it would be overwhelmed by the West, and he worked as diligently and sincerely as any of his comrades to find an acceptable formula for change. Also like a good many others, though, he lacked the imagination to understand the implications such change would have for the traditional world in which he had grown up.

As Saigō was neither the first nor the last to point out, the bakufu deserved to be destroyed simply because in failing either to remove or even to control the Western powers, it had betrayed the trust of both the emperor and the people. Moreover, it had proved itself incapable even of controlling those under its authority within Japan.[12] What Saigō and many others did not realize was that this incapacity was not entirely the fault of the bakufu, or of its officials. Rather, it was a consequence of the strong local autonomy enjoyed by the daimyō under the bakuhan system. The han had always obeyed bakufu directives issuing from Edo, but if they chose not to, only military force could guarantee their compliance. Given widespread faith in the system, such an arrangement was no problem. But by the 1860s, thanks to the accumulated decay of two hundred years, the system was no longer able to inspire faith, and the bakufu, as it demonstrated in a series of embarrassing episodes, was no longer able to force obedience. Because local initiative had always belonged to the daimyō, and because the bakufu no longer had the military power to constrain the exercise of that initiative, it was unable to do anything when some han decided to combine forces in search of an alternative to bakufu rule.

VI

Having taken advantage of this fatal flaw in the bakuhan system to bring it to an end, Japan's new leaders after 1868 realized that the new government they were trying to create could escape the fate of its predecessor only if it could absorb all political initiative to itself. That meant creating new institutions capable of performing the roles assigned to them. And it meant securing unchallenged political authority for the development and administration of those new institutions. Before they could accomplish these things, moreover, Japan's new leaders had to agree on the nature and the relative urgency of the administrative problems they faced, so that they could determine the kinds of institutions to create, and the order in which to address problems. Failure to meet these challenges would mean the failure of the Meiji government, and would invite a repetition of the bakumatsu drama. Needless to say, it might also invite a more aggressive and less benign response from the West.

Thus, an array of closely related problems emerged to constitute the agenda of the Meiji leaders in the decade up to 1878. One of these problems was the consolidation of centralized power – the forging of a working relationship between center and periphery. Another was the distribution of institutional competence and personal authority. And these two problems demanded solutions all the more urgently because of a third – the need to establish a credible national identity for Japan in the international environment of which it had now become a part. Shaped by these problems, the first ten years of Meiji were a time of definition. Until 1868, disparate views of Japan's future had been subordinated to the need for cooperation in the struggle to gain power. Leaders in Satsuma, Chōshū, Tosa, Saga, Fukui, and other han had worked together in part because they understood that none of them could succeed alone. But the new Japan taking shape in the minds of Satsuma's leaders was quite different from that imagined by leaders in Tosa, Saga, Fukui, or Chōshū. Multiple and disparate visions of the future guided the leaders of the anti-Tokugawa coalition, and once these men overcame the bakufu and gained the power they sought, those disparities of vision came to the fore in a contest for control of that power.

The question of institutional competence – of the distribution of bureaucratic responsibility and the setting of national priorities – gave birth to a number of factions, which eventually lined up along a single axis of polarization. Those at one end favored immediate overseas expansion, while those at the other advocated domestic consolidation, and the issue was settled in the series of debates known as seikanron. The question of centralization – of the relationship between the central government and its local extensions – came to a decisive test in a confrontation between government leaders in Tokyo and the remnants of Satsuma's local government in Kagoshima, and ended in the Satsuma rebellion. These two outcomes, in turn, helped to clarify the problem of defining Japan's new international identity.

VII

To view the nineteenth century in the way I have portrayed it here, as marked by a series of major patterns, each of which is coherent within itself, and each of which leads into and informs the next, is to arrive at the two most controversial events in Saigō's life with a somewhat different perspective on both of them. It is to realize, in short, that Saigō's participation in both the seikanron controversy of 1873 and the Satsuma rebellion of 1877 is not the most important thing about those events. To be sure, it was important for Saigō, and his involvement gave those episodes a distinctive quality they would not have had without him. But both events derive their primary historical importance from their place in the process of centralization. In effect, something like both episodes undoubtedly would have happened in one way or another even without Saigō.

Viewed in light of the foregoing postulates about nineteenth-century Japan, seikanron becomes more than a debate over what to do about Korea, and more than a dispute about the relative urgency of internal and external problems. At issue was not the substance of the proposed military action against Korea, but the timing, and even more fundamentally, the question of who in the government should have the initiative in making policy, be it internal or external. No one in the government ever doubted Japan's right to take action against Korea, but it is just such a supposed division of opinion over propriety and justifiability that lies at the heart of the widely accepted view that in seikanron the government was split between a party favoring domestic consolidation and one urging overseas adventure.

Most fundamentally, that is, to the seikanron controversy was a power struggle within the emerging Meiji oligarchy, a part of the process through which they figured out who they were and how they would interact with each other. The main winner in this struggle was Ōkubo Toshimichi, and within the next few years he and his followers showed that it was not overseas adventure they had opposed in the seikanron debate. The Taiwan expedition of 1874 and the Kang Hwa incident of 1876 demonstrated eloquently that Japan's leaders had no aversion to gunboat diplomacy, and that the seikanron controversy was not about the propriety of Western style imperialism for Japan.[13]

In the same way, the Satsuma rebellion becomes more than the last and largest in a series of uprisings by samurai unhappy with the policies of the new government. Certainly samurai discontent was a key factor, and the outcome of the 1877 rebellion did settle the point that the Meiji government had no obligation to preserve the samurai class. At bottom, however, the rebellion and its suppression established the principle that a centralized government cannot allow more than a limited degree of local autonomy. Local interests, in other words, are subordinate to national ones, and local government may neither formulate national policy nor dictate it to the national government. The Satsuma rebellion can be viewed as no more than the last of the samurai uprisings only if one is committed to the thesis that all of the early Meiji uprisings by former samurai (*shizoku hanran*) were identical in motivation and social composition. Even the most casual comparison of those episodes quickly betrays the simplicity of that view.

The issues that arose in 1873 and in 1877 certainly were not inevitable, but the tensions of which they were symptomatic were integral elements in the centralization process. Japan's leaders built their state on the patterns they observed in the West, but with no more than a few visits to Europe and the United States in search of models, there was no reason for them to anticipate the problems they would encounter in adapting those models to Japan's needs. These were things they would have to learn from experience. They had begun in the 1860s with the need to forge a more unified government, so as to solve hitherto intractable social, economic, and political problems. And they were willing to take drastic steps, because they shared a conviction that the price of failure would be the absorption of Japan into the colonial empire of the West. But a firm determination to carry out change is not the same thing as a clear plan for doing it, and I think it would be a mistake to characterize their activities during the first ten years of their rule as anything other than trial and error.

The range of options at the disposal of the Meiji oligarchs was broad, and none of them had the experience or the insight required to make the most appropriate or effective choices. Most of them knew quite well from moment to moment what they wanted, even though their objectives were in constant flux. What they often could not foresee was what the consequences might be of getting what they wanted. Those consequences usually became clear only gradually and well after the event, altering the picture in unexpected ways and calling for further improvisation to avert disaster. For the most part, Japan's new rulers gave an exceptionally good account of themselves in this delicate and demanding political minuet, but some of them were more able and more willing than others to adapt to new circumstances.

Many who had been involved in the transition process since the 1860s had operated on the unacknowledged assumption that the social structure would continue as before, altered somewhat in form, perhaps, but not in substance. For the most part these men were of a different generation from those who had carried out the Tenpō reforms in the early decades of the century, but they were motivated by the same basic impulses. They were unable and unwilling to imagine a world dramatically different from the one in which they had grown up. Modernization, even Westernization, were fine as methods of restoring lost vigor to the old way of life, but they must not be allowed to supplant it, with their unrecognizable customs and their unpalatable values. Thus, for example, in the minds of men such as these, there might be radically new roles for the samurai to play in the new Japan, but the samurai would not disappear, nor would the moral leadership to which they were accustomed. As events began to prove such assumptions wrong, many of these men began to realize too late that they had done away with more than they were willing to do without.

This was nowhere more true than in Satsuma, where most of the steps taken prior to about 1866 were aimed at modifying the old order only enough to make it viable again. From 1866 to 1868, han leaders concentrated their attention on bringing down the bakufu. No one in Kagoshima realized that the world of the Tokugawa shogun, as the world in which the traditional values of Satsuma had evolved, was the only one in which they could exist. What happened in Kagoshima from 1868 to 1877 was fundamentally a series of desperate efforts to regain at least some part of what had been lost, to stem the tide of change sweeping through Japan before it wiped out everything recognizable.[14]

VIII

Saigō became involved in both seikanron and the Satsuma rebellion in part out of a belief that he could rescue some part of the world that he had himself helped to destroy. An important part of that motivation for him was, in fact, the desire to guarantee the survival of the samurai class, if a way could be found to do that without threatening the viability of the new Meiji state. However, Saigō's aims in the 1870s were both broader and narrower than the mere preservation of the samurai class.

They were broader in the sense that he wanted to help create a Japan that could hold its own in the confusing and perilous international environment, but at the same time one in which traditional values and the social relations informed by them could continue to function. Tokugawa Japan, in his eyes, had to be left behind not because its values had lost their force, but rather because its institutions had become incapable of perpetuating those values. And Saigō's aims were narrower in that they were intensely personal. Above all else, he needed to be able to see himself in his world, so that who he imagined himself to be would continue to fit convincingly into the context provided by the society around him.

Moreover, to whatever degree Saigō's motivation in 1873 and 1877 was more or less continuous, it is not that continuity that links seikanron and the Satsuma rebellion together most importantly in the larger tapestry of Japanese history. Rather, it is the character that both of them have as power struggles within the Meiji government. The continuity that runs from 1873 to 1877 is the dynamic of political centralization, and the wrenching dislocations it caused in the society of late nineteenth-century Japan.

To put all of this in the simplest possible terms, Saigō probably did not support the idea of a Japanese invasion of Korea in 1873, and he almost certainly did not hope to overthrow the Meiji government in 1877. Likewise, while the fate of the samurai class was important to him, it was not a major motive behind any of his actions after 1868. So then, if Saigō did not want these things, what did he want?

IX

In the weeks just prior to the seikanron debates in 1873, Saigō wrote a number of letters to Itagaki Taisuke, one of the most outspoken advocates of immediate military action against Korea.[15] In these letters, Saigō argued repeatedly that unprovoked aggression would be morally intolerable, and in any case would discredit Japan in the eyes of other nations, but that his own death at the hands of intransigent Koreans would give Japan a suitable pretext for retaliation. These letters are customarily taken as evidence that Saigō favored the armed seizure of Korea by Japan. His willingness to sacrifice himself to help bring that about is regarded as the decisive confirmation of that reading of his aims.

However, those who take this view have perhaps forgotten that Saigō made the same argument in support of his proposal to attempt a negotiated settlement of the bakufu punitive campaign against Chōshū in 1864.[16] He offered a similar defense for his attempt to prevent the terrorist attacks on officials in Kyoto that samurai from Satsuma and other han plotted in 1862.[17] And in 1868, when he met with Katsu Kaishū to arrange the peaceful surrender of Edo, the same rationale lay behind his actions.[18]

What he argued in these instances was that he should be given a chance to talk, and to work out a peaceful settlement. If talk failed, and the offending parties murdered him, then by that act they would forfeit their own right to fair treatment, and others would then be free to retaliate with honor. In all three episodes, then, Saigō's aim was to avoid violence, and particularly the risk of dishonor inherent in precipitate action, by means of persuasion, and he counted for success on the noble quality of his proposals, and even more on the sheer force of his own sincerity. His willingness to die, as he understood it, was nothing more than the proof of that sincerity.[19]

There is nothing in Saigō's writings to suggest that he had any taste for violent solutions. On the contrary, what he valued was what his heavily Confucian upbringing had taught him to value: harmony, order, and the maintenance of studied propriety and sober decorum in human relations. The pattern discernible in the above three episodes is that of a search for non-violent and mutually acceptable negotiated compromise. If patterns of behavior and motivation are more important than isolated episodes, then it would make sense to conclude that a negotiated compromise was what Saigō hoped to achieve in Korea as well. Out of such a settlement there could then emerge a voluntary association in which Korea would enjoy enhanced security from a Japanese military presence, arranged and approved by both parties, from which both would benefit.[20]

Saigō adopted Itagaki's rhetoric of violence, in other words, not because he approved of it or agreed with it, but because it was the simplest way to gain Itagaki's unqualified support in the Council of State, support that he knew he must have in order to win the chance to carry out his own aims in Korea, according to what he considered a proven formula. If the forceful seizure of

Korea was what Saigō really wanted, one would expect him to have applauded the gunboat diplomacy of the Kang Hwa settlement in 1876. In fact, as we have seen, he condemned that action as unnecessary, unjustified, and unpardonable.

Taking all the evidence together, we may find that we can accuse Saigō of paternalism toward Korea, but assuredly not of aggressive militarism, or of any lust for Japanese territorial aggrandizement. If the samurai class could benefit from the outcome Saigō envisioned, so much the better. But the future of the samurai was not the starting premise behind Saigō's thinking, and was in all likelihood a peripheral issue.

When Saigō's plans for Korea were frustrated in the Council of State, he withdrew from the government and went home to Kagoshima. This action is generally viewed as the first step in a plan to rise against the government.[21] The next step, in the conventional view held by nearly all Japanese scholars, was the establishment of the *shigakkō* school system, which is seen as a private army created expressly for the purpose of rebellion.[22] But again, a careful look at all the evidence suggests that this interpretation is rather artificial.[23]

As early as 1862, Saigō began speaking in letters to his closest confidantes of a desire to retire from public life, and he returned to this theme repeatedly in the following years.[24] His first concerted attempt to withdraw from public affairs came immediately after the end of the fighting in the civil war of 1868–69.[25] There is also considerable evidence that by the early 1870s his health was in such a poor state that he would have had little capacity for public service even if he still had entertained any taste for personal influence in politics. In the final years of his life, he seems to have been relatively free of physical discomfort only when completely immersed in the waters of his beloved hot springs.[26]

Once back in Kagoshima after the seikanron debacle, he spent little time in the city. Rather, like a man genuinely eager to have no more to do with the stress and confusion of public life, he withdrew to the countryside, where he spent his time hunting, working the land, and relaxing at hot springs.[27] Developments in Kagoshima between 1873 and 1877 were mostly the work of others, who looked to Saigō not so much for help as for inspiration. He lent his name and at least his passive support to those developments, certainly, but that by itself does not establish that he plotted rebellion. When angry samurai from other areas came to him asking that he join them in their uprisings, his reception of them was lukewarm at best, and more often overtly disinterested. Some authors suggest that Saigō was biding his time, waiting for the right moment, and his apparent lack of interest in politics was an elaborate ruse. But Saigō was neither that clever nor that patient. On the contrary, both his childhood schooling and his adult temperament gave him an impulsive streak that led him on several occasions to plunge – both figuratively and literally – into life-threatening acts. Had he entertained any genuine desire to do something as dramatic as to rebel against Tokyo, it is unlikely that he would have waited five years to begin.

Saigō supported the shigakko system not as a way to create an army loyal only to him, but rather as a way to inculcate samurai values in what he undoubtedly realized would be the last generation of birthright samurai. If those values could be perpetuated through education, then the hereditary social class with which they were associated could perhaps be allowed to disappear. With proper values, one could behave properly with or without the formal status of samurai. More immediately, with the right sort of education to strengthen their moral fiber, the young men of Kagoshima, whether still samurai or not, might be able to find service with the central government, and help even if only by example to keep some of the traditional values alive. When those whom Saigō had hoped to train for virtuous life in a new Japan chose instead to rebel in defense of the old Japan, Saigō's sense of personal loyalty to his provincial countrymen proved stronger than his sense of abstract loyalty to the government he had helped to create.

Thus he agreed to lead the rebel army, in the hope that he could convince his former colleagues in Tokyo to modify some of their policies. Moreover, persuaded that his boyhood friends had plotted to murder him, he wanted to confront them and learn the truth.[28] Saigō believed his friends in Tokyo had gone astray, in short, and he appears to have decided, at last, to go and remonstrate with them in the time-honored Confucian manner.[29] He believed that he had ample justification for challenging Tokyo; nowhere, however, is there any evidence to show that he wanted to destroy the Tokyo government, or to preserve the samurai class in and of itself.

X

Most interpretations of Saigō's behavior have one thing in common: the Saigō each presents is a contrived image made up of words and phrases chosen from his writings for what they contribute to the pre-ordained picture. Certainly one can take a sentence from here and a phrase from there and assemble almost any Saigō one wishes, be he militarist or pacifist, elitist or egalitarian, traitor or hero. But if one takes all of Saigō's six hundred-odd letters, memorials, poems, and other writings and attends to the patterns that appear throughout them with greatest consistency, most of the dramatic and one-sided interpretations of him are betrayed for the artificial contrivances that they are.

What emerges instead is a man whose most conspicuous features are the simplicity of his tastes, the unforgivingly absolute distinctions of his moral vision, and the unforgettable impact of his physical and emotional presence. We find no brilliant thinker, no awesome military genius, certainly no master of martial arts.[30] Instead, we find a rather ordinary man, remarkably sincere in his beliefs and impressively effective in persuading others to see things his way, but in the end also surprisingly unimaginative, old-fashioned, and downright prudish.[31] These qualities are confirmed repeatedly in the statements of those who knew him.[32]

Taking his own words and those of his associates together, we discover that Saigō became involved in public life not out of personal ambition, but rather out of an irresistible sense of duty to his superiors, primarily his immediate temporal lord, Shimazu Nariakira, and his ultimate spiritual superior, the emperor. He considered himself a samurai in the original sense of the term, as one who serves. Thus, he worked for the restoration of imperial rule because he believed that was what his master Nariakira had sought; and he dedicated himself to Nariakira's goals because that was what one did if one was a vassal of the Shimazu family. Whatever great visions of Japan's future we can find in Saigō's writings are those of the men who impressed him most: Nariakira, the Mito samurai Fujita Tōko, the Fukui samurai Hashimoto Sanai, and the Kyoto loyalist monk Gesshō.

Saigō labored, in other words, mostly to realize the ideas of others, not to carry out ideas of his own. Even his belief in the power of sincerity as a means of persuasion, and of personal integrity and honor as the only reliable guarantees of right conduct, can be traced back to his early upbringing and education in Kagoshima, as can his dedication to the search for non-violent solutions.[33] The durability of the 'Great Saigō' legend says more about the impressions the real Saigō Takamori made on others than it does about the lasting importance of his contributions to nineteenth-century Japanese history. Certainly his contributions were considerable, but there is no basis for the widespread Japanese habit of singling out Saigō as either the most admirable or the most despicable of Japan's nineteenth-century leaders. In the same way, there is no reason to allow the unresolved questions about his life to keep one from understanding the seikanron controversy or the Satsuma rebellion in their proper places as events of fundamental importance in the evolution of the Meiji state.

Thus the key point at issue in 1877 was between Kagoshima and Tokyo, not between Saigō and his former associates in the Meiji government. It had little to do with the frustration of Saigō's aims in 1873, or with the question of whether Saigō and the samurai class should continue to occupy the central place in Japanese society, or even the question of whether the centralized feudalism of the bakuhan system should continue in southern Kyushu. What Kagoshima's leaders hoped to preserve was their personal identities, and they meant to do that by preserving the social, economic, and political conditions that had defined those identities and given them meaning since before the bakuhan system had come into being. Certainly Saigō could identify himself with the spirit of that hope, even if we cannot say with certainty how he felt about the means ultimately chosen for its realization.[34] This sort of motivation was not unique to Japan, or to the samurai of Kagoshima; we need not look very far to find other examples of it.

It was this desire to protect the conditions of personal identity embodied in a particular way of life, as much as anything else, for which Robert E. Lee and tens of thousands of Southerners took up arms and fought so doggedly in the American Civil War. The rebels in Satsuma and in other parts of Japan between 1873 and 1877, though not political conservatives in any way analogous to those of our own time, nevertheless did share with Lee and his followers a set of motives which Russell Kirk, a leading American conservative thinker, has described as based on:

> . . . resistance to the destruction of old patterns of life, damage to the footings of the civil social order, and reduction of human striving to material production or consumption . . . For the conservative, custom, convention, constitution, and prescription are the sources of a tolerable civil social order.[35]

Despite the politically charged overtones of the term 'conservative,' that is, one may apply it to men like Saigō and his followers in Kagoshima accurately if one understands it in the above sense, as an impulse to fend off the unknown and the threateningly unfamiliar by protecting and preserving the known and the comfortingly familiar.

XI

Japan's leading historian of political thought, Maruyama Masao, has made a similar point, by drawing a distinction between being (*de aru*) and doing (*suru*).[36] As he intends the distinction, being entails synchrony, while doing entails diachrony, and Maruyama contrasts early modern and modern Japan on the basis of that difference. Saigō's character, as I understand it, was based on being rather than on doing, and he viewed the world as a synchronous phenomenon. His ethics, and the concepts of society and politics they demanded, were predicated on fixed and lasting relationships. When those relationships changed, as they did relentlessly between 1853 and 1877, Saigō fell prey to profound cognitive dissonance. Like his lifelong friends in Kagoshima, he realized that the world in which he found himself no longer made sense, in the terms he had taken for granted all his life, and that he therefore no longer made sense to himself either.

That discontinuity between Saigō's world and his understanding of himself ultimately proved fatal for him. If he had been left alone to spend the rest of his life hunting and trapping in the hills of the old Satsuma, fishing along its shores, and easing his many physical ills in its hot springs, he probably would have been fine, because he would not have been forced to come to terms with the new Japan that had emerged, with important help from him, out of the ruins of the old one.

Instead, men who looked to him for their own sense of authenticity forced the issue and began a war for which he felt responsible, even though he did not approve of it, precisely because those men had assumed that he would support them. This is a kind of honor that many nowadays would find hard to understand, resting as it does on the belief that a leader is responsible for the behavior of his subordinates, even when the behavior runs counter to his own wishes, but it lay at the heart of Saigō's morality, and in the end, he died for it. Indeed, nothing is more striking about Saigō than the constancy with which he adhered to the values that guided him throughout his life, values of loyalty, duty, service, integrity, sincerity, and honor. Not surprisingly, these are all values characteristic of the samurai, values which Saigō learned as a samurai's son in Kagoshima, and which he cherished right up until his death. In the end, it is these values, and the serious regard in which he held them, that provide the most effective means of understanding Saigō.

For example, many of his biographers, as well as many ordinary Japanese today, have made a great deal of Saigō's attitude toward death, as if his behavior could be explained by appeal to some peculiar obsession with dying. His unsuccessful attempt to commit suicide in 1858 is explained by reference to his expressed willingness to die in Korea fifteen years later, and vice versa, with artful circularity. Ivan Morris, employing the arguments of psycho-biography, has even postulated that Saigō suffered from a death wish. But surely there is a simpler and less exotic explanation.

At the start of the Ansei purge in 1858, one of those marked for arrest by bakufu agents was Saigō's friend and confidante, the monk Gesshō. This man was under the patronage of the court noble Konoe Tadahiro, whose family had a close and long-standing connection with the Shimazu of Satsuma.[37] Since both Tadahiro and Saigō assumed that the Shimazu would honor the requirements of that connection and hide Gesshō from the bakufu, Tadahiro asked Saigō to escort the monk to Kagoshima. When they got there, however, they found the leaders of the han paralyzed by their fear of the bakufu, and ill-disposed to protect a man for whom bakufu agents were searching in Kagoshima even as Saigō and Gesshō arrived there. Thus it proved impossible to offer Gesshō the sanctuary Saigō had thought would be his.[38]

Unable to protect Gesshō, and therefore unable to carry out the promise he had made to Konoe Tadahiro, Saigō saw no alternative but to atone for his failure by taking his own life. For centuries, suicide had been the method of choice among samurai for exonerating themselves. Nothing would have been more reasonable, given that tradition and Saigō's commitment to it, than for him to end his life along with the man he had proven unable to protect. Subsequent remarks, including his description of himself as 'dead bones in the dirt,' appear to support this explanation.[39] Certainly it is not difficult to find references to death and dying in Saigō's writings, some of them quite flamboyant and moving, but this does not distinguish him from most of his contemporaries, and it certainly does not provide a sufficient explanation for his behavior.

A man with no greater ambition than to retire and spend the rest of his life hunting and fishing is not a man obsessed with death. Such an ambition would be appropriate, however, for a man who believed that he had carried out the public duty required of him by his social status, but that it was no longer his place to remain in public office once that duty was done. Such an attitude, unlike the idea of an obsession with death, also has the merit of being consistent with other dimensions of Saigō's ethical code, and the obligation to behave with honor that lay at the heart of that code. That same sense of honor, and of its maintenance through orderly and principled conduct, could plausibly have led him to hope for a mutually agreeable negotiated settlement with Korea, which would obviate the need for conflict and its associated social and ethical chaos. And, as already pointed out, it obliged him to lead a rebel army of misguided young men, who had acted lawlessly in the expectation that he would agree to lead them once the die was cast.

If this interpretation leaves us with a Saigō who appears hopelessly old fashioned even by the standards of early Meiji Japan, that is as it should be. In this limited sense, moreover, it is appropriate to think of Saigō as 'The Last Samurai,' so long as we acknowledge also that it takes more than a sweeping appeal to samurai values to give a satisfying account of who the man was and what he did with his life.

By all the evidence, despite his capacity for occasionally violent emotion outbursts, Saigō was fundamentally a gentle man of uncomplicated tastes and a tolerant nature. The recollections of those who knew him as a father and as a teacher of children portray him as incurably soft-hearted, and he seems to have been unforgivingly strict only in his expectations of faithful adherence to the demands of honor, integrity, and sincerity, both in himself and in others. His program for the creation of a new Japan differed from those of his colleagues less in its final objectives than in the means by which they were to be attained. If he lost faith in the Meiji leaders, and finally lost his life in an ill-conceived attempt to confront them and persuade them to amend their behavior, it was not because he disagreed with their social, economic, or political goals, but rather because of what he saw as their dishonorable ways of pursuing those goals.

His aim, in short, both in the Korean episode and in the Satsuma rebellion, as well as in all of the other main events in his life, was to bring matters to an orderly and mutually acceptable resolution while protecting others in his social group, both peers and superiors, from the indelible stain of dishonor. The dynamics of his life arose from the fact that he had grown up in a relatively simple world where honor could still be the primary criterion for action. Unfortunately for him, it was also a world that was changing even as he grew up in it. Through his own efforts, he helped to bring it to an end, and the new world that took its place was one in which effective action would depend more on Machiavellian qualities than on Confucian ones. Needless to say, qualities of the sort enumerated by Machiavelli were not just beyond Saigō's ken; he found them repugnant, and his most withering condemnations were reserved for those who possessed and practiced them.

Between 1858 and 1877, Saigō's world changed beyond recognition, in no small part because of the things Saigō did, and so perhaps the greatest tragedy of his life is simply that he rendered himself obsolete. And it is out of that paradox that the contradiction and the mystery also arise.

NOTES

1 Ivan Morris, 'The Apotheosis of Saigō the Great,' in *The Nobility of Failure* (London, 1975). Also cf. Mushanokōji Saneatsu, *Great Saigō*, translated and adapted by Sakamoto Moriaki (Tokyo, 1942).

2 Inoue Kiyoshi, *Saigō Takamori*, 2 vols (Tokyo, 1970). Inoue's phrase in Japanese is '*mujun ni michita eiyū*,' *ibid.*, vol. 1, p. i.

3 Cf. Kawahara Hiroshi, *Saigō densetsu: Tōyōteki jinkaku no saihakken* (Tokyo, 1971).

4 Cf. Ueda Shigeru, *Saigō Takamori no higeki* (Tokyo, 1983), and *Saigō Takamori no shisō* (Tokyo, 1990).

5 Japan's historical novelists generally have made better sense of Saigō than have most of its historians. Cf., for example, Shiba Ryōtarō, *Tobu ga gotoku*, 10 vols (Tokyo, 1980); Kaionji Chōgorō, *Saigō Takamori*, 14 vols (Tokyo, 1980); or Hayashi Fusao, *Saigō Takamori*, 11vols (Tokyo, 1986).

6 Cf. Saigō Takamori zenshū henshū iinkai, *Saigō Takamori zenshū*, 6 vols (Tokyo, 1980), vol. 6, pp. 449–534.

7 Cf. Hilary Conroy, *The Japanese Seizure of Korea, 1868–1910* (Philadelphia, 1960), for the standard view of the seikanron episode of 1873. For the Satsuma rebellion, cf. Augustus Mounsey, *The Satsuma Rebellion* (London, 1879), and James Buck, 'The Satsuma Rebellion of 1877,' *Monumenta Nipponica*, vol. 28, number 4.

8 Cf. Umegaki Michio, *After the Restoration: The Beginnings of Japan's Modern State* (New York, 1988).

9 Cf. Tsuchiya Takao, *Hōken shakai hōkai katei no kenkyū* (Tokyo, 1927).

10 An excellent modern study of Satsuma's reforms is Haraguchi Torao, *Bakumatsu no Satsuma* (Tokyo, 1966).

11 Conrad Totman, *The Collapse of the Tokugawa Bakufu, 1862–1868* (Honolulu, 1980), p. 476.

12 Cf. *Saigō Takamori zenshū*, vol. 1, pp. 131–472, and vol. 2, pp. 23–534, *passim*.

13 Saigō, who supposedly had led the pack in pursuit of military action in Korea, condemned the Kang Hwa settlement in the most unsparing of terms, repudiating not only Japan's behavior in that instance, but also the propriety of gunboat diplomacy for the country in any situation. Cf. *Saigō Takamori zenshū*, vol. 3, pp. 479–81.

14 Cf. Mounsey's *Satsuma Rebellion*, as well as Kodera Tetsunosuke (ed.), *Seinan no eki Satsugun kōkyōshō* (Tokyo, 1945), and Kagoshima ken ishin shiryō hensanjo (ed.), *Seinan sensō*, 3 vols (Kagoshima, 1978–80).

15 These letters, eight of them in all, are in *Saigō Takamori zenshū*, vol. 3, pp. 371–95. Three of them have been translated in Ryusaku Tsunoda, Wm. De Bary, and Donald Keene (eds), *Sources of Japanese Tradition*, vol. 2 (New York, 1958), pp. 148–50.

16 Cf. 'Restoration and Rebellion in Satsuma,' pp. 244–63, for a narrative of Saigō's part in the first Chōshū campaign. Also cf. *Saigō Takamori zenshū*, vol. 1, pp. 405–10, 411–17, and 427–31.

17 'Restoration and Rebellion,' pp. 175–7. In *Saigō Takamori zenshū*, vol. 1, p. 192, Saigō explains that it was necessary to join these young terrorists on their 'field of death' in order to convince them of his sincerity.

18 Cf. 'Restoration and Rebellion,' pp. 320–2.

19 In the late summer of 1873, Saigō stated that, while he certainly did not covet long life for its own sake, he was likewise in no hurry to rush to his death, particularly since the emperor had taken a personal interest in his health. Cf. *Saigō Takamori zenshū*, vol. 3, pp. 390–1.

20 Like most of his other ideas, this one apparently did not originate with Saigō, but

with his daimyō, Shimazu Nariakira. Cf. Ichiki Shirō, *Shimazu Nariakira genkōroku* (Tokyo, 1944), pp. 147–50, and Nakamura Tokugorō, *Shimazu Nariakira kō* (Tokyo, 1933), pp. 245–8 and 252–3.

21 Among the most cogent and persuasive of arguments to this effect is Tamamuro Taijō, *Saigō Takamori* (Tokyo, 1960).

22 Again, the most interesting argument is Tamamuro Taijō, *Seinan sensō* (Tokyo, 1958).

23 John Stephan has also examined Saigō's role in the rebellion. Cf. 'Saigō Takamori and the Satsuma Rebellion,' in *Papers on Japan*, vol. 3 (Cambridge, 1965).

24 Cf. *Saigō Takamori zenshū*, vol. 1, pp. 202–3, and ff., esp. vol. 2., pp. 380–2, and vol. 3, pp. 25–6.

25 Cf. *Saigō Takamori zenshū*, vol. 3, p. 27, where he is reported to have been spending all of his time relaxing at a hot spring and roaming in the hills with his hunting dogs.

26 Besides obesity caused by filariasis, Saigō also seems to have suffered from a heart ailment of some kind, as well as complex gastro-intestinal problems. Cf. *Saigō Takamori zenshū*, vol. 3, pp. 40–4, 91–2, 100, 116–17, 119–20, 355, and 363–8. Saigō's autopsy report, including reference to the dropsy caused by filariasis is in Tamamuro, *Saigō Takamori*, p. 194.

27 In 1875, Saigō was so busy with a land reclamation scheme that he declined an invitation to accompany Ōyama Iwao to Europe to observe the Franco-Prussian situation. Cf. *Saigō Takamori zenshū*, vol. 3, pp. 470–1. Also cf. *ibid.*, pp. 473–7.

28 Cf. the works by Inoue and Tamamuro cited above.

29 Cf. 'Restoration and Rebellion,' pp. 137–9.

30 These three qualities are enduring elements of the Saigō myth, but I have found confirmation for none of them. Like his legendary sexual prowess, which is traceable to the enlarged scrotum caused by his filariasis, they are fanciful elaborations of verifiable but unremarkable truths.

31 Cf. 'Restoration and Rebellion,' pp. 118–23, 187–97, and 358–77 for some discussion of Saigō's thought and values. The earliest evidence of his prudery is in a letter from 1854. Cf. *Saigō Takamori zenshū*, vol. 1, pp. 31–3.

32 For some appraisals of Saigō by his contemporaries, cf. *Saigō Takamori zenshū*, vol. 6, pp. 11–270.

33 Cf. Kitagawa Tetsuzō, *Satsuma no gōjū kyōiku* (Kagoshima), 1972.

34 Saigō's own sense of a world lost comes out of a remark he made in 1871, where he expressed the wish that he had died in 1868. Cf. *Saigō Takamori zenshū*, vol. 3, p. 144.

35 Russell Kirk, *The Conservative Mind*, 7th edn (Chicago, 1986), p. iii.

36 Maruyama Masao, 'De aru koto to suru koto,' in *Nihon no shisō* (Tokyo, 1961).

37 Cf. 'Restoration and Rebellion,' pp. 131–3.

38 Cf. 'Restoration and Rebellion,' pp. 139–46, for more detail on this episode.

39 Cf. *Saigō Takamori zenshū*, vol. 1, pp. 131–3 and 135–40. Also, Inoue, *op. cit.*, note 4, vol. 1, pp. 72–8.

Part II

Economic change

9 The Tokugawa period and Japan's preparation for modern economic growth*

E. S. Crawcour

*Source: *Journal of Japanese Studies* 1 (1974): 113–25.

The relationship between pre-Meiji developments and Japan's modern economic growth is one of the central topics of modern Japanese history. That there is some connection would, I suppose, be the *a priori* assumption of most if not all historians. Nevertheless, the first students of modern Japan held the view that the connection was slight or negative, and that the "modern" development of Japan after the Meiji Restoration represented a sharp break with her benighted past. Contemporary foreign observers almost without exception believed that the progress of Meiji Japan stemmed from the introduction of civilization and enlightenment from the West, and to them the rate of progress of the New Japan depended upon the speed with which the Japanese could overcome the ignorance and unenlightened practices that were thought to characterize traditional society. This view was by no means confined to foreign observers but was shared by such influential Japanese educators and intellectuals as Fukuzawa Yukichi and other members of the Meirokusha group. Although extremes of Westernism were followed by an intellectual and political reaction, in the area of material progress the tendency to regard traditional Japan as an obstacle to development remained strong and received a new twist with the introduction of the ideas of the European historical school of economic development theory. The Tokugawa period now became firmly identified with the "feudal" stage of development and as such was regarded as the antithesis of modern economic growth.

The first modification of this view appeared in the late 1920's in the course of a long controversy that arose from the difficulty of fitting all the stages of development between feudalism and capitalism into the inconveniently short period of fifty years or so that had elapsed since the Restoration.[1] One side took the line that developments during the Tokugawa period had already eroded Japanese feudalism and saw the Restoration itself as a victory for these internal economic and social forces rather than as a reaction to external pressures. Thus the penetration of a money economy and the commercialization of economic life led to the dissolution of the peasantry, the impoverishment of the feudal aristocracy, the rise of the merchant class and eventually to the establishment of capitallsm. The implications of this view, exemplified in English by the writings of E. H. Norman[2] and C. D. Sheldon,[3] are that Japan's economic modernization followed directly from the internal dynamics of the pre-Restoration economy and that the impact of the West was significant in influencing the form that economic development would take, rather than in determining whether it would take place or not.

The excellent studies of T. C. Smith[4] as well as a growing volume of Japanese work[5] have convincingly established that change was taking place in Tokugawa Japan and that the tempo of change was quickening in the fifty years before the Restoration. Wage labor was replacing customary labor services, subsistence agriculture was giving way here and there to commercial farming, rural industry was expanding, and new commercial networks were increasingly bypassing officially-sanctioned trade channels. The last years of the shogunate even saw the establishment of a few Western-style industrial plants. At the same time central and local government revenues predicated on subsistence farming were becoming increasingly inadequate to maintain the existing political structure, let alone to meet threats looming from abroad, and the idea of attacking this problem by increasing total output was being widely canvassed and even sporadically applied. But to regard these developments as leading directly into modern economic growth or as preconditions of modern economic growth in Japan may well obscure more than it illumines. Industrial capitalism and modern techniques of production were not invented in Japan and they did not need to be. Attempts to identify in the development of Tokugawa Japan counterparts to the commercial or agrarian developments that preceded the English Industrial Revolution are therefore of little relevance, except to the question of what would have happened to the Japanese economy had news of Western development never reached her shores.

It was considerations like these that prompted Rosovsky to ask, "Is it really necessary to move back farther and farther in time in order to appreciate the significant dimensions of a recent and entirely different past?"[6] He proposed solving the problem of cutting the historical continuum by postulating a transition period with a clear beginning at the Restoration of 1868 and continuing to the end of the Matsukata deflation in 1885. The selection of 1868 as the starting point is not arbitrary. It is justifiable not only on the grounds that it was at that time that Japan was committed to adopting modern ecc-nomic growth as a national objective, but also because the trend rate of change was so much higher after the Restoration than before it that 1868 constitutes a turning point. This turning point is so pronounced that a trend line drawn across it has no explanatory significance. There are also good grounds for regarding modern economic growth itself as beginning only after this transitional phase. Although "economic development" may include qualitative changes and even overtones of movement towards a somehow more desirable state, the term "modern economic growth, " as defined by Kuznets,[7] involves the application of modern science and technology to industry; a sustained and rapid rise in real product per head, usually associated with a high rate of population growth; a rapid decline in the relative importance of agricultural output; and the existence of international contacts.

By this definition the developments of the transition phase did not amount to modern economic growth. Nevertheless, the transition phase was all-important because it was the state of the Japanese economy in 1868 and the developments of the following two decades that explain modern economic growth. Since Rosovsky's interest is primarily in the process of modern economic growth itself, this is an eminently sensible approach and it puts Tokugawa Japan in its proper perspective vis-à-vis modern economic growth.

It is also legitimate, however, to ask how Japan was capable of making the crucial adjustments of the transition phase and it is with this question that this paper is primarily concerned. While a static picture of the Japanese economy as it was in 1868 may well suffice for Rosovsky's purposes as representing the culmination of all that went before, for our present purpose the dynamics linking the late Tokugawa period with the transition phase should form an integral part of our explanation. I have gone to somewhat tedious lengths to make clear that the relevance of these pre-Meiji developments is to the transition phase rather than to modern economic growth itself, but in effect all that I and, for that matter, Rosovsky are suggesting is that one is on safer ground in describing the connection between adjoining links of a chain than in describing the relationship between widely separated links.

Let us first identify the major features of the transition phase that call for explanation. Four stand out and they are a) the adoption of modern economic growth as a national objective; b) institutional change; c) the creation of infrastructure and d) the growth of the traditional economy. All of these features were responses to, or prompted by, contact with the West, or followed Western models.[8] Moreover they interacted with one another and with other events of the Meiji period. What we are interested in here, however, are the ways in which aspects of the late Tokugawa period made these responses possible.

Although the adoption of modern economic growth as a national objective was largely a response to external forces, other responses were conceivable. Presented with the sort of external situation that Japan faced in the 1850's, economically backward countries have been known to accept some restrictions on internal policies or external relations in return for economic assistance or guarantees of maintenance of the political *status quo*, or even to capitulate entirely. One important reason why this did not happen in Japan was an exogenous one. If any Western power was trying to take over Japan, competition with other Western powers in the Far East at the time prevented it and some, for reasons of their own, were actually encouraging Japan to modernize. A second reason had to do with internal politics, since one of the major grounds of opposition to the shogunate was its failure to resist foreign demands for the opening of trade and diplomatic relations.

There was, however, a third set of factors connected with the economic developments of the Tokugawa period that increased the possibility of the adoption of new economic objectives. Although there is much to be said for the view that Restoration leaders adopted the objectives of industrial capitalism because they judged this to be the source of Western power, ideas of economic growth as a solution to financial problems had been current in Japan for a century before the Restoration. Policy had been vacillating between on the one hand attempts to increase revenue by more effectively exploiting taxes in kind based on subsistence agriculture and on the other hand allowing freer rein to developments incompatible with the ideal of a subsistence economy in return for the benefits of economic growth.[9] What inhibited adoption of the latter policy was the correct assessment by the authorities that it would undermine political stability, which was itself an objective of the regime. On the other hand attempts to increase agricultural taxes in kind could also and did provoke disturbing reactions. The likelihood of the growth policy being adopted was thus positively related both to the acuteness of the economic need and to the confidence of the authorities in their ability to preserve political stability both in the countryside and within the ranks of their own administrations. The various "reforms" of both shogunate and daimiates from the mid-eighteenth century on were attempts to restore their finances by one or another of these means.

Financial problems had for a century been pushing the shoganate towards allowing a degree of rural commercial and industrial development provided means could be found to bring it under official control. The reforms of the late Tempō period (1841–43) were somewhat ambivalent on this point. They began with the traditional exhortations to frugality and attempts to stem the movement of people and resources out of agriculture. In abandoning attempts to control the commercial sector of economic life through city merchant capital and recognizing rural commercial development, however, the shogunate's Tempō reforms introduced a change of policy that proved irreversible. Possibly because of its greater internal stability, the shogunate tended to be a leader in this field but daimiates generally followed the same trend though often with a considerable lag. The policies of the remainder of the Tokugawa period were primarily directed towards finding means of controlling this rural development nearer the source and no further attempts were made to reimpose subsistence agriculture. The growth policy clearly had the greater potential for alleviating the financial problems of governments. On the other hand, by countenancing rising rural demand for goods, it reduced the relative economic status of samurai on fixed incomes. Moves towards commercial and general economic development – often prompted by the advice of merchants who hoped to gain by collaborating with the authorities in return for monopoly privileges – were therefore strenuously resisted by lower samurai.[10] These frustrated lower-ranking samural and their allies, the equally frustrated rural businessmen, supported the Restoration for complex and often personal reasons, but in general they worked for the overthrow of the whole *bakuhan* system because they saw no hope of gain from either of the alternatives open to the old regime.

Contact with the outside world brought vastly increased defense costs and the opening of private foreign trade made some commercial development practically inevitable. Yet the Tokugawa government lacked the basis of political power that would have enabled it to adopt a policy of economic growth with any confidence. Very soon after the Restoration, however, it became clear that the requirements of national defense and administration made economic growth essential. In opting for growth the Restoration Government took steps to ensure that such growth did not endanger its own stability. These steps involved creating a power base that depended not on the cooperation of daimyo or the consensus of samurai, but on a monopoly of military power and a central bureaucracy whose members were rewarded broadly according to their ability and loyalty.

Thus the commitment of the new government to economic development involved as a corollary a commitment to controlling potential opposition, and as restrictions on economic growth were progressively removed, corresponding steps were taken to secure internal stability and eliminate the samurai as a source of political opposition.

Between 1868 and 1875 Japan was administratively unified and restrictions on occupation and residence were removed. Commerce and the use and sale of land were freed from restrictions and a national tax payable in cash by the landowner replaced crop taxes in kind. Removal of restrictions on occupation, residence, and disposal of land represented the final abandonment of attempts to increase revenue by extracting a greater surplus from subsistence agriculture. In practice, farmland had been alienated in one guise or another for a long time and involvement of rural population in non-agricultural pursuits was already widespread in important areas of Japan. Removal of legal restrictions in the early years of Meiji was therefore not a radical departure, but represented formal recognition of a situation that had already been first tolerated and then approved in principle. The change in the form of agricultural taxation from collection of a surplus in kind to a cash payment, while far-reaching in its consequences, was in its conception the obvious corrolary of the decision to legitimize commercial agriculture.

The same period saw the removal of the daimyo, the abolition of the military privileges of the samurai and the creation of a conscript army subject to strict central control under a new military code. Garrisons were established, first in the Northeast and Kyushu, and by 1873 at Ishimaki (near Sendai), Kokura (North Kyushu), Tokyo, Osaka, Nagoya, and Kumamoto. The police system was established over the same period. Local uprisings by disappointed samurai and peasants were crushed and with the failure of the Saigō rebellion of 1878 the last hopeless flicker of samurai resistance was easily extinguished.

The comparative smoothness with which a hereditary ruling class was eliminated as an effective opposition calls for some explanation. The daimyo themselves were few in number and had not exercised real authority for some time. Although they lived very well and enjoyed great prestige even at the very end of the Tokugawa period, they did not own any part of their territory. Even their castles and residences were not their personal property, and when a daimyo was transferred from one territory to another he did not seem to have had any claim for compensation in respect of improvements he had made in his former capital. In theory the daimyo received the administration of a territory in trust from the shogunate and was entitled to its revenues to enable him to carry out his duties. The idea that the daimyo were simply returning these responsibilities therefore had a real basis. More importantly perhaps, the administration of a daimiate seldom yielded a profit even in normal times and certainly could not have been expected to do so with the greatly increased financial responsibilities that followed the appearance of Perry. With the development of rural commerce and industry, taxation based on subsistence agriculture had already become inadequate and few daimiates had yet evolved effective means of tapping the new sources of income. One small daimiate actually abdicated without compensation at the earliest opportunity after the Restoration, giving financial difficulties as the major reason.[11] Thus, although the decision to return their territories was in most cases made for them, there was little reason for a daimyo to resist, particularly if, as was often the case, he remained at least initially *in situ* as governor of his former territories. Any regrets he may have had were no doubt dispelled by the Meiji government's offer to release him from liability for the huge debts of his daimiate and to grant him a title that would maintain his status as a member of the nobility and compensation that would allow him to live in appropriate style.

The samurai were to an extent in a similar position. Their real incomes had been falling not only relatively but absolutely over the last decades of the shogunate. Some were finding their careers thwarted by the ascriptive system of appointments still almost universally practiced. They had long been bureaucrats rather than military officers when the 1864 expedition against Chōshū and their obvious inability to defend the country against anticipated foreign attack showed up their military pretensions for the anachronism they had become. Although some resisted the change, most seem to have been resigned to the fact that continuation of the old system could lead only to further deterioration in their position and to have accepted, some eagerly, some perhaps sheepishly, the compensation, social status (as *shizoku*), and opportunities for employment and rehabilitation offered by the new government. Their accommodation to the new régime was made easier by some of the Restoration Government's policies outside the economic sphere. Emphasis on maintenance of the Japanese (= samurai) spirit despite the introduction of Western practical learning (*wakon yōsai*) and in particular the "samuraization" of Japanese culture throughout the Meiji period would have, to some extent, placated ex-samurai even if those policies were not adopted specifically for that purpose. Although the distinction between samurai and popular culture was tending to become a little blurred in some areas even before the Restoration, the distinction was nevertheless real enough, and pockets of resistance to samurai culture (e.g., in *shitamachi* areas of Tokyo) survived until both streams of traditional culture had become so attenuated as to be almost unrecognizable.

The creation of infrastructure was our third feature of the transition phase. Infrastructure here includes not only communications and public utilities but also less prosaic items such as education, public administration, and financial services which might in other contexts be viewed as institutions. The Tokugawa heritage facilitated this most important aspect of the transition phase in two ways. Firstly, this was the area of government activity par excellence and the Meiji government inherited from its predecessors both a traditionally active role in economic life and the means to play it effectively. If we have understood the nature of the transition phase correctly, the contribution of the state in this period should be measured by its success in providing infrastructure rather than by the profitability of its industrial enterprises or its share of industrial investment, and in very few countries has the state been so successful in providing infrastructural facilities at such an early stage. European countries typically depended initially on foreign investment for railway building and other essential services. That Japan was able to move so quickly and effectively and with comparatively little foreign capital undoubtedly owed a good deal to an established tradition of government in this field and to an effective system of taxation that never really ceased to function, putting in the hands of the government from the beginning an unusually large share of the national product.[12]

The role of the government was not confined to direct investment. More important throughout the Meiji period – and probably since – was its role in influencing private investment decisions by guarantees, subsidies, preferential access to bank funds, and by what is now called "administrative guidance." Here the relationship between the government and selected merchants gave the government an influence in key areas of development by means of the same mechanism that had been so bitterly opposed by pre-Restoration "reformers." The role of political merchants (*seishō*) like Mitsui is well-known, but on the local level also the Restoration Government took over early and attempted to unify the trading and commercial control activities of the daimiates. The formation of the Shōhōshi (Commercial Administration) in June 1868 was partly to raise revenue and provide an outlet for the issue of the Dajōkan paper currency in the form of commercial loans. More importantly, however, it demonstrated a decisively positive conclusion to the long controversy over official attitudes to commercial development. It is of some interest that it implemented many features of an abortive proposal by Satō Nobuhiro (Shin'en) to Mizuno Tadakuni in the Tempō Era for nationwide finance and control of commercial development by the shogunate.[13]

Secondly, in a number of important fields the pre-Restoration period provided a substantial basis on which to build as well as providing useful service in the interim until more modern arrangements could be made. The achievements of Tokugawa education, which gave Japan a literacy rate surpassed by only two or three countries in the world at that time are well-known through the work of Ronald Dore, and their importance for the early development of a national system of compulsory education can hardly be overestimated. After the Restoration a large existing educated class provided a useful body of schoolteachers until sufficient numbers could be trained in the new normal schools.[14] Ex-samurai needed little retraining to staff an impressive police force.[15] In the crucial field of commercial law, it was not until 1893, after the end of the transition phase, that a code based on European models was introduced, but in the meantime traditional practice served well. One cannot read the material on Tokugawa commercial law edited by Wigmore[16] without being impressed by its coverage, sophistication, and impartiality. In the cities under shogunal administration at least, courts showed extraordinary understanding of commercial transactions considering the popular conception of the samurai official as completely ignorant of such matters. Ideas of contract, bankruptcy, and a clear distinction between loans and equity capital are especially significant.

The rapid development of banking and insurance provides further examples of the value of Tokugawa experience. Kozo Yamamura has shown that a modern banking system with a nationally integrated structure of interest rates had emerged as early as the 1890's,[17] and this would hardly have been possible without a considerable accumulation of banking experience. The banking system of the late Tokugawa period may seem old-fashioned in its externals, but it was highly sophisticated in operation and the traditional *ryōgae-ya* and their customers were thoroughly familiar with deposits, advances, bill discounting, and exchange transactions, in fact with most of the functions of a modern banking system, including the financing of traditional industry.[18] In Japan, as in other follower countries in the process of industrialization, insurance companies by the end of the transition phase provided an important source of investment funds. The prompt development of insurance business in the Meiji period undoubtedly owed something to the fact that insurance was not unfamiliar to the Japanese. Marine insurance had been a regular part of commercial life for well over a century, and by the end of the Tokugawa period even life insurance was available, implying some familiarity with actuarial concepts.[19] In all these various ways the experience of the Tokugawa period made for a smooth, rapid, and successful transition.

The fourth and final major aspect of the transition phase was the growth of the traditional economy. While the traditional Japanese economy may not have been much more capable than other Asian economies of supporting construction of a modern industrial sector in 1868, output appears to have increased rapidiy over the transition period, so that by the time modern economic growth proper began it was already well ahead of that of its neighbors. Until recently it was generally thought that as pre-modern Japan was overwhelmingly agricultural, the bulk of growth of output during the transition phase occurred in the agricultural sector, and official statistics of agricultural production seemed to confirm this impression. Recently, however, re-examination of the data strongly suggests that the growth of agricultural output before 1900, although substantial, was considerably less than the official figures indicated.[20]

On the other hand the role of traditional industry during this period is being re-evaluated.[21] Since the modern industrial sector was very small indeed in terms of output at this time, the rapid growth of industrial production during the transition phase must have occurred in traditional industries. There are difficulties in quantifying this increase. Y. Yamada's estimates indicate a slightly higher than fourfold increase in the real gross value of both factory and domestic manufacture over the decade 1875–1885, with the domestic component producing twice as much as the factory component.[22] Ohkawa's estimates published in 1957 indicate an increase of about two and a half times in each category between 1878 and 1885.[23] Such rates of growth seem extremely high, and more recent estimates show an increase in the total real gross value of production in manufacturing industry of about 50 per cent from 1874 to 1885, or of 70 to 80 per cent if food products (50 to 60 per cent of the total) are excluded.[24] The same series estimates an increase in the net stock of producers' durables in non-primary industries of about two and a quarter times from 1877 to 1885.[25] As these traditional industries developed they naturally benefited, as for that matter did agriculture, not only from diffusion of existing Japanese technology but also from some imported ideas and materials and from the improvements in infrastructure that characterized the period. Nevertheless they are quite clearly distinguishable from the modern industries whose growth belonged in the main to the following period. Whatever the exact rate of growth, it is clear that traditional industry developed actively during this transitional phase. This contrasts with the experience of most developing economies at a corresponding stage and calls for some explanation.

Throughout the Tokugawa period industry had been spreading from a few old craft centers like Kyoto and Sakai and by the Restoration had penetrated the majority of rural districts. With the development of commercial agriculture, cash demand for industrial products had been rising, producing further rounds of expansion for cottage industry and further rises in rural incomes. All these changes were, however, very gradual and were inhibited by controls and restrictions of all kinds which held back the process in general and directly restricted production, consumption, and markets in particular. Traditional industry had been pressing against these restrictions since at least the beginning of the nineteenth century, and their removal thus released a spurt of demand for the products of industries in which supply was very elastic, producing a corresponding spurt in output. This growth was not itself the growth of modern industry, but it made the later growth of modern industry possible by raising the level of output of the economy, providing a source of capital accumulation, and satisfying the growing demands of a rising population throughout the transition phase and beyond.

We have suggested that the connection between Tokugawa Japan and modern economic growth is to be sought in its relationship to the transition phase rather than to modern growth itself. As Landes says, "The ability of industrializing countries to achieve independence without sacrificing growth unduly has always depended on their success in mobilizing their initially meagre domestic resources, material and human."[26] It was Japan's ability to take these crucial initial steps successfully that distinguished her from other economically backward countries, and this paper has tried to show some of the ways in which her historical experience made this possible.

NOTES

1 See George M. Beckmann, "Japanese Adaptations of Marx-Leninism" in *Studies on Modernization of Japan by Western Scholars*, I.C.U. Asian Cultural Studies, No. 3 (Tokyo, 1962).
2 E. H. Norman, *Japan's Emergence as a Modern State* (New York: Institute of Pacific Relations, 1940).
3 C. D. Sheldon, *The Rise of the Merchant Class in Tokugawa Japan*, Monographs of the Association for Asian Studies, 5 (New York: J. J. Augustin, 1958).
4 Thomas C. Smith, *Political Change and Industrial Development in Japan: Government Enterprise 1868–1880* (Stanford: Stanford University Press, 1955) and *The Agrarian Origins of Modern Japan* (Stanford: Stanford University Press, 1959).
5 For example, Horie Eiichi, ed. *Bakumatsu ishin no nōgyō kōzō* [The structure of agriculture in the late Tokugawa and Restoration periods] (Tokyo: Iwanami Shoten, 1963); *Chihōshi Kenkyū Kyōgikai* [Council for Local History Research] ed., *Nihon sangyōshi taikei* [History of Japanese industry series] (Tokyo: Tōkyō Daigaku Shuppan Kai, 1960); Furushima Toshio, *Sangyōshi* [Industrial history] Vol. III, *Taikei Nihonshi sōsho* [Japanese history series] No. 12 (Tokyo: Yamakawa Shuppansha, 1966); Andō Seiichi, *Kinsei zaikata shōgyō no kenkyū* [A study of rural commerce in the Tokugawa period] (Tokyo: Yoshikawa Kōbunkan, 1958).
6 Henry Rosovsky, "Japan's transition to modern economic growth, 1868–1885," in Henry Rosovsky, ed. *Industrialization in Two Systems: Essays in Honor of Alexander Gerschenkron* (New York: John Wiley & Sons, 1966), p. 92.
7 Simon Kuznets, *Six Lectures on Economic Growth* (Glencoe, Ill.: The Free Press, 1959), Lecture I.
8 The Western world certainly cast its shadow over Japan in the 1830's or even earlier, but it was with Perry's expedition of 1853 that it became a major factor in Japanese politics.
9 See for example Tsuda Hideo, *Edo jidai no san daikaikaku* [The three great reforms of the Edo period] (Tokyo: Kōbundō, 1956).
10 On this point see Horie Eiichi, ed., *Hansei kaikaku no kenkyū* [Studies of reforms in the daimiates] (Tokyo: Ochanomizu Shobō, 1955).
11 Inoue Kaoru, "Hōken hōkaiki ni okeru Kinai shōhan no dōyō [Vicissitudes of a small daimiate in Kinai during the collapse of feudalism], *Historia*, No. 6 (March 1953), pp. 1–24.
12 See Sydney Crawcour, "The Tokugawa Heritage" in William W. Lockwood, ed., *The State and Economic Enterprise in Japan* (Princeton: Princeton University Press, 1965), pp. 29–33.
13 *Fukkohō gaigen* in Takimoto Seiichi, ed., *Satō Nobuhiro kagaku zenshū* [Collected treatises of Satō Nobuhiro and his family] (Tokyo: Iwanami Shoten, 1926), II, 319–37. See also Kitajima Masamoto, "Bakumatsu ni okeru Tokugawa bakufu

no sangyō tōsei" [Industrial control by the Tokugawa shogunate at the end of the Tokugawa period], *Jimbun Gakuhō*, No. 17 (Feb. 1958), pp. 55–83.

14 Ronald P. Dore, *Education in Tokugawa Japan* (Berkeley: University of California Press, 1965), esp. pp. 254–60.

15 Yamamoto Kazuo, *Nihon keisatsu shi* [History of the Japanese police] (Tokyo: Shōkadō, 1934).

16 J. H. Wigmore, ed., *Law and Justice in Tokugawa Japan*, 10 vols., (Tokyo: University of Tokyo Press, 1969–). See also Takayanagi Kenzō, "A Century of Innovation: The Development of Japanese Law, 1868–1961," in Arthur T. von Mehren, *Law in Japan – The Legal Order in a Changing Society* (Cambridge: Harvard University Press, 1963), pp. 23–30.

17 Kozo Yamamura, "The Role of the Samurai in the Development of Modern Banking in Japan," *Journal of Economic History*, Vol. 27, No. 2 (June 1967), pp. 198–220.

18 Matsuyoshi Sadao, *Kinsei no sangyō to ryōgaeshō kinyū* [Early-modern industry and moneychanger finance], Kinyū Kenkyū Kai Series No. 10 (Tokyo: Kinyū Kenkyū Kai, 1938).

19 Tōkyō Kaijō Kasai Hoken K. K. [Tokyo Marine and Fire Insurance Co. Ltd.], ed., *Tōkyō Kaijō 80-nen shi* [Eighty years of Tokyo Marine] (Tokyo: 1964) pp. 16–25.

20 Ohkawa, Shinohara, and Umemura, ed., *Chōki keizai tōkei* [Estimates of long-term statistics of Japan since 1868 (hereafter cited as LTES)] (Tokyo: Tōyō Keizai Shimpōsha, 1966), vol. 9 (Agriculture).

21 See Furushima, *Sangyōshi*.

22 Yamada Yūzō, *Nihon kokumin shotoku suikei shiryō* [Japanese national income estimate data], rev. ed. (Tokyo: Tōyō Keizai Shimpōsha, 1957). From Table 8, p. 48, deflated by Ohkawa's index of non-agricultural prices.

23 Ohkawa Kazushi, *The Growth Rate of the Japanese Economy Since 1878* (Tokyo: Kinokuniya, 1957). Gross value of output in current prices from Table 1, p. 79, deflated by index of non-agricultural prices from Table 6, p. 130.

24 LTES, X (Mining and manufacturing), 144. Table 2.

25 LTES, III (Capital stock), 182. Table 15.

26 David S. Landes "Japan and Europe: Contrasts in Industrialization" in Lockwood, ed., *The State and Economic Enterprise in Japan*, p. 100.

10 British and Japanese economic interaction under the early Meiji

The Takashima coal mine 1868–88*

O. and S. Checkland†

*Source: *Business History* 26 (1984): 139–55.

One of the earliest industrial enterprises heralding the modernisation of Japan was the Takashima coal mine, first sunk in 1868–9. Its story, here considered over a period of some 20 years, the formative phase of the Meiji regime, is one of an uneasy collaboration between Japanese and Westerners, neither of whom could, in the prevailing conditions, have carried through such a pioneering venture alone, but neither of whom was happy with the participation of the other. The Westerners consisted of the great financial houses of Britain and Holland who were the principal source of borrowing in the East, and the lesser men who designed projects and sought funding for them.

In the background was the unsettled state of the country when the venture began as the Meiji politics of industry developed. The new regime, while ensuring its own political position in the face of many dangers, sought to take command of the economic future of Japan, both internally and in relation to the foreigner. In the end the regime entrusted industry, including Takashima, to the newly emerging giant Japanese firms, later called the *zaibatsu*, but it was still dependent on the foreigners for a considerable part of Japan's international business connections, in the form of firms like Jardine Matheson & Co. Takashima also provides a glimpse of one of Japan's first industrial labour forces. The response of this proto-proletariat to their treatment provides an element of drama including explosion, fire, flood and riot and public scandal.

I

The Takashima coal measures are located on a small island of some 133 acres about seven miles from Nagasaki.[1] They had been worked in a primitive fashion when, in 1867, the story of the British–Japanese mining venture begins. The two principals in its formation and early working were the Prince of Hizen, daimyo or feudal lord of the Saga clan in whose fief stood Nagasaki, and Thomas Blake Glover, a Scottish business adventurer in Nagasaki. Hizen was 54 years old; Glover had just turned 30.

Nabeshima Naomasa, Prince of Hizen (1814–71) faced perhaps the most acute case of the 'daimyo's dilemma' in Japan. For the Bakufu government required him to be a Janus, guarding at Nagasaki the gate to Japan, and there importing the new technology (especially as relating to arms and technology), while at the same time loyally suppressing those corrosive developments which were even then threatening the feudal regime.

In 1868 Hizen took his Saga clan into alliance with the other western clans of Satsuma, Choshu and Tosa in their campaigns to restore the emperor to his rightful place and set up a government dominated by their own men. Hizen had already acquired a fleet of steamships[2] powered by coal, then at a premium in Far Eastern waters. It was inevitable that Hizen's thoughts should turn to the exploitation of Takashima.[3] To this end Hizen had provided himself with a hard-headed man of business, Matsubayashi Genzo.[4] Between him and the Prince of Hizen there were various intermediate levels of authority, although Matsubayashi remained in command of Hizen's office in Nagasaki and was therefore Hizen's contact with the Westerner.

What Hizen lacked was mining know-how, ready capital and access to markets. Sinking and operating a coal mine at any depth was, of course, an undertaking requiring skills developed over the generations as in Europe. Hizen, like landlords in many contexts, did not have any great realisable capital; indeed he had contracted large debts. In any case he would not wish to accept the risk of sinking capital in the ground. It was necessary to turn to the Westerners.

The reciprocal of Hizen and Matsubayashi in Takashima terms was Thomas Blake Glover (1838–1911). Glover, like Hizen and Matsubayashi, was indeed ignorant of mining. But he was one of those protean young men of projects and speculations from the more economically advanced part of Europe who seized upon the opportunities of Japan in this period of new beginnings. He was a striking example of those British (and especially Scottish) opportunity searchers who impacted so strongly on India, China and Japan, each in its phase of 'opening up'. He could raise money and he could sell things; moreover he could find and bring out Westerners who could undertake the creation and operation of the mine. He was conversant with most Eastern markets and was involved in many of them. But he had no capital reserves; indeed by 1867 he like Hizen was heavily in debt. These two debt-encumbered men joined together on a capital-intensive project.

Glover had arrived in Nagasaki in 1859 at the age of 21. Although of relatively humble background (his father was a coastguard officer at Bridge of Don, Aberdeen) he was apparently attending, in 1854 at the Gymnasium,[5] a highly regarded school in Old Aberdeen. He may have had a 'far-cousinly' connection with Kenneth Ross Mackenzie, then Jardine Matheson's agent in Nagasaki; at any rate Mackenzie employed him. Glover was soon acting for Jardine Matheson's[6] as well as for others. He quickly became the most active merchant in Nagasaki. He is credited with bringing the first steam engine into Japan, rigging up the first telegraph line from his office to Takashima and building the first slip-dock for the repair of ships in Nagasaki.[7] In the 1860s he became interested in exporting Takashima coal, then being mined by traditional methods. His other activities included selling ships and arms[8] to the restless clans of the west. As a result he was deeply involved with the small group of young samurai who were the driving force behind the Meiji revolution.[9] He was a marvellous fisher in troubled waters, a commercial extemporiser.

But Glover, like Hizen, had overdone himself. He had indulged in too many speculative transactions. The clans for their part had now run out of money and could no longer buy arms or ships; indeed they could not service their debts. There was general depression of trade in Nagasaki with falling prices. Moreover the new treaty ports of Kobe (Hyogo) and Osaka had been opened (1 January 1868), posing a serious rivalry. The tea business was damaged by competition from the Chinese merchants. Though Glover successfully arranged for the sale of the old Hong Kong mint machinery to the new Imperial mint at Osaka, he failed to gain the bullion contract he sought. The development of the coal resources at Takashima seemed a means of recouping his fortunes. It was to be the greatest and most continuous of his speculations.

Hizen and Glover could not act without the support of third parties. These consisted of the dominant Western financial and commercial houses operating in Japan, the only possible source of the necessary capital. Jardine Matheson[10] was the greatest British presence in the East, opening in Japan in 1859; the Netherlands Trading Society was the successor to the Dutch East India Company. These houses responded according to their judgement to approaches from the smaller men, like Glover, for funds to promote their projects. In so doing they had to take into account the profitability aspect, but also the political implications of what was proposed. Jardines and the Netherlands Society were to back Glover in turn.

By the spring of 1867 there was probably an informal understanding between Glover and Hizen through Matsubayashi, for the working of the mine. In the same year Glover travelled to Britain via Hong Kong. In the latter place he had a meeting with James Whittall, senior partner of Jardine Matheson. It seems almost certain that while in Britain Glover made enquiries about coal mining staff, machinery and finance.

On his return to Nagasaki an agreement was signed on 9 June 1868 between Glover & Co. and Matsubayashi as agent of the Prince of Hizen. Lengthy negotiations had been involved in this business, a sustained wrestling between the samurai-factor and the European man of projects, each with his complex background of considerations. The agreement was to be for seven years. The profits were to be equally shared, as was the cost of pumps, machinery and installation. But Glover was to provide coals for Hizen's steamships at cost price, and was in addition to pay one *rio* per ton royalty[11] to the Prince. Hizen was to mobilise the labour force and to provide officials who would in effect be the policing and civil magistracy element of the new island mining community. Glover was to provide the necessary European engineers and superintendents, and pay the colliers.

Glover & Co. thus became the mining company, responsible for setting up and running the venture, providing all that was necessary except the Prince's half of the costs of the machinery, and the 'coolies' as miners. Within these terms Glover had seven years in which to sink his mine, get it operational and make it pay back the investment, together with such profits as would at least cover his debts.

But he had been obliged to lend Hizen $43,750 in order to clinch the agreement.[12] This was to be repaid out of Hizen's royalties and profits, along with Hizen's half of the cost of the gear amounting to some $40,000 additional. Matsubayashi had thus seen to it that his master not only provided no capital, but indeed secured a large advance. Glover, through Jardines and others of his creditors, had to find a sum totalling about $150,000 to add to his already considerable debt. Matsubayashi had struck a hard no-risk bargain for his prince.

For Glover's venture to succeed it was essential that he give it his close and continuous attention. This he did not do. He was busy juggling his other concerns to fend off bankruptcy until the mine could restore his fortunes. Among these preoccupations was the opening of a new office in Osaka and the negotiations necessary to bring the Mint machinery to Osaka for the new Imperial Japanese Mint.[13] The Osaka ventures were intended to compensate for the relative decline in the commercial importance of Nagasaki[14] at this time.

The sinking of Number 1 shaft at 150 feet to the eight-foot seam was a hasty operation to win coal as soon as possible in order to generate some earnings that could be set against the development and wages costs. Coal was first got in January 1870. This haste was contrary to the principle that a mining venture at any depth should be seen in a long-term perspective, with careful planning of the shafts, galleries, winding gear, drainage and ventilation so as to yield their best return over decades rather than a few years.

Yet there had been short-term gains. By March 1870 output was reported by Glover at 300 tons per day. This level of production with a cost price of $2 per ton and a selling price of $4.50 would according to Jardine's calculation using figures supplied by Glover, yield a monthly profit of $15,000, or $180,000 per year. Moreover it was suggested that output could be further raised, perhaps to 500 tons per day. At this level of return Hizen could repay his debts to Glover within a year, and Glover's debts, especially to Jardines, would be greatly relieved.

But in spite of all this Glover was still in great financial difficulty, such as to puzzle and worry his backers, Jardines. Glover tried to go public with the mine but failed: the business community of Yokohama declined to take up the $370,000 of stock he offered. Nor would the Meiji government buy the mine from him as offered at more or less the same price.

What had gone wrong? It seems probable that Glover had presented the affairs of the mine to Jardines in an excessively favourable light. It is highly unlikely that the cost figure of $2 per ton could be a true one. Perhaps even more serious was the state of Glover's affairs in general. It would seem that he was unable to keep up the commercial manipulations that had been his forte so far. Jardines were ready to foreclose on him.

At the last minute, however, Glover was able to persuade the agent of the Netherlands Trading Society in Osaka to assume the Jardine debt. The Society had already advanced a good deal to Glover, and rather than see him collapse it decided, in the spring of 1870, to support him. Even so, Glover was still on a financial tightrope.

The end came when a Captain Forbes, to whom Glover owed $35,000 for building and supplying a gunboat, demanded payment. At this point the Netherlands Trading Society decided that their interest lay in making Glover bankrupt and assuming the role of chief business trustees of his estate. In August 1870 Glover went into liquidation. His debts stood at $564,646 (of which $273,365 was owed to the Netherlands Society)[15] with credits of some $220,000. The credits however did not include the realisable value of the Takashima mine. Henceforth the Society was to operate the mine in an effort to recover its debts,[16] as well as assuming the principal administration of all the other Glover concerns.

II

The Society was not, however, to dispose of Glover. On the contrary for a period of some five years he was working at the mine on behalf of the Society and his own estate in bankruptcy. Indeed he was to be more closely concerned with the mine at this period than he had been as its owner. For having secured from the creditors[17] the discharge of his partner and early mentor in Japan, the ageing Mackenzie, he undertook to work as an employee of the trustees at the mine at a salary of a mere $200 per month, about that of a clerk newly arrived from Britain. The trustees accepted his services 'on account of the Japanese at work in the mine', and because of his marketing ability. His real interest, of course, lay in trying to make the mine pay in order that his estate might be cleared of debt, and perhaps accrue something to himself, should a buyer at a reasonable price be found.

A report of 26 August 1870 was highly critical.[18] It found that 'The present workings are laid out without any system or view to facilitate future work'. There was no plan of the island showing the old workings and the new ones, together with those proposed and their position with regard to the sea. The management was 'very defective', with 'no one responsible and too many masters'. A serious form of waste had been that the machinery ordered from Europe had not been properly planned, requiring expensive alterations on its arrival.

The mining engineer-manager chosen in January 1871 was Frederick Antony Potter of Cromford in the county of Derby. He was to serve at the mine for seven years. His remuneration was to be 'a commission or allowance at the rate of $2\frac{1}{2}\%$ of the gross proceeds of the workings of the mines . . . after deducting therefrom the working expenses including wages, salaries, materials and supplies and also of the cost to the Society of all permanent improvements'. Here was the real accountancy problem! The Society did however undertake to pay Potter a minimum of $350 Mexican per month for the first year; he was also to have an unfurnished house.[19]

It was intended by the Society that Potter should create new workings to exploit the ten-foot seam 150 feet below the eight-foot. He told the Society that no real profits were to be expected until this was done. He described Number 1 pit as having been 'greatly misrepresented, it being no doubt the policy of the Glovers to represent it as of *immense value* when near their bankruptcy'. Poor Potter was harassed both by Glover whom he accused in August 1871 of 'intrigues', and Hizen who 'wanted to press me and the other Europeans to enter into contracts with him, the effect of which would have been to have given him the entire power in Takashima'. Hizen through Matsubayashi tried to coerce Potter and the others by ordering the miners to do no more work, but this tactic was not successful.

Meanwhile in June 1871 Glover had sought to renegotiate the agreement with Hizen. The coal price[20] had collapsed to such a level that the Glover estate was in danger of making a loss. Glover proposed a larger share of the profits to the prince ($\frac{6}{10}$ths), together with a below the market price for supplying the prince's steamers. In return the prince should abandon the royalty. The Netherlands Trading Society pointed out that the quantity of coal required by the prince 'may be so great that Takashima may lose all its profits for the purpose of seeing Hizen's steamers burn its coal'.

In September 1872 the Meiji government sent delegates to negotiate the purchase of the mine, raising Glover's hopes. Terms seemed to be agreed, but the Japanese attitude hardened, and they refused to complete. In December 1872 Hizen, like the rest of the daimyos, voluntarily surrendered his estates to the government. His interest in Takashima passed to the Mining Department of the Ministry of Works (Kobusho). The Netherlands Society, Glover and Potter had henceforth to deal with this arm of government. Its (British) civil servants at once challenged the right of the Society to regard various undertakings given by Matsubayashi as binding on the government.

In January 1874 the Japanese government purchased the mine from the NTS. According to Thomas Smith the price was $400,000.[21] By September 1872 Glover's estate was cleared of much of its debt.[22] By 1877 Glover was out of bankruptcy. It seems likely that the purchase price for the mine may have yielded something additional for Glover. The government did not propose to operate their new acquisition themselves but, consistent with general policy, proposed to privatise it by sale to a Japanese national.

III

The man chosen to succeed to Takashima was Goto Shojiro (1838–97).[23] He was a samurai of the middle rank of the Tosa clan who had played a leading part in the Meiji restoration, becoming a member of the first provisional government in 1868. It was he who had been largely responsible for bringing his clan into the movement for reform.[24] He was a man of independent mind, something of an idealist, a brave man in the samurai tradition. Goto was especially warmly regarded by the British for the courage and valour with which he had defended Ernest Satow and Sir Harry Parkes, decapitating one of their assailants with his sword. He had earlier gained business experience in Nagasaki and Shanghai acting on behalf of his master the Prince of Tosa. This had involved considerable contact with Glover, including the purchase of the gunboat *Nankai*. Dissatisfied, he left the Meiji government in 1873. The sale to him by the government of the Takashima mine on good terms on 20 September 1874, may have been the price of pacifying Goto. This would appear to be a use of the mine as a political counter. Against this view, however, was Goto's business experience and his presumed incentive to run the mine on efficient lines.

What the government did not supply was money. Goto had none. Like Glover before him he had to turn to Jardines. The Japanisation of the mine was thus still incomplete. Surprisingly perhaps, Jardines responded favourably to Goto's overtures. Jardines for their part now had a triple interest in Takashima. They were concerned that there be a relatively cheap supply of fuel for the steamships they chartered, as well as for the general development of Japan on which an important aspect of their business depended. Second Jardines had an incentive to accommodate the Japanese government in disposing of the Goto threat. Third, for all the past difficulties, the mine had real profit potential. Accordingly, Jardines in a 15-year contract agreed to lend Goto the $200,000 down payment, together with the cash and credits necessary to pay for Goto's share of the wages, machinery and materials; on these sums Goto was to pay 10 per cent interest annually. The expenses and profits were to be shared equally. At the end of the period the entire mine would become Goto's property.

Had he attended properly to the business over a period of years Goto could have done very well, for the mine was now a property that could yield some $400,000 per year. But Goto, like Glover in the first phase of the mine, was not to give it proper attention. He returned to Tokyo early in 1875. Jardines had, in effect, to assume the management of the mine but subject to Goto's arbitrary interventions.

The new regime at the mine started well, producing 650 tons per day. But output at this level was unsaleable at the prevailing prices. Should output be cut back or the price reduced? The question was suddenly put in abeyance by the fire and flooding of 1876 (see below). For almost a year there was no production at all. Goto's creditors threatened to sue for a lien on the mine.

Jardines knew full well that they as foreigners would receive little sympathy in the Japanese courts, placing their investment (now about $1,100,000) at risk. Moreover the price of coal had fallen sharply. Optimistically, Jardines hoped that while the mine was being pumped out a buyer would appear. This did not happen, nor did the Japanese government offer to buy it back. Rather, indeed, Jardines were faced with the necessity of paying a further instalment of the purchase price on Goto's behalf. Jardines' only possible card was that they might dismantle and remove the machinery, thus flooding the mine once more. But this, in addition to its doubtful legality, was a council of despair.

Hardly had working been resumed after the fire when in 1877 the Satsuma rebellion broke out, again stopping the mine. Goto's creditors now obtained from the courts under the new Japanese mining laws a levy of 50 cents per ton. Jardines in desperation approached Sir Harry Parkes, Her Britannic Majesty's Minister, to put pressure on the Japanese government to buy out its interest in the mine.

In February 1878 it seemed that this tactic might work, for government agents inspected the mine with a view to purchase. But Goto suddenly reappeared at Takashima with friends and took it over. Jardines' court action to prevent Goto using the machinery failed.[25] There was great confusion. As a senior member of Jardine Matheson's bemoaned, 'You will never get to the bottom of the Goto affair, for the transactions in great part were unrecorded I believe'.[26]

By the spring the mine was again producing 600 tons per day. Jardines had reluctantly made a new agreement with Goto under which he was to ship 120 tons daily to Jardines in China as a contribution toward his debts. The further advances made to Goto were diverted by him elsewhere so that the miners were left unpaid, causing them to riot. Jardines urged to the Japanese government through Parkes that Goto had grossly abused a valuable natural resource. Jardines had recourse to the international court at Tokyo which awarded them $1,100,000 against Goto. Although Goto, being insolvent, could pay nothing, he did enter into yet another agreement. This time both output and selling prices were up: indeed 1,000 tons per day was reached, keeping Goto in business for six months. But by late 1880 he was once more in deep trouble, with three months arrears in wages, provoking the inevitable strike.

In the spring of 1881 Jardines at last found a buyer for their interest in the mine for a mere $200,000, though they retained the agency for coal sales in China. The new owner was the Mitsubishi Steamship Company.

IV

With feudalism still the basic form of Japanese society in 1868 when Glover began operations at Takashima the labour force could be recruited either from Hizen's peasant serfs or perhaps from convict labour.[27] Native sub-officials resident on the island were to keep the workmen to the task and maintain order and discipline among them, providing a kind of police. Under them were the *kagoshira*, a form of sub-contractor who was the immediate employer of the mine workers, setting piece rates for them and organising the immediate operations of cutting and hauling. There were, in addition, the European overseers and technicians. By 10 April 1871 there were 60 coolies underground and 36 at surface labour; these numbers steadily increased.

The sinking of the shaft to the eight-foot seam began in 1868. The stone cutters worked well, encouraged by rewards of sake. One coolie had been killed in the shaft. A priest was paid a fee for purifying the place of the accident; this was the first and only reference to this practice. At least two other coolies had died in this first phase and three boatmen were killed. The company paid modest funeral money.

When completed the eight-foot workings were poorly ventilated, using a small furnace and a chimney at the outcrop with the shaft itself serving as the downdraft. The workings approached the sea without any knowledge of its real proximity. A doctor who, by the modesty of his fee, must have been a native, was retained. The company provided a mine hospital.

The coolies worked eight-hour shifts, but their productivity was very low, at only about one-third that of an English collier. There were some 20 working days per month in 1872: by 1876 there were 26. The stall and pillar method of extraction was used. These tyro miners refused to work in gangs in the English fashion because they distrusted one another. This lack of mutuality made it difficult to introduce improved European practice. The *kagoshira* organised and paid the coolies, apparently[28] doing so on a shift basis at a rate agreed with the company; they then recovered from the company. It was found impossible at first to get the Japanese to use the light double picks (because of back injuries when swinging the pick). It also took time to train them to undercut and wedge down the coal. Failure to do this resulted in large quantities of dust and small coal of little value. Van der Pot of the Netherlands Trading Society described the Japanese labour in 1871 thus:

> With a little good management they will do a good deal, but it must be born in mind that in Japan, as in all countries of the East, the people are attached to their customs and habits, which must not be interfered with. Anyone who would attempt to introduce suddenly Western ideas and manners would meet with great difficulties, whereas a little sympathy and indulgence would far better promote the object in view.[29]

The Western overseers had thus to have a careful regard to the susceptibilities of the miners if they were to get them to perform at any reasonable level.

The miners' recalcitrance concerning the method of working, and the warning that they must be treated in a manner consistent with their traditions, suggest that, though they were certainly under compulsion and discipline, they were able to assert some degree of control over their tasks. They learned a mode of common action toward their employers: thus when Glover, in an attempt to lower production costs, reduced the coolie rates they petitioned Matsubayashi and so had the reduction restored. Moreover wages rose a good deal between 1870 and 1873 suggesting bargaining power on the miners' side. On the other hand, in their isolated situation, they were vulnerable to the truck system which made necessities on the island very expensive. When pressed too hard the coolies simply rioted, as they did in the sixth moon. Additional police had to be hired and brought to the island to arrest the rioters, reinforced by men armed with firearms.

A far more serious outbreak of violence occurred between Sunday 15 December and Monday 16 December 1872. The Hizen officials were withdrawn to give place to the new Meiji authorities.[30] The latter failed to materialise, leaving a dangerous vacuum. An armed crowd of coolies drove the British engineers from the workings and forcibly stopped the pumps, thus endangering the new and costly Number 2 workings involving the 12-foot seam. They destroyed houses and other property. The British staff, finding their lives threatened, fought a defensive action with rifles against their labour force, killing some and wounding more.

By 1875 the coolie labour force had considerably expanded, amounting to several hundreds, hewing and carrying underground, labouring on the surface and loading the junks. There was a continuous seepage of sea water, against which the pumps were the miners' protection. Even more serious, fire damp began to be encountered. A man was killed by inhaling lighted gas, an accident which caused *The Rising Sun* and *Nagasaki Express* to remark that because the incident was so mysterious the 'burning to death of one man . . . was not sufficient to awaken any keen feelings of the danger to which they are subjected'. Nor did the Europeans seem to respond to the warning. The inevitable came early in December; there was a vast explosion, with 44 dead, 24 injured and five missing. Japan had suffered its first great industrial accident.

At the end of July 1876 a small fire at the west end of the works filled the whole of the mine with smoke and gas. The ceilings were weakened, causing two heavy falls. For two weeks the miners fought the fire that had seized hold of one of Japan's major sources of coal. But it could not be extinguished. There remained no choice for the European management but to order the pumps to be reversed and the pits flooded with sea water.

The recovery, however, was quickly begun. Seven new pumps with the appropriate piping were brought from Britain and the existing pumping was reorganised. To hurry things up Potter built his own casting and forging shop, thus adding to the responsiveness of the mine and to the skills available to the workers. By mid-September the pumping out was going well and by early November much of the mine had been cleared. Altogether the mine was out of production for almost a year.

The response to the emergency did, however, suggest that the Japanese miners, after only some eight years learning the job were able, like their kind in the West, to respond with vigour to the challenge of calamity, working under the leadership of their European managers and overseers.

Within a year the entire labour pattern was again disrupted. This time the cause was rebellion, breaking out in Satsuma province in March 1877. The Meiji government stripped the mine of most of its workers to act as porters and to build fortifications. Not until late September was production really resumed. Then came epidemic. The returning workmen brought cholera with them. Within three days there were 44 dead and 60 in the mine hospital. There were many more unreported cases, with the miners refusing to bring their sick friends for treatment. But the greatest losses of manpower came from the exodus of miners fleeing from the tight confines of the island. The working ceased. By the end of the epidemic in November 163 deaths were recorded.

By July 1878 wages were months in arrears. Goto, the ostensible operator of the mine, had no money. The miners struck. They soon worked themselves into a terrifying fury. Police sent from Nagasaki armed only with sticks wisely refused to land on the island. The foreign management spent a terrifying night hiding in the hills while the miners burned their houses and belongings together with the workshops. Relief came in the morning when the police returned armed with rifles and restored order.

In a desperate short-term strategy Goto closed off the workings furthest from the shaft and began to remove the pillar coal left to support the workings. By September 1880 three months of wage arrears had again accumulated. Goto wrote to Jardines setting out his view of the Takashima miners. They are, he said, 'not people to be looked at in the same light as ordinary mankind, as they are animals like beasts or birds which begin to seek for food or drink when they feel hungry or thirsty and know today but not tomorrow'.[31] Goto then enunciated sentiments not far from those of Arthur Young, a century or so earlier in England. 'If they were paid as their work were done and plentifully supplied with their food and drinks, they would have one by one run away.' There was no doubt some truth in this latter statement, for men suddenly made flush by the back pay of months would not be easy to keep at work, preferring to go on sake-sodden visits to Nagasaki. In November 1880 the men struck again, quickly stopping the winding gear and the machinery of the main workings. With the Mitsubishi purchase of the mine in the spring of 1881 the enterprise passed finally into Japanese hands.

It was the colliers who were the greatest sufferers from the under-capitalisation of the mine, the instability of coal prices, and the imposition by the Meiji government of Goto on the mine. Labour organisation was difficult if not impossible. The *kagoshira* were the only form of leadership at the worker level, but they were in a sense in league with the Company. A strike was a blind and instinctive affair: it meant an attack on the installations, followed by riot, burnings and a threat to the lives of Europeans. Perhaps under the aegis of a concern with capital resources and proper organisation like Mitsubishi the circle of difficulty, stress and violence could be broken.

V

The agreement with Iwasaki Yataro (1835–85) founder and head of Mitsubishi was dated Yokohama, 30 March 1881. The mine probably cost Mitsubishi a million and a half dollars. Mitsubishi was by this time a leading Japanese company, driven by the force of its founder and sustained by the Meiji government as a leading case of native enterprise.[32] To Mitsubishi had fallen, since the new government transport policy of 1875, lavish favours, including subsidies and guarantees.[33] Mitsubishi had no real rival for such treatment until 1882. Steamships were among the first major business successes arising from the government's efforts to supersede the foreigner, doing so in sea carriage in the great nexus between Japan and China and the West. Much of the coal for the Japanese steamships came from the Takashima mine: indeed coal mining in this phase could be regarded in a sense as an extension of transport and communications. It was highly appropriate, both for the Company and the government that Mitsubishi should own Takashima.[34]

But Japanese management was not yet total. Glover now reappeared at the mine, acting as commercial manager chiefly concerned with sales. It was his job, in addition to supplying the Mitsubishi ships, to feed the coal onto the Nagasaki and Shanghai markets in such a fashion as to maintain a good price in both. Nagasaki had first claim, but the Shanghai market must be neither starved nor flooded. The mine, though now comfortably producing 900 tons per day, had no great reserve stocks.

In this way Glover, now 43, began a new career as servant and adviser to Mitsubishi. He had known Iwasaki, its founder, from pre-Meiji days. Indeed they had almost certainly been associates in the heady years around 1868 when Iwasaki, in charge of the Nagasaki office 'was buying all the arms he could find for the militant Tosa Han'.[35] At that time Iwasaki and Glover, both buccaneering spirits, had shared in the excitement of the great days of Nagasaki. But there were other, more hard-headed considerations. The newly emerging *zaibatsu* like Mitsubishi were aware that Japan had as yet no great supply of entrepreneurial talent and eagerly seized upon and perhaps indeed monopolised such talent as there was. Glover had enormous knowledge of Japanese affairs acquired from the time the first treaty ports were opened, together with his justifiable claim to have been a promoter of the new Japan.[36]

The takeover of the mine by Mitsubishi did not, in fact, put an end to its troubles. On the contrary the mine became a *cause célèbre* brought to the public attention of the new liberal Japan by investigative journalism. A young idealist, Koichi Matsuoka, obtained employment at the mine from November 1885 to the spring of 1886. He observed the condition and treatment of the miners and in 1888 published an exposé of Takashima. The matter was taken up by journalists, of whom the most prominent was Tsuyoshi Inukai, writer and politician, who was later to become prime minister. Matsuoka described conditions as very bad indeed. There were more than 2,000 miners crowded onto the small island; only 50 women were present. About half the men had come direct from the land as very poor peasants. The second largest group of 428 had been in petty trade. A further 275 were miners, formerly employed on traditional shallow workings. Severe agricultural depression in 1885–86 in Japan had made men willing to accept mining employment.

The miners were illiterate and often did not understand the engagements into which they had entered with the contractors who had employed and bound them. Many were in debt to the mining company, and were victims of the truck system. Bad health was general, with some 900 of the miners having suffered a serious disease or disability.

On the other hand, Inukai conceded that the mining company was caught in something of a dilemma. The miners, for whatever reason, were hard cases, and had to be subjected to a pretty strong discipline. Mitsubishi, as the owners of the mining company, seem not to have fully understood how bad things had become as the labour force expanded. The mine was still not really profitable, tempting the management to squeeze the miners through cutting the piece rates and so increasing the tensions. The revelations conveyed to Mitsubishi the economic unsoundness of an abused and exploited labour force, together with a realisation of the serious adverse public response to such conditions. It would seem that Mitsubishi, having taken over the mining company in 1881, had left it to its own devices, failing to scrutinise the working of its new possession.

VI

The Takashima story provides a kind of microcosmic cross-sectional view of early Meiji Japan. The enterprise itself had its own developmental logic: its history throws light on the general picture of an economy in the first phase of modernisation.

Two leading characteristics of a traditional/transitional economy are illuminated by Takashima, namely the scarcity of liquid capital and the need to import technique. Such capital as Japan could command at this period was largely invested in public works, construction and railways, mainly under government aegis. But private investment was urgently needed as the mediator of economic modernisation. In the Takashima case it came from the foreign agency houses making their money from Japan's external nexus, namely trade and foreign exchange. Shipping (to which coal supply was an auxiliary) was thus a strategic sector in which, indeed, one of the first *zaibatsu*, Mitsubishi, the eventual owner of the mine, was formed.

Because the capital and technology in the initial phase were foreign, a complex set of Japanese–foreigner relationships was involved. The Glover–Hizen interface illuminates the relationships that arose before the Meiji revolution was secure. In the next phase the object of the game for Jardines was not only to get their loans serviced and eventually repaid, but to assist the growth of commerce by helping to power the ships which carried it so that their own business might continue to expand. They also wished to establish a good relationship with a strongly interventionist Japanese government. The latter needed such collaboration in the short run, but quite soon realised the strength of its own bargaining position, treating even so great a house as Jardines pretty roughly.

Takashima also throws light on the processes governing Japan's early acquisition of social capability. The pioneering mine quickly became a kind of college of technical diffusion with visitors converging from many parts of Japan to see modern mining demonstrated.[37] There are glimpses too of how an early industrial labour force performed and were regarded by the Japanese. The absence of the traditional social cohesion of the rice-growing village, together with the need to confront very different natural forces in the form of earth, fire and water constituted a new set of challenges for Japanese peasants. At the same time they had to accept the discipline of a new kind of work, together with the need to trade work for wages and build a new kind of life on the wages received. The circle was completed when the undercapitalisation of the mine, inherent in the historical situation, led to short-term policies including pressures on the miners and non-payment of their wages.

Takashima also reveals important aspects of Japanese culture. The strict definition of relationships as required for a Western form of law of contract was alien to the Japanese. If Glover had insisted on an explicit and enforceable arrangement with Hizen he would never have got the mine started.[38] Indeed, Japanese informality had served well enough in many of Glover's early buccaneering activities, but it probably lay at the root of the difficulties leading to his bankruptcy.[39] When, from the early 1870s onwards, the Meiji regime could employ British professional men, these could be used in fighting the claims of British traders against the Japanese government.[40]

Finally the whole complicated story of Takashima between 1868 and 1888 reflects the strong demand for coal in the Far East. With the expansion of trade and the new predominance of steam ships there was great competition to supply steam coal. Britain, the United States, Australia, Japan and Formosa were all eager suppliers. Indeed, in 1865, 50 per cent of the total imported coal to Shanghai (the great coal market) was from Britain. By 1873 British coal had been completely replaced by Japanese on the Shanghai market. Even Australian coal, with a relatively short haul and low carrying costs, was unable to compete and by 1880 Japanese mines were supplying 81 per cent of the coal imported at Shanghai.[41] Despite the crises which punctuated the Takashima story, those who had the faith to develop the mine were justified by the overall success of Japanese coal in Far Eastern markets.

NOTES

† We are indebted to N. Nambu, M.E.A. Pamplin, A. Reid, Dr S. Sugiyama and Dr M.E. van Opstall for their kind help.

1 In Japanese the principal references are Egashira Tsunoharu, 'Takashima Tanko

ni okeru Nichi-Ei Kyodo Kigyo' (Joint Anglo-Japanese enterprise at the Takashima Coal Mine) in *Bakamatsu Keizai-shi Kenkyu* (Studies in Bakumatsu Economic History) (Tokyo, 1935), pp. 27–28, 43–47. Hattoir Kazuma, 'Takashima Tanko to Jardine Matheson & Co.' (The Takashima Coal Mine and Jardine Matheson & Co.) in Kindai-ka to Kogyo-ka (Modernization and Industrialization) (Tokyo, 1968) and Mizunuma Tomoichi, 'Meiji Zenki Takashima tanko ni okeru gaishi to Sono haijo katei no tokushitsu' (Foreign capital in the Takashima Coal Mine during the early Meiji period and the nature of the process by which it was expelled), in *Rekishigaku Kenkyu (Journal of Historical Studies)* February, 1963, pp. 28–37. In English see J. McMaster, 'The Takashima Mine: British Capital and Japanese Industrialization', *Business History Review*, Volume XXXVII, 1963, 217–39, S. Sugiyama, 'Japan's export trade 1859–1899 with special reference to silk, tea and coal', University of London Ph.D. 1981, and M. Sumiya and K. Taira eds, *An Outline of Japanese Economic History, Major Works and Research Findings* (Tokyo 1979).

There are two main primary sources in English. The first of these is in Algemeen Rijksarchief, The Hague, Netherlands, where the archives of the Netherlands Trading Society are housed. See Tweede Afdeling Nederlandische Handelmaatschappij, Nr. 5935, hereafter NA Box 5935. Secondly there are the Jardine Matheson Archives held in Cambridge University Library, hereafter JMA.

2 New or second-hand ships were bought through various agents, including Glover and Jardine Matheson. For an example of a contract for a new ship, the Jho Shu Maru (dated 1 July 1868), between Alexander Hall Shipbuilders of Aberdeen and Charles Thomas Glover, merchants in Aberdeen (NA Box 5935).

3 Stanleigh H. Jones Jr., 'Early industrialization in Japan: the example of the Saga-Han, *Columbia University East Asian Institute Studies*, No. 6 (New York 1959), pp. 16–19.

4 In the law suits which followed Glover's bankruptcy the lawyers of the Ministry of Works (*Kobusho*) attempted to discredit Matsubayashi. It was claimed that he was not competent, because of his lowly rank (4th rank Shosok'wan) to sign legal documents on Hizen's behalf, *Memoire of Plaintiffs*, n.d., p. 5. (NA Box 5935).

5 Shewan, A., *Spirat adhuc Amor, the Record of the Gym, Chanonry House School, Old Aberdeen* (Aberdeen 1923), p. 384.

6 Glover's relationship with Jardines was less formal than the usual agency system which operated in the Far East and which is explained in M. Greenberg, *British Trade and the Opening of China* (Cambridge, 1951), Chapter 6.

7 Interested visitors can still see its remains at Nagasaki harbour. There was always an acute shortage of ship repairing facilities in the Far East. Glover wrote that he had sold the ship dock to the Japanese government at $130,000, 'which will give us a large profit and bring some of our locked-up funds back'(sic), letter from T.B. Glover to F.B. Johnson, Cobe, 23 January 1869 (JMA B/10/2/31).

8 It is believed in Japan that Glover's prosperity in the 1860s resulted from his successful trade in arms to the dissatisfied clans and that his bankruptcy in August 1870 was subsequent upon the Restoration of 1868 and the drying-up of the markets. In Glover's Accounts (n.d. but presumed *c.* August 1870) there are references to stocks of rifles still held (NA Box 5935).

9 There are entries in Glover's Accounts (n.d. but presumed *c.* August 1870) referring to the debts of young Japanese leaders, including Ito, Endo, Matsuda and Sano, which Glover claimed were still outstanding (NA Box 5935).

10 McMaster, J., *Jardines in Japan, 1858–67* (Groningen 1967). *Jardines Centenary in Japan 1859–1959* (Tokyo 1959). Keswick, M., ed., *The Thistle and the Jade* (London 1982).

11 'One rio per ton royalty', admitted on all sides to be excessive, amounted to $66\frac{1}{2}$ cents per ton, *Memoire of the Plaintiffs*, legal proceedings between Glover's creditors and Ministry of Public Works, n.d., p. 9 (NA Box 5935).

12 Joseph Heco, *Narrative of a Japanese*, n.d. 2 vols. (Yokohama, 1899), Vol. II, p. 186. All dollar figures quoted are Mexican.

13 Glover claimed to have made 'not one cent profit' from the 'Hong Kong Mint' transaction because of the heavy charges levied by JM (Letter from T.B. Glover to F.B. Johnson, Cobe 23 January 1869, JMA Cobe (B10/2/31).

14 *The Nagasaki Express* (No. 80, 22 July 1871) reported 'Beyond having a trade in Coal and Tea, both of which articles are likely to cause few firms to remain, Nagasaki has but little business of any other description worth speaking of, so that literally the port, year by year, continues on its downward course'.

15 These figures are from a memorandum by J.J. Van der Pot, Trustee in the Estate of Glover & Co. in liquidation (NA Box 5935). There are several accounts of Glover's position at the time of his bankruptcy. The figures given here differ from those presented by Dr Sugiyama. The discrepancy relates in part to the manner in which various liabilities and assets were valued, to some degree an arbitrary calculation. Presumably the figure for 'Property' given by Dr Sugiyama includes an estimate of the value of the mine.

16 Dr Sugiyama has suggested that the NTS believed in the ultimate profitability of the mine and hoped to operate it until 1876 when the lease ran out.

17 Reports of some of the meetings of the creditors of Glover & Co. are available (NA Box 5935).

18 Unsigned report (NA Box 5935).

19 Details of Potter's Appointment (NA Box 5935).

20 There were constant problems with the quality control of the coal. 'A NOTICE (dated Nagasaki 17 December 1870) to prevent inferior descriptions of Japanese coal being sold as TAKASHIMA the proprietors of this Colliery beg to notify that for the future no coal will be sold without a certificate' (*The Nagasaki Express*, No. 54, 21 January 1870).

Later, 'Respecting the failure of the Nagasaki coal to compete with that from Australia and Formosa, we fear that the rascality of the native merchants engaged in the trade has much to do with its want of success. The propensity these people have for watering and supplying coal dust instead of coal renders it indispensibly necessary for some responsible person to be on board vessels during the whole time it is shipped, to prevent either of the above contingencies arising.' (*The Nagasaki Express*, No. 54, 21 January 1871).

21 Thomas C. Smith, *Political Change and Industrial Development* (Stanford, 1955), p. 12.

22 By late 1872 the NTS had recovered all but $94,747.71 of the original Glover debt, J.J. Van der Pot to JM, 10 September 1872, JMA Nagasaki (B10/4/877).

23 See W.G. Beasley, *The Meiji Restoration* (London, 1973), p. 432, and *Hakushaku Goto Shojiro Den* (Tokyo, 1926), Chapters 24 and 27, Bunzo Hashikawa and Soichiro Goto ed. *Distinguished Figures in Meiji* (Tokyo, 1970), see chapter on 'Goto Shojiro: A Machiavellian in Meiji'.

24 See W.G. Beasley, 'Political Groups in Tosa, 1858–1868', *Bulletin of School of Oriental and African Studies* (BSOAS), No. 30, 1967, pp. 382–90.

25 The Japanese courts were on strong ground for Japanese Mining Law forbade foreigners any form of ownership in Japanese mines.

26 F.B. Johnson to J. Bell-Irving, 29 June 1877 (Private Copy Letter Book Shanghai to Japan JMA/C44/1, p. 150).

27 See R. Mathias, 'The Recruitment and Organization of labour in the coal-mining industry of Northern Kyushu', in I.H. Nish and C.J. Dunn, *European Studies in Japan* (Tenterden 1979), pp. 24–30, Murakushi Nisaburo, *Nihon Tanko Chin-Rodo*

Shi Ron (Studies on the History of Wages and Labour in Japanese Coal-mines) (Tokyo, 1976), and Ueno Hidenobu: *Kofu (Miners): Kindai minshi no kiroku*, Vol. 2 (Tokyo, 1971), pp. 529–37.

28 The European managerial staff may not have known how the miners were paid. In Glover's evidence he said 'The money expended on labour was sometimes paid direct to the labourers and sometimes to small contractors and sometimes to Hizen's officials.' (See NA Box 5935).

29 Van der Pot's advice to F.A. Potter on taking up his post as Mining Engineer in 1871 (NA Box 5935).

30 In 1872 the old *Han* or clan tenure gave way to the *Ken* or prefectural system. See W.G. Beasley, *Select Documents on Japanese Foreign Policy* (London 1955) and *The Meiji Restoration* (London 1973).

31 Letter from Goto Shojiro to JM, 24 September 1880 (JMA B10/4/1386).

32 Matsumura Kan'ichi (compiler) *Mitsubishi Jukogyo Kabushiki Kaishi Shi* (History of Mitsubishi Heavy Industries) (Tokyo 1956). Also *Mitsubishi Goshi Kaisa* (The Mitsubishi Company Ltd.) (Tokyo 1911).

33 See Kobayashi, M., *Nihon no Kogyo-Ka to Kangyo Haraisage* (Japan's Industrialisation and the transfer of government enterprises) (Tokyo, 1977) and 'Policy of encouraging industry by the Meiji government' *Kanto Gakuin University Economic Review*, No. 1, 1978, pp. 29–41.

34 Miike, another important coal-mine, was controlled by Mitsui.

35 Yamamura, K., *A Study of Samurai Income and Entrepreneurship* (Cambridge, Mass., 1978), p. 145.

36 Glover died in 1911 a legendary figure. He had lived in Shiba Park, Toyko, a merchant prince, although still maintaining the closest connections with Nagasaki. He and his wife Tsuru, are buried in the Foreigners Cemetery, Nagasaki. See *The Japan Times*, 19 December 1911 and Glover photograph albums preserved at the prefectural archives Nagasaki.

37 'The Takashima mine is more than a mere trading speculation. It is a sort of practical school, visited by a vast number of Japanese anxious to gain practical knowledge, to whom the mine officers invariably afford every facility and instruction.' *Takashima Colliery, Case of the Japanese Government, Statement and Argument*, n.d., p. 5 (NA Box 5935).

38 'The Japanese rarely make absolute statements or absolute promises' and 'almost invariably use language of a non-positive character'. *Reply of the Plaintiffs to the 'Case Statement and Argument' of the Kobusho*, n.d., p. 4 (NA Box 5935).

39 'The evidence of Mr Van der Pot, Mr Glover and Mr Burmeister show clearly that the non-payment by Hizen of his quota was the main cause of Glover & Co.'s suspension.' *Memoire of the Plaintiffs*, n.d., p. 13 (NA Box 5935).

40 The body of papers which we have used here give ample evidence of the tenacity of those English lawyers and engineers who were employed by *Kobusho*, the Ministry of Public Works: as they strove to get the best result for their Ministry out of a confused and controversial situation.

41 See S. Sugiyama, 'Trends of Japan's Coal-Export and the Shanghai Coal Market in the late Tokugawa and Early Meiji period', *Shakai Keizai Shigaku (Socio-Economic History)*, Vol. 43, No. 6, 1978.

11 Early modern farm ideology and the growth of Japanese agriculture, 1870–1895*

T. R. H. Havens

*Source: *Farm and Nation in Modern Japan: Agrarian Nationalism, 1870–1940* (Princeton: Princeton University Press, 1974), Ch. 2, pp. 15–55.

The steep mountain slopes, narrow valleys, and sharp seaside cliffs that dominate Japan's fifteen-hundred-mile-long volcanic archipelago scarcely create an ideal locale for one of the world's most productive agricultural economies. Only 15 percent of the total land area is available for farming, and much of it is deficient in natural fertility and irrigation. On the other hand, most of the country is blessed with a mild climate, abundant and well-distributed rainfall, and a long growing season, permitting double cropping in many areas. Throughout much of the country, the lowlands and gentler slopes are reserved for rice paddies, irrigated for many centuries by a network of dikes and canals that draw on short, swift streams. Except in the northeast, winter wheat, barley, and other cool-season crops fare well on drained paddy fields during the relatively dry, gentle winters. Vegetables and fruits grow in great numbers, with the steeper hills often given over to orchards or the ubiquitous bamboo. Only in the northeast are sizeable lands devoted to pasture, although most farms include small barnyard animals and fowl.

Lush and beautiful though the countryside is, ever since antiquity human ingenuity and hard labor have been more responsible than Japan's modest environmental assets for the economic well-being of society. The wet rice agriculture practiced in Japan at least since the time of Christ requires intensive care, especially at the time of transplanting seedlings and at the harvest. Such methods demand a high labor to land ratio, and together with the terrain they account for the small size of the typical Japanese farm, both historically and today. Although oxen and other draft animals have always been widely used, the scale of farming has inhibited mechanization as a substitute for human labor, even in the twentieth century when farm machinery could be efficiently produced in Japan.[1]

The family has long been the basic unit of rural labor; clusters of households have been grouped into communities known as *buraku*. These settlements of a few dozen or, at most, a few hundred persons have served as the building-blocks of rural society, just as their slightly larger administrative counterparts, the *mura* or villages, have been the smallest legal and political entities for nearly a century. (When modern bureaucratic agrarianists referred to farm villages, or *nōson*, they usually meant the *mura* imposed by the central state in 1888–1890. Popular Nōhonshugisha, however, ordinarily used farm villages to mean the traditional *buraku*.)

THE TOKUGAWA BACKGROUND FOR MODERN FARM THOUGHT

When the armies of Tokugawa Ieyasu (1542–1616) ended a century of feudal warfare with their decisive victories at Sekigahara (1600) and Osaka (1615), Japan entered a long period of peace and rural prosperity. The Tokugawa era, extending from 1603 to the Meiji restoration in 1868, is also called the Edo period, because Ieyasu and his successors built their permanent capital in the city of Edo (now Tokyo) in the heart of the country's richest farmland, the Kantō plain. There they instituted a unique form of mature feudal rule, known as the *bakuhan* system, in which the military government of the Tokugawa family (*bakufu*) acted as overlord, beneath which some two hundred and fifty fiefs (*han*) exercised regional hegemony.

Although this form of government was a striking innovation, the shift of political power from Kyoto to Edo also reaffirmed a number of historical practices and traditions that affected the development of people's thinking about agriculture. First of all, wealth in land once again became the economic foundation for rule. The Tokugawa family controlled about one-fifth of the productive land area in Japan, sufficient to meet most *bakufu* expenses, whereas Ieyasu's earlier rivals in the Kansai (Kyoto–Osaka–Kobe) area had depended considerably on trade for their income. Second, power returned to the east, a stronghold of traditional, farm-oriented Shinto beliefs when compared with western Japan, where Buddhist and Christian influences were strong. Third, the political capital was once more situated in a region with distinctly hierarchical social patterns, whereas the Kansai district by this time was somewhat more egalitarian. Finally and most importantly, the move to Edo in time came to signify a switch in economic policy from promoting international trade, which had flourished in the sixteenth century, to encouraging diplomatic isolation, containing commerce, and fostering agricultural production.

These trends did not, of course, comprise a frozen monolith throughout the long centuries of Tokugawa rule, and indeed great economic growth occurred.[2] But to a remarkable degree the favorable attitude of the *bakufu* toward agriculture remained the prevailing official view of economics until Commodore Matthew C. Perry's squadron reached Uraga Bay in 1853, exposing Japan to the liberal economic orbit of the nineteenth-century West. Since the Edo period was truly "the womb and hothouse"[3] of both forms of modern Japanese agrarianism, bureaucratic and popular, it will be useful to sketch the range of farm-centered thought, both official and nonofficial, during this late feudal era.

"Agriculture is the root, trade and industry, the branches."[4] This arid but time-honored maxim had been a canon of state economic policy for many centuries in Japan. To this the Tokugawa *bakufu* added a great outpouring of rhetoric to justify its profarming policies. One reason for the Tokugawa fondness of agriculture was that many *bakufu* advisers were adherents of the orthodox Shushi (Chu Hsi) school of Confucianism, and as a result most of them regarded as axiomatic the *Ta hsüeh* idea, "Let the producers be many and the consumers be few. Let there be activity in the production and economy in the expenditure. Then the wealth will always be sufficient."[5] Because Confucian counsel was kept in Edo, it was natural that the static Shushi view of national wealth should prevail.

Second, it is easy to imagine that an abundantly landed regime, eager to maximize its own revenues while depriving its rivals of potential sources of new wealth, would uphold farming even to the point of urging the cultivator to be "the docile instrument of a feudal policy."[6] Some Neo-Confucian fundamentalists even spoke of relocating the warrior class (samurai) on the land, to offset the attractions of life in the castle towns. Yet when times were bad in the countryside, Edo officials wasted little time before pinning the blame on the sloth and indolence of the farmers; surely, they reasoned, the cultivators were at fault for failing to live up to the ideals of rural life. Government agricultural pronouncements routinely began with such phrases as "peasants are stupid people" or "since peasants are people who lack sense or forethought."[7] However unrealistic and disdainful these ideas may have been in an economy that was slowly but irrepressibly maturing, most Tokugawa officials accepted placid Confucian views that glorified farming and resisted commercialization,[8] whether out of intellectual conviction or the instinct for survival.

A third consideration is that the state extolled agriculture out of a concern for social stability. To put an end to decades of turbulent and sometimes violent social change, the *bakufu* classified the public into four broad groups: samurai, farmers, artisans, and merchants (*shi-nō-kō-shō*). Although the stated model was the fourfold Confucian stratification of Chinese society, the Tokugawa rulers' real aim seems to have been merely to set off the warrior class as a distinct elite, since it was upon the samurai that the *bakufu*'s own political power was based. Ambivalent though the Tokugawa family may have been about enforcing class lines among commoners, its intellectuals in residence spent a great deal of time urging each member of society to lead a style of life appropriate to his status. As Ogyū Sorai (1666–1728), the scholar of Chinese classics and *bakufu* adviser, wrote in 1728: "To prize the root and suppress the branches was the rule of the ancient sages. The root is agriculture. The branches are commerce and industry. Clearly throughout history agriculture declines when commerce and industry rise. Samurai and farmers have permanently fixed occupations and depend entirely on the land for their survival. This is a proper basis for government."[9] Sorai's leading disciple, the great Sinophile Dazai Shundai (1680–1747), expressed most clearly the Confucian moral opprobrium of commerce and dim view of peasant proclivities:

> Agriculture is the foundation of all other productivity. All classes are fed by the farmer. When artisans and merchants increase, they merely stimulate the luxury of the people because they produce useless commodities. As the labour of the farmer, however, is essentially disagreeable, farmers are generally anxious to get out of their kind of work. This must be strictly forbidden by law, else the production of the necessities of life will fall below the amount required.[10]

Notable throughout such writings of the mid and late Edo period is not merely the call for freezing class lines in a feudal political system based on farming but also the implicit acknowledgment that the fate of the warrior was tied to the peasantry, since farmers paid the taxes that underwrote samurai salaries. As the quip went, *nō* (farming) meant *nō* (tax payment). When Sorai pointed out that the warrior and cultivator were each bound to "the land for their survival," without the right to change occupations, he conceded that to a great degree the elite class was helpless to forestall the slow erosion of its privileged position caused by the growth of commerce. The farmer, in practice, could flee to the city, whereas the samurai was legally and ethically obliged to eschew any other calling. Until very late in the era, remarkably few warriors, other than masterless samurai (*rōnin*), yielded to the temptation.

An added reason for promoting agriculture was that it was the economic basis for a sound army. The state accepted the autarkic premise that self-sufficiency was vital to the Tokugawa family's own military strength, but since samurai were set apart by virtue of their monopoly on arms-bearing, the government officially rejected the ancient idea of the farmer-soldier (*nōhei*).[11] Most *bakufu* administrators saw the economic value of farming to government defense policy, but few connected it to a clear conception of nation, before the end of the Edo period. Instead, their orientation was toward protecting the state against its internal enemies.

In short, the Edo regime lionized farming, perhaps in word more than in deed, for diverse reasons: to implement the economic views of the Confucian ideology it patronized, to maximize its own revenues, to deprive potential rivals of commercial wealth, to stabilize Japanese society, and to assure its own defense. It is tempting to view *bakufu* agrarianism as the exploitative hypocrisy of a state founded on a "serf-like 'poor peasant economy,' "[12] but it seems more appropriate to say that the government's support of farming drew at least as much strength from moral and political conviction as it did from desperation, scorn, or envy about socioeconomic developments beyond its control. Although a sound merchant economy was emerging by the late Tokugawa period, the official outlook on farming throughout the era remained truly conservative, trying to retain a time-honored system that still worked quite well. It was only with the rise of industrial Japan in the late nineteenth century that the state, under new political leadership, endorsed any really backward-looking farm policies, in an effort to restore a prior condition of Japanese farming.

Farm thought in the Edo period was not confined to the abstract intellectualizing of court Confucianists, who, as Sansom put it, thought highly of agriculture but not of agriculturalists. Agrarianism also had an important existence as a body of optimistic natural philosophy that was deeply rooted in the countryside long before Confucian blandishments about the virtues of cultivation began to pour out from Edo. In the broadest sense, agrarian fundamentalism – a positive view of society based on small village farming – was a formless concept linked to Japan's climate (*fūdo*), natural setting, distinctive forms of social organization, and indigenous deities.[13] Agriculture connoted not merely the fact but also the consciousness of living close to nature. Most Japanese have long regarded their climate as agreeable and their land as fertile, sometimes to the point of treating nature as a benevolent force to be trusted rather than a fearsome phenomenon to be respected.[14] Such an idealistic, optimistic outlook laid a basis for village solidarity in pre-modern Japan, insofar as the common worship of local gods was connected with fertility in the agricultural cycle.

These assumptions provided the Tokugawa leaders with a deep reservoir of general proagriculture sentiment, but in several respects Confucian agrarianism conflicted with the natural philosophy of the countryside. The latter emphasized family ties, whereas *bakufu* Confucianism attempted to direct loyalties to feudal overlords. The folk outlook on farming also differed from the state position in its stress on the oneness of gods and man (*shinjin gōitsu*).[15] What is more, the corporate consciousness of villagers pointed up communal harmony and discouraged the strict class divisions enunciated by the state. Finally, the pre-Confucian ideal of the unity of politics and religious ceremony (*saisei itchi*) was founded on the village as the primary locale of corporate Shinto ritual and basic unit of self-government. While the *bakufu* in practice exercised little control over farm villages, nevertheless Confucian canons of centralized rule ran counter to the longstanding custom of village autonomy. Still it would be unwise to exaggerate the divergence between state and popular attitudes. In many respects Tokugawa pronouncements about farming had a wide appeal precisely because this inchoate corpus of rural beliefs was so widely diffused throughout Japanese society.

More tangible was a second stream of nonofficial farm thought in the Edo period, the practical teachings of men who promoted agricultural improvements, aptly labeled "technologists" by Thomas C. Smith.[16] As persons concerned with increasing the material prosperity of the countryside, the technologists were not preoccupied with overall questions of politics or society, and thus they were only indirect forebears of the modern Nōhonshugisha. Nonetheless such men as Miyazaki Yasusada (Antei; 1623–1697), Ōkura Nagatsune (1768–1844), Andō Shōeki (late seventeenth to mid-eighteenth centuries), and Satō Nobuhiro (1769–1850) did a great deal to reify popular thinking about farming, and their refrain served as a distinct counterpoint to the official ideology. They believed that education and technical improvements, not Confucian frugality and diligence, grew more grain.[17] Hence they differed not just from the orthodox *bakufu* position but also from the amorphous agrarian naturalism, which shared their belief in the capacity of humans to improve themselves but emphasized simple gathering of the bounty of nature rather than progressive technology.

Satō was especially noteworthy because he was drawn to the thought of the advocate of National Learning Hirata Atsutane (1776–1843) late in his career and began to couple technical progress in farming with Shinto natural philosophy. Satō believed that remote gods had patronized agricultural productivity, and ever since it was an imperative of nature "for rulers to employ every means in their power for the sake of agriculture . . . [this] is the way to carry out the divine will of creation and to assist in the cultivation of nature."[18] Satō's economic centralism distinguished him sharply from both the self-sufficient village communalism of his own times and the economic localism of most subsequent popular Nōhonshugi partisans, but his preliminary attempts to yoke farms and deities in the early nineteenth century within a reasonably coherent conception of nation foreshadowed the Shinto-inspired agrarian nationalism of more outspoken farm ideologues in the twentieth century.

The treatises of technologists and utopians, together with the hazy rural natural philosophy grounded in Shinto beliefs, suggest that the range and diversity of agrarian thought in the Edo period soared far beyond the Confucian interdictions and exhortations of the *bakufu*. These writers and schools of thought by no means exhaust the ideological options which existed during the intellectually rich Tokugawa period, but they clearly indicate the continuing prominence of agricultural considerations during Japan's late feudal era.

Popular agrarianism in the Edo period peaked with the practical and moral teachings of Ninomiya Sontoku (Kinjirō; 1787–1856). Ninomiya and his colleagues shared a commitment to practical improvements in Japanese farming, but from their private positions outside the state they also reasserted the importance of moral exhortation and agreed that the cultivators should raise production and pay their taxes. Ninomiya acted as a reformer within the feudal hierarchy and mounted no direct challenge to the economic basis of Tokugawa rule. So noteworthy was his success as a technologist that the state finally put him in an official post; so remarkable were his ethical maxims that Ninomiya was ultimately lionized as a paragon of virtue in the national ethics textbooks in the 1930s.[19] The Hōtoku (Repaying Virtue) movement founded by his followers was both a magnet and an organ of popular agrarianism after the Meiji restoration. The Ninomiya tradition became a central thread binding multiple strands of agrarian thought, both official and nonofficial, moral and practical, feudal and modern, as Japan gradually shifted from a rural economy to industrial capitalism.

Ninomiya's central teaching was *hōtoku*, the idea that the benefits received from heaven, man, and earth should be repaid. If people collectively repaid their blessings, he believed, a peaceful and prosperous country (*fukoku anmin*) would be created and a "true society" would result – one in which all persons would be ennobled. The means of achieving *hōtoku*, he taught, consisted of sincerity (*shisei*), diligence (*kinrō*), thrift (*bundo*), and yielding to others (*suijō*).[20] All but the last had been prominent virtues in Tokugawa Confucian ethics, but Ninomiya combined them in a novel fashion, transforming these seemingly pious qualities into a practical code with powerful impact.

Although the concepts of *bundo and suijō* assumed a static economy, Robert N. Bellah has correctly asserted that Ninomiya's doctrines subsequently played a social role not unlike that of Christianity in the rise of European capitalism. Although Bellah has probably overemphasized the degree to which economic recovery and spiritual salvation were fused in Hōtoku thought,[21] it is easy to imagine that the new urban work force, bringing such values as hard work and thrift from the farms, proved immensely helpful in the industrialization program of the Meiji state after 1868.

But Ninomiya's teachings themselves stressed self-improvement within the stable social and administrative structure of Tokugawa Japan. By exhorting the individual to act in concert with his neighbors for the common good, Ninomiya directed attention away from reliance on the initiative of the state, which had heretofore been primarily responsible for economic relief. Yet if he prodded men into resisting the ravages of nature, Ninomiya proposed no measures to relieve the heavy tax burdens borne by the farm villages. In no sense was he a rural leveler;[22] the direction of his dogmas was upward, toward individual self-improvement within a communal village society dominated by the political overlordship of the *bakuhan* system. Although Ninomiya encouraged a degree of rural industrialization, he forcefully asserted that agriculture was the most important calling: "The masses of the people are the foundation of a State and of all occupations agriculture is the basic one. . . . It must be highly valued and strongly encouraged. If the root is adequately nourished, there is no doubt that the branches will flourish."[23]

As a consequence, Ninomiya's thought, like that of various court Neo-Confucianists, rural technologists, and partisans of village natural philosophy before him, as yet represented no fundamental challenge to the ideological consensus underpinning the Japanese polity and society. Instead, his teachings confirmed two centuries later the static policy implications of moving the political capital to Edo back in 1603; the primacy of wealth in land rather than trade, of Shinto beliefs and gods, of social hierarchy and knowing one's station, and of encouraging farm production. Ninomiya both affirmed and conserved the central importance of intensive wet rice agriculture and the *buraku* communities in which its practitioners have lived, close to nature, since earliest times.

THE SETTING FOR AGRICULTURAL DEVELOPMENT, 1870–1895

> The wealth of the country is dependent on the quantity of goods produced. . . . The people's industries have not had sufficient encouragement from the government as they have just begun to develop. Skill and knowledge must be given to the people and complete regulations established.

> The government and officials must all exert every effort to encourage industry and to increase production.[24]

With these words Minister of Home Affairs Ōkubo Toshimichi (1830–1878) inaugurated the modern era of Japanese economic growth in 1873. Ōkubo was a leading figure in the small oligarchy of samurai from western Japan who had overthrown the Tokugawa *bakufu* in a nearly bloodless coup and "restored" the teenaged Meiji emperor to political authority in January 1868, closing out Japan's eight-hundred-year history of feudal rule.

The insurgents seemed to agree that language is the dress of thought: their choice of the term "restoration" (*ishin*) to characterize their action was deliberate. They consciously portrayed the Meiji restoration as a metaphor for the ancient Japanese ideal, honored above all in the farm villages, of the unity of politics and religious ceremony. By theoretically reuniting the sacred functions of the emperor, deriving from his ceremonial position as chief priest of Shinto, with his renewed temporal duties as political sovereign, the Meiji oligarchs used the venerable imperial institution as a focus of new public loyalties emerging in response to decades of diplomatic pressure from abroad and political incompetence at home. In practice, Ōkubo and his associates had simply replaced the Tokugawa family as thurifers of the imperial regalia, using the throne to legitimize decisions taken among themselves, without the emperor's personal discretion. Yet this note of functional continuity from Tokugawa to Meiji is offset by the remarkable innovations that were made in the 1870s, in law, administration, education, military affairs, the economy, and virtually every other sector of national life. So broad and permanent were the changes that many persons have come to regard Meiji less as a restoration than a revolution.[25]

When Ōkubo Toshimichi spoke of working "to encourage industry and to increase production," he set the tone not just for the Meiji government's economic policies but also, in the long run, for the performance of the country's entire economy. Under active state guidance that continues in altered forms even today, the Japanese economy sailed steadily toward the national goal of enriching the country and strengthening the army (*fukoku kyōhei*). As in many modernizing countries, economic policy became a trustworthy tool of national integration and political development, so that Japan could compete successfully in a world of rich and powerful states. From this it is evident that within less than twenty-five years official attitudes toward economics had been greatly transformed by the chain of events, both internal and external, that propelled Japan into the modern era.

Ōkubo and the other Meiji oligarchs knew that industrialization was the main path to national wealth, but they also understood that an overwhelmingly agricultural economy, with 80 percent of the labor force employed in farming, could not be converted to industrialism overnight. Like state planners everywhere, they realized that farm production set the limits for industrial growth, by feeding the expanding urban population, creating capital for investment, providing raw materials for manufacturing, and, ideally, supplying a surplus for export, thereby earning foreign exchange with which the state could import capital equipment to launch new enterprises. Thus the Japanese leaders fashioned policies that, paradoxically, exploited and nurtured agriculture at the same time: to make farming pay for industrialization, it must pay to be engaged in farming.

Although my chief concern is with attitudes toward farming, it is important to outline the economic context within which agrarian thinking, both official and popular, took place during the years from the Meiji restoration to the Sino-Japanese War of 1894–1895. There can be no shred of doubt that, with government encouragement, farm output grew almost without interruption from the 1870s right up to the rural depression of the 1920s. Table 1 suggests that general agricultural production more than doubled between 1880 and 1915. Especially noteworthy is the fact that this great increase occurred despite an almost constant average farm size (about 1.0 hectares) and rural labor force (15.5 million in 1878, 14.5 million in 1912).[26] Although population growth in the countryside was relatively high during this period, the urban economy expanded fast enough to absorb unneeded rural workers without notable labor shortages or excesses in either sector until the 1920s. At the same time, agricultural growth was strong enough to allow even more spectacular increases in industrial output, especially in the years following the Sino-Japanese and Russo-Japanese wars.[27] Japan in these years was an unusual example of an industrializing country that raised its agricultural productivity within a system of small-scale farming, without major reductions in rural population or the dislocations of village life that might have accompanied mass migrations to the cities.

Table 1 Agricultural output, 1878–1937 (five-year averages)

Year	*Agricultural output, constant million yen*	*General agricultural production index*
1878–1882	904	100
1883–1887	1,032	114
1888–1892	1,196	132
1893–1897	1,308	145
1898–1902	1,558	172
1903–1907	1,628	180
1908–1912	1,875	207
1913–1917	1,966	217
1918–1922	2,189	242
1923–1927	2,057	228
1928–1932	2,287	253
1933–1937	2,534	280

Source: Agriculture and Economic Growth: Japan's Experience, ed. Kazushiu Ohkawa, Bruce F. Johnston, and Hiromitsu Kaneda (Princeton and Tokyo: Princeton University Press and University of Tokyo Press, 1970), p. 38.

Despite the modern determinist contention that Japan's economic development before World War I took place atop a traditional agricultural base characterized by "feudal production relations,"[28] a number of technological and institutional innovations affected rural life during the period 1870–1895. On the one hand, the national government carried out Ōkubo's injunction that "skill and knowledge must be given to the people" by energetically promoting new farming techniques, especially during the 1870s. Land improvement schemes, better irrigation and drainage, more rational soil use, improved seeds, more fertilizers, and the like had an important long term impact on farm output.[29] On the other hand, the state enacted major revisions in the tax and landholding systems in 1873, further discrediting the notion of an unchanging rural Japan.

Briefly put, the land tax law of 1873 granted legal land ownership by deed to the customary possessors who had previously occupied it in their own names under feudal regulations. Henceforth land could be freely bought and sold. Government surveys accompanying the new law "discovered" so many previously unregistered lands that the recorded tax base was increased by 48 percent.[30] Taxes were fixed at 3 percent cash payment per annum, based on land price, which was approximately the same level as when payments were made in kind during the Edo period. Estimates of the real burden vary, but it seems to have been little heavier in the Meiji era than earlier in the century.[31] The effect of the new tax law was to recognize legally a large landlord class (many of them petty owner-cultivators), a sizeable group of part owners, part tenants, and a smaller class of tenants, roughly in the proportion of 45: 35: 20.[32]

From the perspective of state planners, the new tax system had certain evident merits. It permitted year-to-year budgeting, since tax obligations were fixed regardless of output. It created a nationwide mechanism for accumulating revenue for the expenses of governing and for industrial subsidies. It brought previously untaxed lands under the law, spreading tax obligations more equitably and reducing potential unrest. The new scheme benefited large landlords the most and tenants the least, because rents continued to be paid in kind (about half the crop, as in the Edo period). Since population pressure on the land remained relatively strong throughout the Meiji era, rents also stayed high. By contrast, landlords' tax obligations were somewhat lower than previously (because of a broader tax base), and they were fixed at definite cash levels.

In a generally inflationary age, both tenant and landlord could obtain favorable prices for the crops they marketed directly or indirectly, but the value of the tenant's rent also rose. On the other hand, the landlord's taxes rose much more slowly, and then under the impact of local levies.[33] To the landlord it was generally advantageous to rent surplus lands to tenants, not only because of the prevailing high rates that renting commanded but also because it was expensive to hire the field hands that intensive rice growing demanded, should the landlord try to cultivate the land himself.

The drift toward tenancy accelerated in the 1880s as a result of stiff deflationary measures taken by the oligarchy in 1881 under the new Minister of Finance, Matsukata Masayoshi (1835–1924). Rice prices quicky fell to 4.8 yen per koku, half their level in 1880. After a number of relatively fat years, this sudden pinch effectively doubled the proportion of a landlord's income given over to taxes.[34] Many small landowners were consequently forced into debt to pay taxes, and a large number of owner-farmers, perhaps as many as five hundred thousand families, lapsed into tenant status.[35] Tables 2 and 3 display the classifications of farm families and the proportion of land in tenancy from the restoration to World War I. The land thus defaulted fell into

Table 2 Farm families classified by land status

Year	*Owner-farmer* %	*Part owner-farmer, part-tenant* %	*Tenant farmer* %
1868	ca. 45.0	ca. 35.0	ca. 20.0
1883–1884	37.4	42.9	19.7
1888	33.3	45.1	21.6
1899	35.4	38.4	26.2
1902	33.9	38.0	28.1
1907	33.7	37.7	28.6
1912	32.5	39.8	27.7

Source: Ronald P. Dore, *Land Reform in Japan* (London: Oxford University Press, 1959), p. 17; *Agricultural Development in Modern Japan*, ed. Takekazu Ogura, 2nd ed. (Tokyo: Fuji Publishing Co., 1968), p. 18.

Table 3 Proportion of land area cultivated by tenant farmers to total cultivated land

Year	*Proportion* %
1868	ca. 30.0
1883–1884	36.8
1887	39.3
1892	40.0
1903	44.5
1908	45.4
1913	45.5

Source: Ronald P. Dore, *Land Reform in Japan* (London: Oxford University Press, 1959), p. 17; *Agricultural Development in Modern Japan*, ed. Takekazu Ogura, 2nd ed. (Tokyo: Fuji Publishing Co., 1968), p. 18.

the hands of large landlords and, more and more, city merchant speculators. By World War I, the percentage of land in tenancy had stabilized at about 45 percent, where it remained until the U.S. occupation land reform of 1946. Likewise the number of tenant families grew steadily as a result of the Matsukata deflation, reaching a peak early in the twentieth century. The effects of these changes in the 1880s were long lasting: a concentration of landownership in fewer hands, absentee landlordism by the 1890s, diminished face-to-face relationships between owners and tenants, a debt spiral that made it difficult to escape tenant status, and a gradual weakening of community ties and customary contacts, as control over landed wealth was no longer entirely in the hands of village residents.

While overall agricultural production climbed quite steadily from the Meiji restoration to World War I, the Sino-Japanese War of 1894–1895 is a good bench mark for gauging the effects of the land tax and the landholding system it fostered. In 1888–1892, despite two decades of stimulating industrialization, the government still derived 85.6 percent of its tax revenues from the land tax. Twenty years and two wars later, the land tax accounted for only 42.9 percent of total state tax income, despite a doubling of the absolute value of the land tax from 38 million yen to 79 million yen.[36] Farming clearly was crucial for the solvency of the government until the mid-1890s, but thereafter new taxes on new revenue sources sprouted rapidly as industrialization spread. This created an uneasy situation in which landowners' real tax obligations to government at all levels were growing heavier, whereas the state depended on farming less completely than in the early Meiji period. No small part of the rural unrest that emerged after 1900 can be attributed to these changing relationships between taxpayers and the state.

FARM POLICY IN THE EARLY MEIJI PERIOD

When the Meiji government decided to lift both indusrial and agricultural production in the 1870s, it decisively set aside the Tokugawa canon that farming should be preserved as the unchanging economic foundation of society. The goal of government agricultural policy in the early Meiji years was distinctly modern and clearly nationalist: farm output must be increased to create a rich country and strong people. In practice, agricultural exports (mainly tea, silk, and silkworm eggs) accounted for 70 to 80 percent of total exports in the early Meiji period.[37] No longer was farming officially to be regarded as a virtue in itself; instead it must be articulated with a larger economic policy that would bring Japan wealth, power, and international respect.

The means to be employed were both modern and traditionalistic. On the one hand, the state quickly introduced technical improvements and agricultural education, and some leading statesmen advocated the commercialization of agriculture on a large scale. On the other hand, the government echoed the Tokugawa encouragements to thrift and diligence, especially in the 1880s, although it did so for modernizing, not conserving, purposes.

The first official agency for farm policy was the Kannōkyoku (Office for Encouraging Agriculture), created within the Minbushō or Ministry of Public Affairs, in 1870. After many changes, this unit reemerged as the new Ministry of Agriculture and Commerce (Nōshōmushō) in 1880. The agency's policies were shaped in part by the report of the Iwakura mission to America and Europe in 1872–1873, which concluded that (1) agricultural development varied among Western countries, but all were more advanced than Japan; (2) agricultural growth required education and experimentation; and (3) agricultural science and techniques were best spread through schools and colleges, such as those founded under the 1862 Morrill Land Grant Act in the United States.[38] With farmers no longer legally bound to their occupations, the government maintained, it was critically important that a new class of progressive cultivators take the lead in raising output.

As a consequence, beginning in 1877 the government set up agricultural experiment stations throughout Japan to demonstrate Western techniques, products, and machinery. As was true for many other government programs in the 1870s, foreign advisers were hired to accelerate farm improvements. The state also opened a series of agricultural schools. These various efforts required many years to take full effect, and their part in enhancing productivity must be weighed against the many other factors which spurred output. These activities reveal the government's conviction, as Matsukata put it in 1879, that "the development of agriculture must not rely merely on practical experience. First you must have science and only then will you begin to have success."[39] Strapped by other heavy budget commitments, the Meiji state invested relatively little in rural technical education and public works[40] in the years before the Sino-Japanese War, but Matsukata's words were a firm denial of the Tokugawa belief that farmers were too stupid to need any education and show that the Meiji oligarchs hardly intended to preserve Japanese farming in its premodern condition.

Most emblematic of the early Meiji view that agriculture should serve national economic policy was the enthusiasm of some government leaders for large-scale commercial farming. Well aware that land consolidation and big farms had caused great spurts of productivity in Western countries, men such as Ōkubo, Matsukata, Itō Hirobumi (1841–1909), and later Inoue Kaoru (1836–1915) called for mechanization and extensive farming wherever possible. Although their attempts to implement ranch farming met with some success in Hokkaido and Iwate prefectures,[41] the deck was stacked against large-scale agriculture: rice was the richest crop in most areas of Japan and required vast amounts of labor, the rural population was too large to be thrown off the land as ranching demanded, and there was a scarcity of capital and machinery for large-scale operations. Perhaps the most salutary result of the government's extensive farming doctrine was to bring more lands under cultivation, especially in northern Japan.[42] The fact remains that renting lands out to tenants was more profitable for large landowners than ranch-scale operations, and after Ōkubo's assassination in 1878 the state placed less hope in large farming.

During the same period the bureaucracy also unveiled a program to promote agricultural development within the existing small-scale structure of Japanese farming by creating a system of itinerant veteran farmers (later replaced by trained agronomists) to spread new techniques throughout the countryside.[43] The government also sponsored the Dai Nihon Nōkai (agricultural Society of Japan), formed in 1881. A quasi-official organization based on local farm discussion groups which had arisen in the mid-1870s, the Dai Nihon Nōkai emphasized experience equally with science. Its announced purpose was to "exchange agricultural knowledge and experience and especially to plan the reform and improvement of agriculture."[44] Under chief secretary Shinagawa Yajirō (1843–1900), then an official in the new Ministry of Agriculture and Commerce and later a cabinet minister under several premiers, the Dai Nihon Nōkai held discussions all over the country to promote production through the cooperation of the "conscientious" landlords who dominated village society.

Moral uplift also had a place in the Meiji scheme of fostering farm development, but the assumptions and purposes underlying the oligarchs' exhortations to farmers were substantially different from those prevalent among Tokugawa Confucianists. Hard work and frugality had specific monetary advantages to the new leaders, who believed in economic growth, whereas in the premodern view these qualities were ethically desirable for their own sakes in a static agrarian economy. Thus the Meiji emperor could tell the guests at the opening of the Komaba Agricultural School in January 1878, "We think that agriculture is the foundation of the country," but his words had lost the Confucian freight of a century before. Now, the emperor continued, "let production continue to increase, and let the people continue to prosper. We must practice the study of agriculture."[45] Science and progress, not eternal economic stasis, were moral in their own right.

The Confucianist educator Nishimura Shigeki (1828–1902), an influential Meiji bureaucrat, stressed that the countries of Europe were thriving because their people were frugal and diligent.[46] Such notes were struck repeatedly in the 1880s, especially when the government exported rice to improve its trade balance after the collapse of 1881, all the while urging the farmers to restrict consumption. An edict from the Nōshōmushō in 1885 urged that labor and thrift were the means to escape the poverty imposed by urbanization.[47] As one observer put it, "the export of rice in this period was, so to speak, a 'hunger export.'"[48] However pious and self-serving these exhortations, the theme of sacrifice for the sake of modernization runs throughout, and the emphasis is no longer on the glorification of self-denial for its own sake.

By the mid-1880s, the state had switched most of its attention to working within the small-scale farm system, and it had begun to accommodate its earlier interest in technical education to the realities of a rural society dominated by landlords. Increasingly it had to cope with practical problems hindering farm growth. In 1884, for example, the Nōshōmushō was obliged to upgrade the quality of market rice through rigid inspection programs, since much rice was rotting and sake production was affected.[49] These changes seemed to constitute appropriate adjustments to a decade's experience with promoting output – especially in light of the farm depression of the 1880s – but in no sense did they indicate a policy swing away from stimulating agricultural production as a part of the overall quest for wealth and power. Despite tactical shifts, the Meiji oligarchs remained firmly wedded to their modernizing outlook on farming.

POPULAR FARM THOUGHT AND THE NINETEENTH-CENTURY HŌTOKU MOVEMENT

The new government was quite secure enough to set farm policy as it saw fit during the 1870s and 1880s without fears of a serious challenge to its own power from the countryside. At the same time the cooperation, or at least acquiescence, of farmers large and small was highly desirable if agriculture was to play the modernizing role cast for it by Ōkubo. Part of the impetus for rural improvements in the early Meiji period came from the farm villages themselves, where after the land revision of 1873 "conscientious farmers" (*tokunō*) and other progressive landlords pressed both technical improvement and moral uplift upon the cultivators, in order to grow bigger crops and increase the landlords' own incomes.[50] Most progressive landlords realized full well that the state's motive for advocating technical education in the 1870s and 1880s was primarily to increase tax revenues by means of expanded farm production, although this had the side effect of feathering landowners' nests as well. But, since their own interests coincided with those of the government, *tokunō* generally took the lead in land improvement in their own districts. In the earlier Meiji period, these progressive farmers usually supported the state's technological innovations, but by the 1890s many of them began to demand that the government do more for the landholding classes, both technologically and fiscally. One especially prominent organization of conscientious farmers was the Meiji period Hōtokusha (Repaying Virtue Society), several of whose leaders became persuasive exponents of popular farm thought in the 1870s and 1880s.

Taken together, the Hōtoku societies founded by Ninomiya Sontoku's pupils in the late Tokugawa period formed a sizeable farm-improvement movement in the Meiji era, under the leadership of landlords who were at once innovative and didactic.[51] These organizations by no means encapsulated the full range of opinion found within the very diverse landowning class. To some progressive local leaders, the echoes of feudal moralism rendered the Hōtoku societies too anachronistic to deserve their loyalty. To more traditional farmers, the Hōtoku interest in self-improvement and technical change was too great a departure to warrant allegiance. But the movement merits attention, first because of its appeal to precisely that village leadership class which became the object of official patronage after 1900, and second because, of all the popular agrarian ideologies in modern Japan, Hōtoku teachings eventually came to enjoy the greatest favor within the government.

Although Ninomiya Sontoku preached the virtues of 'sincerity, diligence, thrift, and yielding to others throughout the first half of the nineteenth century, his impact on the Hōtoku movement was more inspirational than organizational.[52] The earliest Hōtokusha were apparently started in Tōtōmi in the 1840s by Agoin Gidō (1789–1863) and Okada Saheiji (1812–1878),[53] both of whom applied Ninomiya's principles to farm management and shopkeeping with great profit. These small predominantly landlord organizations were most notably credit societies. The man most responsible for spreading Hōtoku thought was Tomita Takayoshi (1814–1890), a scholar and technologist who helped to establish Hōtoku societies in present-day Fukushima, Kanagawa, and Shizuoka prefectures in the 1850s.[54] Tomita wrote *Hōtokuron* (Theory of Repaying Virtue) in 1850, explaining that the purpose of the movement was to make the country thrive and build a "true society" by "making sincerity the foundation, emphasizing diligence, making one's lot in life the substance, and practicing self-restraint and aiding others."[55] Both this work and *Hōtokuki* (Record of Repaying Virtue), which Tomita wrote right after Ninomiya's death in 1856, were realistic guides based on experience, not sophisticated bodies of theory, and their impact was understandably less intellectual than practical.

With the overthrow of the *bakuhan* system in 1868 and the consequent tax and landholding reforms, the Hōtoku movement grew somewhat discredited, insofar as it was tied to the feudal land relations and stratified social system of the Tokugawa era. The spirit of the new age, typified by the "civilization and enlightenment" (*bunmei kaika*) outlook of the Meiji Six Society, flowed directly against the notion of accepting one's inherited social position. However helpful the Hōtoku stress on self-help and free credit may have been to certain late Tokugawa villages, its premodern overtones would plainly require modification if the movement was to remain dynamic in the 1870s. This task of adaptation fell to another of Ninomiya's disciples, the National Learning advocate Fukuzumi Masae (1824–1892).[56]

Fukuzumi organized the Meiji period's first Hōtokusha in 1874 and defined its goals in these terms:

> The purpose of the Hōtokusha is to help the poor and to aid them to unite in helping one another, first by opening their hearts and developing goodness of character among them, and secondly by assisting them to open up wild lands, improve irrigation and roads, repair bridges and river banks, and, in general, doing all that is of benefit to the poor. It begins by helping the poorest and encouraging and rewarding the good.[57]

Here Fukuzumi expressed the twin themes that brought so many progressive landlords into the Hōtoku movement: character-building and practical improvements. These remained the primary emphases of the Hōtoku societies until they were taken over by the state early in the twentieth century.

There was more to Meiji Hōtoku thought, however, than ethics and technology (which after all had been staples since Ninomiya's time). Fukuzumi offered a reinterpretation of the Hōtoku tradition in *Fukoku shōkei* (Shortcut to Enriching the Country), written during 1873–1874. For Ninomiya's teachings to remain valid, he believed, men must understand that the way of nature meant the way of the Shinto gods (*kami*). He claimed that farm growth was not inconsistent with the new economic policies of the Meiji era:

> Making every effort to protect against poor crops, starvation, and epidemic, to assist the very poor, and to reverse declines, we place priority on encouraging both agriculture and industry to flourish, thus increasing production, causing wealth to accumulate, enriching the country, making all the people prosperous, carrying out the divine will of creation, and supporting the evolution of nature.[58]

It was now the "divine will of creation" that both agriculture and industry prosper – quite a departure from the farm-centered teachings of Ninomiya within a static, feudal understanding of economics. Yet both saint and disciple served the state to which each was loyal. Just as Ninomiya's doctrines appeared after 1868 to be conservative and tied to the feudal political culture of his era,[59] so Fukuzumi's enthusiasm for linking agricultural improvement to the way of the gods and the development plans of the Meiji oligarchy seemed flawed by his ingenuous attachment to the religious and economic motifs of the new age.

Fukuzumi's only peer as a Hōtokusha organizer in the early Meiji period was the progressive landlord Okada Ryōichirō (1839–1915), who was less concerned than he with Shinto and correspondingly more interested in economic growth.[60] Most striking was Okada's belief that rural industrial development must parallel agricultural growth. One of his motives for entrepreneurship through the Hōtokusha was to provide employment for village residents and to stimulate productive activity that would improve rural conditions. More important seems to have been his assumption that national economic development depended on farming, by exporting rice, tea, and silk. More open to the rise of manufacturing than other Hōtoku leaders, Okada nevertheless insisted that industry be scattered throughout the countryside,[61] underlining his belief that the rural areas must be the foundation of national prosperity. Okada's outlook seems to have been affected by a utilitarian conviction that the simultaneous development of agriculture and industry would benefit the most persons (he is known to have read works by Jeremy Bentham and J. S. Mill).[62]

As a progressive rural entrepreneur in sericulture and food processing, Okada helped to update Hōtoku teachings by accommodating, to a degree, the drive for industrial growth of the Meiji period. At the same time he criticized the state for policies that favored manufacturing over farming, and he was a strong opponent of centralized industrialization induced from above. His ideas formed a type of producer class philosophy: within the limits of the landlord system and his belief in the primacy of agriculture, he was a great innovator, both in spreading credit, technology, and job opportunities and in encouraging individual initiative as a part of overall national economic growth.

By Okada's time, Hōtoku thought had clearly come very far from Ninomiya's outlook in the late feudal period. But Okada's seemingly progressive position was tenable only so long as farming dominated the economy. By the 1890s, as industrialism spread, the limitations of Okada's producer class assumptions became apparent, and the Hōtoku movement took on an increasingly conservative hue. Indeed, by the mid-1880s Okada had lost touch with local farming and devoted most of his time to administering national Hōtoku activities. In 1890 he moved to Tokyo, where he sat in the lower house of the Diet and contented himself with his sugar enterprises.

The fortunes of the Hōtoku movement in the first half of the Meiji period depended to a great extent on the practical leadership of Fukuzumi and Okada, but local economic conditions also had a bearing on the formation of new societies. To be sure, both Fukuzumi's focus on Shinto and Okada's concern for entrepreneurship were signs of a specific national consciousness not evident in Ninomiya's teachings a few decades earlier. This new consciousness helped them attune their movement to the new ideological requirements of the Meiji period and explains in part why Hōtoku societies continued to attract members. Yet the large number of new Hōtokusha formed in the mid-1880s showed a direct relationship to the economic miseries of the Matsukata deflation.[63] In the face of dropping farm prices and total rural debts of 200,000,000 yen, many peasants turned to rioting, most notably in the Chichibu uprising of November 1884.[64] Landowners, meanwhile, found the favorable Hōtokusha credit arrangements to be one of the few avenues of escape from debt, especially in the rock bottom years 1884 and 1885. It seems likely that specific local problems of credit, debt, and taxes, rather than a theoretical commitment to the doctrines of Fukuzumi and Okada, prompted most landlords to join the Hōtokusha.[65] No doubt some progressive farmers shared their enthusiasm for national growth, but on the whole the movement's vicissitudes probably turned on immediate problems facing landowners in their day-to-day operations.

By the 1890s the Hōtoku organizations were approaching the limits of their effectiveness in promoting rural growth. The capital they mustered for village rehabilitation was modest in relation to the need, and small owner-farmers continued to slide into tenancy. More generally, Fukuzumi's echoes of Shinto mythology had an odd ring to many persons educated in the new school system or otherwise affected by the cosmopolitan influences of *bunmei kaika* in the earlier Meiji period. Even Okada's progressive Hōtoku doctrines appeared to many observers to be anachronistic, formalistic, and too cautious in tempo for the economic expansion and aggressive speculation of the

1890s.[66] Nevertheless the Hōtoku movement remained powerful in many regions through the end of the century and provided considerable backing for government farm proposals in the 1890s.

Just as the Hōtokusha played an important institutional part in the transition from an agrarian to a capitalist economy, they also contributed to a changing awareness of the economic significance of agriculture in many landlords' minds during the period 1870–1895. Having restyled Ninomiya's premodern teachings to suit the fashion of a new age, Hōtoku thought in the Meiji era stretched the farm-first tradition but never burst it. Because agriculture remained its central pillar, the Hōtoku outlook gradually turned into a special-interest ideology with the rise of industrial Japan. By the early twentieth century the Hōtoku approach was so tamed that it received support and encouragement from the same central government whose policies Okada had vigorously attacked a generation earlier. When it became apparent that traditional farm-centered ideologies such as Hōtokushugi could not remain vital in an age of onrushing capitalism, the ground was cleared for true Nōhonshugi – a body of ideas designed to counteract industrialism and reconstruct Japanese society by regaining the virtues of an agricultural era now irretrievably past.

EARLY MEIJI FARM POLICIES AND JAPANESE AGRARIANISM

Both the official attitudes and policies toward farming and the thought of conscientious farmers during the 1870s and 1880s unquestionably played a critical part in the nation's economic growth and permanently redirected the course of agricultural development in Japan. Just as Fukuzumi and Okada recast Hōtoku ideas to fit their times, so too the state farming programs and pronouncements differed both in substance and in sentiment from the agricultural outlook of the Tokugawa government. To some specialists, this difference is sufficient to mark out the first half of the Meiji period as the initial phase of the official profarming ideology known as bureaucratic Nōhonshugi. Sakurai Takeo, a provocative observer, regards Nōhonshugi as primarily a political doctrine created by the Meiji oligarchy to preserve the farm villages on which their own power was based.[67] Whereas the Tokugawa *bakufu* had revered agriculture "for its own sake" (*jūnōshugi*), Sakurai has written, Nōhonshugi now emerged as "a reflection of the contradiction between the development of bourgeois elements and feudal production relations (i.e., petty serf economics)."[68]

Okutani Matsuji, another modern scholar, has echoed Sakurai's view: "The formation of Nōhonshugi thought is premised on a crisis in the original feudal system, that is, the development of the commercial economy to a fixed stage, corresponding to the absolutist stage in politics"[69] (in the early Meiji period). Okutani acknowledges that an agricultural revolution had not yet taken place in Japan at this time, so that the oligarchy protected its rural base by resorting to premodern farm ideas. Also characteristic of early Meiji state agrarianism, Okutani maintains, was its strong support of the emperor system,[70] a carry-over from premodern society. Despite these wrinkles peculiar to Japan, Okutani concludes that official Nōhonshugi in the early Meiji period closely resembled the physiocratic economics of eighteenth-century France. He cites François Quesnay (1694–1774), Anne Robert Jacques Turgot (1727–1781), and Jean-Charles Léonard Simon de Sismondi (1773–1842) as critics of capitalism who upheld farming in an age of industrialization.[71] Like Japanese agrarian thinkers in both Tokugawa and Meiji times, they regarded agricultural labor alone as productive and saw it as the foundation of all other enterprise.

Although Sakurai and Okutani have properly noted that Nōhonshugi developed as a response to the growth of trade and industry, each appears to be premature in timing insofar as bureaucratic agrarianism is concerned. As diligent as the state may have been in stimulating industrial enterprises in the 1870s and 1880s, it is beyond dispute that the economy was still predominantly rural before the Sino-Japanese War, with insufficient capitalism for agrarian ideologies to react against. However elusive a concept Nōhonshugi may be, few of its primary attributes appear to have been present in the agricultural thinking of the early Meiji state. No important bureaucrats as yet trumpeted the merits of village communalism; little was heard of the subsequent theme that farming was at the heart of Japan's national essence. Indeed, the weight placed on Nōhonshugi as a political doctrine should not be permitted to obscure its equally important place in popular thought. It was not just an ideology of the establishment; in time its main stream became essentially antiestablishment. Most importantly, state agricultural thought stressed farm policy as a key element in Japan's overall program of modernization; true Nōhonshugi advocates, whether bureaucrats or private citizens, made farming a foil to the complications produced by that program.

What is more, to say that the oligarchs tried to preserve the farm village in its premodern condition in order to maintain their own political power is to overlook the growth-oriented objectives and progressive technical-educational programs of state farm policy after the restoration. Farm life was no doubt nearly as dull and burdensome in the late nineteenth century as it had been a hundred years earlier, but it seems unwarranted to portray Japanese agriculture by the mid-Meiji period as unchanged since antiquity.[72]

When Okutani identifies agrarianist thought with the "absolutist" politics of the earlier Meiji period, he appears to regard it as a response to political feudalism rather than to economic modernism. Indeed, by tying Nōhonshugi ideas to the physiocratic doctrines of prerevolutionary France, Okutani has virtually conceded that the so-called bureaucratic agrarianism of the period 1868–1890 was grounded in a preindustrial farm economy which merely wanted preservation, not yet restoration. Moreover, his emphasis on the connection between farming and the imperial institution seems to slight the nationalist objectives of the Meiji bureaucrats. As in all major state policies after 1868, service to the emperor was urged upon the cultivators not just to reinforce old bonds which had been neglected in the feudal era but primarily to pursue the new goals of wealth and power, symbolically sanctioned by the Meiji emperor.

One might well ask whether it is proper to equate physiocratic economics with Japanese farm thought in either the Tokugawa or Meiji eras. The French physiocrats believed that land was the only source of wealth, a proposition congenial to Neo-Confucian economics. Quesnay is rumored to have put it tersely: "Poor peasants, poor kingdom; poor kingdom, poor sovereign."[73] Physiocrats opposed the mercantilistic view that money was the essence of wealth and should be accumulated by each nation by minimizing imports. Instead, they believed in free trade, an unrestricted flow of capital, and reduced taxes.[74] To this end, Turgot advocated a single tax or *impôt unique*, on the net product of the land – the income of the landowning class.[75]

Free trade was almost unknown in Japanese agricultural discourses, either before the restoration or after. The prevailing view of the Edo period was that of the Neo-Confucianist Arai Hakuseki (1657–1725), who feared that foreign trade would harm the state. Even in the mid-nineteenth century, exclusionists in Japan clamored in a most unphysiocratic manner that the country was importing useless woolens in exchange for the substance of wealth: gold, silver, and copper.[76] Kanda Takahira (1830–1898), a Meiji modernizer and otherwise no exclusionist, also took these precious metals, not land, to be the real source of wealth. In the Meiji era the state's near-mercantilist development policies obviously transcended physiocratic economic philosophy, and much later, in the twentieth century, those who advocated the return to a society based on village farming also looked on international trade with suspicion. The French physiocrats' interest in lower taxes likewise struck no responsive chords among government officials in Japan, before or after 1868, although the same cannot, of course, be said of the taxpayers themselves. Both the French physiocrats and the popular agrarian ideologues in Japan arose during hard times on the farms, and both resisted exorbitant taxes imposed from above, which in the case of France were as high as 82 percent of net produce.[77]

The physiocratic conception of politics was grounded on a natural order in which few disputes arose so long as men obeyed the rules of nature.[78] In this respect there was a resemblance both with the Confucian idea of man and nature in the universe and with the communal natural philosophy of the Japanese countryside, with its Shinto overtones. To insure that equal conditions and uniform rules prevailed, the physiocrats favored a single despot whose prerogative would be strictly limited to identifying the true natural law in cases of conflict. This outlook was theoretically congenial with the Confucian notion of rule by virtue and nonaction, although the Tokugawa state rarely conformed to this ideal. Clearly the activism of the Meiji state exceeded by far the limited despotism envisioned by Quesnay and Turgot. The real parallel seems to arise in the village self-rule scheme of Gondō

Seikyō (1868–1937) in the 1920s, since Gondō accepted the emperor but distrusted almost all other authorities above the village level.

Important exceptions to this overall pattern of dissimilarity between Japanese and French agrarianism can be culled from the vast body of economic thought bequeathed by the Tokugawa era. Dazai Shundai shared with the physiocrats not only the notion that all wealth came from the soil but also the idea that taxation should be based on the net product of the land.[79] Andō Shōeki sought a citizen-state of independent farmers who lived within the laws of nature under a limited political authority.[80] Still, it must be granted that the analogy between Japanese farm thought and French physiocratic economics is only partial. Not only did the two societies inherit different cultural traditions and confront different economic problems, but also the diversity of Japanese agrarianism makes it difficult to establish a precise correspondence with physiocratic ideas. As a rule, Japanese farm ideologues (with the exception of Ōkubo and others in the early Meiji period) favored small-scale agriculture, whereas Turgot and the other physiocrats held that large farms were the key to progress.[81]

In this respect Thomas Jefferson's vision of a nation of small farmers may come closer to the ideal sought by Japan's agrarian ideologues after the middle of the Meiji era. The physiocrats cared little more for the individual peasant's welfare than did the lofty Tokugawa Confucianists; they saw agriculture as a source of wealth, whereas to Jefferson it was a wellspring of human qualities that were requisite for self-rule. He wrote John Jay in 1785: "Cultivators of the earth are the most valuable citizens. They are the most vigorous, the most independent, the most virtuous, and they are tied to their country, and wedded to its liberty and interests by the most lasting bonds. . . . I consider the class of artificers as thc panders of vice, and the instruments by which the liberties of a country are generally overturned."[82] Yet while Jefferson stressed liberty and citizenship, his Japanese counterparts usually emphasized subjecthood, communalism, and men's obligations to others within the self-ruling village.

Two conclusions seem to emerge. First, the evidence for similarity between French physiocratic thinking and Japanese agrarianism is conflicting, sometimes contradictory. Second, the official view of agriculture during the earlier Meiji period was neither especially physiocratic nor very harmonious with the thought of those subsequent agrarian ideologues known as Nōhonshugisha. It is to the growth of their ideas that I shall now turn.

NOTES

1 For a description of the Tokugawa land system, see Thomas C. Smith, *The Agrarian Origins of Modern Japan* (Stanford: Stanford University Press, 1959), pp. 1–11.

2 Furushima Toshio, *Nihon nōgakushi* [History of Japanese Agriculture] (Tokyo: Nihon Hyōronsha, 1946), I, is a standard source for Tokugawa agricultural history. For a survey of the Edo period merchant economy, see Charles D. Sheldon,

The Rise of the Merchant Class in Tokugawa Japan, 1600–1868 (Locust Valley, N.Y.: J. J. Augustin, Inc., 1958).

3 Sakurai Takeo, "Nōhonshugi – sono rekishi, riron, jiban" [Agrarianism – Its History, Theory, and Foundation], *Rekishi kagaku* [Science of History], IV, 3, March 1935, p. 119.

4 *'Nō wa moto nari, shōkō wa sue nari.*

5 *Ta hsüeh* [Great Learning], ch. 10, 19, quoted in John W. Hall, *Tanuma Okitsugu (1719–1788): Forerunner of Modern Japan* (Cambridge, Mass.: Harvard University Press, 1955), p. 157.

6 E. Herbert Norman, *Andō Shōeki and the Anatomy of Japanese Feudalism, Transactions of the Asiatic Society of Japan*, series 3, II (Tokyo,1949), 276.

7 Ibid.

8 See Hall, pp. 60–61.

9 Ogyū Sorai, *Seidan* (Political Discourses), 1728, quoted in Sakurai, p. 121.

10 Dazai Shundai, quoted in Garrett Droppers, "Some Economic Theories of Old Japan," *Transactions of the Asiatic Society of Japan*, series I, XXIV, 1896, vii.

11 On *nōhei*, see Kumazawa Banzan, *Daigaku wakumon* [Questions on the Great Learning], ch. 12, quoted in *Sources of Japanese Tradition*, comp. Ryusaku Tsunoda, ed. William T. deBary (New York: Columbia University Press, 1958), pp. 391–392. See also Norman, pp. 11–12, 277.

12 Sakurai, p. 122. Tsukuba Hisaharu, "Nihon nōhonshugi josetsu" [Introduction to Japanese Agrarianism], *Shisō no kagaku* [Science of Thought], No. 18, June 1960, pp. 6–7, recognizes the multiple motives of the Tokugawa family in supporting farming.

13 See Takeuchi Tetsuo, "Nōhonshugi bunseki e no zenteiteki shomondai – shu to shite bunseki shikaku ni tsuite" [Preliminary Problems in Analyzing Agrarianism – With Emphasis on Analytical Viewpoints], *Shimane Nōka Daigaku kenkyū hōkoku* [Shimane Agricultural University Research Reports], No. 9, A-3, March 1961, pp. 54–56. For a modern outlook on *fūdo*, see Watsuji Tetsurō, *Fūdo* (Tokyo: Iwanami Shoten, 1935), translated as *A Climate – A Philosophical Study* by Geoffrey Bownas (Tokyo: Japanese National Commission for UNESCO, 1961). Also see Iinuma Jirō, *Nihon nōgyō gijutsushi* [History of Japanese Agricultural Technology] (Tokyo: Miraisha, 1971).

14 On this point, see Tsukuba, pp. 4–7.

15 Takeuchi, p. 54.

16 Thomas C. Smith, "Ōkura Nagatsune and the Technologists," *Personality in Japanese History*, ed. Albert M. Craig and Donald H. Shively (Berkeley: University of California Press, 1970), p. 127.

17 See Miyazaki Yasusada, *Nōgyō zensho* [Farmer's Compendium] quoted in Katayama Seiichi, "Meiji zenki nōgyō shidōsha no nōgyō kyōikukan" [The Farm Education Outlooks of Early Meiji Farm Leaders], *Nihon Daigaku Seishin Bunka Kenkyūjo-Kyōiku Seido Kenkyūjo kiyō* [Bulletin of the Nihon University Cultural Research Institute and Educational System Research Institute], IV, June 1967, 207. See also Norman, passim.

18 Satō Nobuhiro, "Yōzō kaikuron" [Creation and Cultivation], *Keizai taiten* [Compendium of Economics], XVIII, quoted in *Sources of Japanese Tradition*, p. 574.

19 See Robert K. Hall, *Shūshin: The Ethics of a Defeated Nation* (New York: Columbia University Teachers College, 1949), p. 204f. Even today in many Japanese schoolyards can be found statues of Ninomiya, absorbed in a book held in one hand, with a bundle of faggots slung over his shoulder grasped in the other.

20 For a study of Ninomiya's ethics and a detailed bibliography, see Thomas R. H. Havens, "Religion and Agriculture in Nineteenth-century Japan: Ninomiya Sontoku and the Hōtoku Movement,"*Japan Christian Quarterly*, XXXVIII, 2, Spring 1972, 98–105.

21 Robert N. Bellah, *Tokugawa Religion: The Values of Pre-Industrial Japan* (Glencoe, Ill.: The Free Press, 1957), p. 128.

22 Robert C. Armstrong, *Just Before the Dawn: The Life and work of Ninomiya Sontoku* (New York: Macmillan, 1912), p. 255.

23 *Ninomiya Sontoku: His Life and "Evening Talks,"* ed. Ishiguro Tadaatsu (Tokyo: Kenkyūsha, 1955), pp. 243–245. This book is primarily a translation, by Yamagata Isō, of *Ninomiyaō yawa* [Ninomiya's Evening Talks], written down from memory between 1884 and 1888 by Fukuzumi Masae (1824–1892), one of Ninomiya's ablest followers, in *Fukuzumi Masae senshū* [Selected Works of Fukuzumi Masae], *Ninomiya Sontoku zenshū* [Complete Works of Ninomiya Sontoku] (Shizuoka: Ninomiya Sontoku Igyō Sen'yōkai, 1931), XXXVI, 666–853. See also Nakamura Yūjirō, *Kindai Nihon ni okeru seido to shisō* [Thought and Institutions in Modern Japan] (Tokyo: Miraisha, 1967), pp. 294–296.

24 Okubo Toshimichi, 1873, quoted in Hugh Borton, *Japan's Modern Century*, 2nd ed. (New York: Ronald Press, 1970), p. 129.

25 See, e.g., Thomas C. Smith, "Japan's Aristocratic Revolution," *Yale Review*, L, 3, Spring 1961, 370–383; Marius B. Jansen, "The Meiji State: 1868–1912," *Modern East Asia: Essays in Interpretation*, ed. James B. Crowley (New York: Harcourt, Brace & World, 1970), pp. 102-108.

26 *Agricultural Development in Modern Japan*, ed. Takekazu Ogura, 2nd ed. (Tokyo: Fuji Publishing Co., 1968), pp. 618–619 (hereafter cited as Ogura). For detailed statistics on Japanese economic growth, see *Chōki keizai tōkei, suikei to bunseki* (English title: *Estimates of Long-Term Economic Statistics of Japan Since 1868*), ed. Ohkawa Kazushi, Shinohara Miyohei, and Umemura Mataji, 13 vols. (Tokyo: Tōyō Keizai Shinbunsha, 1966–), esp. vols. 9 and 13.

27 For data and analysis of industrial growth, see William W. Lockwood, *The Economic Development of Japan: Growth and Structural Change 1868–1938* (Princeton: Princeton University Press, 1954), pp. 18–37. See also Henry Rosovsky, *Capital Formation in Japan, 1868–1940* (Glencoe, Ill.: The Free Press, 1961); James I. Nakamura, *Agricultural Production and the Economic Development of Japan, 1873–1922* (Princeton: Princeton University Press, 1966); *Agriculture and Economic Growth: Japan's Experience*, ed. Kazushi Ohkawa, Bruce F. Johnston, and Hiromitsu Kaneda (Princeton: Princeton University Press, and Tokyo: University of Tokyo Press, 1970); *Economic Growth: The Japanese Experience Since the Meiji Era*, ed. Lawrence Klein and Kazushi Ohkawa (Homewood, Ill.: Richard D. Irwin, Inc., 1968). The problem of using reliable statistics is treated in Henry Rosovsky, "Rumbles in the Ricefields: Professor Nakamura vs. the Official Statistics," *Journal of Asian Studies*, XXVII, 2, February 1968, 347–360.

28 Sakurai, p. 122.

29 See Ogura, p. 624.

30 Ronald P. Dore, *Land Reform in Japan* (London: Oxford University Press, 1959), pp. 14–17.

31 Ibid.; Ogura, p. 108. An additional local tax of up to one percent was also permitted. On land taxes, see also Smith, *Agrarian Origins*, pp. 100–101, 159f.

32 See Dore, p. 17. The figures are estimates for 1868. It is almost impossible to distinguish mathematically among large, medium, and small landlords at any time between 1873 and World War II, nor did the later agrarianists who spoke optimistically of the small and medium landlords as ideal special types attempt to define them in terms of precise landholdings. In general a large landlord was one who could live entirely on rents from tenants. Usually at least ten hectares of good paddy or the equivalent in upland fields was needed for this purpose. Lands in the single-crop regions of the northeast were, of course, less productive than those in the multiple crop areas further south. A small landlord might own one or two hectares, a part of which he rented to tenants whereas a *jisakunō*, or owner-

farmer, usually held one half to one hectare and worked it by himself. The medium landlord, who rented part of his land and worked the rest, might own something like five hectares. As large landlords drifted off to the cities and became absentee owners, the small and medium landholder, and later the owner-farmer, was regarded as the backbone of village society by Nōhonshugisha. I am grateful to Ann Waswo, in private correspondence, for advice on this point.

33 Ogura, p. 18.

34 Ann Waswo, "Landlords and Social Change in Prewar Japan," Ph.D. dissertation in history, Stanford University, 1969, p. 54.

35 Ogura, p. 654.

36 Ibid., p. 22.

37 Ibid., p. 153. On Ōkubo's attitude toward agriculture and national strengthening, see Denda Isao, *Kindai Nihon nōsei shisō no kenkyū* [Studies on Modern Japanese Agricultural Administration Thought] (Tokyo, Miraisha, 1969), p. 61.

38 Katayama, pp. 164–165, 209–210.

39 Matsukata Masayoshi, "Nōshō hensan no gishi" [The Meaning of Compiling Farm Books], 1879, quoted in Katayama, p. 186.

40 Lockwood, p. 247, suggests that 10 percent of tax revenues, a low figure, went to these activities, with half supplied by local governments. On the experiment stations, see Sakurai Takeo, *Nihon nōhonshugi* [Japanese Agrarianism] (Tokyo: Hakuyōsha, 1935), pp. 151–153; Niwa Kunio, "The Reform of the Land Tax and the Government Programme for the Encouragement of Industry," *The Developing Economics*, IV, 4, December 1966, 470–471; Ogura, pp. 3–15, 152, 320–322.

41 Ogura, p. 152. On large-scale farming, see Denda, p. 72; Sakurai, Nōhonshugi – sono rekishi, riron, jiban," pp. 123–126; Sakurai, *Nihon nōhonshugi*, pp. 14–15, 80–82, 147–151; Ogura, pp. 150–153; Ogura Takekazu, *Agrarian Problems and Agricultural Policy in Japan* (Tokyo: Institute of Asian Economic Affairs, 1967), pp. 11–12.

42 Ogura, *Agrarian Problems*, p. 11.

43 See Takeuchi Tetsuo, "Nōhonshugi to nōson chūsansō" [Agrarianism and the Farm Village Middle Class], *Shimane Nōka Daigaku kenkyū hōkoku* [Shimane Agricultural University Research Reports], No. 8, A, March 1960, p. 229. On veteran farmers, see Ogura, pp. 15–16, 157–158, 299–301; Shūjirō Sawada, "Innovation in Japanese Agriculture," *The State and Economic Enterprise in Japan*, ed. William W. Lockwood (Princeton: Princeton University Press, 1965), p. 340; John R. McEwan, "The Confucian Ideology and the Modernization of Japan," *The Modernization of Japan*, ed. Tōbata Seiichi (Tokyo: Institute of Asian Economic Affairs, 1966), 1, 237.

44 "Denda, p. 76. On the Dai Nihon Nōkai, see Sawada, p. 340; Okutani Matsuji, *Shinagawa Yajirō den* [Biography of Shinagawa Yajirō] (Tokyo: Kōyō Shoin, 1940), p. 169; McEwan, p. 238; Ogura, p. 302; Morita Shirō, *The Development of Agricultural Cooperative Associations in Japan* (Tokyo: Japan FAO Association, 1960), p. 16.

45 Meiji emperor, January 24, 1878, quoted in Katayama, p. 209.

46 Donald H. Shively, "Nishimura Shigeki: A Confucian View of Modernization," *Changing Japanese Attitudes Toward Modernization*, ed. Marius B. Jansen (Princeton: Princeton University Press, (1965), p. 208.

47 Fukutake Tadashi, *Nihon no nōson shakai* [Japanese Rural Society] (Tokyo: Tokyo Daigaku Shuppankai, 1953), pp. 180-181.

48 Ogura, p. 183.

49 Waswo, pp. 47–66; Ogura, pp. 163-165.

50 Waswo, pp. 40–45; Dore, pp. 44–50.

51 See Dore, pp. 44–53.

52 Kiyoshi Ogata, *The Co-operative Movement in Japan* (London: P. S. King & Son Ltd., 1923), p. 26.

53 Emori Itsuo, "Meijiki no Hōtokusha undō no shiteki shakaiteki haikei" [Historical and Social Background of the Meiji Period Hōtokusha Movement], *Hōritsu ronsō* [Collection of Legal Theories], Meiji University, part 1, XL, 1, October 1966, pp. 86–87. See Haraguchi Kiyoshi, "Hōtokusha no hitobito" [Hōtokusha Members], *Nihon jinbutsushi taikei* [Outline History of Talented Persons in Japan], ed. Konishi Shirō (Tokyo: Asakura Shoten, 1960), V, 255–264; Naramoto Tatsuya, *Ninomiya Sontoku* (Tokyo: Iwanami Shoten, 1959), pp. 162–169; Ogata, pp. 39–40; Saitō Osamu, "Hōtokusha undō no kuronorojii – 19 seiki kōhan ni okeru keizaiteki henka e no nōmin no taiō" [Chronology of the Hōtokusha Movement – The Response of Farmers to Economic Changes in the Latter Half of the Nineteenth Century], *Mita Gakkai zasshi* [Journal of the Mita Gakkai], LXIV, 8, August 1971, 227–228.

54 For Tomita see Koide Kōzō, *Kyōdo o okoshita senjin no omokage* [Memories of Forebears who Revived Their Home Towns] (Tokyo: Nihon Jichi Kensetsu Honbu, 1958), pp. 140–166; Naramoto, pp. 155–160; Emori, part I, pp. 95–98; Hirose Yutaka and Hirose Toshiko, *Ninomiya Sontoku no kōtei Tomita Takayosbi* [Tomita Takayoshi, Ninomiya Sontoku's Senior Disciple] (Tokyo: Nihon Kōshikai, 1953), pp. 226–244.

55 Tomita Takayoshi, *Hōtokuron* [Theory of Repaying Virtue], I850, quoted in Hirose, p. 228.

56 For Fukuzumi see Haraguchi, pp. 264–272; Nakamura, *Kindai Nihon ni okeru seido to shisō*, p. 297; Yoshimoto Tadasu, *A Peasant Sage of Japan: The Life and Work of Ninomiya Sontoku* (London: Longmans, 1912), pp. 227–228; Emori, part I, pp. 90–109.

57 Fukuzumi Masae, as recorded by Yoshimoto Tadasu, quoted in *Sources of Japanese Tradition*, p. 586.

58 Fukuzumi Masae, *Fukoku shōkei* [Shortcut to Enriching the Country], 1873–1874, quoted in Haraguchi, p. 268.

59 On this point see Ogata, pp. 29–31; Denda, pp. 108–109; Hirose, p. 226; Okutani Matsuji, *Ninomiya Sontoku to Hōtokusha undō* [Ninomiya Sontoku and the Hōtokusha Movement] (Tokyo: Kōyō Shoin, 1936), p. 201; Haraguchi, p. 272.

60 For Okada see Denda, pp. 88–114; Haraguchi, pp. 272–282; Naramoto, pp. 170–175; Nakamura, *Kindai Nihon ni okeru seido to shisō*, p. 297.

61 See Deñda, pp. 107–108.

62 Ibid.,109–110.

63 Of the 103 societies founded between 1874 and 1889, 64 were begun during the three years 1884 to 1886. Emori, part 1, p. 117.

64 See Mikiso Hane, *Japan: A Historical Survey* (New York: Charles Scribner's Sons, 1972), pp. 304–306; Irwin Scheiner, "The Mindful Peasant: Sketches for a Study of Rebellion," *Journal of Asian Studies*, XXXII, 4, August 1973. At the University of California, Berkeley, Stephen Vlastos is preparing a study of the Fukushima peasant movement in mid-Meiji.

65 See Saitō, p. 234; Okutani, Ninomiya Sontoku, pp. 262–274; Emori, part 1, pp. 98–99.

66 Haraguchi, p. 272; Sakurai, *Nihon nōhonshugi*, p. 211; Nakamura, *Kindai Nihon ni okeru seido to shisō*, pp. 297–298.

67 Sakurai, *Nihon nōhonshugi*, p. 81. See also Sakurai, "Nōhonshugi – sono rekishi, riron, jiban," pp. 119–120; Sakurai Takeo, "Shōwa no nōhonshugi" [Agrarianism in the Shōwa Period], *Shisō* [Thought], No. 407, May 1958, pp. 42–54; Tsunazawa Mitsuaki, *Nōhonshugi no kenkyū* [Studies on Agrarianism] (Nagoya: Fūbaisha, 1968), pp. 10–12; Nakamura, *Kindai Nihon ni okeru seido to shisō*, pp. 278–281;

Adachi Ikitsune, "Nōhonshugi no saikentō" [A Reappraisal of Theories on Agrarianism], *Shisō*, No. 423, September 1959, p. 57.

68 Sakurai, "Nōhonshugi – sono rekishi, riron, jiban," p. 122.

69 'Okutani Matsuji, "Nihon ni okeru nōhonshugi shisō no nagare" [Trends in Agrarian Thought in Japan], *Shisō*, No. 407, May 1958, p. 3. See also Tsunazawa, pp. 17–19; Nakamura, *Kindai Nihon ni okeru seido to shisō*, pp. 281–285; Adachi, p. 52f.

70 Okutani, "Nagare," p. 3.

71 Ibid., pp. 1–2.

72 See Adachi, p. 58.

73 Léon Say, *Turgot,* trans. Melville B. Anderson (Chicago: A. C. McClurg & Co., 1888), p. 47.

74 "Physiocratic School," *Encyclopedia Britannica* (Chicago, 1959), XVII, 885–886; Douglas Dakin, *Turgot and the* Ancien Régime *in France* (London: Methuen & Co., 1939), p. 295.

75 See Mario Einaudi, *The Physiocratic Doctrine of Judicial Control* (Cambridge, Mass.: Harvard University Press, 1938), p. 11; Dakin, p. 296; Henry Higgs, *The Physiocrats* (London: Macmillan, 1897), pp. 11–13.

76 William G. Beasley, "Introduction," *Select Documents on Japanese Foreign Policy, 1853–1868*, ed. William G. Beasley (London: Oxford University Press, 1955), p. 9.

77 Higgs, p. 10.

78 See "Physiocratic School," p. 885; Einaudi, pp. 10–28.

79 Droppers, pp. xi–xii.

80 Norman, pp. 299–303.

81 Say, p. 51.

82 Thomas Jefferson to John Jay, August 23, 1785, quoted in A. Whitney Griswold, *Farming and Democracy* (New York: Harcourt Brace, 1948), p. 31.

12 The role of the samurai in the development of modern banking in Japan*

K. Yamamura†

*Source: *Journal of Economic History* 27 (1967): 198–220.

Unquestionably the samurai – the lower samurai, the experts will add – carried out the Meiji Restoration; they also supplied the administrators for the new government. It was the samurai who provided the essential dynamic force that turned Japan away from the Tokugawa status quo and toward rapid modernization.[1]

That the modernization of Japanese political and economic institutions during the Meiji period was spearheaded by the government and the samurai class that manned the government is a widely accepted view. One could, with little effort, assemble numerous quotations (in English or Japanese) reiterating this theme with little or no variation.[2] Government–samurai endeavors such as pioneering in modern technology, subsidy programs (tangible and intangible), dissemination of new knowledge (to include modern business practices), and other aspects of "community-centered entrepreneurship"[3] all support the theme. The purpose of this article is to question this well-entrenched view by submitting the findings of a close examination of the emergence of modern banking in Japan. Although this is only one aspect of the general theme, few students of Japanese economic history would deny that it has been often cited as one of the most typical examples of samurai leadership and of government initiative in the modernization of Japan. Eiichi Shibusawa, a former samurai, has invariably been linked with this development, in an attempt to stress that modern banking was a creation of the samurai class.[4]

The first section of this article summarizes the events leading up to the 1876 amendment to the Banking Act of 1872; the second section argues that the general thesis – to the effect that the so-called "old vibrant spirit of samurai" provided the primum mobile of modern banking in Japan – considerably overstates the case; and the third section presents evidence to show that the data often cited to demonstrate the importance of the *kazoku* (the former *kuge* group and top-ranking members of the samurai class) and samurai (*bushi*),[5] overstate and even misrepresent their role in the development of the banking system. Instead, the paper concludes that the force majeure of the success of the modern banking in Japan was the profit incentive of the *heimin* (nonsamurai[6]) class and that the implications of such a conclusion are significant for the nature of the emerging modern industrial sector in Japan.

I

Immediately following the Meiji Restoration (1868), the new government faced a dire need to establish a sound – or at least less chaotic – monetary system. Nonconvertible currencies issued by 240-odd *han* (feudal clans), increasingly debased coins, and the many counterfeits numbered, according to at least one estimate, 1,694 kinds in the years preceding the Restoration.[7] To compound the confusion, the new government issued its own nonconvertible notes called *dajōkan-satsu* (notes of the Privy-Councillor) in large quantities to finance its war against the remnants of shogunate and to support the administrative apparatus of new government.[8] The Meiji Government, which financed a large part of its military operations by forced loans from rich merchants, admitted frankly that those *dajōkan-satsu* were issued "to overcome the urgent crises at hand."[9] During the initial years of the new government a modern unified tax system had not yet been instituted. Debts and the deteriorated finances of the shogun and *daimyo* (feudal lords) provided far less than a satisfactory foundation for the exhausted coffers of the Meiji Government faced as it was with mounting expenditures.

Because of these strained financial circumstances the government established the Commerce Bureau (*Shohō-shi*) in April 1868. Though it has been said that this Bureau was established "to facilitate the means of communication among the businessmen (*shōgyōka*) and to lend them capital in order to stimulate the commerce,"[10] Katō was correct in noting that "the Bureau was to facilitate the circulation of the *dajōkan-satsu*."[11] The *dajōkan-satsu* were failing to circulate even in such large cities as Tokyo and Osaka; and even when accepted they were discounted up to 40 per cent of their face value.[12] Local offices, popularly called "handling offices of *dajōkan-satsu*" (*kinsatsu kashisage toriastukaisho*),[13] were established to increase the acceptance of these notes. But the whole operation had to be discontinued in March 1869. "At that time," one Japanese economic historian wrote, "the *dajōkan-satsu* had little acceptance and the venture failed to get off the ground."[14]

Anticipating this failure, the government formed a new bureau to replace the Commerce Bureau, and in February 1869, the Trade Bureau (*Tsushō-shi*) was established. Its goals were ambitious: (a) to assure stable prices and flow of goods; (b) to organize money-exchange operations; (c) to maintain flows and stable relative prices of gold and silver; (d) to promote exports and imports at ports open to foreign traffic and guide international transactions; and (e) to establish *shosha* (trading firms).[15]

To accomplish these ends, the Trade Bureau established 8 *kawase kaisha* in port cities. *Kawase kaisha* literally means bills of exchange companies, but this was a translation of the English word "bank," since there existed no word in Japanese for a direct translation. *Kawase kaisha* had "characteristics of banks and were authorized to issue their own notes."[16] The capital for these *kawase kaisha* was supplied by wealthy merchants, rich farmers, money-exchangers who had established large houses during the late Tokugawa period, and the government, which nearly matched the capital supplied from these private sources.

But all these *kawase kaisha* failed save one in Yokohama. The reasons for the failures included: (a) the lack of motivated interest on the part of those wealthy merchants who subscribed nearly half of the capital, because of the degree of government control;[17] (b) an administrative reorganization that eliminated the Trade Bureau; and (c) the unstable economic conditions of the first years after the Restoration.[18] *Kawase kaisha*, like its predecessor, was an unsuccessful attempt by the government to find a means to increase the acceptance and circulation of its own *dajōkan-satsu*, and hopefully to stimulate the economy by an increased flow of private and government credits.

Seeing the failure of these government attempts, the rich merchant Houses of Mitsui and Ono asked permission to establish their own respective banks[19] financed by their own capital. Though the government "welcomed such intentions,"[20] it withheld permission lest such banks fail without a better legal foundation. Such a legal foundation, following the model of U.S. national banks, was then in the making upon recommendation of Hirobumi Ito, then a high-ranking officer of the Ministry of Finance.[21]

The first Banking Act (*Ginkō jōrei*) built on Ito's recommendation, was decreed in November 1872. The Act required national banks to pay 60 per cent of their cash holdings to the government, which in return provided banks with government securities bearing 6 per cent interest. It authorized national banks so established to circulate convertible bank notes of their own up to the total value of the government securities they held. A main reason for the requirement to issue convertible notes was the government's expectation that "part of the government's inconvertible note issue would be replaced by notes convertible into gold, and that effective banking machinery to serve the needs of the new economic system would be brought into being."[22]

Strong government pressure established four banks under the Act. The First National Bank was the largest, with a capital of three million yen. Sixty per cent of this capital came from the Houses of Mitsui and Ono, which were, against their wishes, forced to pool their resources.[23] The Second National Bank, capitalized at 250,000 yen, was established mainly by the Yokohama silk-yarn merchants by transforming the only *kawase kaisha* that had not failed.[24] The Fourth was started by *gōnō* (wealthy landowners) of Niigata Prefecture[25] and the Fifth by four Kyushu merchants and one samurai. A charter for the Third was granted to some wealthy merchants in Osaka, but an internal squabble prevented its formation.

These banks, formed reluctantly under the compelling influence of the government, proved to be failures. The two major reasons for the failures, and for the need for government pressure approaching coercion, seem clear. In the first place, the banks were in effect investing 60 per cent of their initial capital in government bonds that were earning 6 per cent while the prevailing rate of return was 10 per cent. Moreover, these banks had difficulty in keeping their notes in circulation. As Allen put it:

> Since these notes were convertible into specie, whereas the government paper money of the same face value was at a discount, merchants who had to pay for imports naturally found it profitable to present the bank notes at the issuing bank and so to obtain gold for their foreign payments. In this way the national banks were drained of their reserves.[26]

As late as 1876 outstanding bank notes totaled only 62,456 yen, and loans made by these four banks came to slightly over 2 million yen. At their peak loans reached only 3.25 million in 1873, or just about the combined paid-in capital of the First and the Second National Banks.[27]

In retrospect one can conclude that government efforts to stimulate modern banking in Japan failed because of the continued issuance of nonconvertible notes by the government and of stringent restrictions (mainly the required conversion) placed on the national banks. The failure, in short, was due to the unprofitability of these banks, and this was sufficient to stifle a development of genuine modern banking. The politico-economic pressures exerted by the government clearly failed to found a new institution called *ginkō* (bank).

The government's thwarted wish to establish a viable modern banking system soon became an urgent necessity when it decided to issue compulsory samurai commutation bonds amounting to 174 million yen. The magnitude of the bond issue was staggering, five times the total government revenue in 1876. Under the circumstance it was clear that if this large volume of bonds was not absorbed quickly by the monetary system, their value would depreciate rapidly and the economic status of the samurai class would be depressed further.[28] The government could ill afford such a result, considering the smoldering resentments of the de facto declassed samurai and under threats of rebellion by the die-hard shogun supporters. Thus, as a device to maintain the price of bonds and provide replacements for the earlier unsuccessful attempts to build a modern banking system, a new banking act was decreed "to give an avenue of employing the [commutation] bonds, and to maintain their price level, and to facilitate flow of private funds."[29] The Banking Act of 1876 authorized the new national banks to issue nonconvertible bank notes up to 80 per cent of their respective capitals. This portion of the capital was to be paid to the government which, in turn, would supply government bonds yielding 4 per cent to the new banks.

The new venture showed all the signs of success. The number of banks chartered under the Act of 1876 increased rapidly from 6 in 1876 to 153 in 1879, when the originally stipulated total capital of 40 million yen and circulating notes of 34.4 million yen were reached.[30] No further charters were therefore issued after this date. Observing this, Hirschmeier wrote, as many others had done before him:

> The rush of the samurai to found banks stands out in striking contrast to the attitudes of the wealthy merchant houses, which had to be forced to establish the first four national banks in 1872. Correspondingly, in this early phase the merchants also fell far behind the samurai as contributors of capital to the whole banking system.[31]

He then cited the following oft-used figures to make his point.[32] The breakdown of the contribution of the total capital by class was: *kazoku*, 44.1 per cent; samurai, 31.9; merchants, 14.6; farmers, 3.5; artisans, 0.1; and others, 5.6.[33] On the basis of this finding the thesis was advanced that *kazoku* and samurai contributed initiative and over three-fourths of the capital to found the first successful modern banks in Japan. *Heimin*, many wrote, were passive followers in this new venture and contributed less than one-fourth of the total capital to found these new institutions.

II

Notwithstanding the long-accepted view and the oft-cited data Hirschmeier presented, it can be argued that the main source of capital and initiative for the success of modern banking was the *heimin* (commoners) class. To show this, an attempt was made to examine, for as many banks as possible, the exact proportion of capital contributed by each class of individuals, the class composition of the initial organizers of each bank, the distribution of officers by class, the purposes and business practices of each bank, and other relevant factors. It was possible to examine 62 banks for which some information, ranging from detailed, excellent records to bare outlines, was available.[34] The recent interest by Japanese scholars in more empirically oriented research in the development of the banking system provided a useful check, though (as will be shown below) in several instances their anxiety to make their point appears to overemphasize their findings.[35]

Of the 62 banks (out of a universe of 153) for which some information was available, it is possible to classify 38 banks as to the "dominant" class. As shown in Table 1, K stands for *kazoku*-dominated, S for samurai-dominated, M for merchant-dominated, and GM for gōnō-merchant-dominated. Combinations of letters signify cases that do not fall into a single category but involve more than one class. An SM denotes a case of combined dominance in which S was stronger in influence, while an MS denotes the opposite.

In some instances, especially when combined dominance such as MS or SM is involved, the writer had to make a subjective judgment. But this procedure required far less need for the writer's judgment than anticipated, as the "deciding factors" column in Table 1 makes clear. To illustrate the classification procedure and the meaning of "dominance," and also to show the degree of subjective judgment used, the "deciding factors" are elaborated for the following seven cases. The first two cases clearly illustrate the meaning of "dominance".

Table 1 "Dominant" class, capital, and year of charter

Bank	*Year of charter*	*Capital (in 1,000 yen)*	*Shares owned by heimin (percentage)*[a]	*"Dominant class"*	*Deciding factors*
1	1876	1,500	49.5	M	Through 1876–1885, the Mitsui family owned approximately 50 per cent of total shares; except for E. Shibusawa, bank officers were Mitsui appointees. (See text.)[b]
2	1876	250	98	M	See text.
3	1876	200	Complete	M	Owned and operated by Yasuda and Kawasai (two well-known wealthy merchants).[c]
4	1876	300	91.8	GM	See text.
5	1876	300	50-plus	SM	Initial *heimin* capital contribution was 53 per cent. (See text, also footnote 38).
6	1876	100	80-plus	GM	Initiated and operated by *gōnō* and merchants of Fukushima; 50 out of 60 who owned over 10 shares were *gōnō* or merchants.[d]
7	1877	100	Complete	M	Evolved from a *ruiji-ginko* established earlier by merchants in Kōchi.[e]
11	1877	100	Complete	M	Exclusively owned and operated by cotton goods and rice merchants of Nagoya.

Notes:

[a] Where an exact figure is given, it indicates that a complete listing of shareholders classified by class origin is available. "Complete" and "nil" refer to those cases where either the *heimin* class owned 100 or 0 per cent of the total shares or almost all or no shares. The latter is caused by the fact that a complete list of shareholders, including the smaller ones, is not available in some cases, and the only available observations are those which state that a specific bank is "almost" completely *heimin*-owned or samurai-owned.

[b] The First National Bank has been an object of frequent study. See for example Katō and Ōuchi, *Kokuritsuginkō no Kenkyū*, p. 54 which concludes, after a detailed study of the bank, "It is clear that this bank has characteristics which are totally different from that of those banks known as samurai banks."

[c] This bank, however, was under the personal control of Zenjiro Yasuda. For detailed description, Chapter 4, *Yasuda Ginko 60-nen-shi* (a 60-year history of Yasuda Bank) (Tokyo: Yasuda Bank, 1940), pp. 33–44, is very useful. Also, one of Yasuda's biographies, Yasuda Gakuen (school), *Yasuda Zenjiro* (Tokyo: Yasuda School, 1958), pp. 100–6, has an interesting description as to why Yasuda established a national bank along with his own private bank.

[d] In the first few years of bank's existence, the *heimin* share could have been higher. See Tōhata and Takahashi, *Meijizenki no Ginkōseido*, p. 62.

[e] A *ruiji-ginko* is a quasi-bank which began to perform bank-like services before the Banking Act of 1876. Many of these became fully-fledged banks under the Act.

Table 1 (Continued)

Bank	*Year of charter*	*Capital (in 1,000 yen)*	*Shares owned by heimin (percentage)*[a]	*"Dominant class"*	*Deciding factors*
13	1877	250	Complete	M	Exclusively owned and operated by Konoike, a wealthy merchant of Osaka.
15	1877	17,826	Nil	K	The *kazoku* bank, as described in the text.
16	1877	50	Complete	MG	All initiators and 22 out of 32 initial shareholders were merchants and *gōnō*; operated by and did business mostly with the local merchants in Gifu. Samurai participation could be as high as 10 per cent of initial capital.
17	1877	105	53	SM	Initiative came from samurai. In 1878 samurai shares stood 2:1 over merchant shares – an unusual case. *Heimin* occupied 4 out of 6 officerships and "ran" the bank.
18	1877	90	Complete	M	Evolved from a *ruiji-ginko* established earlier by Nagasaki merchants; operated for and by them.
19	1877	100	Complete	GM	Mostly owned and operated by gōnō of Nagano; some Nagano merchant capital.
23	1877	50	50-plus	M	Most likely 75 per cent of original capital was supplied by merchants in Oita; evolved from a *ruiji-ginko* established by merchants but which saw a marginal samurai participation; operated for and by local merchants.
29	1878	120	Complete	M	Developed from a *ruiji-ginko* established by merchants in Ehime; "run" by merchants and $\frac{3}{4}$ of its business was for merchants.
32	1878	120	Complete	M	Established by former Osaka moneychangers; operated for and by merchants.
34	1878	100	Complete	M	Osaka merchants' bank; owned, operated by and for themselves.
37	1878	150	17	S	Samurai initiative and capital; "run" by and for samurai (samurai borrowers exceeding *heimin* borrowers 5:1).[f]

[f] Katō and Ōuchi, *Kokuritsuginkō no Kenkyū*, pp. 175–215, has a detailed study on this bank.

Table 1 (Continued)

Bank	*Year of charter*	*Capital (in 1,000 yen)*	*Shares owned by heimin (percentage)*[a]	*"Dominant class"*	*Deciding factors*
39	1878	350	Nil	S	Established and "run" by samurai capital for samurai in Maebashi (Gumma).
40	1878	150	Nil	S	A replica of the 39th above in Tatebayashi (Gumma).
50	1878	100	Nil	S	Capital supplied by, " run" by and for samurai; evolved from the *han*-operated business agency of former Tsuchiura-*han* (Ibaragi).
52	1878	70	Nil	S	Begun with samurai capital for samurai; " run" by samurai of former Matsuyama-*han* (Ehime); soon became a *heimin*-controlled bank.
56	1878	50	Complete	M	Exclusively owned and operated by former moneychangers of Akashi (Hyogo).
59	1878	200	Nil	S	"Run" by and for samurai; *heimin* capital about 2.5 per cent.
62	1878	100	20-plus	SM	A *heimin* contributed the required cash, but samurai outnumbered *heimin* 5:1 as initiators; details not available but *heimin* capital could reach 50 per cent of total capital.
63	1878	100	32	MS	4 out of 6 initiators were merchants; though 68 per cent of the capital was supplied by samurai and only 32 out of over 400 shareholders were *heimin*, silk (yarn and cocoon) merchants of Nagano " ran" the bank and over a half of the loans were made to local silk merchants.
74	1878	250	80	M	See text.
77	1878	250	50-minus	S	See text.
81	1878	60	20	M	See text.
85	1878	200	Complete	M	Exclusively owned and operated by former moneychangers of Kawagoe (Saitama).

Table 1 (Continued)

Bank	*Year of charter*	*Capital (in 1,000 yen)*	*Shares owned by heimin (percentage)*[a]	*"Dominant class"*	*Deciding factors*
98	1878	120	20	SM	See text.
107	1878	100	Complete	MG	Begun with the capital of a silk merchant and moneychanger Yoshino; supplemented by *gōnō* capital of Fukushima, while local samurai made a token participation (2 to 3 per cent); operated by and for local merchants.
114	1879	50	10	S	All initiators and all shareholdings except 4 *heimin* out of 159 shareholders were samurai; operated by and for samurai in Takamatsu.
116	1878	50	20-plus	GS	6 largest shareholders (over 2,000 yen) consisted of 5 *gōnō* and 1 samurai; out of 257 shareholders 236 were samurai; *Gōnō* "ran" the bank in spite of large samurai holding as small (mostly 100 to 200 yen per samurai) holders.[g]
117	1879	50	41.5	MS	See text.
133	1879	100	53	MS	See text.
148	1879	100	Complete	M	Fully owned and operated by an Osaka merchant, Yamaguchi.

[g] The classification of the One Hundred Sixteenth National Bank was determined on the basis of Shirō Morita's *"Chichō-Kigyo to Jinushi tōshi"* (local industries and investments by landlords), *Shigaku Zassi* (journal of history), Vol. 68, No. 11, 1958. This source notes that *heimin* (*gōnō*) owned 20 per cent plus the amount owned by 9 *heimin* who owned between 50–100 yen and 7 *heimin* who owned less than 50 yen, p. 4.

Sources: As important sources are cited elsewhere in this article and additional notes in those cases demanding special explanations are added in the notes, above, the following is supplied in lieu of citing all sources. The greatest problem in identifying sources is to discover which history of an existing or defunct bank contains the information pertinent to a specific national bank. For example, the information regarding the Seventy-fourth National Bank is found in *Yokohama Koshinginkō 30-shunenshi* (a history of Yokohama Credit Promotion Bank in the 30th year), 1950. This is true for most of the cases. As the Japanese authors cited in footnote 32 are not helpful on this aspect, one should begin by consulting the sources cited in footnote 34. In addition, the knowledge of location of each bank is extremely helpful in tracing necessary sources through the histories of existing large banks in that locale.

The Seventy-Fourth National Bank (M)

This bank was established mostly by capital supplied by silk merchants in Yokohama. When the bank was established in 1878, 21 of the 30 largest shareholders were *heimin* and held nearly 80 per cent of the total shares. It is also evident that the bank was initiated and operated by Yokohama merchants, as seen in the fact that all the officers of the bank were Yokohama merchants and merchant-landlords who resided in Yokohama. Having virtually no government deposits, the merchants contributed nearly all of the bank's deposits and received most of the loans made by the bank. Thus, "this was a bank which evolved around the Yokohama merchants, i.e., functioned as a credit agency for merchants, especially local merchants. From the composition of the bank's capital and deposits . . . it is clear that this is a merchant's bank."[36]

The Seventy-Seventh National Bank (S)

This bank was initiated by samurai with the express purpose of aiding impoverished samurai of Miyagi Prefecture, and two-thirds of the largest shareholders (owning over 50 shares) were samurai. Unlike the *heimin*-oriented Seventy-Fourth, the bank enjoyed a large government deposit amounting to from 30 to 40 per cent of the total deposits for the first several years of its existence. Though data on loans and private deposits are not available for the earlier years, it is known that as late as in 1884 over 80 per cent of the total deposits were made by samurai, and the number of loans made to samurai was over twice that made to *heimin* (204 vs. 91). The bank also continued to be managed by samurai directors.[37]

The following are the five less clear-cut cases involving the judgment of the writer:

The Fifth National Bank (SM)

This has often been called a samurai bank, but the contribution made by merchants is sufficient to label it SM. The initiators (*hokkinin*) were four merchants of Northern Kyushu and one samurai. The former jointly subscribed 2,350 shares and the latter 2,000. The bank was established explicitly for the purpose of aiding local samurai. Given the continued strength of the shareholding and an increasing share of deposits made by merchants, one is tempted to classify this bank in an MS category. But since it was established for the purpose of aiding samurai under the apparent leadership of a samurai, an SM classification was given.[38]

The Eighty-First National Bank (M)

This has also been called a samurai bank, but the initiative came from eleven rice merchants of Yamagata Prefecture. They provided the required cash (20 per cent) and solicited the remainder from samurai to invest their bonds. Though the nominal breakdown of capital by class yields an 8 to 2 ratio on this basis, it is clear in the available records that the merchants "ran" the bank. The samurai interest was passive from the beginning and dwindled rapidly over the following years to less than one per cent of the total shares by 1883. Other information available on patterns of deposits and loans also strengthens the classification made for this bank.[39]

The Ninety-Eighth National Bank (SM)

This was classified SM since the largest shareholder was a samurai (6,000) and the other four initiators were merchants with joint holdings of 18,000 shares. This means that the merchant class provided the required cash portion as was the case of the Eighty-First. This could very well be classified MS rather than SM if some evidence existed to indicate that the bank was "run" by the merchants or operated for or by merchants, but because of rather inconclusive evidence SM classification was given.[40]

The Hundred and Seventeenth National Bank (MS)

This bank began its operation in 1879, and no detailed information is available for the first two years. However, it is known that of seven initiators, five were merchants and two were samurai. The shareholding pattern in 1881 was 58.5 samurai and 41.5 *heimin*, but by 1882 the samurai holding fell to 26 per cent. In spite of this shareholding pattern, however, we may agree with the assessment made by T. Hayashi: "This bank has been called a *tonosama*[41] bank because of the nature of its beginning and of the fact that many bank employees were samurai – but by examining the initiators and the distribution of large shareholders, the initiative to found the bank did not necessarily come from samurai, but rather it came from *heimin*, i.e., merchants and *gōnō*."[42]

The One Hundred and Thirty-Third National Bank (MS)

This is a case in which the participation of a former *daimyo* as the largest shareholder has been considered sufficient to classify this bank S-dominated. But 53 per cent of the original shares were owned by *heimin* and individual samurai shareholding was (except for the *daimyo*) much smaller than the average shareholding of *heimin*. In this case either an S or SM classification would be inappropriate.[43]

More than two-thirds of the sample were readily classified as to their dominant class. In those cases in which classification was less than clear-cut, classification procedures analogous to those used in the above five cases were adopted. The result, as shown in Table 1, is: 1 *kazoku* bank, 12 samurai-dominated banks (S-8, SM-4), and 25 *heimin*-dominated banks (M-16, MS-3, GM-3, MG-2, GS-1). That is, in terms of "dominance" as the term has been used in this article, *heimin*-dominated banks outnumber the samurai-dominated banks nearly 2 to 1. It should also be noted that in the sample those banks established during the first two years (1876 and 1877) were overwhelmingly M-dominated while S- and SM-dominated banks began to appear more frequently in the third year (1878). One could perhaps give credit to *heimin* initiative in the temporal sense as well on the basis of this observation.[44]

A crucial question to be asked then is: Does the sample of 38 cases out of possible 153 (24 per cent) provide a sufficient basis with which to conclude that the modern banking system, initiated under the Banking Act of 1876, was led by *heimin* initiative rather than by that of samurai? The writer believes that the answer is affirmative for two reasons: One reason is that those banks whose records are available today were usually larger in size of capital than the average and were more successful, thus playing a larger role in establishing the foundation of modern banking. Those banks whose records are not available in some cases were those banks which either existed in name only with virtually no real business transactions or failed shortly after formation, or ceased to exist for various reasons, including almost immediate absorption.[45] The second reason is that the sample includes only those banks which, in the writer's view, could be judged for their respective "dominance" with reasonable certainty. Other authors on this subject have included several banks which could be included as *heimin*-dominated if a less rigid requirement was made.[46]

III

Before questioning the meaningfulness of the frequently quoted data on the breakdown of the sources of the total capital for 153 banks by class, one specific point must be made. The Fifteenth National Bank, established by 480 *kazoku* (most of them former *daimyo*) should not be included in this discussion because the Fifteenth was not one of the 153 banks established under the same Act. Moreover, the way it was established, the degree of special privileges it enjoyed from the government, and its mode of operation disqualify the Fifteenth National Bank from being called a bank in the same sense that the others were. The Fifteenth was literally forced upon *kazoku* by the government, especially by Tomomi Iwakura, Vice-Privy-Councillor, and himself a *kazoku*. His concern for the status of *kazoku* was such that his office lent enough funds to 294 *kazoku* to enable them to join their wealthier fellow noblemen. (Though 480 *kazoku* as a group received 20 per cent of the total commutation bonds, the distribution of bonds was extremely skewed, reflecting their respective former economic status.)[47] With such an origin, the bank from the beginning behaved as if it were a branch of the government. For several years it enjoyed large deposits of the government funds and virtually no private deposits. Its "customer" was almost exclusively the government or government-guaranteed "investments" such as financing government forces to crush the Satsuma Rebellion or the Aomori–Tokyo Railroad for which the government guaranteed a return of 10 per cent. Katō and Ouchi, noting these developments, concluded that the Fifteenth National Bank was "built" to prevent *kazoku's* bonds from scattering out of their hands and to raise the earning of these bonds for *kazoku*.[48] Professor Patrick's observation on the Fifteenth National Bank is revealing. He wrote:

> The Fifteenth National Bank was unique. . . . Apparently its immediate purpose was to make a 15 million yen loan at 5 per cent to the government to assist in putting down the Satsuma Rebellion. In as much as the government could have issued its own paper notes without paying interest, this was a further means by which the government bought off the *daimyo*. Continued coddling was evident in subsequent government relations with the Fifteenth National Bank.[49]

The privileges extended by the government – what Patrick aptly called "coddling"—were extensive and present another aspect of the Fifteenth's uniqueness in more explicit terms:[50] (1) The Fifteenth was authorized to issue notes up to 95 per cent of its capital while the Banking Act of 1876 restricted all others from exceeding 80 per cent of their capital. (2) The liquid asset (specie) reserve required for redemption of all banks was 25 per cent of the value of notes issued, but 5 per cent for the Fifteenth. (3) When liquid assets were not available for redemption, the government would "lend" cash up to the amount which the Fifteenth lent to the government. (4) The government bonds purchased by the Fifteenth were guaranteed not to depreciate below a specified figure (an effective rate of interest), while other banks received no such guarantee. (5) The Fifteenth was not restricted by the ceiling of 10 per cent of all loans to any one borrower as all other banks were. (6) The Fifteenth was not required to set aside 10 per cent of the annual profit for capital accumulation as all others were.

From these factors it is clear that this was a very politically oriented "bank" established in the hope of alleviating the wounded pride and financial status of former *daimyo*. The concern shown by the Meiji Government for *kazoku* contrasted sharply with that shown for the plight of ordinary samurai.

Assuming the above to be true, we can examine the breakdown of contributions to the total capital of 152 banks by class excluding the Fifteenth National Bank. With the large *kazoku* contribution eliminated, the respective shares for samurai and *heimin* appear as shown in Table 2.

The impression obtained from Table 2 is quite different from the general-

Table 2 Contribution of capital by class, 1880–1889 (in 1,000 yen)

Year	*Samurai*	*Heimin*	*Ratio – heimin to samurai*
1880	13,340	11,070	0.83
1881	11,355	13,906	1.22
1882	11,863	13,704	1.15
1883	11,147	14,736	1.32
1884	10,895	15,430	1.41
1885	10,289	15,508	1.50
1886	9,962	15,747	1.58
1887	9,765	15,794	1.62
1888	9,222	16,114	1.75
1889	9,577	16,404	1.71

Source: Computed from Asakura, *Meijizenki Nippon Kinyū Kōzō-shi*, p. 121.

ization advanced by Hirschmeier.[51] When the Fifteenth is eliminated, the *heimin* contribution was not significantly behind that of samurai in 1880. Then, beginning in 1881, the *heimin* contribution rose rapidly relative to that of samurai. This could be considered to reflect the case typified in the example of the Eighty-First National Bank where the samurai bonds contributed to the initial capital began to occupy a secondary position to *heimin* capital. This was perhaps to be expected, since the growth of capital depended on merchants and *gōnō* while the samurai's economic status deteriorated in a fashion typical of rentier classes during rapid inflation and social deracination.[52] As a result, the commutation bonds supplied by the samurai were a "passive" contribution – lacking alternatives – while the contribution made by *heimin*, who saw the potential profits to be made out of the new banks, was "active." The fact that the samurai's share was larger than that of the *heimin* during the initial years of banking in Japan does not mean that "the samurai were able to generate a good deal of entrepreneurial dynamism." Nor was it due to "the old vibrant spirit of samurai."[53] However well samurai dominance in the development of modern banking in Japan fits the accepted thesis that the initiative for the modernization of Japan came "from the top," the role of the *heimin*, as we have seen can hardly be called that of "ignorant merchants following the prodding of the samurai class."[54]

This, however, is not the whole story. Along with these national banks, private banks were established in 1876.[55] The first of them was the Mitsui Bank with an initial capital of 2 million yen. The founders of private banks, which continued to be established in a large number, "were almost all from the merchant-landowner-financier group, but were usually among their wealthiest elements, especially in rural areas."[56] Table 3 shows the number and the total capital of these private banks.

It should be noted that the total capital of private banks easily exceeded

Table 3 Number and total capital of private banks, 1880–1889

Year	*Number of banks*	*Total capital (1,000 yen)*
1880	39	6,280
1881	90	10,447
1882	176	17,152
1883	207	20,487
1884	214	19,421
1885	218	18,758
1886	220	17,959
1887	221	18,896
1888	218	17,472
1889	217	18,976

Source: Asakura, *Meijizenki Nippon Kinyū Kōzō-shi*, p. 187.

the contribution made by samurai after 1882. The average size of these banks was smaller than that of national banks, but the contribution made by the private banks in establishing a modern style credit system in the modernization of Japan in 1880's should not be underestimated. Several large private banks, such as the Mitsui and Yasuda Banks, were larger than most national banks and rapidly evolved into giant modern banks. Small ones also played a key role in financing small-scale, often rural, enterprises in cocoon-raising, silk-spinning, tea-growing, and wholesale and other agricultural and handicraft activities. Many of these small banks continued to grow and became, by the turn of the century, important local banks.

One could strengthen this argument further by commenting on the so-called quasi-banks (*ruiji-ginko*) and other financial intermediaries which flourished during the 1880's; a tentative examination of these institutions reveals their predominantly *heimin* origin.[57] But one is justified, on the basis of the evidence presented above, in concluding that the role of *heimin* has been underrated while that of samurai has been overrated in the development of modern banking in Japan.

IV

Professor Patrick seems quite correct in his judgment that "by the mid-1880's, Japan had a well-established commercial banking system based on the twin foundations of national banks and private banks."[58] If this assessment is accepted, an important inference may be suggested from the observations contained in this article. If E. H. Norman is correct in emphasizing the importance of bank capital (as against industrial capital) in the development of Japanese industries,[59] this could mean that it was largely *heimin* initiative and capital which opened the way for the beginning of economic development in Japan. Though this is a tempting syllogism – that modern banking was built by the initiative of *heimin*, industries depended on bank capital, and therefore *heimin* initiative and capital played a major role in spurring industrial development during the 1880's – one must be extremely cautious in presenting such a sweeping generalization on this complex and controversial topic.

Norman's assertion has never been demonstrated to the writer's knowledge. In short there exists no conclusive study to answer the question: Whence did the firms in the modern sector obtain their capital to industrialize? Even if the argument and evidence presented in this article are correct, research on the second link (between banks and industrial firms) of the syllogism remains to be undertaken. The initial results of investigation in this area, such as that conducted by Miss Murakami on the large Mie Textile, indicate that Norman was essentially correct in his assertion [60]

Pending further research on the second link of the syllogism, one may suggest the need for critical re-examination of some conventional generalizations.[61] The economic development and modernization of Japan, we have been told, stemmed from government initiative, inspired by the "samurai spirit." The multitude of *heimin* who participated in these historic processes were merely following passively the leadership of government officials and former samurai. Can this interpretation be maintained? In the financial field, one able student of Japanese economic history has asserted that "the state not only created modern fiscal and financial institutions – it also played a leading part in mobilizing resources for transfer from the traditional economy to the young modern sector."[62] In the light of the evidence presented in this article, can this generalization be supported? Surely not. The attempts to introduce Commerce and Trade Bureaus, *kawase kaisha* and the banks under the Banking Act of 1872, failed in spite of the strong initiative shown by the government. The lack of enthusiasm shown by the *heimin* class, which saw few profitable opportunities in these government-initiated schemes, should be considered one of the major reasons for their failure.[63] But when the *heimin* class displayed an active interest, or when the House of Mitsui was willing to establish its own bank without strong pressure from the government, the first secure foundations of modern commercial banking were laid. The role played by samurai in this process was, on the whole, a passive one. The role of the government was not to coax and coerce a reluctant and lethargic *heimin* class – a class which had in fact actively begun to establish banks on its own initiative – but rather to restrict the number of banks to only one hundred and fifty-three.

NOTES

† I am grateful to Professor Henry Rosovsky who provided valuable comment and criticism. Also, Professor Hugh T. Patrick was kind enough to make available to me his "Banking in the Early Stages of Industrialization: Japan, 1868–1914" (mimeo).

While I was collecting the necessary sources in Tokyo, Professors Keiichiro Nakagawa and Tsunehiko Yui were extremely cooperative, as was the Economics Library of the University of Tokyo. A Research Professorship granted by The Brookings Institution made possible my stay in Japan, the purchase of source materials, and the research needed for this paper. I also wish to express my appreciation for the opportunity to participate in stimulating and helpful discussions on the substance of this article with Professors R. Hidy, A. Johnson, F. Redlich, J. Baughman, and M. Klein.

1 Johannes Hirschmeier, *The Origins of Entrepreneurship in Meiji Japan* (Cambridge: Harvard University Press, 1964), p. 44.
2 Professor Yasuzo Horie expressed this view articulately in his "An Outline of the Rise of Capitalism in Japan," *Kyoto University Economic Review* (July 1936). Its date and the fact that it was written in English seem to account for its influence, as repeated quotations from his article indicate. More recently, the widely used N. S. Buchanan and H. S. Ellis, *Approaches to Economic Development* (New York: The Twentieth Century Fund, 1955), p. 118, offers a typical presentation of this view.
3 This is a phrase coined by Gustav Ranis. See his "The Community-Centered Entrepreneur in Japanese Development," *Explorations in Entrepreneurial History*, VIII (Dec. 1955).
4 Professor Takeo Tsuchiya, who has written many volumes on Japanese economic history, exemplifies this thinking. His view is best summarized in his *Nippon Shihon-shugi no Keieishi-teki Kenkyū* (a business history study of Japanese capitalism), (Tokyo: Mimizu-Shobō, 1954), p. 189. For what I consider an overrated assessment of Shibusawa's role, see Hirschmeier, *Entrepreneurship in Japan*, pp. 167–75.
5 *Kazoku* was the newly created nobility composed of *kuge* (the former court members) and high-ranking samurai. Samurai and *bushi* are identical. Japanese historians seem to prefer *bushi* to samurai in their writings.
6 *Heimin* means commoners. This class consisted of former *chonin* (merchant), *nomin* (peasant), and artisan classes, i.e., all nonsamurai.
7 Torajiro Takagaki, *Kindai Nippon Kinyū-shi* (a history of banking in modern Japan), *Local Banking Association Monograph No. 20* (All Japan Banking Association, Tokyo, 1955), p. 28.
8 Akira Sawada in his *"Dajōkan-satsu Hakkō no Shushi to Shokusankogyō"* (the intent of the issuance of *dajōkan-satsu* and industry promotion) *Shakai Keizaigaku Shigaku* (journal of social and economic history), III (Oct. 1937). This excellent article on *dajōkan-satsu* shows how the initial intent was subverted by the needs of the time.
9 Toshihiko Katō, *Hompō Ginkō-shiron* (a historical treatise on Japanese banking), (Tokyo: Tokyo University Press, 1957), p. 10.
10 *Meiji Zaisei-shi hensankai* (editorial association of Meiji financial history), *Meiji zaisei-shi* (Meiji financial history) (1905), XII, 328. Hereafter *MZS*.
11 Katō, *Hompō Ginkō-shiron*, p. 19.
12 Takagaki, *Kindai Nippon Kinyū-shi*, p. 37.
13 Sawada, *Dajōkan-satsu Hakkō*, p. 24.
14 Y. Matsunari, T. Miwa, and Y. Chō, *Nippon ni okeru Ginkō no Hattatsu* (the development of banks in Japan) (Tokyo: Aoki-shoten, 1959), p. 28.
15 *MZS*, XII, 331.
16 Katō, *Hompō Ginkō-shiron*, p. 18.
17 In *ibid.*, p. 22, article 1 of the Kawase Kaisha Act is cited, which reads in part: "The *kawase kaisha* were established for the benefit of . . . enriching the nation and . . . the government shall exercise its authority when loans are not repaid upon the promised date." The government directed *kawase kaisha* to lend for "international trade, tea-growing and purchasing cocoons," all of which were risky long-term loans.

18 Katō, in *ibid.*, pp. 22–23, also notes that: "*Kawase kaisha*, except one in Yokohama, accumulated large debts, and had nowhere to go. They received a large sum of government aid, or were given moratorium on past aids and dissolved themselves." Also see Naoichi Takizawa, *Kōhon Nippon Yūshi-ron* (a monograph on the theory of Japanese finance) (Tokyo: Yūhikaku, 1912), p. 60.
19 See footnote 23.
20 *MZS*, XII, 496.
21 *Ibid.*, XIII, 18.
22 G. C. Allen, *A Short Economic History of Modern Japan* (London: George Allen & Unwin Ltd., 1946), p. 38.
23 A Mitsui source wrote: "for Mitsui which wished to establish a bank of its own . . . the concurrence to establish the joint bank (with Ono as suggested by the government) was given as it (Mitsui) was unable to cope with the strongest of the government pressure. Mitsui's hope was to make the bank its foundation for its own bank some day." It is clear that Mitsui resented the facts that it had to take Ono as its partner and that it was forced into establishing a bank which it considered would be unprofitable. Mitsui Bank, *Mitsui Ginkō 80-nen-shi* (the history of eighty years of the Mitsui Bank) (Tokyo: Dekoban-Insatsu, 1957), p. 68. In an older history, also published by the Mitsui Bank, the bank expressed its resentment in no uncertain terms. The "course forced upon" it by the government and the virtual government order to use the Mitsui House (the first large Western-type building which was intended to be a headquarters of the Mitsui Bank) for the First National Bank caused "crises" for Mitsui which "necessitated Hachinōemon Mitsui to call all his relatives into a conference as he was concerned with the 200 year tradition of the House of Mitsui." Mitsui Bank, *Mitsui Ginkō 50-nen-shi* (the history of 50 years of the Mitsui Bank) (Tokyo: Mitsui Bank, 1927), p. 25. It should not be forgotten that the government had a potent weapon to cow Mitsui – a threat to withdraw its funds from Mitsui's vaults.
24 A best source on a detailed discussion and analyses of the Yokohama *kawase kaisha* and the Second National Bank is Shirō Hara, *Meiji-zenki Kinyūshi* (a history of early Meiji finance) (Tokyo: Toyōkeizai Shimposha 1965), especially pp. 51–86, and 99–190.
25 On the role played by *gōnō* and for a well-researched work on the Fourth National Bank, see T. Katō and T. Ōuchi, eds., *Kokuritsuginkō no Kenkyū* (a study of national banks) (Tokyo: Keisō-Shobō, 1963), pp. 89–141.
26 Allen, *Economic History of Japan*, p. 38. As to the reasons for the failure of these four banks, T. Akashi has an excellent summary. He ascribes the failure to: (a) the fact that these banks were established under the American model but were required to redeem their notes in gold; (b) the continued issuance of the government notes which caused steady inflation; and (c) the banks and the public which correctly viewed the Banking Act of 1872 as a transitional policy rather than a permanent one. For these reasons "the operation of these banks remained unsuccessful and the banks' existence was barely maintained." Teruo Akashi, *Meiji Ginkōshi* (a history of banking in Meiji Japan) (Tokyo: Kōbun-do, 1935), pp. 30–31.
27 *MZS*, XIII, 297.
28 For an excellent discussion of the Japanese economy during the early Meiji period see Henry Rosovsky, "Japan's Transition to Economic Growth, 1868–1885," in H. Rosovsky, ed., *Industrialization in Two Systems* (New York: Wiley, 1966). This essay includes a good discussion of the background and economic reasons for the samurai commutation bonds, pp. 125–31. Also see: Harry D. Harootunian, "The Economic Rehabilitation of the Samurai in the Early Meiji Period," *Journal of Asian Studies*, XIX (Aug. 1960).
29 *MZS*, XIII, 112.

30 Katō, *Hompō Ginkō-shiron*, pp. 30–31.
31 Hirschmeier, *Entrepreneurship in Japan*, p. 58.
32 For example this figure has been quoted by Katō, *Hompō Ginkō-shiron*, p. 33 and in Takeo Tsuchiya's *Chihōginkō Shōshi* (a small history of local banks) (Tokyo: Hosokawa Kappansho, 1961), p. 27. The original source is Ministry of Finance, *Ginkō-kyoku dai niji hōhoku* (the second report on the Banking Bureau) (Tokyo: Ōkura-sho, 1880), p. 129.
33 Due to rounding, these figures do not add up to 100 exactly.
34 In collecting sources, T. Katō's *"Ginkōshi shōkai"* (introduction to bank histories) *Shakai-kagaku Kenkyū* (research in social science), Vol. 6, No. 4, October 1955; Shiga University's *"Hompō Shashi Mokuroku"* (listings of Japan's company histories) *Hikone Ronsō* (annals of Hikone), Vol. 33, 1956; and University of Tokyo's *Shashi, Jitsugyōkadenki Mokuroku* (listings of company histories and businessmen's biographies), November 1964, were use to trace the available publications. But these were found to be incomplete, as nearly thirty bank histories have been published since the end of World War II and especially during the past several years. For those interested in these sixty-two cases and an equally large number of histories on *Zaibatsu*-connected banks and special banks (*Tokushu Ginkō*), the writer can furnish pertinent information upon request.
35 In this connection see Katō and Ōuchi, *Kokuritsuginkō no Kenkyū;* Matsunari, Miwa, and Chō, *Nippon ni Okeru Ginku no Hattatsu;* Hara, *Meiji-zenki Kinyūshi,* S. Tōhata and T. Takahashi, eds., *Meijizenki no Ginkōseido* (the banking system in early Meiji Japan) (Tokyo: Toyōkeizai Shimpōsha 1965); and K. Asakura, *Meijizenki Nippon Kinyū Kōzō-shi* (a history of financial structure, early Meiji Japan) (Tokyo: Iwanami, 1961) are valuable. Asakura's work is most comprehensive and directly pertinent to this paper. He examined sixty-nine banks, some very sketchily and some in detail, but seven more than I was able to examine. See footnotes 38, 40, and 46 for my comments and criticisms on Asakura's method.
36 Hara, *Meiji-zenki Kinyūshi*, p. 119. Observations on this bank are based on the source cited in note (a) of Table 1 and Hara, *Meiji-zenki Kinyūshi*, p. 111–13.
37 Based on *Nanajunanen-shi* (the 77-year history) (1954), and Katō and Ōuchi, *Kokuritsuginkō no Kenkyū*, pp. 217–66. The former is by far the best history of a bank. This 724-page volume is in effect a good economic history of Miyagi prefecture as a part of the rapidly changing Japanese economy, and detailed examinations of industries, banks, and other financial institutions during the period between 1868 and 1952 provide many valuable analyses of the local economy.
38 Tsuchiya's work on local banks, *Chikōginko Shōshi*, p. 28, classified this bank as a samurai bank. Asakura, *Meijizenki Nippon Kinyū Kōzō-shi*, does not reach a conclusion on this bank. He observes: "Here again we could say that the largeness and strength of merchants' capital were shown" (p. 118). This is one example of numerous uses of nonconclusive phrases found in Asakura's work. Subjunctives and suggestive but unanswered questions are replete in his book.
39 This is one of the rare cases in which two good histories on the bank are found. In addition to the one published in 1916, a postwar publication, *Ryōu Ginkō 60-nen-shi* (sixty-year history of the Ryōu Bank), 1956, is an excellent source exceeding 500 pages. Ryōu Bank was established by a merger between the Eighty-First National Bank and the One Hundred Twenty-Fifth National Bank in 1899.
40 In addition to those listed in footnote 46, this is another instance of my disagreement with Asakura, *Meijisenki Nippon Kinyū Kōzō-shi,* pp. 102–3. On the basis of the initial shareholding and the fact that "the operating fund was borrowed from Mitsui Bank," he classifies this bank as "established by merchant." As noted in the text, the most we could call it is SM-dominated rather than S-dominated. A slim 172-page history of this bank, which became one of the three to form the

Chiba Bank in 1933, does not yield sufficient evidence to warrant M or MS classification.

41 Tonosama is a leader of samurai, usually *daimyo* but sometimes a high-ranking samurai.

42 Katō and Ōuchi, *Kokuritsuginkō no Kenkyū*, p. 268. Although Asakura does not include this bank in his study, the Katō-Ōuchi volume has a chapter on it by Takehisa Hayashi. My classification of this bank is based upon the latter's detailed study.

43 This classification agrees with that of Asakura's, *Meijisenki Nippon Kinyū Kōzō-shi*, p. 101. Though the One Hundred Thirty-Third Bank was absorbed by Shiga Bank, an excellent 600-page history, *Shiga-ginkō 20-nen-shi* (twenty-year history of Shiga Bank), 1953, provides information which leaves no room for disagreement in classification.

44 Excluding the giant Fifteenth National Bank (see Section IV of this article), the mean capital of all 152 banks is approximately 130,000 yen. The mean capital of *heimin*-dominated banks in our sample was 180,000 yen and the same for samurai-dominated banks was 158,000 yen. But, given the smallness of the sample and the observed variability of the data (standard deviation and range), one cannot conclude that the *heimin*-dominated banks were larger on the average. In the universe (153 banks), there exists no significant temporal pattern in the size of capital, i.e., small (50,000 yen or about) and relatively large (over 150,000 yen) were found all through the period when charters were granted (1876–1879).

45 It is possible that my efforts have failed to unearth existing histories of banks which are not in this category.

46 A few examples to show my disagreement with Asakura, *Meijisenki Nippon Kinyū Kōzō-shi*, illustrate this. Asakura classifies the Seventeenth National Bank as "merchant-samurai, and operated by merchants" (pp. 107–8). Though merchants contributed a larger capital at the beginning (M-55,800 yen vs. S-49,200 yen), this bank was clearly organized under the leadership of Kazuo Kuroda, the chief minister (*rōshoku*) of the Kuroda *han* (a feudal clan) and the majority of the officers were samurai. In 1871, when the capital was increased, samurai contributed nearly twice the amount supplied by merchants. Neither *Fukuoka Ginkō soritsu 25-nen-shi* (a twenty-five-year history of Fukuoka Bank since its origin), published in 1918 by Fukuoka Bank which was absorbed by the Seventeenth in 1923, nor *Kabushiki Kaisha 17 Ginkō 60-nen-shi* (a sixty-year history of the Seventeenth Bank, Ltd.), published in 1941, provides reasons to change my classification of this bank to SM.

On the Sixty-Second National Bank, Asakura wrote: "Though it is called a samurai bank, merchants have taken initiative" (p. 105). My classification for this bank is SM because of a 5 to 1 dominance of samurai in the composition of initiators. The fact that one merchant provided the largest amount of initial capital is not sufficient to classify this bank as Asakura did. See: *Jyōyo Ginkō 20-nen-shi fu Ibaragi-ken Kinyūshi* (a twenty-year history of Jyoyo Bank with a financial history of Ibaragi Prefecture), 1955. This is one of the best bank histories, and the Financial History of Ibaragi Prefecture appended is detailed and well-documented.

This list could be lengthened by adding my further disagreements with Asakura, but the documentation would become unduly long, as the two examples above show. This process, in several instances, would also be tedious as Asakura's style is to write, for example, on the Seventy-Seventh National Bank, "I think that this bank cannot necessarily be considered to belong to samurai" (p. 79).

47 Katō and Ōuchi, *Kokuritsuginkō no Kenkyū,* p. 154.

48 *Ibid.*, p. 158.

49 Patrick, "Banking in the Early Stages" (mimeo).

50 *Nippon Zaisei Keizai Kenkyushō* (Japan financial economics research center), *Nippon Kinyu Zaisei-shi* (a history of Japanese finance) (Tokyo: Sakuma-Seihon, 1957), p. 41.

51 The data he quoted were for 1879–1880, one year previous to the year at which the series in Table 2 begins.

52 Rosovsky, "Japan's Transition," p. 131.

53 Hirschmeier, *Entrepreneurship in Japan*, p. 58.

54 This remark made by Eiichi Shibusawa was quoted in Tsuchiya's *Nippon Shihonshugi*, p. 183.

55 When the Banking Act of 1876 was decreed amending the Act of 1872, it became possible to establish "private" as opposed to "national" banks. A private bank could be established with a smaller capital than that required for a national bank, but it was not authorized to issue its own notes.

56 Patrick, "Banking in the Early Stages" (mimeo).

57 See *ibid.,* for the total capital of these quasi-banks and description. Asakura, *Meijizenki Nippon Kinyū Kōzō-shi,* devotes four chapters on private banks, quasi-banks, pawn shops, *mujin* (revolving credit association), and similar institutions. He then concludes that: "The strength of these low-level financial institutions and private money-changers could be considered to have exceeded that of banks. In any case one should not underestimate the functions performed by these money-changers and the low-level financial institutions in our economy, especially in finance" (p. 323).

58 Patrick, "Banking in the Early Stages" (mimeo).

59 E. H. Norman, *Japan's Emergence as a Modern State* (New York: Institute of Pacific Relations, 1940), pp. 111–12.

60 Hatsu Murakami, "*Mie Bōsekikaisha no Shikinchotatsu*" (financing of the Mie Textile Company) *Shakai Keizai Shigaku*, Vol. 31, No. 1, 1965, pp. 18–38. She found that in the case of this firm bank capital was supplied directly as long- and short-term loans and indirectly as loans to large shareholders who used the shares of the firm as collateral. But one notes in her data a sharp increase of accumulated profits which exceeded the direct loans in 1896, p. 23.

61 Among the active students of Japanese economy, Professor Patrick must be mentioned as one expressing this view explicitly. See footnote 63. One could also discern an emphasis in profit-motivation rather than the "community-centered entrepreneurship" approach in Hugh Patrick, "Lessons for Underdeveloped Countries from the Japanese Experience of Economic Development," *Indian Economic Journal,* IX, (Oct. 1961), pp. 150–66.

62 E. S. Crawcour, "Problems of Japanese Economic History," *Journal of Economic History*, XXIII (Dec. 1963), p. 625.

63 Or, to put it positively, Professor Patrick's insight gained by his study of Japanese banking is to the point: "Too much emphasis should not be placed on the role of the government in the establishment and development of Japan's financial system, since it was mainly through the initiative of profit-minded individuals that most Japanese financial institutions were born." Patrick, "Banking in the Early Stages" (mimeo).

13 Private entrepreneurs and the Meiji government*

B. K. Marshall

*Source: *Capitalism and Nationalism in Prewar Japan: The Ideology of the Business Elite* (Stanford: Stanford University Press , 1967), Ch. 2, pp. 13-29. Cross references citing chapters etc. relate to the original publication.

Vested interest, religious piety, the commitment to "history,"[1] sheer inertia – the psychological barriers to industrialization are as manifold as they are formidable. The core of the powerful ideology that sanctioned the efforts to overcome those barriers and to transform Japanese society in the late nineteenth century was "reactive" nationalism:[2] that is, the appeal to all Japanese to put aside personal, class, and regional differences in order to defend Japan against foreign intrusion. Industrialization, in other words, was advocated first and foremost as a means of avoiding humiliation at the hands of the Western powers. The fact that the Meiji Restoration and the far-reaching changes it set in motion took place in and derived their justification from a sense of national crisis colored all subsequent Japanese political, social, and economic thought. Nationalism played an especially important role in shaping the ideology of the modern Japanese business class, in that it provided a ready-made rationale for government aid to private business, and for the rejection of the doctrines of laissez-faire economics.

REACTIVE NATIONALISM AND THE INDUSTRIALIZATION OF JAPAN

From the beginning of the nineteenth century onward, the fear of foreign encroachment grew steadily in Japan. However, by the 1860's the recognition of the superiority of Western military power had served to convince even the most xenophobic of patriots that some degree of intercourse with the foreigner was essential if Japan was to acquire a knowledge of modern military technology.[3] The effects of the opening of foreign trade, moreover, soon led to an awareness that the economic challenge posed by the West was every bit as urgent as the military threat. Trade with the West not only caused serious dislocations in the existing handicraft economy, but also created a need for specie. Since the commercial treaties that Japan had signed with America and the European nations under duress forbade such measures as protective tariffs, the Japanese government had little control over the quantity or type of foreign goods being imported. Japanese leaders were thus faced on the one hand with a massive outflow of specie that undermined the stability of the national currency and the value of government tax revenue fixed in money, and on the other with an influx of foreign goods superior to and less costly than domestic products, which posed a serious threat to the rural handicraft industries and thus to the standard of living of large numbers of the peasantry. Confronted with the problems of a depreciating currency and growing unrest among the peasantry, the new Meiji government moved as quickly as its resources permitted to stimulate industrial development, hoping thus to increase exports and reduce dependency upon imports.[4]

But though military and economic considerations were unquestionably the most compelling reasons put forth by the advocates of rapid industrialization in Japan, military strength and a favorable trade balance were not the only goals of the Meiji reformers. There was a third aspect to the nationalistic reaction to foreign intrusion: i.e., the intense desire of the Japanese leaders to stand on an equal psychological footing with the advanced nations of the West. The material and cultural achievements of late nineteenth-century Europe and America made a profound impression on the increasingly large number of Japanese who traveled abroad. Earlier visitors, the influential Fukuzawa Yukichi in particular, had written vivid accounts of their travels in Europe and America; but even the best-informed traveler was not fully prepared for the sights that greeted him on his first trip abroad. The effects of such experiences on Japanese attitudes toward industrialization are attested to in numerous diaries and autobiographies. According to one biographer, even the able Okubo Toshimichi, who as one of the inner circle of the new government had good reason to feel satisfied with his own accomplishments, came home from Europe in 1873 with an "inferiority complex."[5] Okubo and others like him were determined to bring "civilization" and "enlightenment" to Japan – a motive as important to them as any military or economic reason for placing their energies in the service of industrial development.

The interplay of these motives can be seen in the careers and thought of many of the pioneers of Japanese industrialization. Inoue Shōzō (1846–1886), a Chōshō loyalist who spent his career in government, was sent to Germany in 1870 to learn military science. Instead, he devoted himself to studying the woolen industry, and after his return he played a leading role in the establishment of the government-owned Senjū Woolen Mill. Of his decision to go into industry he wrote:

> I want to make our country the equal of Europe and America. Today even the small children of Japan talk of enriching the country and strengthening the military, and they call for civilization and enlightenment. But there are few men who really have attempted to discover the tree that has brought forth the fruit of civilization and enlightenment in Europe. . . . After having read something of world history and geography in my search for the source of the wealth, the military power, the civilization, and the enlightenment of present-day Western nations, I realized that the

source must lie in technology, industry, commerce, and foreign trade. In order to apply these precepts and make the nation rich and strong, we must first of all instruct the people about industry. Then we can manufacture a variety of goods and export them, import those articles we lack, and accumulate wealth from abroad.[6]

GOVERNMENT VIEWS OF PRIVATE ENTERPRISE

The story of the extensive measures taken by the Meiji government to promote economic development has been told in detail elsewhere.[7] Our concern here is with the attitudes the Meiji business elite expressed regarding government participation and intervention in the economic sphere. However, in order to understand the position taken by business leaders on this issue, it is first necessary to consider how the Meiji political oligarchy envisioned the economic role of government.

Although the Meiji government rejected in practice the doctrines of the Western laissez-faire economists, government leaders had no desire to repudiate the private enterprise system. On the contrary, political spokesmen lamented the fact that the government had been forced to shoulder a burden properly belonging to the people. It was only the backwardness of the economy and the immaturity of the people, they claimed, that compelled the government to take action. When in 1874 Okubo Toshimichi – the key figure in government economic planning until his death in 1878 – submitted an outline of his proposals for promoting industry, he bemoaned "the weakness of spirit of the people," and stated that it was the duty of the government to encourage and guide them.[8] Nevertheless, Okubo took pains to avoid any direct repudiation of either the principles of private enterprise or the theory of laissez-faire economics. Instead he advanced the argument that economic policies should fit the level of development of the nation, and pointed out that in England laissez-faire policies had not been deemed appropriate until the economy had reached a fairly high level of development. Only after there was no longer the need for government initiative or protection had England become the champion of laissez-faire and free trade. In Okubo's view, Japan was then at the same stage of development reached by England in the seventeenth and eighteenth centuries, and it was the England of that period, rather than contemporary England, that Japan should take as her model. Implicit in Okubo's statement was the view that once neo-mercantilist policies had propelled Japan well down the path toward industrialization, it would be feasible to adopt, as England had, the philosophy of the Manchester school.[9]

These views were echoed in the formal proposals for each new venture that the Home Ministry, which Okubo headed, presented to the Council of State (the *Dajōkan*). They were also repeated in the official statements of principle that accompanied public announcement of new undertakings: for example, the March 1876 request by the Home Ministry for approval of its plan to establish a government-operated woolen mill stated, "It is the natural task of the people to undertake such an enterprise," and indicated that the Home Ministry foresaw the time when the woolen mill could be "entrusted to the people."[10] This emphasis on the temporary character of the government's involvement in the management of industry was repeated frequently by government officials. It is evident that these men wanted it clearly understood by the public that once a venture was "sufficiently developed," private enterprise should "take it over from the government,"[11] and that the government had every intention of eventually transferring the burden to those "among the people" who desired it.[12] Meanwhile, government spokesmen said, the government wished only to "give the people a profitable example"; and they denied that government attempts to establish modern industrial enterprises were in any way efforts to "compete for profit with the people."[13]

Each new government enterprise was thus carefully justified on the grounds that the people were still unable to establish and operate the needed industries themselves, and that therefore the government had no choice but to take the initiative. Failure to do so at a time when "the very existence of the nation was in peril" would mean disaster.[14]

BUSINESS VIEWS OF THE ECONOMIC ROLE OF GOVERNMENT

The basic position expressed by the spokesmen of private enterprise on the question of the economic role of government was in complete accord with that of the Meiji political leaders. Indeed, Meiji entrepreneurs were seldom satisfied that the government was as active as it might be. They produced a steady stream of speeches, articles, and petitions aimed at obtaining increased government aid in developing the banking system, expanding transportation facilities, increasing provisions for commercial and technical education, enlarging overseas markets, and so on.

In stressing the need for this aid, business leaders repeatedly referred to the "crisis" that faced the nation, and consistently sought to take advantage of the prevailing mood of reactive nationalism.[15] For example, in an 1875 petition for a change in the regulations governing the formation of commercial companies, Minomura Rizaemon, the chief manager (*bantō*) of the Mitsui enterprises, bolstered his arguments with references to the dangerous drain on the nation's specie holdings and the threat to Japan's sovereign rights posed by the activities of foreign merchants.[16] Godai Tomoatsu, the president of the Osaka Chamber of Commerce (Osaka Shōkō Kaigisho) in 1880 and a leading promoter in that city, told the government that it was impossible to "lay the foundations of wealth and strength" in Japan unless the government increased its efforts to give protection to the businesses run by "the people." Like Okubo, Godai pointed out that laissez-faire economics were not appropriate to Japan's present situation. "Consider the progress of national development in the various countries abroad. Countries like England, America, and France, which are the very models of civilization, prosper today because their government exerted sufficient effort and protected commerce and industry at the time when these had yet to flourish."[17]

Businessmen expressed even greater concern for the nation's future after the Diet was created in 1890 and the representatives of rural interests who opposed higher land taxes attempted to reduce government spending. If the government did not continue to give special attention to the needs of commerce and industry, business spokesmen warned, the nation would be in grave danger. An editorial in the *Tōyō Keizai Shimpō (The Oriental Economist)*, for example, called attention to the plight of China as an example of what would befall Japan if the government cut back expenditures for the promotion of industry: "Anti-business attitudes have been an evil in China since ancient times; and despite the wealth of resources in that country, industry has not developed. The fact that China is a weak country ridiculed by the rest of the world is the result of anti-business attitudes."[18] The petitions that business organizations regularly sent to the Diet contained similar warnings. The leaders of the Nagoya Chamber of Commerce, complaining that the existing election rules gave too much weight to rural constituencies, claimed that because the Diet was dominated by agrarian landholders, it continually ignored "problems involving the prosperity of the country's commerce and industry. Truly this is cause for great fear for the future of the nation!"[19] The Osaka Chamber of Commerce, petitioning for increased measures to "encourage and protect the enterprises operated by the people," struck an even more ominous note when it proclaimed that "the very survival of the nation" depended upon "a comparatively great advance [in industry] in a relatively short span of time."[20]

It is hardly surprising to find private entrepreneurs urging the use of state resources to promote business interests. Even the ardent economic individualists of nineteenth-century America usually favored tariff protection, subsidies to vital industries, land grants to railroads, and the like.[21] The more significant question is how business reacted to other forms of government intervention, especially public ownership and management of economic enterprises.

The issue of direct government participation in the management of business enterprises did not cause concern among the Japanese business community until late in the Meiji period.[22] The absence of serious opposition to the establishment of government enterprises in the 1870's can be easily understood in terms of two interrelated factors. In the first place, government enterprise in the early period was confined largely to areas where no private entrepreneur had yet shown a serious intention or capacity to venture. The majority of the old Tokugawa business class were either too shaken by the rapid turn of events in the early Meiji period to do so, or were quite content to remain within their traditional fields of endeavor. The more progressive entrepreneurs who were to form the new business elite had yet to attain sufficient experience or size to undertake the Herculean task of creating large-scale modern industries. As already noted, it was the vacuum created by the lack of private capital and experience that drew the government into the field of industrial entrepreneurship. Not until the 1880's, when the government had largely withdrawn from the field by selling the majority of its enterprises, did private investment in the modern industrial sector reach significant proportions; hence government-owned enterprises at no time posed a direct challenge to private business, except in the armament and railroad industries. Therefore, it is not surprising that the issue of private-versus-public enterprise remained largely an academic one in the early decades of the Meiji period.[23]

Secondly, as we have seen, the economic principles that served as guideposts in the formulation of government policy during these early years did not constitute a threat to private business. Private business leaders apparently believed the government's assurances that it had no desire to encroach permanently upon that sector of the economy which, according to both tradition and the example of Western industrial nations, belonged properly to private enterprise. When announcing the sale of government factories, Matsukata Masayoshi (Okubo's successor as the chief architect of government economic policy) had given the business community more reassurance by stating unequivocally: "The government should never attempt to compete with the people in industry and commerce. It falls within the sphere of government to look after matters of education, armament, and the police, while matters concerning trade and industry fall outside its sphere."[24]

Nevertheless, the question of government ownership of economic enterprises did arise in the 1890's, when a heated debate broke out over the issue of railroad nationalization. In 1892, Matsukata, then serving as Prime Minister, proposed to the Diet a bill authorizing government purchase of private railroads. Matsukata and the bill's supporters reasoned that private companies could not undertake the expansion of services essential to the rapid growth of the economy, because such expansion would require a huge outlay of capital with little immediate return.[25] The Diet, however, consistently refused to vote the necessary funds until 1906. But the failure of Matsukata's plans was not brought about by business opposition. On the contrary, the nationalization proposal had the active support of the majority of the business community in all three of the nation's economic centers, as was evidenced in the resolutions passed by the Chambers of Commerce of Tokyo, Osaka, and Nagoya.[26] The Tokyo Chamber of Commerce, for instance, agreed that private enterprise lacked the ability to carry out the task of creating an efficient nationwide rail network. Masuda Takashi, who represented the Mitsui firm on the committee that endorsed the original proposal in 1891, stated that although he was not in principle an advocate of government ownership of railroads, he was convinced that the purchase was unavoidable "in view of the prevailing conditions of the economy."[27]

Although the majority of the business community favored nationalization, there were prominent businessmen who disagreed. Shibusawa Eiichi, for one, opposed the plan, but his arguments were not based on opposition to public ownership per se. Shibusawa was concerned rather with the special problem of the influence of the military on the planning of railroad development. He had long argued that decisions on new routes should be made primarily on the basis of economic factors. In his view it would have been detrimental to the economy to give undue weight to the military's concern for inland routes less vulnerable to foreign attack; and he feared that the military would have too great a say if the government were to operate the railways.[28]

A second source of opposition to nationalization was the Mitsubishi Company. Here we find one of the major exceptions to the generalization that Japanese businessmen shunned arguments based on laissez-faire doctrines. Shoda Heigorō, Mitsubishi's chief executive in Tokyo, skilfully invoked the central tenets of the classic Anglo-American argument in his fight against government ownership. In December 1898, for instance, Shōda told the Railroad Council (Tetsudō Kaigi):

> [The advocates of nationalization] argue that there are so many competing lines that profits have shrunk and capital and labor are wasted. But does there exist any enterprise in which there is not some waste of capital or labor? The progress of enterprise in this world depends upon the fact that there are both those who make profits and those who suffer losses. I say that if we expect enterprises to progress, they must be left alone – left to natural selection and the survival of the fittest – without artificial intervention.[29]

In 1908, after the nationalization bill had passed the Diet, Shōda wrote: "I opposed the nationalization of railways from the beginning. My reasons were that it confiscated the property produced by private individuals, thus disregarding the guarantees under the law, and that the result of unification would be a reduction of competition."[30] Mitsubishi's allies in the Kaishintō, the Progressive Party, also opposed nationalization; and the party's leader, Okuma Shigenobu, claimed that he too was an advocate of laissez-faire economics. Speaking as Minister of Agriculture and Commerce in 1897, Okuma told the press: "There is much debate about whether the Ministry of Agriculture and Commerce should intervene in business or leave business alone. From the beginning I have agreed with the principle of laissez-faire, and have been opposed to intervention. Free competition is very essential to the development of business. It is necessary to promote a spirit of independence in businessmen."[31] Shimada Saburō, another Diet leader who opposed the nationalization plan, also invoked the principle of free competition, declaring: "Unless competition continues, all progress in railroading will cease, for the same reason that it ceases in other instances."[32]

The majority of business leaders, however, continued to support nationalization on the grounds that economic progress as well as national defense required the early creation of a nationwide transportation system.[33] In reply to Shōda and the others who opposed government ownership, business leaders who favored nationalization argued that the shortage of investment capital in a country such as Japan, which was still in the early stages of economic development, made government ownership essential. Advocates of laissez-faire, according to Masuda Takashi, simply did not understand this.[34]

The railroad nationalization bill was the only instance in which government ownership gave rise to any serious debate among the business community in the Meiji period. Although an occasional voice was heard calling for the government to limit the scope of the manufacturing enterprises it had retained after 1880,[35] government ownership of economic enterprises other than railroads did not constitute an issue about which the majority of the Meiji business class felt compelled to argue.

THE QUESTION OF GOVERNMENT REGULATION OF BUSINESS

The support and protection of industries and the development of transportation facilities were not the only forms of intervention practiced by the Meiji government. Two other major types of intervention influenced business attitudes toward the role of government: 1) the regulation of relations between management and labor; and 2) the regulation of competition between private entrepreneurs. The question of labor relations will be treated at length in Chapter 4. The issue of government regulation of competition was of much less importance, and can be summarized briefly here.

The commerce and industry of Tokugawa Japan had been organized for the most part within a tight framework of associations (*nakama*) not unlike the European guilds.[36] Shortly after the Meiji Restoration, these associations were ordered to disband on the grounds that they encouraged monopolistic practices unsuited to the new age: "For the sake of their own private profit [businessmen] form associations to prevent others from entering the same occupation, and this causes prices to rise. . . . Since today is a time for spreading civilization and enlightenment, all so-called *nakama* will henceforth be dissolved."[37] The rapid changes following the Restoration, however, brought severe economic dislocations, and it was not long before some merchants were blaming their difficulties on the dissolution of the old guilds.[38] Mitsui's Minomura Rizaemon, for example, pointed out to the Council of State in 1875 that the *nakama* had served to provide essential facilities for credit, and that the production of exportable goods such as silk and tea was being hindered by the lack of these facilities.[39] Three years later, the newly formed Osaka Chamber of Commerce gave similar reasons for requesting permission to organize *dōgyō kumiai* – literally, "associations of those in the same occupation." The Osaka leaders blamed the business slump in the city on the decline of cooperation between merchants: "Even those in the same occupation have no means of mutual assistance, and each man runs after his own profit without regard for the harm done to the country as a whole. Business is steadily falling into decline."[40] The proposal to create *dōgyō kumiai* to perform some of the same functions that the old *nakama* had performed was discussed at length by the Tokyo Chamber of Commerce in the spring of

1879.[41] Opinion was divided. Shibusawa spoke in favor of such associations, saying that they would promote the mutual benefit of their members and also provide a basis for closer liaison with the government. Masuda Takashi, who had taken over the reins of the Mitsui firm when Minomura died in 1877, expressed his fear that government supervision and regulation of commercial associations would result in "governmental interference in commerce."[42] Shibusawa's reply to Masuda illustrates the attitude toward government regulation of competition held by the majority of businessmen as well as by most government leaders. The question of whether government intervention is beneficial, said Shibusawa,

> is a matter that basically depends upon the degree to which the customs of the people are advanced . . . and should not be discussed in the abstract. Although free trade is the highest principle in England, it is not [necessarily] appropriate in other countries. Can there be any question that in our country at the present time it is to the general good that the guidance of the [economic] system should be entrusted to the government?[43]

Masuda's doubts were not allayed, however, and the Mitsui-controlled *Chūgai Bukka Shimpō (Domestic and Foreign Price Reporter)* took the occasion to editorialize on the dangers of relying too heavily on government regulation of competition:

> There are those who say that theoretically it is good to leave management alone, yet argue that merchants have nothing to fall back upon and consequently are unable to secure credit and are thus ruined. . . .What sort of talk is this? Business is opportunity; the thing that merchants should depend upon is their own diligence. If they cease to be diligent they should not have anything to fall back upon. If we build them something to lean upon, they will become indolent.[44]

No further action was taken on the petition to create *dōgyō kumiai* until January 1883, when the Ministry of Agriculture and Commerce asked the Tokyo Chamber of Commerce to discuss the question again. Once again Masuda expressed fear of the "evils of government intervention" and argued that the authorization of such associations by the government in the Tokugawa period had led inevitably to monopolistic practices. Masuda proposed that instead of setting up officially regulated organizations, the government allow legal force to be given to trade agreements between businessmen under existing laws covering private contracts, and argued that matters of trade were properly left to "the self-rule (*jiji*) of those in commerce and industry." Those who favored the *dōgyō kumiai* system, however, replied that private agreements could not be made sufficiently binding to provide an adequate foundation for cooperation between businessmen; and Okura Kihachirō, their leader, argued further that such cooperation was essential if the quality of Japanese exports was to be raised and the nation was to attain its proper position in the sphere of foreign trade.[45] Despite Okura's arguments, the

Chamber of Commerce voted to advise the Ministry that the matter was best left to private agreement, and that no special regulations were necessary.

The issue was still not resolved. In the following year (1884) the government instructed the representatives of the Kangyō Shimonkai – the regional committees of businessmen and officials created by the government to advise on economic matters – to discuss the question at their general conference. The type of objections set forth by Masuda apparently carried little weight with those from outside Tokyo who attended the conference, for there was general agreement that competition, if left unchecked, would degenerate into the practice of "harming others to profit one's self."[46] The conference endorsed the *dōgyō kumiai* system; and in November 1884 the government promulgated the Standard Regulations for Occupational Associations (Dōgyo Kumiai Junsoku).[47]

Thus the majority of the Meiji business class accepted not only the principle of restricted competition but also the view expressed by Shibusawa that it was the proper function of the government to enforce such restrictions. Again, as in the case of government management of economic enterprises, those in favor of government intervention used the argument that such intervention was justified by the backward condition of the Japanese economy and the need to meet the economic challenge of the West.

There is one further noteworthy instance of the Meiji government's intervention to control competition. This was occasioned by the famous duel between the Mitsubishi shipping lines and the Kyōdō Un'yū Kaisha (The United Transportation Company), a company that had been formed originally with government support to challenge Mitsubishi's domination of Japan's shipping industry. The struggle between the two companies was the fiercest industrial battle of the period. By 1885, the cutting of shipping rates in the attempt to drive the opposition out of business had pushed both companies deep into the red, and a number of business leaders feared that both would collapse if the duel were to continue. In August 1885 a group led by Okura Kihachirō, one of the most prominent businessmen of the period, asked the Tokyo Chamber of Commerce to appeal to the government to intervene. The petition warned of the harm that would be done to the nation if both of Japan's modern shipping firms were to fall into bankruptcy. Not only would this open the way for foreigners to handle an even larger share of Japanese foreign trade, but it would also undermine the country's military position, since Japan depended on the merchant marine for defense in the event of war.

Mitsubishi's Shōda Heigorō entered a written objection to the petition, taking the position that the government should not be called upon to regulate competition. On the other hand, Shōda claimed, there was not room for two companies in the shipping field; and he suggested that a merger be negotiated between the parties involved. Okura, supported by Shibusawa, opposed the idea of a merger on the grounds that competition was generally desirable, but stated that since unchecked competition might in this case endanger the shipping trade of the nation, the government should supervise the competition between the two companies in order to keep it within reasonable bounds. Shibusawa agreed that since shipping was crucial to the nation's economy, such government supervision could not be said to be "unwarranted interference." Significantly, Shōda, who thirteen years later fought the nationalization of railroads on the grounds that progress demanded competition, based his case for a merger on the plea that "if it is left to the survival of the fittest, the inferior will certainly suffer a crushing defeat."[48]

These examples of the view taken by businessmen of the proper role of government in the economic life of Meiji Japan reveal how little appeal the main tenets of laissez-faire economics had for the majority of private entrepreneurs. The relative absence of expressions of hostility toward government of the sort that pervades the classic Anglo-American business ideology is striking. But this restraint was not simply the result of that fear or sense of inferiority vis-à-vis government officials sometimes attributed to the Meiji businessman;[49] we have seen that Meiji business leaders did not hesitate to openly oppose government policies when they felt it was in their interest to do so. The chief reason for their willingness to accept intervention was simply that at this time government intervention posed little threat to private business interests. Government leaders were convinced that they must do everything in their power to encourage private enterprise, if the economy was to grow and the nation to become great and business leaders, for their part, were acutely aware that the fate of individual private enterprises, as well as the expansion of the economy and of business opportunities, depended greatly upon the active participation of the government. Moreover, businessmen were able to take advantage of both the government's commitment to rapid industrialization and the nationalistic temper of the times to obtain the types of intervention most favorable to private business.

Mitsubishi's opposition to railroad nationalization and Mitsui's opposition to the *dōgyō kumiai* clearly demonstrate the ability of Meiji business leaders to seize on lassez-faire principles when they believed government intervention was threatening their interests. The point is that these were simply not the sort of weapons business generally felt the need of, since in most instances the government was firmly on the side of private enterprise. Nevertheless, the willingness of government leaders to support and protect private enterprise was by no means the only reason that Japanese business spokesmen had little recourse to laissez-faire justifications. In order to fully understand the differences between business attitudes toward government in Japan and those in the United States and England, it is necessary to turn to the related problem of the doctrine of economic individualism.

NOTES

1 In the sense described in Joseph Levenson's brilliant essay, "'History' and 'Value': The Tensions of Intellectual Choice in Modern China," in Wright, pp. 148–94.

2 I have borrowed the phrase from Rostow, pp. 26–27. For insights into the role of ideologies in the initial stages of industrialization, see Gerschenkron, in Hoselitz, esp. pp. 23–25.

3 See Ienaga, *Gairai bunka*, pp. 148–256. Jansen's *Sakamoto Ryōma* is an excellent account of the life and times of one of the more important of such converts.

4 There is a detailed account of the origins of Meiji government economic policy in Thomas C. Smith, *Political Change*. The existence of a large samurai class, the majority of which were without useful function and quite frequently unable to support the style of life their rank entailed, was also a prime factor in the decision to embark upon industrialization, for industrialization was envisaged as a means of samurai employment.

5 Sidney Devere Brown, pp. 189–90. Okubo is recorded as having told one of his traveling companions, "I had wanted to overthrow the Bakufu and establish the rule of the Emperor. That task being almost complete, [I felt that] we had done our part. But now I am sorely troubled, for having traveled through the West I see that we cannot measure up to a world so advanced." Quoted in Tsuchiya Takao, *Nihon shidōshatachi*, p. 25. Kuroda Kiyotaka, onetime president of the House of Councillors, underwent an even more dramatic conversion to the cause of industrialization. He left for his European tour one of the chief opponents of extensive railroad development. Upon his return, he apologized publicly and became one of its most ardent advocates. See Hirschmeier, *The Origins of Entrepreneurship*, p. 123.

6 Quoted in Ienaga, *Gairai bunka*, p. 260.

7 See Thomas C. Smith, *Political Change*, for an account of government efforts in the crucial first decade. Lockwood, *Economic Development of Japan*, gives the most thorough overall survey of the role of the government; see especially Chap. 10, pp. 499–592.

8 The "Memorial on the Promotion of Industry," submitted to the Dajōkan in May 1874, *Okubo Toshimichi monjo*, IV, 561–64. The Memorial is also summarized in Sidney D. Brown, p. 190, and in Iwata, pp. 237–38.

9 Okubo had just returned from a lengthy tour of Europe, including Germany, and the terms in which he couched his views suggest strongly that he had been exposed to the ideas of Friedrich List. List's works, however, did not become well known in Japan until the 1880's; see Sumiya Etsuji, *Nihon keizaigaku shi*, pp. 92ff.

10 Quoted in Thomas C. Smith, p. 65. Okubo's original thought had been to subsidize Okura Kihachirō, a rising young entrepreneur who was interested in a government contract for manufacturing woolen army uniforms. Okubo said to Okura when they met in Paris in 1872: "Since you are an entrepreneur starting a new venture, there is the possibility of failing, in which case others who subsequently may wish to enter the field would hesitate to do so. The government should therefore aid you, and after the enterprise is well established, it can be sold back to you." Quoted in Iwata, p. 158.

11 From the "Opinion Paper on the Establishment of a Steel Works" (undated, ca. 1890), in Itō Hirobumi, *Jitsugyō kōgyō shiryō*, pp. 70–74.

12 From the government announcement of the establishment of the Tomioka filature. Reprinted in Inoue Kaoru Kō Denki Hensankai, II, 458.

13 *Ibid.*, p. 459; also quoted in Thomas C. Smith, *Political Change*, p. 59. For another example of the denial that the government intended to compete with the people, see Shōkō Gyōseishi Kankokai, I, 51–52.

14 See the quotations in Thomas C. Smith, *Political Change*, p. 26.

15 It should be noted again that we are not here concerned with the ultimate *motives* of the entrepreneurs. Although Meiji businessmen as a group gave every appearance of having been as sincere in their professions of patriotic devotion as any other segment of their society, this is beside the point. What is significant here is

the use to which they were able to put patriotic slogans in furthering the development of private business.

16 This document can be found in Okuma, *Okuma monjo*, II, 138–49.

17 Godai, pp. 448, 449.

18 March 25, 1898, p. 6.

19 Petition submitted in January 1899 by the Nagoya Chamber of Commerce, reprinted in *Nagoya Shōkō Kaigisho*, II, 121.

20 Petition submitted in 1900, reprinted in *Osaka Shōkō Kaigisho*, p. 68.

21 See, for instance, Fine, pp. 97–98, 111–13. For an interesting study of the "myth" of *laissez-faire* and the role of state governments in the American economy during the first half of the nineteenth century, see Louis Hartz, esp. pp. 287–320.

22 A search through the annals of the Chambers of Commerce of Osaka, Nagoya, and Kōchi, and the records of the Tokyo Chamber of Commerce reprinted in Shibusawa, *Shibusawa Eiichi denki shiryō* (hereinafter cited as *SEDS*), failed to uncover any trace of opposition to government-owned enterprises prior to the debate over railroad nationalization discussed below. See also Thomas C. Smith, *Political Change*, pp. 92–95.

23 This is not to deny that there was a great deal of theoretical discussion of the principles of laissez-faire economics. For a survey of the introduction of Western laissez-faire and protectionist doctrines in the 1870's and 1880's, see Sumiya Etsuji, *Nihon keizai gakushi*, pp. 32–150.

24 Quoted in Thomas C. Smith, *Political Change*, p. 95.

25 Tokutomi, II, 466–72, 556; see also *Nihon tetsudōshi* II, 797–830. There is a lengthy study in English by a former Assistant Councilor of the Imperial Board of Railways, Watarai Toshiharu, titled "Nationalization of Railways in Japan," in *Studies in History, Economics and Public Law*, The Faculty of Political Science of Columbia University, LXIII, 2 (1915), 189–339.

26 SEDS, XIX, 664–68; XXI, 356–65 and 713–17; *Osaka Shōkō Kaigisho*, p. 451; *Nagoya Shōkō Kaigisho*, Part I, pp. 320–22. The businessmen of Nagoya, then still relatively isolated from the major urban markets of Osaka and Tokyo, were particularly interested in the development of transportation facilities; see *Nagoya Shōkō Kaigisho*, Part II, pp. 35–36, 104–5, and 151–52.

27 SEDS, XIX, 666.

28 See Shibusawa's article in the August 30, 1898, issue of *Jiji Shimpō*; reprinted in SEDS, XXI, 364–65.

29 The speech is reprinted in its entirety in Tsubotani, pp. 42–56.

30 Article in *Tōyō Keizai Shimpō*, February 15, 1908, p. 206.

31 Interview in *Jitsugyō no Nihon*, August 23, 1897, pp. 37–38.

32 Speech before the 22nd Session of the House of Representatives, March 17, 1906; reprinted in *Shimada*, I, 295.

33 See the Tokyo Chamber of Commerce petition of 1898; SEDS, XXI, 358–59.

34 See his article in *Jitsugyō no Nihon*, January 1898, pp. 10–12.

35 See, for example, the 1898 petition submitted to the government by the Tokyo Chamber of Commerce. Fujiyama Raita, who initiated the petition, protested that the government-owned factories were producing a wide variety of goods, many of which were non-military in character, and thereby were hindering the growth of private enterprise; SEDS, XXI, 737–39.

36 See Miyamoto Mataji, *Kabunakama no kenkyū*; and Sheldon.

37 Quoted from an Osaka ordinance of 1872 in Miyamoto Mataji, *Nihon no girudo no kaihō*, pp. 27–28.

38 *Ibid.*, pp. 37–42.

39 See the memorial reprinted in *Okuma monjo*, II, 138–49.

40 *Osaka Shōkō Kaigisho*, pp. 9–10; also Godai, pp. 434ff.

41 The relevant portions of the *Tōkyō Shōkō Kaigisho yōkenroku* [The Records of the Tokyo Chamber of Commerce] are reprinted in SEDS, XVII, 112–21.

42 *Ibid.*, pp. 112–13.

43 For the view of an influential government bureaucrat, see Maeda Masana, *Kōgyō iken* [Views on Promoting Industry], reprinted in Ouchi and Tsuchiya, XVIII, 82–83.

44 Reprinted from the March 15, 1879, issue in Ouchi and Tsuchiya, p. 122.

45 SEDS, XVIII, 140ff.

46 For these discussions, see the excerpts from the *Kangyōkai, Kōmubu nisshi* [Proceedings of the Section on Industry of the Conference on the Encouragement of Industry], in SEDS, XVIII, 159ff. For similar views expressed in 1899 in support of stricter enforcement of the regulations for *dōgyō kumiai*, see *Nagoya Shōkō Kaigisho*, Part II, pp. 123–24.

47 See Shōkō Gyōseishi Kankokai, I, 272–74.

48 SEDS, XVIII, 359–79.

49 Cf. Scalapino, *Democracy*, pp. 271–72.

Guide to further reading

Beasley, W. G., *Select documents on Japanese foreign policy* (Oxford: Oxford University Press, 1955).

Beasley, W. G., *The Meiji Restoration* (Stanford: Stanford University Press, 1972).

Beasley, W. G., 'The foreign threat and the opening of the ports', *Cambridge history of Japan*, vol. 5 (Cambridge: Cambridge University Press, 1989).

Beasley, W. G., *Great Britain and the opening of Japan: 1834–1858* (Folkestone: Japan Library, 1995).

Beasley, W. G., *Japan encounters the barbarian: Japanese travellers in America and Europe* (New Haven, Conn.: Yale University Press, 1995).

Beauchamp, E. R. and Iriye, A., eds, *Foreign employees in nineteenth-century Japan* (Boulder, Col.: Westview Press, 1990).

Blacker, C., *The Japanese enlightenment: a study of the writings of Fukuzawa Yukichi* (Cambridge: Cambridge University Press, 1964).

Burks, A. W., ed., *The Modernizers: overseas students, foreign employees, and Meiji Japan* (Boulder, Col.: Westview Press, 1985).

Craig, A. M., *Choshu in the Meiji Restoration* (Cambridge, Mass.: Harvard University Press, 1961).

Fox, G., *Britain and Japan: 1858–1867* (Oxford: Oxford University Press, 1969).

Hirakawa, S., 'Japan's turn to the West', *Cambridge history of Japan*, vol. 5 (Cambridge: Cambridge University Press, 1989).

Hoare, J. E., *Japan's treaty ports and foreign settlements: the uninvited guests 1858–1899* (Tenterden, Kent: Japan Library, 1994).

Huber, T. M., *The Revolutionary origins of modern Japan* (Stanford: Stanford University Press, 1981).

Jansen, M. B., *Sakamoto Ryoma and the Meiji Restoration* (Princeton: Princeton University Press, 1961).

Jansen, M. B., 'Modernization and foreign policy in Meiji Japan', in R. E. Ward, ed., *Political development in modern Japan* (Princeton: Princeton University Press, 1968).

Jansen, M. B. and Rozman, G., eds, *Japan in transition: from Tokugawa to Meiji* (Princeton: Princeton University Press, 1986).

Jones, H. J., *Live machines: hired foreigners in Meiji Japan* (Vancouver: University of British Columbia Press, 1980).

Kiyooka, E., trans., *The autobiography of Yukichi Fukuzawa*, revised edn (New York: Columbia University Press, 1966).

Lehmann, J.-P., *The image of Japan: from feudal isolation to world power, 1850–1905* (London: George Allen & Unwin, 1978).

Lensen, G. A., *The Russian push toward Japan; Russo-Japanese relations, 1697–1875* (Princeton: Princeton University Press, 1959).

Nagai, M. and Urrutia, M., eds, *Meiji ishin: Restoration and revolution* (Tokyo: The United Nations University, 1985).

Totman, C., *The collapse of the Tokugawa Bakufu, 1862–1868* (Honolulu: The University Press of Hawaii, 1980).

Umegaki, M., *After the Restoration: the beginning of Japan's modern state* (New York: New York University Press, 1988).

Wakabayashi, B. T., 'Opium, expulsion, sovereignty: China's lessons for Bakumatsu Japan', *Monumenta Nipponica* 47 (1992): 1–25.

Westney, D. E., *Imitation and innovation: the transfer of Western organizational patterns to Meiji Japan* (Cambridge, Mass.: Harvard University Press, 1987).

Wilson, G. M., *Patriots and redeemers in Japan: motives in the Meiji Restoration* (Chicago: University of Chicago Press, 1992).